Dental Nursing –
The EDNA Way

Clare Morvan BDS (London)

Clare Morvan
15 Millennium Court
Greve D'Azette
St Clement
JE2 6GS

www.ednaweb.com

Dental Nursing – The EDNA Way

Publisher and copyright
Clare Morvan

Printed and bound in Great Britain.

ISBN 970-0-9560527-0-4 2008

www.ednaweb.com

Acknowledgements

I would like to thank all the staff at Webreality and especially Phil Balderson and David Barton who gave me time, invaluable advice and an insight into the world of teaching, academia and computer technology.

I would also like to thank Ben Hickingbotham and his superb team of illustrators and printers. Ben has the remarkable ability to immediately understand a brief and produce a fabulous creative team to make the product a reality. I would like to thank Dave Ellis for the excellent presentation of this book.

A warm thanks goes to Cedric Bird of Jersey Enterprise and best wishes for his forthcoming English Channel swim.

I would like to give a special thank you to Dr "Joe" Omar who regularly gives informative and entertaining lectures in medical emergencies. He has a unique insight into dentistry as an anaesthetist who also provides conscious sedation for dental patients. Joe's attention to detail has provided many solutions to the best way of caring for the collapsed patient in the dental chair.

Thank you to Nobel Biocare and especially Jo Lakeman, dental nurse and tutor, for showing me exactly how the dental nurses set up the surgery for implant placement. Again her attention to detail and teaching skills are exemplary.

It is always a pleasure to catch up with my old college friend Consultant John Turner and his family. I greatly appreciate his input and experience in the field of orthodontics.

My final thanks go to Minerva and their suppliers who provided the vast majority of the illustrations. Minerva showed outstanding efficiency at providing these illustrations and Scott Allott, from Minerva's graphic design department was a pleasure to work with.

There are many others who played a part in producing this book and my appreciation goes to them all.

ABOUT THE AUTHOR

Edna was created by Clare Morvan. Clare has taught candidates dental nursing ever since she qualified. Not as a tutor at university but as an ordinary general dental practitioner teaching candidates while carrying out the work of dentistry and maintaining the high standard of care rightly expected from patients. Sounds familiar? This is the way most dental nurses learn their profession and the way most dentists teach them.

The world of dentistry is dynamic and Clare feels strongly in providing high quality education to both undergraduate and postgraduate dental nurses. This education should not be a "hand-me-down" from a dentist's lecture but lectures specifically written for the dental nurse containing relevant information.

Dental nurses live full and busy lives. EDNA recognises this and provides affordable knowledge which the nurse can access whenever and wherever they are.

"Dental Nursing the EDNA Way" also supports today's dentists teaching new dental nurses by providing comprehensive explanations to modern dentistry and practical solutions to the challenges we all meet every day in the surgery.

If you have found this book beneficial, you may like to look up our website www.ednaweb.com for continuing professional development for dental nurses.

Table of Contents

Characteristics of a Dental Nurse

Is Dental Nursing for you?

Dental nursing is a busy worthwhile career. You will literally be working alongside the dentist and patient as an important member of the dental team. Dental nurses require certain qualities. Nurses are:

Caring

Dental nurses have a duty to care for their patients. The welfare of your patients must always be at the forefront of your mind.

Practical

Dental nursing is a practical career that involves such tasks as mixing dental materials to specific requirements and passing instruments to and from the dentist in a precise manner. The dental nurse needs to be able to perform these tasks while monitoring the patient.

Organised

Your working environment is small so you must work in a neat and organised manner. Appointments are arranged back-to-back which necessitates working methodically to maintain strict infection control policies. Dental nurses work with the dentist in a fluid controlled manner. The nurse should be able to anticipate the dentists needs for routine procedures.

Trustworthy

Dental nurses witness confidential conversations. The information may not seem important to you but it may be highly sensitive to the patient. The patient's privacy must be respected at all times. Dental nurses must be trusted to carry out their tasks diligently even when unsupervised.

Personable

The nurse should be aware of other people's rights. They should be respectful of patients and colleagues without prejudice to the diversity of background, opportunity, language and culture.

Hygienic

Dental nurses should wear a clean and presentable uniform. They must be neat and tidy at all times.
Dental nurses must be aware that the hygiene regime of dental instruments, equipment and the surgery is of paramount importance.

Knowledgeable

A dental nurse, especially a student nurse, must be aware of their personal limitations. They should willingly seek help where necessary.
Qualified dental nurses must maintain their high level of competence and knowledge by continuing professional development.

Punctual

Dental nurses should be punctual and reliable. A nurse who is late will delay every patient in that session. A dental nurse who is unreliable puts an intolerable strain on the rest of the dental team. Dental nurses should also understand that although dentists try to keep within working hours there may be occasions when treatment times unavoidably overrun.

THE THREE GOLDEN RULES OF DENTAL NURSING

1. The most important person in the practice is the patient.

2. Hygiene is everything.

3. Never ever breach confidentiality.

Dental nursing is a fulfilling career that is rarely dull. People who are interested in helping and caring for others make great dental nurses.

How to study – the rules!

1. Make a timetable of the hours that you are going to study each week and then stick to it! The hardest part of studying is beginning! Once you're in a routine it will become a habit.

2. If you are invited out during one of your designated study sessions, make up those missing hours IN ADVANCE. That way you will enjoy yourself more when out as you know you've earned it and when you return to your study you will not feel demoralised as you will still be on schedule.

3. We all study at are own pace but after half an hour stand up and have a 5 minute break away from your desk. No more than 5 minutes mind you!

4. Have a glass of water beside you while you are studying and take sips regularly. Dehydration lowers concentration.

5. Reward yourself AFTER study by giving yourself a small treat such as watching your favourite TV program or phoning a friend etc.

6. If you keep to your timetable you won't waste your free time worrying about studying. You will savour your free time knowing that you've got it covered. Be smug!

7. Remember you are passing this exam for YOU. Don't get pushed into studying at someone else's speed whether faster or slower. SET YOUR OWN PACE. Beware of "know alls". They are trying to undermine you.

8. Every day at work you are gaining practical experience. You are not studying dry facts. You know their practical application so connect the two.

9. Don't give up. Persevere. Study on a regular basis and it will become a habit. It is better to study say four times a week for 1 hour than to study just once a week for 4 hours.

10. The final exam should not be feared. IT IS YOUR CHANCE TO BOAST ABOUT HOW MUCH YOU KNOW.

11. While studying the book, read the questions before each section and try to find the answers within the text. After reading that section answer the multiple choice questions and check the answers to see if you have answered them correctly. If you have not, reread that section.

1. Communication and Confidentiality

" **The most important person in the surgery is the patient and the most important patient is the one in your dental chair".**

COMMUNICATION

While reading the text answer the following;

1. Why is good communication important?

2. Besides talking how do we communicate?

3. How should we treat people who are different to us?

4. Define open and closed questions.

5. What is a trigger word?

Good communication is imperative. It builds patient's trust and confidence in you. It also involves the patient in their dental health so that they become part of the team empowering them to make informed decisions about their treatment, to give consent and to take responsibility for the daily maintenance of their mouths.

Up to 70% of communication is non verbal. Patients expect to see a nurse in a clean neat uniform, with tided back hair and a friendly smile. Why? Because this tells them that they're in the right place. A professional nurse who's hot on hygiene is going to care for them.

An open posture and good eye contact tells the patient that you're listening-you care about their concerns, you have time for them. A steady gentle voice tells them you know what you're doing, they're safe. Oh and remember when you're talking to patients on the telephone, smile. A smile will travel down the line but beware so will a frown!

A dental surgery is an unusual environment for most people, filled with strange sights, sounds and smells. Some patients find it down right scary. A nervous patient will not remember what was said to them on the first visit but they will remember the

atmosphere! Communicate well and the patient will leave with the overall impression of a caring professional team who's on their side. They will say, "That wasn't as bad as I thought it was going to be." Well done. That's a huge compliment!

As a nurse you will get an insight into different peoples' lives-a mixture of religions and races, rich people and poor, gifted and challenged and everyone in between! Every person must be treated with respect and dignity. The diversity of their view points should be given merit. You don't have to agree with them but you do have to respect their right to be different from you.

People of different cultures may dress differently and have a different concept of personal space. People of different religions will have different diets and may have periods of fasting. You do not have to be an expert on various religions but you do have to be respectful and aware that differences may exist and be sensitive to them. If your patient has limited English ask them to bring an interpreter. This is usually a relative or friend and may be a child.

Disabilities can include a wide range of impairments such as deafness, epilepsy or mental health problems. Only offer help if it seems appropriate and the patient has accepted your offer. Only make the same physical contact that you would make with anyone else. Do not treat disabled adults as children. Speak to the patient in the wheelchair at their eye level. Do not ignore them or speak above their head. A physical disability does not make the person stupid. Never stare. Make eye contact.

If your patient is visually impaired your tone of voice becomes more important. Don't shout. Let them know you are there. Lead them into the surgery by letting them rest their hand on your arm. Don't grab them. Always give a running commentary

on what procedures are about to take place. And remember a guide dog is a working dog not a pet. Let it get on with its job. If your patient is deaf do not talk though your mask. They need to lip read. Speak slowly and clearly. Touch is important. If someone has a hearing aid minimise background noise such as the radio. Above all give patients time and be non judgemental. For example a person with impaired speech is usually perfectly intelligent.

When meeting people for the first time you will find out more about them and avoid false assumptions and offence by asking open rather than closed questions. An open question involves an explanation for the answer. For example, "Where do your children go to school?" Whereas a closed question has a yes or no answer. "Do your children go to St. Mark's School?" Even the shyest person can speak about themselves. Ask open questions and listen to the answers. Do not interrupt. Put people at ease.

When you first start as a dental nurse pay attention to the way the dentist describes procedures especially to young children and nervous patients. With children treatment is fully explained using words appropriate for their age. Be honest with patients but do not inflame their anxiety. A trigger word is one that triggers a strong emotional response in a patient. Notice how the dentist replaces words which would elicit a strong negative response with softer, less intimidating words. For example do not tell a child "You're very brave". Tell them "You're very good". If you say the word "brave" they will wonder what they have to be brave about! As soon as you tell a patient "This won't hurt" they will think "Something painful is going to happen". Who wouldn't?

Also you will have noticed the way instruments, which often appear foreign and hostile to the patient, are kept out of view. This fear may even be triggered by the metallic glint of a basic mirror and probe. This is one of the reasons why we pass the instruments out of the patient's vision behind their head or under the chin. Be sensitive to your patient's needs.

Q1. Good communication allows the patient to make informed decisions about their dental care. True or false?

Q2. Good communication involves which of the following;

    a. listening to the patient
    b. using a raised voice
    c. crossing your arms in a closed posture
    d. smiling and having an open body posture

Q3. When treating a patient in a wheelchair it is best to talk to their companion about the various treatment options. True or false?

Q4. "Do you like football?" is an open question. True or false?

Q5. A trigger word is one which elicits a strong emotional response in a patient. True or false?

How well did you do?
    A1.True   A2.a,d   A3.False
    A4.False   A5.True

PATIENT CONFIDENTIALITY

While reading the text answer the following

1. When can a nurse breach confidentiality?

2. What is the consequence to the nurse if confidentiality is breached?

For most people the sight of a white coat symbolises care and trust. Your patients will confide in you and tell you things that they may not have even revealed to their nearest and dearest. This is an honour which has been bestowed on the medical profession and allows us to help the individual to the greatest extent possible. It is UNETHICAL AND ILLEGAL TO BREACH THIS TRUST. Regard any breach in confidentiality as a dismissible offence. It is unacceptable as it builds a barrier between the clinician and patient which can prove life threatening. So however tasty the tit bit of local scandal, when it is told in the dental surgery it stays there.

Confidentiality is taken so seriously that you do not even have the right to say if a patient attends your dental practice or not. It is very easy to unintentionally breach confidentiality. For example, it is breached if you discuss, without permission, an 18 year old's treatment with his mother who will be paying the bills. Or if you tell a patient's work colleague how wonderful it is to hear that she's pregnant. She may not have told her office yet. In fact she may not have even told the father.

Patients have the right to their own records under the Access to Health Records Act 1990. However only the dentist can approve access. Under strict laws other parties such as the Dental Practice Board or the police may be allowed access to a patient's records under extreme circumstances for example to identify a body. But remember, ONLY THE DENTIST CAN RELEASE THE PATIENT'S RECORDS NEVER THE DENTAL NURSE however persuasive the person is being. Confidentiality is protected by law under the Data Protection Act 1998.

Q1. When can a dental nurse breach confidentiality?

    a. when the patient's husband wants to know the results of his wife's x-rays
    b. when a policeman is investigating a criminal
    c. when out socialising you tell your friends that Jane is a patient at your practice
    d. never

Q2. A breach of confidentiality by any member of the dental team constitutes grounds for dismissal. True or false?

How well did you do?
    A1.d   A2.True

4

2. Getting Started

"For the things we have to learn before we can do them, we learn by doing them." Aristotle

HEPATITIS B VACCINATION

Before you become a dental nurse you must be vaccinated against the hepatitis B virus. This consists of a series of three injections; an initial injection, then another one month later and the final six months after that. To be immune to the hepatitis B virus your antibody level should be greater than 100 IU/ml.

SEATING POSITIONS

I will assume that the dentist is right handed. If the dentist is left handed then the surgery is set up for a left handed person and is the mirror image of the following description. Sorry, but the dentist always dictates the seating arrangements! The working area of a dental surgery is compact as the surrounding instruments and equipment need to be in arms reach of the dentist and dental nurse. The working areas are well defined to prevent accidents and ensure the smooth flow of procedures.

While attending to a patient the dentist usually works in the 9 o clock to 12 o clock position and the dental nurse in the 3 o clock to 6 o clock. If a lower tooth is being filled the nurse usually sits or stands at 3 o clock. Standing provides a better vantage point as you are looking down on the tooth. When an upper tooth is being restored the nurse usually sits facing the patient. By sitting on a lowered stool you can look up at the tooth. Always watch your back by positioning the stool correctly. The dentist gets priority on viewing vantage as the dentist is doing detailed work. This may limit your view. Make sure that you do not obscure the dentist's vision by placing your head in front of the overhead light!

When the nurse is mixing materials they should use the work surface on their side of the room. The working area of a dental surgery is very small so the dentist and dental nurse should not "crowd" each other but keep to their side of the dental chair.

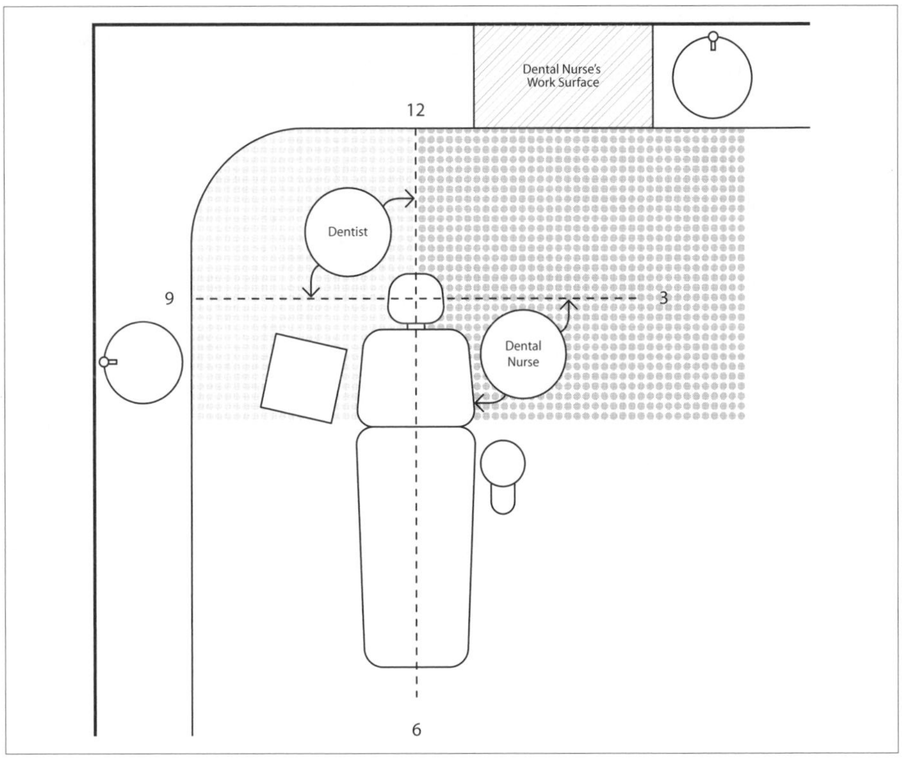

If the nurse tries to use cupboards and drawers on the dentist's side while the dentist is operating on a patient, they may inadvertently nudge the dentist causing an accident. Never go between the patient and the dentist. The dental nurse should organise the surgery to maximise the use of space.

PASSING INSTRUMENTS

Instruments must be passed smoothly and firmly between the nurse and dentist. The nurse may have to hold several instruments at once while doing the suction. You should hold the suction in your right hand while in your left hand you stack the instruments individually between each of your fingers. This allows you to hold up to four instruments and let go of each instrument individually without dropping the lot.

Figure 2.2 Stacking the instruments.

Instruments should be passed out of the vision of the patient either behind their head or low under the chin. Never pass anything over the patient's face. If an instrument is accidentally dropped it should not fall on their face. Sometimes the dentist has to keep focussed on the patient's tooth. In this instance, you have to place the instrument firmly and precisely into the dentist's hand. Do not expect the dentist to fumble blindly for it. The instruments should be placed into the

Figure 2.1 The seating positions of the dentist and dental nurse in a typical dental surgery.

exact working position of the hand. This ensures a smooth flow of movement that the patient equates to competency. It is also efficient and avoids accidents.

SUCTION

The wide bore suction has three functions;

1. MOISTURE CONTROL

    It sucks up water, saliva and debris.

2. RETRACTION

    It retracts the tongue and cheek allowing physical and visual access.

3. PROTECTION

    It protects the tongue and cheeks from traumatic injury from burs and sharp instruments. When you are working on the left hand side of the patient's mouth the nurse's role is to protect the left cheek. When working on the patient's right you must protect the tongue at all times.

All three functions should be borne in mind as you use the suction.

Imagine the mouth is like a bowl. Any fluid will always fall to the bottom of the bowl. When aspirating make sure that the suction tip is as close to the tooth as possible or down where the water will flow. Never place the suction on the back of the patient's tongue or palate as this will make them retch. Do not press the suction into the gum as this can traumatise the gingivae and never lean it against the dentist's hand or handpiece. Be careful not to obscure the dentist's hand mirror with the suction tip. Keep the suction tip still while the dentist is drilling to prevent accidents and to allow the dentist to fully concentrate on the tooth without being distracted by your movement. The suction is used precisely as the working field is very small (often just one tooth).

BASIC INSTRUMENT TRAYS

These are typical trays. However every dentist works differently and you must learn to set up the instruments that your dentist specifically requires.

1. EXAMINATION TRAY

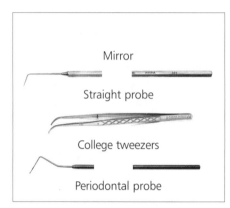

Figure 2.3 A typical examination tray.
(Courtesy of Minerva.)

2. FILLING TRAY

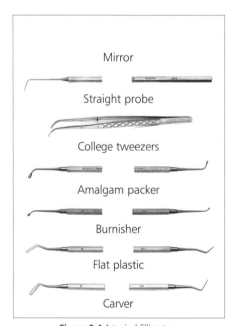

Figure 2.4 A typical filling tray.
(Courtesy of Minerva.)

3. EXTRACTION TRAY

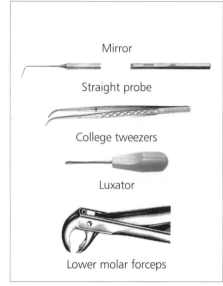

Figure 2.5 A typical extraction tray for a lower molar.
(Courtesy of Minerva and SDI Director.)

BASIC CHARTING

Many dental nurses find this confusing at first so you are not alone!
The chart is a schematic method of representing the teeth in the mouth. It represents every surface of each tooth. It shows us the past treatment of the tooth and any future treatment required.

6

THE MOUTH

Obviously there are upper and lower teeth. The upper teeth are placed above the horizontal line and the lower teeth below.

The mouth is also divided into right and left along an imaginary line running down the centre of the face. This is called the midline.

Figure 2.6 *Upper and lower.*

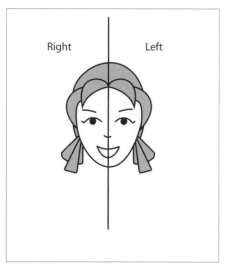

Figure 2.7 *The patient's right and left.*

Remember you are not looking at yourself in the mirror but are facing the patient. You must chart <u>their</u> left and <u>their</u> right NOT yours.

Put this information together and the mouth becomes divided into four quadrants.

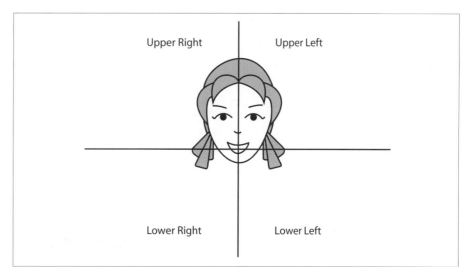

Figure 2.8 *The four quadrants.*

THE TEETH

Every permanent tooth is designated a number as follows;

1 = central incisor
2 = lateral incisor
3 = canine
4 = first premolar
5 = second premolar
6 = first molar
7 = second molar
8 = third molar

For example the lower right first molar = lower right 6 = LR6.

For example the upper left canine = upper left 3 = UL3.

THE SURFACES OF THE TEETH

Each tooth is represented as a box. Every surface of the tooth is represented within the box. Molars and premolars are posterior teeth. Incisors and canines are anterior teeth.

Posterior (back) tooth   Anterior (front) tooth

Figure 2.9 The teeth.

The biting surface of a **posterior** tooth is called the **occlusal** surface. The occlusal surface occludes with the opposing teeth. The **anterior** teeth do not have a big grinding surface but a blade-like edge for cutting and nibbling. This is called the **incisal edge**.

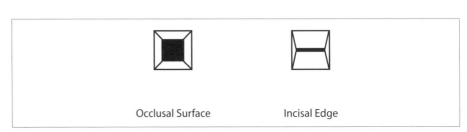

Occlusal Surface   Incisal Edge

Figure 2.10 Occlusal and incisal surfaces.

The inner surfaces of the teeth are those closest to the tongue or palate.
In the upper teeth the inside surface is closest to the palate and is known as the **palatal** surface.
In the lower teeth the surface closest to the tongue is called the **lingual** surface. Both the palatal and lingual surfaces are represented as the side closest to the horizontal line.

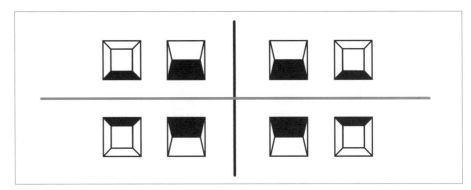

Figure 2.11 Palatal and lingual surfaces.

The outer surfaces of the teeth have one of two names.
All posterior teeth are next to the cheek. Their outer surface is called the **buccal** surface. Buccal comes from the word buccinator which is your cheek muscle. The outside surface of your anterior teeth are next to the lips and are called the **labial** surface.
The buccal and labial surfaces are represented as the side furthest away from the horizontal line.

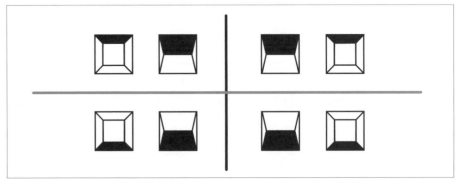

Figure 2.12 Buccal and labial surfaces.

8

The last surfaces that we chart are the surfaces between the teeth called the interproximal surfaces.

In each tooth one surface will be close to the midline and the other surface will be faraway from the midline. The surface closest to the midline is called the **mesial** surface. So the mesial is near the middle.

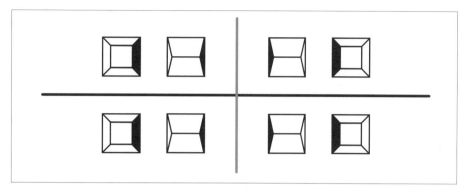

Figure 2.13 Mesial surface.

The surface furthest away from the midline is called the **distal** surface. So the distal is at a distance from the midline

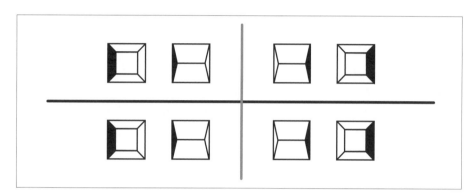

Figure 2.14 Distal surface.

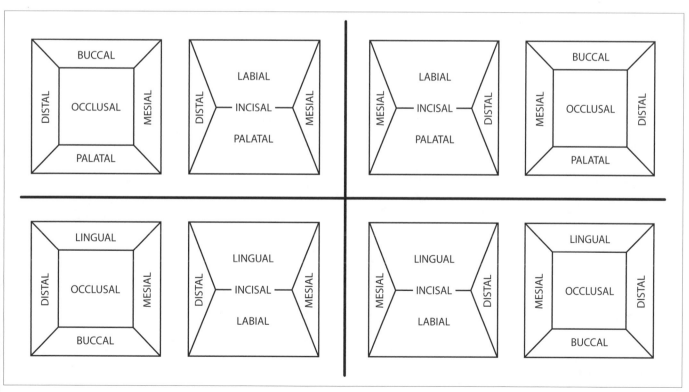

So to summarise front and back teeth can be represented as such;

Figure 2.15 The surfaces of the teeth.

Congratulations!

You now know the name of every tooth surface and how to chart it. The rest is easy!

By putting all this information together you can now chart fillings. Charts are a pictorial method of recording information efficiently. Here are some examples;

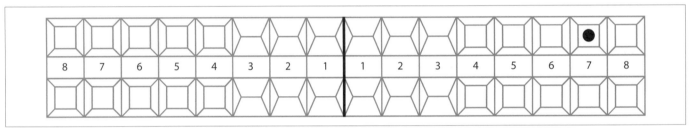

Figure 2.16 *An occlusal filling in the upper left second molar (UL7).*

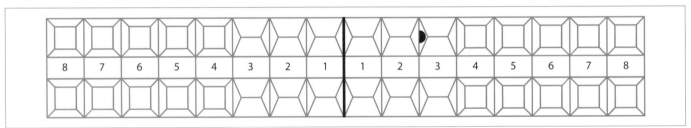

Figure 2.17 *A mesial filling in the upper left canine (UL3).*

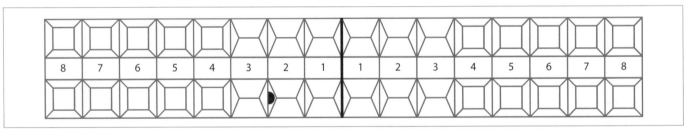

Figure 2.18 *A distal filling in the lower right lateral incisor (LR2).*

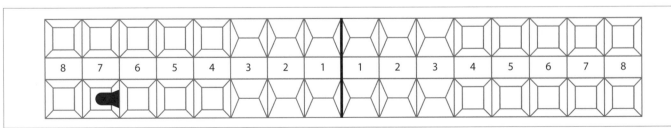

Figure 2.19 *A mesial-occlusal filling (known as an MO) in the lower right second molar (LR7).*

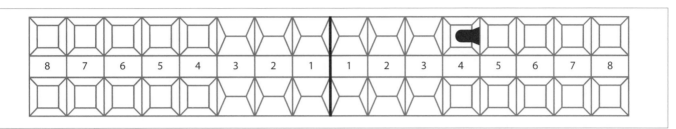

Figure 2.20 *A distal-occlusal filling (known as a DO) in the upper left first premolar (UL4)*

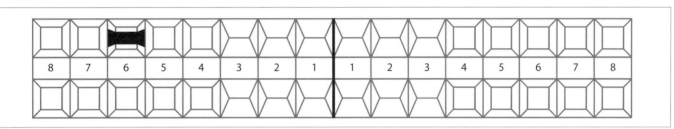

Figure 2.21 *A mesial-occlusal-distal (known as a MOD) in the upper right first molar (UR6).*

Most paper charts have an inner grid and an outer grid. The **inner grid** is for work already present in the mouth. This is called a **base charting**. The **outer grid** is for **work to be carried out or recently completed**. Many computer charts use the same grid for both. Whichever system you use the charting should be updated at the end of every appointment.

On a paper chart, a filling that already exists is shaded in. A filling that needs to be done is charted as an outline. As soon as the filling is completed it is shaded in on the chart.

A tooth that needs to be extracted is represented as a diagonal line. As soon as it has been extracted it is marked with a cross. If the tooth is already missing it is represented as a horizontal line.

| Tooth to be extracted | Recently extracted tooth | Missing tooth |

Figure 2.23

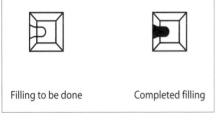

| Filling to be done | Completed filling |

Figure 2.22

Q1. Fill in all the tooth surfaces on the diagram.

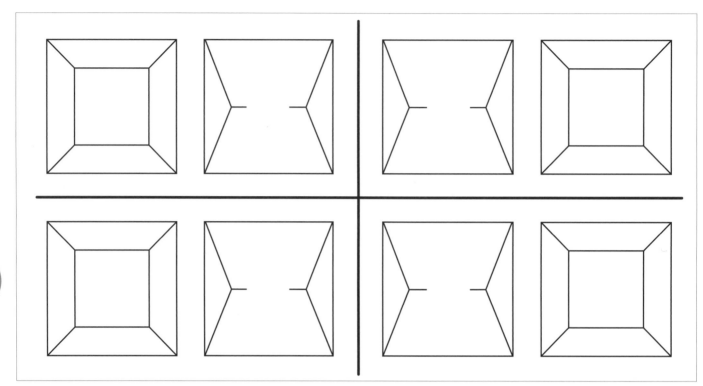

Q2. Please chart the following on the dental chart below.

Upper right second molar has an occlusal filling.
Upper right canine has a mesial filling.
Upper right lateral incisor has a palatal filling.
Upper left lateral incisor has a palatal cavity.
Upper left first premolar has a buccal cavity.
Upper left first molar has a distal-occlusal filling.

Lower left second molar has a mesial-occlusal-distal cavity.
Lower left first premolar needs to be extracted.
Lower left central incisor has recently been extracted.
Lower right lateral incisor has a distal-incisal filling.
Lower right second molar is missing.
Lower right third molar has a lingual cavity.

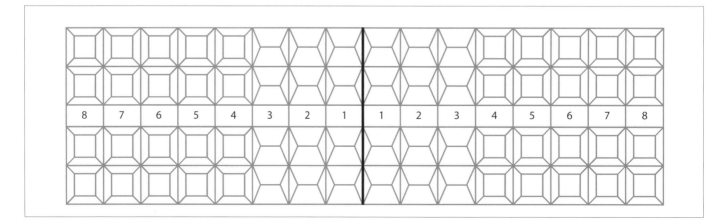

How well did you do?

A1.

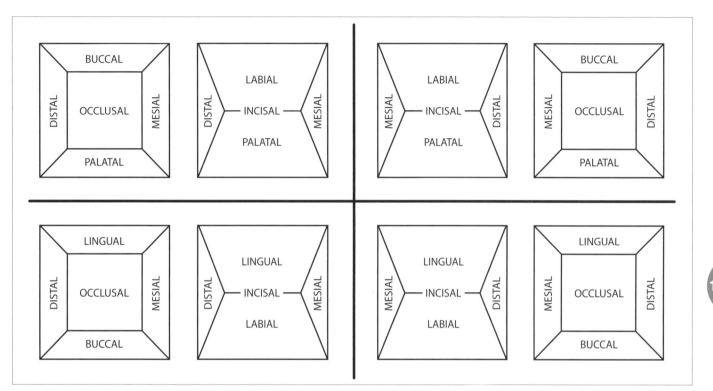

A2.

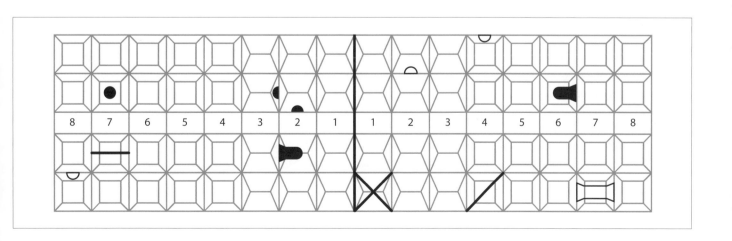

3. Cross Infection Control

"First do no harm."
Why do I need to know about bugs?

MICRO ORGANISMS

While reading the text answer the following;

Q1. How do bacteria survive unfavourable environments?

Q2. Name three types of bacteria.

Q3. How large is a virus?

Q4. How does a virus multiply?

Q5. Name an important fungus of the mouth.

Q6. Name two oral infections caused by fungi.

Q7. What are prions?

Q8. How do they differ to bacteria, viruses and fungi?

Q9. What is a biofilm?

Micro organisms/germs/microbes are tiny organisms which cover every surface of our body. The mouth is a warm, moist and protective environment where microbes can flourish. Some are harmless but others can cause diseases which can be spread from one person to another. Microbes which produce disease are called pathogens. Microbes are the organisms that you kill every time you autoclave instruments and disinfect work surfaces. This is cross infection control. It is one of the most important roles of the dental nurse. Every member of the dental team has a legal obligation to follow Health and Safety requirements to prevent cross infection in order to protect their patients, colleges, themselves and their families.

BACTERIA

- Bacteria are single celled organisms which can be seen under the microscope. They are similar in size to human cells.
- Bacterial infections are treated with antibiotics.
- Some bacteria can survive unfavourable environments by forming protective coatings and becoming spores. These are very tough and can only be killed by sterilisation.
- Bacteria are defined by their shape;

1. Bacilli (singular, bacillus) are rod shaped. For example fusiform bacilli are found in acute necrotising ulcerative gingivitis (ANUG).
2. Cocci (singular, coccus) are round. For example staphylococci are found in nose infections while streptococcus mutans causes tooth decay.
3. Spirochetes are spiral and can also be found in ANUG.

VIRUSES

- Viruses are about 1000 times smaller than bacteria and can only be seen with an electron microscope.
- They live within the cells of other organisms. A cell which has been infected by a virus is called a host cell.
- The virus takes control of the host cell and makes it produce thousands of new viruses. This process ends up killing the host cell which bursts open releasing the newly formed viruses. These viruses then proceed to infect new host cells and the cycle continues.
- They are responsible for a wide range of diseases such as colds, flu, German measles (rubella), Chicken pox, Glandular fever, mumps, herpes, shingles, hepatitis and AIDS.
- Some viruses can be treated with anti-viral drugs (not antibiotics) but many are unaffected by any drugs.

- Viral infections are very difficult to treat as the viruses inhabit our own cells. This is a classical case of "prevention is better than cure". Specific vaccines have been developed to provide immunity against many of the more serious viral infections.

FUNGI

- Fungi are larger than bacteria. In fact if there are enough fungi on the tongue they can be seen as a white coating with the naked eye.
- The most important fungi in the mouth is Candida albicans.
- It causes denture stomatitis under dentures which are continually worn.
- It also causes oral thrush in people with a low resistance to infection such as patients with AIDS or debilitated people who cannot clean their mouths properly.
- Candida is treated with anti-fungal drugs.

PRIONS

- These are not living organisms but special proteins. Disease producing prions are made of abnormal proteins.
- They are associated with nerve tissue.
- Prions are found in people suffering from the rare neurological disease called CJD (Creutzfeldt-Jakob Disease).
- Unlike bacteria, viruses and fungi they cannot be destroyed by sterilisation (autoclaving).This means that there is a theoretical risk of cross infection with reusable endodontic files so these files are now discarded after a single use.

BIOFILMS

Bacteria can exist in two ways. They can either live as free floating single cells or as a biofilm. Biofilms occur in aqueous environments when bacteria stick to a surface and each other.

BACTERIA + SURFACE + WATER
= BIOFILM

The bacteria secrete a sticky glue-like substance that allows them to stick to all types of surfaces such as metal, plastic, teeth and tissue. The sticky matrix protects the bacteria. Biofilms may be composed of one type of bacterium but usually consist of several different types. They can also include other micro organisms such as fungi. Biofilms are important in two main areas of dentistry.

1. Biofilms may cause cross infection if they are allowed to flourish in our water lines within the dental unit/chair, autoclaves, handpieces and ultrasonic equipment. The small bore plastic tubing of our dental waterlines are ideal surfaces to accommodate well established biofilms if they are not properly maintained. This would be detrimental to patients with a compromised immune system.

2. Plaque is a biofilm. It is a collection of bacteria which produces a sticky matrix allowing them to adhere to each other and the teeth. Plaque causes dental decay and periodontal (gum) disease.

Q1. Bacteria can form protective coatings to become spores. True or false?

Q2. A spirochete is round. True or false?

Q3. How large is a virus?

a. a thousand times smaller than a human cell
b. a thousand times smaller than a bacterium
c. a hundred times smaller than a bacterium
d. ten times smaller than a bacterium

Q4. A virus invades a host cell and makes it produce thousands of new viruses, killing the host cell in the process. True or false?

Q5. Which of the following are fungi;

a. Candida albicans
b. Penicillin
c. Hepatitis B
d. HIV

Q6. Which of the following are caused by fungal infection;

a. denture stomatitis
b. denture hyperplasia
c. oral thrush
d. oral herpes

Q7. What are prions?

a. micro organisms
b. special carbohydrates
c. special proteins
d. special viruses

Q8. Prions cannot be destroyed by autoclaving. True or false?

Q9. Biofilms only form on dry surfaces. True or false?

How well did you do?
A1.True   A2.False   A3.a,b
A4.True   A5.a   A6.a,c   A7.c
A8.True   A9.False

STERILISATION AND DISINFECTION

While reading the text answer the following;

Q1. What is the definition of sterilisation?

Q2. What is the definition of disinfection?

Micro organisms can spread from patient to patient via dirty instruments. They can also be passed directly from patient to clinical staff and vice versa. We prevent cross infection by the use of sterilisation, disinfection and the careful disposal of contaminated articles.

STERILISATION

Sterilisation is the process of killing all micro organisms. This means that no bacteria, viruses, fungi or spores remain. Sterilisation is an absolute term-the instrument is either sterile or not.

DISINFECTION

Disinfection is the process of eliminating most micro organisms but not all. This is a relative term-disinfectants work to various degrees. Most disinfectants will kill the majority of bacteria and fungi but may be ineffective against viruses and spores. Disinfection is useful because it cuts down the number of micro organisms that the body would have to defend itself against.

DISPOSABLES

Disposable items are those which are used on a single patient and then safely thrown away. This eliminates the chance of cross infection. Disposable items include syringes, needles, scalpels, sterile dressings, cotton wool rolls, gloves, rubber dams, matrix bands and local anaesthetic cartridges.

Q1. Which of the following is true of sterilisation;

a. it is a relative term
b. it is an absolute term
c. all pathogens are destroyed
d. most microbes are destroyed

Q2. Which of the following is true of disinfection;

a. it is a relative term
b. it is an absolute term
c. all pathogens are destroyed
d. most microbes are destroyed

How well did you do?
A1.b,c   A2.a,d

SURGERY DESIGN

While reading the text answer the following;

Q1. What special design features should be present in a dental surgery?

Q2. What is found in the sterile zone?

Q3. What is found in the disinfected zone?

Q4. What is found in the dirty zone?

Q5. How does zoning maintain cross infection control?

Q6. What is the aerosol effect?

Q7. How should dental unit waterlines be treated?

Surgeries should be designed to promote cross infection control. They have the following features;

- Simple, uncluttered layout.
- Wash basins should have arm controlled taps and liquid hand wash dispensers.
- It should be well ventilated.
- The work surfaces should be smooth.
- The floor covering should be laid in one piece with sealed joints to cope with any spills. The flooring should ideally curve up at the walls. Carpet must not be used.
- Light switches, door, cupboard and drawer handles should be easy to disinfect.
- The dental unit should have foot controls.
- The opening of bin lids should be foot operated.

ZONING

In an operating theatre the surgeons work in a sterile environment. They do not have the public walking in and out.

In a dental surgery, quite correctly, the patients expect all dental work to be carried out using sterile instruments in a very clean environment. However they also expect to be able to nip into the dentist to have their treatment during their lunch break, after picking the kids up from school etc. This means that the surgery has to be accessible to a great volume of people every day. So how do we maintain a high standard of hygiene for routine dentistry?

Through zoning. Zoning is usually described as two areas; clean and dirty. However for **routine** dental work I like to subdivide both zones into two further areas. The clean zone consists of the sterile zone and disinfected zone. The dirty zone consists of the contaminated zone and the remaining areas. For **surgical** procedures such as implant placement I have described the cross infection control method in Chapter 20.

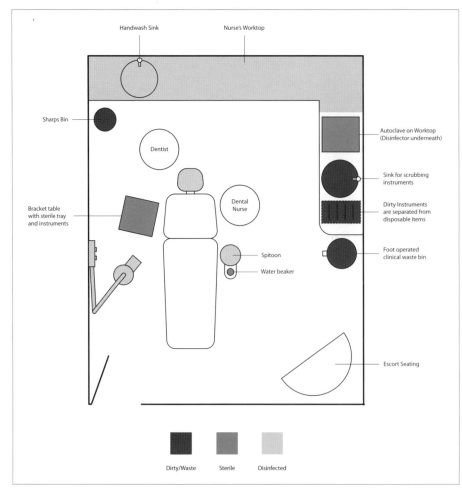

Figure 3.1 Zones in a typical dental surgery.

Look at the above diagram of a typical dental surgery. It has been shaded to represent the various zones.

A. CLEAN ZONE

1. STERILE ZONE

Everything in this zones must be able to be sterilised (autoclaved) or disposable (for single use only). This includes all hand instruments which should be placed on a sterile tray, handpieces, burs, suction tips and 3-in-1 nozzles. It also includes items such as paper points, gutta percha points and pins. Basically anything that goes in the patient's mouth.

2. DISINFECTED ZONE

Everything in this zone must be able to be disinfected between every patient. This applies to all worktops, handpiece tubing, aspirator tubing, dental unit including overhead light handles and x-ray machine. Basically every surface which may have become contaminated through touch or the aerosol effect but has not been in the patient's mouth. It is important to keep work surfaces free from clutter so that they can easily be disinfected. All unnecessary equipment and items should be stored in cupboards. (During procedures such as implant placement these areas must be covered with sterile drapes and plastic film which must all be disposed of in the clinical waste after a single use.)

B. DIRTY ZONE

1. CONTAMINATED ZONE

Despite the name this area should be kept as clean and tidy as possible. This area is very small and contains contaminated instruments and a sink in which they are scrubbed prior to sterilising. All instruments from this contaminated zone should be sterilised before entering the sterile or disinfected zones. If a sterilised instrument is inadvertently placed in the contaminated zone it has to be sterilised again before being replaced on the bracket table even though the area may look clean to the naked eye. Why? Because as soon as an instrument touches this zone it will be contaminated by micro organisms and is no longer sterile.

2. REMAINING AREAS

This includes the floor, coat stand, wall mirror, paintings etc. These areas are cleaned on a regular basis throughout the week to the standard expected of a hygienic kitchen. From a dental perspective no instrument should ever touch this area. If an instrument is accidentally dropped it is left on the floor until the end of treatment. If a nurse picks it up during treatment they will need to change their gloves immediately as the instrument and gloves have become contaminated by the floor. The dropped instrument needs to be re-sterilised before it can be used again and should be immediately placed in the contaminated zone.

It is important for everyone to adhere to these zones during treatment. For example the dentist and nurse should not open the surgery door with gloved hands to talk to the receptionist. Patient escorts, such as friends and family, should remain in their area. Toddlers and young children should not be allowed to wander freely touching disinfected and sterilised areas.

THE ONE WAY CYCLE OF STERILISATION

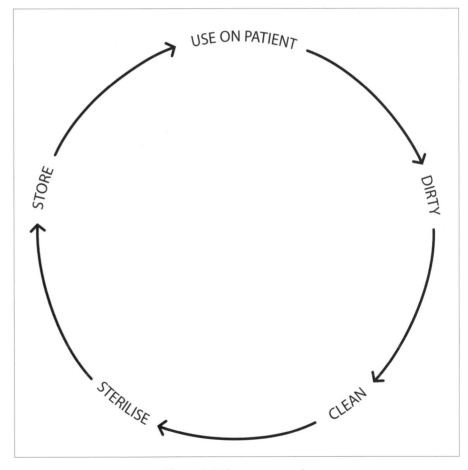

Figure 3.2 *The one way cycle.*

At the end of an appointment, dirty instruments and their tray are taken from the dentist's bracket table and placed in the contaminated zone to be cleaned. They are then autoclaved. Both tray and instruments are then stored until they are required. While storing, if any matter is seen on an instrument that instrument should be cleaned again and re-sterilised.

WHICH AREAS NEED TO BE DISINFECTED BETWEEN PATIENTS?

Easy. Both you and the dentist wear gloves whilst treating a patient. Imagine that both pairs of gloves have been dipped in red paint. Every time either one of you touch something imagine that a red mark is left. Every mark must be wiped away, i.e. disinfected, before the next patient is seen. Think about this next time you are in surgery. Have you disinfected everything? Did you include door handles, pens and dental material containers such as tubes of paste?

This exercise makes you very aware of cross infection control and how easy it is to inadvertently contaminate an area. It also disciplines you to work within a narrow area. After all, the less areas you contaminate the easier it is to disinfect between patients.

For every patient, the nurse should always have a sterile set of tweezers on their work top. If the nurse then needs to open a drawer to retrieve another instrument they can use the tweezers. This way there is no contamination of the drawer handles or the contents of the drawer. The tweezers must be autoclaved at the end of the appointment. New patient, new tweezers.

Work surfaces must be disinfected between patients as there is an aerosol effect from the use of handpieces, 3-in-1 syringes and the ultrasonic scaler. A cloud of water and saliva particles are released which may fall on worktops. It is also good practice to place a clean paper napkin on the disinfected surface and to use this as your workstation for a particular patient and after the appointment to dispose of this, re-disinfect and place a new paper napkin for the next patient. And so the cycle continues.

WATERLINES

At the beginning and end of the day water should be discharged for three minutes from the handpieces, 3-in-1 syringes and the spittoon to eliminate microbes that may have multiplied in the water lines over night. This is extremely important on Monday as the biofilms have had longer to become established over the weekend. All drinking water contains bacteria. The most common bacteria found in the dental unit waterlines are pseudomonas and Legionella. The build up of these bacteria must be prevented as they could cause problems especially in immunocompromised patients. Legionella causes pneumonia. Pseudomonas thrives in distilled water and is a highly resistant bacteria.

Figure 3.3 Dental unit cleaning/disinfecting solution. (Courtesy of Minerva and Durr Dental.)

At the end of the day, after the last patient has been seen, the dental unit waterlines are flushed through with the appropriate cleaning solution. First the dental nurse puts on heavy-duty rubber gloves and cleans out the filters in the dental unit. All dental chairs come with a customised plastic basin. The cleaning solution is placed in this basin following the manufacturer's instructions. Both aspiration nozzles are places in their designated slots within the customised basin and are allowed time to suck up all the cleaner. When it is empty the aspirators are put back in their holders. The chair is raised to it's highest level (so that the floor can be washed easily) and the dental unit is then switched off at the mains.

Which of the following features are best for a dental surgery?

    a. carpet
    b. smooth surfaces
    c. cluttered units
    d. swing bins

Q2. What is found in the sterile zone during routine dentistry?

    a. autoclaved handpiece
    b. new paper point
    c. x-ray machine
    d. used flat plastic

Q3. What is found in the disinfected zone?

    a. handpiece
    b. new paper point
    c. x-ray machine
    d. used flat plastic

Q4. What is found in the contaminated zone?

    a. handpiece
    b. new paper point
    c. x-ray machine
    d. used flat plastic

Q5. Zoning maintains cross infection control by rotating instruments in a one way cycle from used/dirty to clean, sterilised, and stored again. True or false?

Q6. Which of the following creates an aerosol of microbes?

    a. sneeze
    b. high speed handpiece
    c. carver
    d. 3-in-1 syringe

Q7. How should dental water lines be treated?

    a. autoclaves and ultrasonic baths should be emptied of water at the end of the day
    b. midday the dental unit should be flushed with cleaning solution
    c. after the last patient the dental unit should be flushed with cleaning solution
    d. water should be discharged for three minutes from handpieces, 3-in-1 syringes and the spittoon at the beginning of the day.

How well did you do?
    A1.b A2.a,b A3.c A4.d
    A5.True A6.a,b,d A7.a,c,d

SO WHAT DO I DO?

METHOD OF STERILISING INSTRUMENTS IN THE SURGERY

While reading the text answer the following;

Q1. Why is it important to clean instruments?

Q2. What are the functions of the ultrasonic bath and disinfector?

Q3. How are autoclaves maintained?

Q4. Name two other types of sterilization.

In the dental surgery instruments are sterilised by autoclave. Before being placed in the autoclave they must be cleaned of all obvious matter.

CLEANING

Most student nurses think that if an instrument is autoclaved it will automatically be sterile. Wrong! Instruments have to be cleaned thoroughly first to remove all visual matter. Remember, micro organisms are minute. To understand this try to visualise one cubic millimetre of blood. This small volume of blood contains five million red blood cells and several thousand white blood cells. So a dried spot of blood contains millions and millions of cells including any pathogens. On a microscopic level the cells in the centre are protected by the cells in the outer layers of dried blood.

These inner cells could be infected with a virus and may survive autoclaving to infect the next patient. That is why all dental nurses need to be diligent at cleaning contaminated instruments.

As a dental nurse, you are handling contaminated instruments so you should be fully immunised, especially against Hepatitis B. You must take care not to injure yourself on sharp instruments. Heavy duty gloves should be used when handling and washing contaminated instruments. Under no circumstance should a dental nurse scrub instruments with ungloved hands. Nurses with latex allergy can use the double glove technique with vinyl gloves.

There are three methods to clean instruments; scrubbing, ultrasonic and disinfector.

1. SCRUBBING

Scrubbing is the least effective method of cleaning the instruments. The instruments may be pre-soaked in an enzymatic solution. They are fully immersed in warm water. Plastic items should be scrubbed with a long handled plastic brush. The inside of reusable wide bore suction tips can be cleaned with a long handled bottle brush. These brushes should be autoclavable. Metal instruments, handpieces and burs are scrubbed with a wire brush. The hand pieces are scrubbed with the bur in place. After scrubbing, the bur is removed and the handpieces are oiled before placing in the autoclave. The

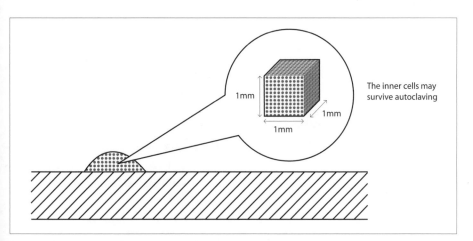

Figure 3.4 A drop of blood on the surface of an instrument.

slow handpiece should be separated into two before oiling and autoclaving. The oil can should be shaken first to ensure that the contents are well mixed. A tissue is held against the head of the handpiece to absorb excess oil. (If the manufacturer recommends oiling the handpieces again after autoclaving this should be done with clean oil cans. The nurse should mark the oil cans with "clean" or "dirty"). Cleaning and maintenance systems are available which clean and lubricate handpieces. They flush the air and water channels with cleaning fluid and oil the internal parts automatically.

2. ULTRASONIC BATH

An ultrasonic bath contains detergent (not disinfectant) which vibrates at high frequency to dislodge small particles. First the instruments are scrubbed manually. Then they are placed in a basket and fully submerged in the detergent. The lid is placed and the machine switched on for 15 minutes. Handpieces should not be placed in the ultrasonic bath as this may damage them. The detergent in the ultrasonic bath should be changed frequently (twice daily in a busy surgery) and emptied, cleaned and dried at the end of the day to prevent the formation of biofilms.

3. DISINFECTORS

Disinfectors are the most effective method of cleaning instruments. They pre-wash the instruments at a temperature lower than 35°C with high pressure spray. Disinfectors take longer to clean the instruments and are expensive. However they are a safer method of cleaning instruments for the dental nurse as they eliminate the need to scrub manually. They also release the nurse for other duties.

AUTOCLAVING

Anything that is placed in the patient's mouth must be autoclaved or disposed of after every patient. An autoclave works like a pressure cooker as it uses steam under pressure to sterilise.

Downward displacement autoclaves have the following characteristics;

- They reach a temperature of 134°C and hold this temperature for 3 minutes.
- At this temperature they maintain a pressure of 2.25 bar.
- This kills all bacteria, spores, viruses and fungi.
- A complete cycle usually takes between 15 to 20 minutes to allow the temperature and pressure to build up and then reduce.
- The cycle cannot be interrupted and the door cannot be opened during the cycle.

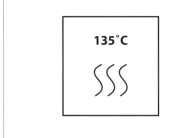

135°C

Figure 3.8 Sterilisation symbol.

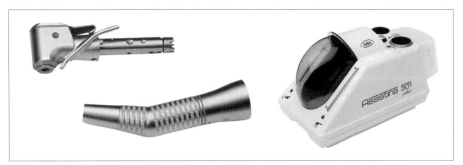

Figure 3.5 The head and shank of a slow speed hand piece and a cleaning and maintenance system. (Courtesy of Minerva, Kavo and W&H.)

Figure 3.6 A disinfector. (Courtesy of Minerva and Eschmann.)

All metal instruments can be sterilised but some plastics melt at high temperatures. Plastic equipment which needs to be sterilised will have a symbol on it with the temperature to which it can safely be heated. This includes items such as the nozzles of the 3-in-1 syringes and wide bore suction tips. Look for this symbol. If in doubt ask the dentist first before autoclaving. Most can be sterilised at 134°C for 3 minutes but some have to be sterilised at 126°C for 10 minutes. Most autoclaves have this second setting.

Figure 3.7 *An autoclave.*
(Courtesy of Minerva and Eschmann.)

Figure 3.9 *Trays with perforations to allow effective sterilization. (Courtesy of Minerva and Nichromnox.)*

In order to sterilise, the steam must be able to perculate all around the instruments. Always ensure that the instruments are evenly spread on perforated trays. Do not pile up instruments in the autoclave.

After autoclaving the instruments should be stored away to prevent contamination by airborne microbes. Instruments should be dry before being stored. Handpieces and surgical instruments can be kept in pouches or covered kits. Instruments should not be stored in liquids.

TYPES OF AUTOCLAVES

1. NON-VACUUM AUTOCLAVES

These are called downward displacement autoclaves as the air is displaced downward by steam during autoclaving. However hollow instruments such as handpieces may not always be fully sterilised by this type of autoclave.

2. VACUUM AUTOCLAVES

Vacuum autoclaves suck out all the air first before releasing steam. These autoclaves will sterilise handpieces. Unfortunately these autoclaves require a longer cycle. Vacuum autoclaves will sterilise bagged instruments.

MAINTAINANCE OF THE AUTOCLAVE

1. Each morning the nurse fills the water chamber to the recommended level with distilled water. The chamber is emptied at night to prevent microbes colonising the water system. The autoclave is left open to dry.
2. A test cycle of the autoclave should be run at the beginning of each day. The autoclave should be monitored by the nurse and a log of temperature, pressure and length of one complete cycle recorded. Many autoclaves have a printout to record each stage of the cycle automatically. These should be kept for eleven years. (Indicator strips can also be used. They change colour to show that the correct temperature has been reached. However this does not guarentee sterility as they do not test the pressure.)
3. The nurse should make a weekly inspection of the door seal.
4. The autoclave must be tested annually by a trained engineer to ensure that it conforms to health and safety regulations.
5. Dental insurance policies must cover third person liability for autoclaves (and compressors) as they are pressurised systems.

OTHER TYPES OF STERILISERS

1. GLASS BEAD STERILISER

These are used during endodontics to sterilise files while operating on a single patient. The glass beads are heated to 218°C and the files are dipped in the beads for 20 seconds to re-sterilise. By continually re-sterilising the files, the dentist prevents bacteria from an infected canal being introduced into another clean canal.

2. INDUSTRIAL STERILISER

Ionising radiation is used to sterilise manufactured dental products such as needles, scalpels, suture needles and sterile dressings. These products arrive sealed to maintain their sterility and are made for single use only.

Q1. All instruments must be thoroughly cleaned before autoclaving to ensure sterilisation. True or false?

Q2. What is the function of an ultrasonic bath?

   a. it is used to remove calculus from teeth
   b. it removes small particles from contaminated instruments
   c. it sterilises endodontic file
   d. it sterilises instruments

Q3. Every morning the nurse should run a test cycle to ensure that the autoclave does which of the following?

   a. reaches 134°C
   b. reaches 143°C
   c. at 2.25 bar
   d. at 1.34 bar

Q4. Which of the following are other types of sterilization.

   a. ultrasonic bath
   b. hot glass beads
   c. ionising radiation
   d. industrial

How well did you do?

A1.True   A2.b   A3.a,c
A4.b,c,d

DISINFECTING

While reading the text answer the following;

Q1. What is the disadvantage of bleach?

Q2. How is blood spillage managed?

Q3. What personal hygiene measures should a nurse take?

Q4. Describe the hepatitis B vaccination.

Q5. How should clinical staff wash their hands?

WORK SURFACES

Sodium hypochlorite (bleach) can kill bacteria, spores, fungi and viruses including hepatitis B virus and HIV. Bleach is useful for disinfecting work tops at the end of the day. However bleach will corrode metal items.
Gloves, gown and glasses should be worn as sodium hypochlorite can irritate the skin, airway and eyes and splashes will bleach clothes. Always have the surgery well ventilated. Bleach should be stored carefully.

An effective and efficient method of disinfecting surfaces between patients is the use of alcohol based wipes. These wipes should be fully wet with disinfectant not just damp. They come in plastic tubs/dispensers which help to prevent the evaporation of the disinfectant within. The wipes are disposed of after a single use in the yellow bins. Disinfectant sprays are also available. The advantage of disinfectant wipes over disinfectant sprays is that there is no aerosol effect of chemicals. Masks and safety glasses should be worn when using sprays in addition to gloves.

Work surfaces and handles may be covered with plastic film. However the protective plastic coverings must be discarded and replaced with new ones between every patient.

IMPRESSIONS AND APPLIANCES

The surgery is responsible for ensuring that impressions and appliances are disinfected before being sent to the laboratory. Impressions and appliances should be rinsed under water. Appliances can be placed in the ultrasonic bath. Both should be immersed in disinfectant for 10 minutes. They are then rinsed, dried and bagged. The label should confirm that they were disinfected. The exception is alginate impressions which should not be dried but wrapped in damp tissue before bagging to prevent dehydration and distortion. The label of returned laboratory work should be checked to ensure that it has been disinfected before placing in the patient's mouth.

RADIOGRAPHS

After taking an x-ray the tube head and switches should be cleaned with a disinfectant wipe. The exposed film packet should be wiped before processing.

MIXING PADS

Dental nurses usually mix dental materials on a paper or plastic mixing pad. Never place the whole pad on the dentist's bracket table as you will contaminate the underlying sheets for the next patient. Always tear the top sheet off and place this on the bracket table.

BLOOD SPILLAGE

Heavy duty gloves should be worn. A blood spillage should be treated with 10,000 ppm (parts per million) hypochlorite solution (bleach) or a powder disinfectant such as Virkon™. The blood and disinfectant is then covered with a disposable towel for three minutes. After this the soaked towels are disposed of into yellow plastic bags and the area cleaned with detergent.

ROOM VENTILATION

The surgery should be well ventilated to prevent an increase in the number of air born bacteria. This may mean opening a window, using an extractor fan or a ventilation system. Air recycling systems are not recommended.
About 100 million bacteria will be released into the air throughout the day. By the competent use of high volume suction, during dental treatment this aerosol effect is greatly reduced.

PERSONAL HYGIENE AND PROTECTION

PERSONAL HYGIENE

Long hair must be tied back. All jewellery including watches must be removed. No nail varnish or nail extensions are permitted as they can harbour microbes. Be aware that odours can be overpowering in a confined space. This includes perfumes, aftershaves and body odours.

UNIFORM

Nurses must wear a uniform to protect themselves from splatter from infected materials. Uniforms should only be worn in the surgery, not to and from work. They should be placed in a separate bag when being transported. All uniforms should be washed separately from other clothes at 65°C. Dental uniforms should be short sleeved so that your arms may be washed. For certain procedures a plastic bib may be worn over your uniform. Shoes should be flat and closed to protect the feet.

GLOVES

These are normally made of latex but vinyl gloves should be worn if you or the patient has a latex allergy. A new pair of gloves are used for each patient. If the gloves become punctured they must be removed immediately and your hands washed in disinfectant liquid soap before replacing with new gloves.

Heavy duty gloves should be worn when scrubbing instruments.

GLASSES

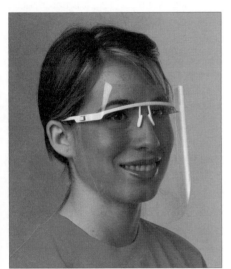

MASK

Disposable face masks should be worn to cover both the nose and mouth, not just the mouth alone. Masks should be worn under visors. Masks and visors guard against splatter (not microscopic organisms). Remove masks by the ties only. Never handle the filter.

Figure 3.10 *Safety visor and glasses. (Courtesy of Minerva and Codent.)*

Plastic safety glasses or visors prevent eye injury from infection and trauma. Sharp shards of filling can hit the eyes when drilling. Glasses should have side protection. If the patient has a cold sore use a rubber dam or place petroleum jelly over the sore. A rubber dam minimises the number of micro organisms in the aerosol and helps cross infection control. Cold sores are caused by the herpes virus and are highly infectious. Due to the aerosol effect they could be passed from an infected patient to a nurse's unprotected eyes. If possible treatment should be postponed until the sore has healed.

VACCINATIONS

As a dental nurse you should be immunised against hepatitis B before starting clinical duties. The vaccination consists of a series of three injections. Your blood is then tested to make sure that you have developed sufficient antibodies. Your antibody level should be greater than 100IU/ml. It is important for you to keep a written record of this. Every 3 to 5 years your blood should be retested and if needed a booster can be given.

As well as hepatitis B you should have had the routine childhood vaccinations including diptheria, pertussis, poliomyelitis, rubella, tetanus and tuberculosis.

HAND WASHING

Hands should be washed thoroughly at the start and finish of each session. As long as you go straight from one pair of gloves to the next without contaminating your actual hands, there is no need to wash between glove changes but you should use an alcohol hand rub instead. (Excess washing may cause dermatitis and dry skin lesions leaving you more exposed to infection.) If your hands become soiled at any time they will need to be rewashed.

1. All jewellery and watches should be removed.
2. Taps should never be turned on or off using your hands. Use your **elbows** to turn on the tap and to dispense liquid hand disinfectant such as Hibiscrub™.
3. Hands should be washed under warm running water thoroughly and methodically for at least 30 seconds using a disinfectant liquid soap. Your nails should be kept short and free from nail varnish and nail extensions to prevent the build up of underlying debris.
4. Rinse your hands keeping them at a higher level to your elbows so that any excess water drains away from your hands. If it drips the other way then your hands will be recontaminated.
5. Dry your hands with a clean disposable paper towel.
6. Any cuts should be covered with a waterproof dressing before putting on your gloves.
   At the end of the day after washing your hands you should moisturise them to keep the skin supple.

Q1. What is the disadvantage of bleach?

    a. it does not destroy hepatitis B
    b. it does not destroy spores
    c. it does not destroy HIV
    d. it rusts instruments

Q2. How is blood spillage managed?

    a. use heavy duty gloves
    b. treat with 10,000 ppm sodium hypochlorite
    c. treat with 1,000 ppm sodium hypochlorite
    d. treat with 10,000% sodium hypochlorite

Q3. What hygiene measures should a nurse make?

    a. tie back long hair
    b. wear nail varnish
    c. wear a wrist watch
    d. wear a mask

Q4. The hepatitis B vaccination consists of two injections taken six months apart. True or false?

Q5. How should clinical staff wash their hands?

    a. with ordinary hand soap
    b. for a minimum of 45 seconds
    c. by keeping your elbows higher than your hands
    d. under running water

How well did you do?
    A1.d   A2.a,b   A3.a,d   A4.False
    A5.d

MICROBES WHICH ARE OCCUPATIONAL HAZARDS IN DENTISTRY

While reading the text answer the following;

Q1. How do hepatitis B and C differ?

Q2. How is HIV spread?

Q3. What precaution is taken to prevent the spread of prions?

Q4. What is MRSA?

At the beginning of this chapter you learnt about different types of micro organisms. Some of these are particularly important in dentistry as they are an occupational hazard and may cause life threatening illnesses.

HEPATITIS B

Hepatitis is inflammation of the liver. Symptoms include poor apatite, aching muscles and joints, mild fever and jaundice. However the patient may get a sub-clinical infection and be unaware that they have been infected. Long term damage may result in liver cancer or cirrhosis. Hepatitis B is caused by the hepatitis B virus. This is a highly infectious virus. It is also difficult to destroy. The virus can be found in the blood, saliva and other bodily fluids of those infected. It is diagnosed with a blood test.

The hepatitis B vaccination is very effective. All dental nurses should be immunised against hepatitis B. People who are most at risk include;

- Health care workers as they frequently deal with blood.
- Drug abusers as they often share needles.
- The sexually promiscuous.
- People living or working in institutions such as prison and rehabilitation centres.
- Family members of people with chronic hepatitis B.
- People who have lived in Africa or China.

Most people who are infected with hepatitis B virus will produce antibodies and clear the virus from their body. Some people cannot eradicate the virus and so become carriers. They may have no symptoms, indeed they may not even be aware that they have the virus but they are infectious. As a dental nurse you will treat patients with hepatitis B many of whom will not know that they are carriers. Statistically it is estimated that a typical dental practice treats one hepatitis B patient every seven days. 0.0001ml of infected blood is

enough to transmit the virus. It is highly virulent. This is why your cross infection control routine for all patients is paramount. As an extra precaution, known carriers should be treated at the end of the day which allows more time for cross infection control procedures.

HEPATITIS C

Hepatitis C is inflammation of the liver caused by the hepatitis C virus. Patients with hepatitis C are more likely to develop serious liver problems. Hepatitis C is diagnosed by a blood test. It is transmitted by blood contact. Patients are unlikely to contract the virus through other bodily fluids. High risk groups include;

- Drug abusers.
- Haemophiliacs and patients who received contaminated blood before 1991. All donor blood is now tested for hepatitis C.

The greatest risk of catching hepatitis C is through needlestick injuries. Hepatitis C is less common than hepatitis B but there is no vaccine.

HIV (HUMAN IMMUNODEFICIENCY VIRUS)

HIV infection can develop into AIDS (Acquired Immune Deficiency Syndrome). The virus destroys certain white blood cells in the patient's immune system leaving them open to other infections. Patients may have no specific symptoms and so may be unaware that they are HIV positive. Diagnosis is by blood test. HIV can be detected in most bodily fluids. It is usually spread by having unprotected sex and sharing needles. High risk groups include;

- Drug abusers.
- Male homosexuals.
- Sexually promiscuous.
- People who have lived in Africa.
- As with hepatitis B, mothers can infect their children during childbirth.

There is no vaccine. Fortunately HIV is not very infective and can be easily destroyed by diligent cross infection control procedures. Again nurses should take care to avoid needlestick injuries. It is prudent to treat known HIV carriers at the end of the day.

CJD (CREUTZFELDT-JAKOB DISEASE)

CJD causes a rapid fatal degeneration of the nervous system. CJD is transmitted by prions. As you know these are unaffected by sterilisation. There is a theoretical risk of cross infection during root treatment so all endodontic files are discarded after a single use.

MRSA (METHICILLIN RESISTANT STAPHYLOCOCCUS AUREUS)

MRSA stands for Methicillin Resistant Staphylococcus Aureus. Staphylococcus Aureus bacteria are found in the nose, throat, mouth and on the skin of many healthy people. Unfortunately some strains of Staphylococcus Aureus have become resistant to antibiotics (including Methicillin).
MRSA tends to occur in debilitated patients. As these people are treated in hospitals it is easy for whole wards to become infected. MRSA is no more infectious than other strains of Staphylococcus Aureus but it is harder to treat and so is life threatening. MRSA infected patients are treated in isolation. Fortunately the spread of MRSA can be prevented by effective hand washing. Chlorhexidene can kill MRSA in 30 seconds (as can Listerine™). All medical staff and hospital visitors must be scrupulous in washing their hands before and after seeing patients.

Q1. Which of the following is true of hepatitis B and C?

   a. both are transmitted by blood
   b. both are transmitted by the sexually promiscuous
   c. both attack the liver
   d. both have vaccines

Q2. How is HIV spread?
   a. by shared needles
   b. by the sexually promiscuous
   c. by needlestick injuries
   d. by touching people with AIDS

Q3. What precaution is taken to prevent the spread of prions?

   a. disposal of endodontic files
   b. autoclaving endodontic files
   c. sterilising endodontic files
   d. scrubbing endodontic files

Q4. What is MRSA?
   a. a resistant bacteria
   b. an incurable disease
   c. a disease resistant to treatment
   d. a disease resistant to antibiotics

How well did you do?
   A1.a,c   A2.a,b,c   A3.a
   A4.a,c,d

CONTAMINATED NEEDLESTICK INJURY

While reading the text answer the following

Q1. What should you do if you prick yourself with a contaminated needle?

Q2. How should you assess the risk of cross infection?

Q3. How is the surgery waste disposed?

A needlestick injury refers to an injury caused by a sharp object which pierces the skin. The sharp object may be a needle, scaler, bur or scalpel.

1. Immediately squeeze the wound to encourage bleeding and continue to squeeze under running water.
2. Inform the dentist.
3. Disinfect the wound. Then dry and apply a waterproof dressing.
4. Check the medical history of the patient.
5. Record the accident and the name of the patient.
6. Get your blood tested by your doctor depending on the status of the patient.

Every practice should have a written policy for needlestick injuries and the whole clinical team should be trained to handle an incident should it occur. The extent of the injury should be assessed as you are cleaning and disinfecting the wound. Was the needle sterile or contaminated? Is it a deep wound? Is the wound bleeding? After tending the wound it is important to quickly assess the patient risk factors.

- Are they a known hepatitis B carrier or HIV positive?
- Are they a drug user?
- Have they lived in Africa or the Far East.
- Have they had a blood transfusion prior to 1991?
- Have they had sexual intercourse with a prostitute?
- Have they had male to male sexual intercourse?

To save patient embarrassment rather than asking these questions individually you can keep a standardised list and simply ask the patient if they fall into any of the categories.

If the answer is yes or you have any concerns you must seek medical advise promptly to have your blood tested and to begin post exposure prophylaxis. Post exposure prophylaxis involves taking anti-viral medication for one month starting immediately. Every clinical member of staff should know their antibody level against hepatitis B.

To prevent needle stick injuries always take great care when handling and passing any sharp instrument. The dentist should recap the needle using a needle guard as soon as it has been used. The dentist is also responsible for disposing the needle and empty cartridge into the sharps bin at the chairside.

Figure 3.11 Sharps bin. (Courtesy of Minerva.)

SHARPS

Sharps are any items that could pierce the skin for example needles, scalpels, extracted teeth, burs and local anaesthetic cartridges. The sharps bin is a yellow plastic puncture proof container. It has a self locking lid which should be sealed when the container is two thirds full. It is then collected and incinerated by authorised contractors. The signed transfer note should be kept for two years.

WASTE DISPOSAL

CLINICAL WASTE

Clinical waste is collected in yellow plastic bags within a foot operated bin. This waste includes any item that might be contaminated with saliva or blood such as swabs, gloves, masks, cotton wool rolls and disposable plastic aspirator tips. It is then collected and incinerated by authorised contractors.

SPECIAL WASTE

This includes all amalgam waste including extracted teeth with amalgam fillings. The amalgam is stored in special containers which prevent the escape of mercury vapour. It is collected by authorised contractors for recycling.

Special waste also includes the lead foil in radiographic films, x-ray developer and fixer. This is gathered separately and again collected by authorised contractors. Consignment notes must be signed and kept for three years.

CLERICAL WASTE

Clerical waste such as paper is collected in black plastic bags and disposed in the same manner as household waste.

Q1. What should you do if you prick yourself with a contaminated needle?

    a. panic
    b. encourage the wound to bleed
    c. wash under running water
    d. record the accident

Q2. After a needle stick injury the risk of cross infection is assessed by asking which of the following questions;

    a. was the needle sterile or used?
    b. is the patient in a high risk group?
    c. has the patient ever lived in Canada or USA?
    d. has the patient ever lived in Africa or the Far East?

Q3. How is the surgery waste disposed?

    a. sharps are placed in yellow bags
    b. clerical waste is placed in yellow bags
    c. clinical waste is placed in yellow bags
    d. sharps are placed in ridged yellow plastic containers

How well did you do?
    A1.b,c,d   A2.a,b,d   A3.c,d

4. Biomedical Sciences

I'm a Dental Nurse. Why do I need to know about Biomedical Sciences?

Biology =
   The study of living organisms.
Anatomy =
   The study of the body structure.
Physiology =
   The study of the body functions.

Well, you are dealing with many people and not all of them are going to be a 100% fit and well. Some will have high blood pressure, diabetes, epilepsy or a hundred and one other complaints. You need to know how a healthy body works to understand what's going wrong when there is a medical problem.

Also you will be assisting while the dentist is injecting, sedating or performing surgery on a patient. These things affect different patients in different ways, especially if the person is on medication. You need to know how your patient will be affected. Their general well being should always be at the forefront of your mind.

So what's the norm?

Circulatory System

BLOOD

While reading the text answer the following;

Q1. What is the pigment found in red blood cells?

Q2. What is the function of white blood cells?

Q3. What is the function of platelets?

Q4. What is plasma composed of?

Q5. List eight functions of the blood.

RED BLOOD CELLS

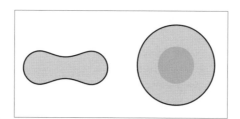

Figure 4 *Red blood cells.*

- Red blood cells carry oxygen around the body.
- A red blood cell is the shape of a concave disc.
- They contain a red pigment called haemoglobin.
- In the lungs oxygen binds with the haemoglobin. The red blood cells then carry the oxygen to the various cells throughout the body where it is released.
- Oxygen bound to haemoglobin gives arterial blood it's bright red colour. When the oxygen is released the blood darkens. This is why venous blood is darker than arterial blood.

WHITE BLOOD CELLS

- White blood cells defend the body against infection.
- They attack germs (micro organisms) and repair damaged tissue.
- There are several different types of white blood cell.

PLATELETS

- Platelets stop wounds bleeding excessively by forming blood clots.

PLASMA

- Plasma is a straw coloured liquid.
- 90% of plasma is water. The rest consists of plasma proteins.

FUNCTIONS OF BLOOD

1. Carries oxygen from the lungs to the cells.
2. Carries carbon dioxide away from the cells to the lungs.
3. Carries food from the intestine to the cells.
4. Carries waste products from the cells to the kidneys.
5. Carries hormones from the specific glands around the body.
6. Defends the body against disease.
7. Along with the skin, the blood maintains the body temperature at 37°C.
8. Blood clots at the site of injury to prevent excessive bleeding and blood loss.

SO WHAT CAN GO WRONG?

DISORDERS OF THE BLOOD

- Anaemia. People who do not have enough haemoglobin are said to be anaemic. There is less haemoglobin for oxygen to bind with so less oxygen reaches the cells. Patients with anaemia are pale and tire easily.
- Sickle cell anaemia and sickle cell trait. The red blood cells are an abnormal sickle shaped due to sickle haemoglobin.
- Leukaemia. Another name for white blood cells is leucocytes. Patients with leukaemia produce too many leucocytes. Leukaemia is cancer of the white blood cells.
- Bleeding and clotting disorders for example haemophilia. When the patient has a cut it will not stop bleeding as the blood cannot clot.

Q1. What is the pigment found in red blood cells?

    a. haemostasis
    b. haemoglobin
    c. iron
    d. oxygen

Q2. What are the functions of white blood cells?

    a. to circulate oxygen
    b. to fight infections
    c. to repair tissue damage
    d. to clot blood

Q3. What is the function of platelets?

    a. to circulate oxygen
    b. to fight infections
    c. to repair tissue damage
    d. to clot blood

Q4. What is plasma composed of?

    a. water
    b. saliva
    c. protein
    d. carbohydrate

Q5. Which of the following are functions of the blood?

    a. maintains body temperature at 27°C
    b. maintains body temperature at 37°C
    c. circulates hormones
    d. circulates nutrients

How well did you do?
    A1.b A2.b,c A3.d A4.a,c
    A5.b,c,d

THE HEART

While reading the text answer the following;

Q1. List the four chambers of the heart.

Q2. Name the two heart valves.

Q3. What is the pacemaker?

The function of the heart is to pump blood around the body.

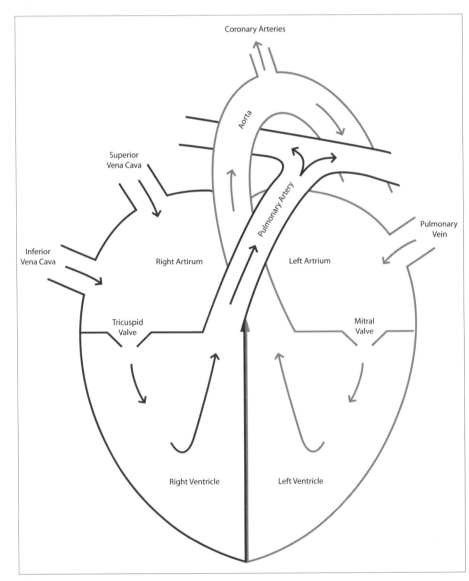

Figure 4.2 *Diagram of the heart.*

The heart is divided into four chambers; the left and right ventricles and the left and right atriums. The two chambers on either side of the heart are separated by valves but there is no communication between the right and left side of the heart. The right side contains only deoxygenated blood and the left side contains only oxygenated blood.

Deoxygenated blood returning from the body, except the lungs, enters the right atrium via the vena cavas. The superior vena cava carries blood from the head, neck and arms. The inferior vena cava carries it from the rest of the body. The blood then passes through the tricuspid valve into the right ventricle. It is pumped out of the right ventricle through the pulmonary artery to the lungs.

Here the blood releases waste carbon dioxide and takes up oxygen. This oxygenated blood travels from the lungs through the pulmonary vein to the left atrium. The blood passes through the mitral valve into the left ventricle. It is then pumped out of the left ventricle through the aorta to the rest of the body. The first branches of the aorta supply the heart muscles themselves and are called the coronary arteries.

The heartbeat itself starts in a group of specialised cells called the "pace-maker". These are found on the top surface of the right atrium. The beat spreads throughout the heart like a wave. The blood is prevented from flowing backwards by the heart valves. The pacemaker can speed up or slow down the heart as necessary. For example during exercise as more oxygen is required by the body the heart speeds up.

SO WHAT CAN GO WRONG?

DISORDERS OF THE HEART

- Heart murmurs. These are irregular heart sounds. They are due to holes in the walls between the right and left chambers. This results in oxygenated and deoxygenated blood mixing.
- Irregular heart beat. This is due to poorly functioning pace maker cells.
- Leaky valves. Weak valves will allow blood to flow the wrong way within the heart.
- Damaged heart tissue. This may be due to previous heart attacks. Scarred heart tissue affects the contraction of the heart muscle.
- Angina. The amount of blood reaching the heart muscle is restricted due to partially blocked coronary arteries.

Q1. Which of the following are chambers of the heart?

    a. right atrium
    b. left ventricle
    c. tricuspid
    d. mitral

Q2. Which of the following are heart valves.

    a. right atrium
    b. left ventricle
    c. tricuspid
    d. mitral

Q3. The pacemaker is a group of specialised cells which regulate the heart beat. True or false?

How well did you do?
    A1.a,b   A2.c,d   A3.True

THE CIRCULATORY SYSTEM

While reading the text answer the following;

Q1. What is internal respiration?

Q2. What is external respiration?

Q3. What are the main differences between arteries and veins?

Blood travels from the heart in arteries and to the heart in veins.

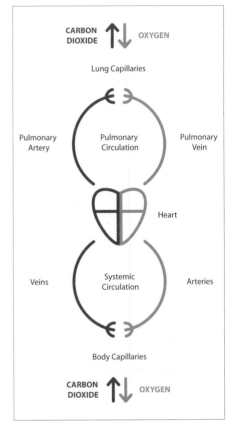

Figure 4.3 *The circulatory system.*

SYSTEMIC CIRCULATORY SYSTEM AND INTERNAL RESPIRATION

The heart is a pump. Oxygenated blood leaves the left side of the heart in the aortic artery. This artery divides into finer arteries carrying oxygenated blood all around the body. These arteries divide further until they are so small that they become the body's capillaries. Capillaries have very thin walls which allows gaseous exchange to take place. So in the body oxygen is passed to the cells and waste carbon dioxide passes into the capillaries. This is called internal respiration. The blood is now deoxygenated. The capillaries join up to become small veins. The veins become larger and larger as they approach the right side of the heart. The deoxygenated blood enters the right side of the heart. This is the systemic circulation.

PULMONARY CIRCULATORY SYSTEM AND EXTERNAL RESPIRATION

Deoxygenated blood from the right side of the heart leaves the heart in the pulmonary artery. The pulmonary artery is the only artery to carry deoxygenated blood. The large artery splits into finer and finer blood vessels until they are so fine they become the lung's capillaries. Carbon dioxide passes out while oxygen enters the lung capillaries. This is called external respiration. The blood is now oxygenated. These capillaries unite to form the pulmonary vein which enters the left side of the heart. The pulmonary vein is the only vein to carry oxygenated blood. This is the pulmonary circulation.

STRUCTURE OF BLOOD VESSELS

1. ARTERIES

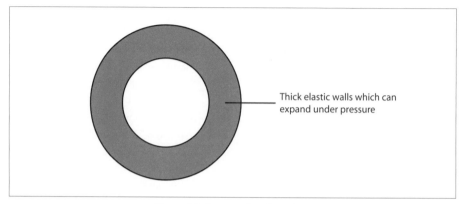
Thick elastic walls which can expand under pressure

Figure 4.4 *A cross-section of an artery.*

Arteries have strong elastic walls which can take the force of blood being pumped into them from the heart.

2. VEINS

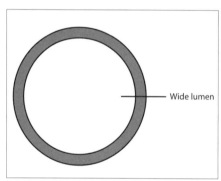
Wide lumen

Figure 4.5 *A cross-section of a vein.*

Veins have thin walls and wide lumens. They offer little resistance to the flow of blood back to the heart from the capillaries. To keep the blood flowing towards the heart they have many one-way valves along their length.

3. CAPILLARIES

Capillaries are the smallest blood vessel. Their walls are only one cell thick to facilitate the exchange of oxygen and carbon dioxide. This also allows them to easily exchange nutrients for waste products. It allows white blood cells to enter the tissues to fight infection and remove toxins when necessary.

THE MAIN FEATURES OF THE CIRCULATORY SYSTEMS

- Oxygenated blood is bright red.
- Deoxygenated blood is much darker.
- The blood in arteries is under high pressure as it has just been pumped from the heart. A cut artery spurts blood.
- The blood in the veins is under low pressure as it has just been through the capillaries. A cut vein will gush blood. (A cut capillary oozes blood slowly.)
- Veins unlike arteries have valves to stop the blood flowing backwards.
- The left side of the heart pumps oxygenated blood from the lungs to the rest of the body.
- The right side of the heart pumps deoxygenated blood from the body to the lungs.

Q1. What is internal respiration?

a. breathing indoors
b. the exchange of oxygen and carbon dioxide in the lungs
c. the exchange of oxygen and carbon dioxide in the tissues
d. it is the respiration which occurs in the systemic circulation

Q2. During external respiration the blood becomes deoxygenated. True or false?

Q3. What are the main differences between arteries and veins?

    a. arteries have valves
    b. veins are under low pressure
    c. veins carry bright red blood
    d. cut veins spurt blood

How well did you do?
    A1.c,d   A2.False   A3.b

BLOOD PRESSURE

While reading the text answer the following;

Q1. What is blood pressure?

Q2. What is the normal blood pressure of an adult at rest?

Q3. What causes a pulse?

The pumping of the heart produces pressure to send the blood flowing around the body. When a patient has their blood pressure taken there are two readings. The upper value is the pressure of the arterial blood when the heart contracts. The lower value is the pressure of the arterial blood when the heart relaxes. The normal blood pressure of a resting adult is 120/80.

PULSE

Following every heart beat, the elastic arteries expand as a wave of blood passes through them and then relax to their usual size again. This surge of blood can be felt as a pulse. So as your heart rate increases during exercise so does your pulse.

SO WHAT CAN GO WRONG?

DISORDERS OF THE CIRCULATORY SYSTEM

- High blood pressure. If the arteries become less elastic the patient's blood pressure increases. The heart has to pump excessively hard as thickening of the arteries is resisting the flow of blood.
- Varicous veins. The veins become enlarged and more prominent due to weak valves and a sluggish circulation.

Q1. Blood pressure is the arterial pressure of blood when the heart contracts over the pressure when it relaxes. True or false?

Q2. What is the normal blood pressure of an adult at rest?

    a. 80/100
    b. 100/80
    c. 80/120
    d. 120/80

Q3. The surge of blood being pumped from the heart can be felt as a pulse. True or false?

How well did you do?
    A1.True   A2.d   A3.True

Respiration

While reading the text answer the following;

Q1. Describe the airway and lungs.

Q2. How much oxygen and carbon dioxide enters and leaves the lungs during normal adult breathing?

Q3. How do we breath?

Q4. How many litres of air do we breath?

Q5. How does nature guard against airway obstruction?

The purpose of respiration is to draw fresh air into the lungs where oxygen can enter the blood system and waste carbon dioxide can leave. We have two lungs which lie in the chest either side of the heart. The lungs are protected by the ribs.

The air enters the nose. It then passes down the trachea (windpipe) which is found in the neck. When it reaches the chest it divides into two branches called the left and right bronchi. The bronchi enter the lungs and divide up into smaller and smaller tubes. At the end of each tube are microscopic air sacs called alveoli. Gaseous exchange occurs between the thin walls of the alveoli and the capillaries. Oxygen enters the circulation and carbon dioxide leaves. This is external respiration. Inspired air contains 20% oxygen and a negligible amount of carbon dioxide. Expired air contains only 16% oxygen and 4% carbon dioxide.

The air does not enter the lungs passively but is actively sucked in by the movements of the chest. Between the ribs lie the rib muscles and separating the chest from the abdomen is a sheet of muscle called the diaphragm. When a person inhales these muscles pull the ribs upwards and out-wards and the diaphragm is pulled down. This expands the chest and the air is sucked in. When the muscles relax the chest returns to its normal size and the air is pushed out. At rest an adult will breath about 8 to 20 times a minute, exchanging 0.5 litre of air with each breath. During exercise this increases.

NATURE'S WAY OF KEEPING AN OPEN AIRWAY

People can die within minutes if their airway is completely blocked. We have several natural mechanisms of keeping the airway clear from debris.

- The nostrils are guarded by hairs which filter out dust.
- Sneezing expels foreign bodies from the nose.
- Coughing expels foreign bodies from the throat.
- The epiglottis automatically blocks the windpipe when swallowing to prevent food inhalation.
- The lining of the respiratory system before it enters the lungs is covered with mucous and has specialised cells that have tiny hair like projections called cilia. Dust particles get caught in the sticky mucous and the cilia flick them back towards the throat where they are swallowed or coughed out.

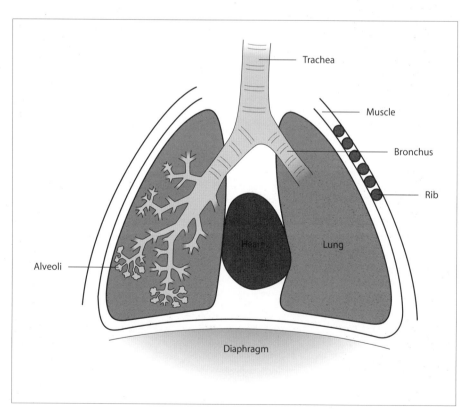

Figure 4.6 *The chest.*

During dental treatment the clinical team must always protect the patient's airway from inadvertently inhaling dental instruments. The right bronchus is almost vertically in line with the trachea so a dropped crown, for example, may fall straight into the right lung. This can happen even in a conscious patient and has serious consequences. It is important for the nurse to realise this and help protect the airway during treatment. It is far better for a crown or extracted tooth to go up the high speed suction than down into the lung!

If a patient collapses and becomes unconscious, they completely loose their reflexive protective mechanisms. They cannot sneeze, cough or swallow. Guarding the airway of an unconscious patient is of paramount importance to ensure unobstructed breathing.

SO WHAT CAN GO WRONG?

DISORDERS OF THE RESPIRATORY SYSTEM

- Asphyxia. Suffocation due to a blockage of the airway.
- Asthma. Inflammation of the airways characterised by periods of wheezing and shortness of breath.
- Allergies. These can cause swelling of the airway making breathing difficult or impossible.
- Bronchitis. Inflammation of the bronchial tubes from infection or irritation.
- Sinusitis. Inflammation of the lining of the sinus (in the maxilla).

Q1. Inspired air enters the airway in which of the following orders?

  a. nose, trachea, alveoli, bronchi
  b. nose, alveoli, bronchi, trachea
  c. nose, trachea, bronchi, alveoli
  d. nose, bronchi, trachea, alveoli

Q2. How much oxygen and carbon dioxide enters and leaves the lungs during normal adult breathing?

  a. inspired air contains 20% oxygen and negligible carbon dioxide
  b. inspired air contains 16% oxygen and 4% carbon dioxide
  c. expired air contains 16% oxygen and 4% carbon dioxide
  d. expired air contains 20% oxygen and 4% carbon dioxide

Q3. Our rib muscles pull the ribs upwards and outwards when we expire air. True or false?

Q4. How many litres of air do we exchange per breath at rest?

  a. 5 litres
  b. 0.5 litres
  c. 0.05 litres
  d. 50 litres

Q5. How does nature guard against airway obstruction?

  a. coughing
  b. with cilia
  c. using hair as a filter
  d. vomiting

How well did you do?
  A1.c   A2.a,c   A3.False   A4.b   A5.a,b,c

Digestion

Food is ingested into the intestine. Here enzymes break the food down into their basic units. These units are small enough to then be absorbed into the body. This process is digestion.

Food is needed for growth, to provide energy to function and to repair tissues. Our "diet" simply refers to the food we eat. (Do not confuse it with slimming diets!) For a balanced diet we need food from every food group i.e. carbohydrates, proteins, fat, vitamins and minerals. The body also requires over a litre of water per day. Excess water is excreted in urine but excess food is stored as fat. This increases body weight causing a strain on the heart.

CLASSIFICATION OF FOOD

While reading the text answer the following;

Q1. What are carbohydrates?

Q2. What are proteins?

Q3. What are fats?

CARBOHYDRATE

- All carbohydrates are broken down into glucose.
- Carbohydrates provide cells with energy.
- There are two types of carbohydrate. The first type is found in sweet foods e.g. sugar, soda, sweets, cakes, biscuits and ice-cream. These sweet foods release energy quickly as they are broken down into glucose quickly. They should be eaten sparingly as they cause dental decay and diabetes.

- The second type of carbohydrate is found in starchy savoury foods e.g. bread, pasta, rice, oats, bran and potatoes. These starchy carbohydrates release energy slowly over a long period of time as they are broken down into glucose slowly. They also provide fibre which prevents constipation. They are healthy and normally form one third of your diet.

PROTEINS

- Protein is broken down into amino acids.
- Proteins allow the cells to grow and repair.
- They are found in fish, meat, poultry, lentils and beans.

FAT

- Fat is broken down into fatty acids.
- Fats are high in energy.
- They can be stored as a layer of fat under the skin as an insulation layer and as a reserve source of energy. Fats should be eaten in small quantities to avoid obesity.
- They are found in margarine, butter, chocolate, crisps and vegetable oils.

Q1. Which of the following are carbohydrates?

    a. meat
    b. margarine
    c. icing sugar
    d. bread

Q2. What are proteins broken down into?

    a. fatty acids
    b. minerals
    c. amino acids
    d. glucose

Q3. What are the functions of fat?

    a. to provide energy
    b. to allow growth
    c. to form an insulation layer
    d. to repair tissues

How well did you do?
    A1.c,d   A2.c   A3.a,c

VITAMINS

While reading the text answer the following;

Q1. Why do we need vitamin A?

Q2. Why do we need vitamin B?

Q3. Why do we need vitamin C?

Q4. Why do we need vitamin D?

Q5. Why do we need calcium?

Q6. Why do we need iron?

- Vitamins are essential but only needed in small quantities.
- There are many different vitamins. For example;

1. Vitamin A. Vitamin A is found in the pigment carotene and so is found in red/orange coloured vegetables such as carrots and tomatoes. It is needed for growth.
2. Vitamin B complex. Vitamin B is found in liver, yeast and cereals. It helps form red blood cells. Deficiency causes anaemia and sore tongue syndrome.
3. Vitamin C. This is found in citrus fruit. It is needed for healthy skin and the absorption of iron. Deficiency causes bleeding and gum disorders. In the past British sailors were called "Limeys" as they were known for stocking up on citrus fruit to prevent scurvy.
4. Vitamin D. This is found in fish and dairy products. It is important for healthy teeth and bones. Deficiency causes rickets (deformed bones). Vitamin D is the "sunshine" vitamin as it can be made in the skin on exposure to sunlight.

MINERALS

- Minerals are also essential but only needed in small quantities.
- Again there are many different minerals. For example;

1. Calcium. This is found in milk and cheese. Calcium is required to form teeth and bones. Deficiency causes deformed teeth and bones.
2. Iron. Iron is found in leafy green vegetables and red meat. It is required to form haemoglobin. Deficiency causes anaemia and sore tongue syndrome.

Q1. Vitamin A is found in which of the following?

    a. carotene
    b. carrots
    c. bran
    d. fish

Q2. Why do we need vitamin B?

    a. to form white blood cells
    b. to form red blood cells
    c. to prevent anaemia
    d. to prevent scurvy

Q3. Vitamin C is found in which of the following?

    a. oranges
    b. red meat
    c. dairy products
    d. fish

Q4. Why do we need vitamin D?

    a. for healthy teeth
    b. to prevent anaemia
    c. for healthy bones
    d. to prevent rickets

Q5. Why do we need calcium?

    a. for healthy teeth
    b. to prevent anaemia
    c. for healthy bones
    d. to prevent sore tongue

Q6. Iron is found in which of the following?

    a. leafy green vegetables
    b. red meat
    c. blood
    d. haemoglobin

How well did you do?
    A1.a,b   A2.b,c   A3.a   A4.a,c,d
    A5.a,c   A6.a,b,c,d

MASTICATION

While reading the text answer the following;

Q1. What is mastication?

Q2. What is salivary amylase?

Q3. How is the airway blocked off during swallowing?

Q4. What is peristalsis?

Chewing food is called mastication. Your teeth chew the food, physically breaking it down. The saliva starts to digest carbohydrates with an enzyme called salivary amylase and lubricates the ball of food before it is flicked to the back of the mouth by the tongue and swallowed. Saliva flow increases when eating and even on the anticipation of food.

SWALLOWING

When food is swallowed it is firmly directed down the oesophagus. The sinuses are momentarily blocked off from the mouth by the soft palate. At the same time the airway is momentarily blocked off by the epiglottis. These two mechanisms prevent food entering the airway during swallowing. When a patient is unconscious these reflex mechanisms do not work. Unfortunately unconscious patients can still vomit. If a patient is unconscious we place them in the recovery position. In this position if vomiting occurs, it should not enter the open airway.

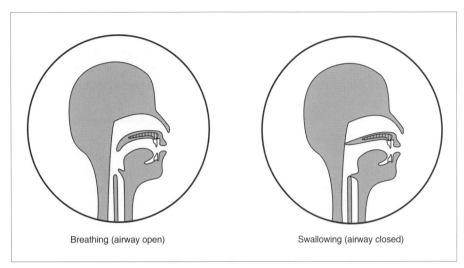

Breathing (airway open)   Swallowing (airway closed)

Figure 4.7 Open and closed airway.

As soon as the food is in the oesophagus it is propelled downwards by the wave like contraction of the muscles in the wall of the oesophagus. This is called peristalsis. Peristalsis occurs all the way along the alimentary canal (which is 10 meters long!) to keep the food moving towards the anus.

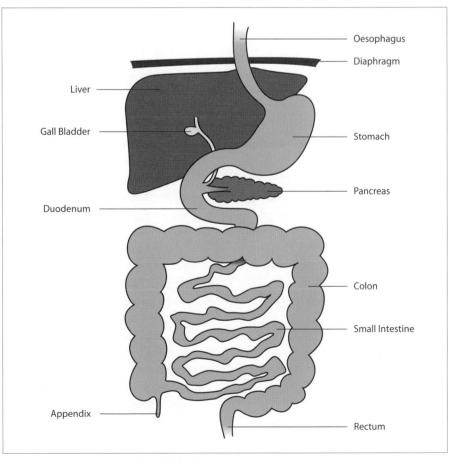

Liver
Gall Bladder
Duodenum
Appendix

Oesophagus
Diaphragm
Stomach
Pancreas
Colon
Small Intestine
Rectum

Figure 4.8 The digestive system (alimentary canal).

Q1. What is mastication?

    a. swallowing food
    b. chewing food
    c. absorbing food
    d. ingesting food

Q2. What is salivary amylase?

    a. an enzyme
    b. it digests fat
    c. it digests carbohydrates
    d. it digests proteins

Q3. How is the airway blocked off during swallowing?

    a. sinuses are momentarily blocked off by the soft palate
    b. the airway is momentarily blocked off by the epiglottis
    c. the sinuses are momentarily blocked off by the epiglottis
    d. the sinuses are never blocked off as food cannot travel upwards

Q4. Peristalsis is a wave like contraction of the walls of the alimentary canal to keep food moving towards the mouth. True or false?

How well did you do?
    A1.b A2.a,c A3.a,b A4.False

STOMACH

While reading the text answer the following;

Q1. How does food enter the stomach?

Q2. What is the name of the first loop of the small intestine?

Q3. Which two ducts enter the duodenum?

Q4. Where is bile formed?

Q5. What is the colon?

Q6. What happens in the colon?

- Food travels from the oesophagus to the stomach.
- The stomach produces acid which helps to kill any germs present.
- Stomach enzymes start to digest protein.
- Food is churned around in the stomach for about five hours. (Patients must fast before a general anaesthetic to ensure that no food remains in the stomach. If food was present and was refluxed it could enter the windpipe and obstruct breathing. Remember an unconscious patient looses their protective reflexes.)

SO WHAT CAN GO WRONG?

DISORDERS OF THE STOMACH

- Acid reflux. The stomach has a strong lining to cope with the acid it produces. If acid is refluxed into the oesophagus and mouth it can cause ulcers and tooth erosion.
- Peptic ulcers. These are stomach ulcers. These patients should not take aspirin which can cause further ulceration and bleeding.

SMALL INTESTINE

- Most of digestion takes place in the small intestine.
- The duodenum forms the first loop of the small intestine.
- The small intestine produces its own enzymes but also receives enzymes from the pancreas and bile from the gall bladder.
- Bile is produced by the liver and stored by the gall bladder. It passes into the duodenum via the bile duct.
- Pancreatic juice is made in the pancreas and passes into the duodenum via the pancreatic duct. Pancreatic juice contains enzymes which digest carbohydrate, protein and fat.

- Most food absorption takes place in the small intestine. Digested food enters the blood supply and is sent to the liver.

LARGE INTESTINE

- The large intestine is also called the colon.
- The remaining undigested remnants contain a lot of water. The large intestine absorbs this water and remaining minerals. The waste remnants are excreted through the anus as stools (faeces).

Q1. How does food enter the stomach?

    a. through the duodenum
    b. through the oesophagus
    c. through the colon
    d. through the small intestine

Q2. What is the name of the first loop of the small intestine?

    a. the duodenum
    b. the oesophagus
    c. the colon
    d. the small intestine

Q3. Which two ducts enter the duodenum?

    a. bile duct
    b. submandibular duct
    c. sublingual ducts
    d. pancreatic duct

Q4. Where is bile formed?

    a. gall bladder
    b. liver
    c. duodenum
    d. colon

Q5. What is the colon?

    a. small intestine
    b. large intestine
    c. anus
    d. duodenum

Q6. What happens in the colon?

    a. absorption of protein
    b. absorption of water
    c. absorption of minerals
    d. absorption of vitamins

How well did you do?
    A1.b   A2.a   A3.a,d   A4.b
    A5.b   A6.b,c

LIVER

While reading the text answer the following;

Q1. What is unique about the blood supply of the liver?

Q2. What are the functions of the liver?

The liver is a large smooth, red/brown organ partially protected by the ribs. It is the centre of your metabolism and can be thought of as the large chemical factory of the body. Unlike any other organ, the liver has a double blood supply; one from the heart and the other from the intestine. It receives oxygenated blood from the heart and nutrients from the intestine. All of the liver's blood leaves the liver via the hepatic vein.

The oxygen powers the "factory" and the nutrients provide the raw materials. Like all factories products are manufactured and waste is produced.

The liver also produces bile which is collected in the gallbladder.

FUNCTIONS OF THE LIVER

The liver carries out hundreds of separate processes. Here are a few;

- It distributes nutrients derived from food
- It provides many of the constituents of blood.
- It produces bile which digests fat in the intestine and it neutralises acid from the stomach.
- It filters chemicals and waste products from the blood.

- It protects the body by removing bacteria and neutralising toxins.
- It stores vitamins.
- It regenerates itself. It creates new cells as old or damaged ones die off.

SO WHAT CAN GO WRONG?

DISORDERS OF THE LIVER

- Cirrhosis. The most common cause of liver disease is too much alcohol. This causes hepatitis (inflammation of the liver) and eventually cirrhosis (liver cell death and scaring).
- Hepatitis. Hepatitis can also be caused by virus. This is called infective hepatitis.
- Congenital defects of the bile ducts. This may cause jaundice giving babies a yellow colour.
- Liver cancer.

Q1. What is unique about the blood supply of the liver?

    a. it has two veins
    b. it has two arteries
    c. it has three veins
    d. it has three arteries

Q2. What are the functions of the liver?

    a. stores vitamins
    b. neutralise toxins
    c. filters chemicals
    d. produces urine

How well did you do?
    A1.b   A2.a,b,c

Hormones

While reading the text answer the following;

Q1. What is the function of insulin?

Q2. What is the difference between type 1 and type 2 diabetes?

Q3. What is the function of thyroxin?

Hormones are chemicals which regulate the various systems within the body. They are produced by special cells within glands. Hormones travel around the body via the blood system. There are many different types of hormones but two are particularly relevant to dentistry.

INSULIN AND GLUCAGON

The pancreas secretes glucagon and insulin. Glucagon raises the level of glucose in the blood while insulin lowers it. In diabetes this mechanism does not function properly. All diabetics need to control their diet and some need to take insulin daily. Insulin removes glucose from the blood and moves it into the cells where it is broken down to produce energy. If the pancreas does not make enough insulin the blood glucose level can become too high. Over time, high blood glucose levels will cause damage to the blood vessels which in turn may lead to organ damage for example of the eyes or kidneys. The inability to control blood glucose levels is called diabetes. There are two types;

TYPE 1 OR INSULIN DEPENDENT DIABETES

These patients need insulin supplements for the rest of their lives. They also need to control their sugar intake.

TYPE 2 OR NON-INSULIN DEPENDENT
DIABETES

This type of diabetes is usually linked with
obesity. These patients do not need insulin
supplements but do need to learn to eat a
healthy diet to control their blood glucose
levels.

The normal blood glucose level is between
3.5 and 5.5. Most people can control the
level of glucose in the blood. After a meal
glucose is absorbed into the blood. The
pancreas secretes enough insulin to remove
excess glucose from the blood and place it
in the cells. Initially the blood glucose level
rises but within two hours after a meal, a
healthy person will have regulated their
blood glucose level back down to the
normal level. However, diabetics have
difficulty controlling the level of glucose in
the blood so two hours after a meal the
blood will still have an excessive amount of
glucose. This can be diagnosed with a
blood test.

THYROXIN

Thyroxin is produced by the thyroid gland
which is found in the front of the neck.
The thyroid controls metabolism.
Metabolism is the speed at which the body
consumes energy.

HYPERTHYROIDISM

When too much thyroxin is produced the
metabolism increases. The patients are
energised. They may loose weight rapidly
and cannot relax. Their pulse rate is high
even when they are sleeping. The thyroid
gland is often enlarged.

HYPOTHYROIDISM

The thyroid gland does not produce
enough thyroxin. The metabolism slows
down. The patient lacks energy and puts
on weight easily. Women are affected six
times more often then men.

Q1. What is the function of insulin?

   a. to regulate the blood fat levels
   b. to regulate the blood glucose levels
   c. to regulate the metabolism
   d. to regulate the blood flow

Q2. Which of the following statements
   are true?

   a. type 1 diabetics need to regulate
   their sugar intake
   b. type 2 diabetics need to regulate
   their sugar intake
   c. type 1 diabetics need to inject
   insulin
   d. type 2 diabetics need to inject
   insulin

Q3. What is the function of thyroxin?

   a. to regulate the blood fat levels
   b. to regulate the blood glucose levels
   c. to regulate the metabolism
   d. to regulate the blood flow

How well did you do?
   A1.b   A2.a,b,c   A3.c

Pathology

The body has several defences to prevent
injury occurring. For example the skin is a
great protector of the underlying organs.
However the body also responds in a
specific way when injury has occurred to
minimise the damage and prevent future
damage.

INFLAMMATION

While reading the text answer the
following;

Q1. List the five characteristics of
   inflammation.

Q2. How are infections fought at tissue
   level?

Q3. What is the difference between acute
   and chronic inflammation?

Inflammation is a defence reaction to an
irritant. The irritant may be physical
(e.g. a cut), chemical (e.g. an acid burn)
or infective (e.g. a cold virus).
Inflammation has five characteristics;

1. Swelling
2. Redness
3. Heat
4. Pain
5. Loss of function

So, if you hit your thumb with a hammer
it would swell up, look red and angry,
become warm, hurt like crazy and you
wouldn't want to use it for a while! So
what's happening? Well as you know the
white blood cells are the body's great
defence against disease. They also repair
damaged tissue. So as soon as we are
injured there is a huge increase in blood
flow to the effected area to bring a large
number of white blood cells to fight any
microbe which may have caused the
inflammation and to repair any damaged
tissue. The blood vessels dilate allowing
blood to rush in causing redness, heat and

swelling. The swelling puts pressure on the nerve endings causing pain and that prevents us using that part of the body until it returns to normal.

When the inflammation is caused by an infection white blood cells, antibodies, antitoxins and plasma pass through the capillary walls to fight the bacteria. The plasma dilutes the bacterial toxins and the antitoxins actually neutralises them. The antibodies and the white blood cells fight the bacteria literally to death. Dead white blood cells and bacteria collect to form pus. A localised pocket of pus is called an abscess. (If the infection continues, pus spreads diffusely through the tissues. This is called cellulitis. Cellulitis is rarely seen in the mouth in western countries due to the availability of dental treatment and antibiotics.) The damaged tissue is then repaired. This involves the formation of granulation tissue.

Granulation tissue is a temporary repair tissue. It allows damaged cells to be removed and replaced. Granulation tissue is vascular to allow the necessary components to get to the injured site. During extraction, you will have seen granulation tissue around the apices of chronically abscessed teeth. It is a sac of soft tissue attached to the apex of the root. The extraction sockets of these teeth bleed profusely due to the increased blood supply. However they heal quickly for the same reason. (Note, if the cause of the infection is removed, for example the infected pulp is removed and the tooth is root filled, then the granulation tissue would be able to complete it's job and repair the periapical bone.)

Acute inflammation occurs suddenly and lasts a short time but is often very painful. Chronic inflammation builds up over a long period of time and tends to be less painful.

All words ending in -itis indicate inflammation. For example pulpitis is inflammation of the pulp and gingivitis is inflammation of the gingivae.

Q1. Which of the following are characteristics of inflammation.

    a. heat
    b. cold
    c. redness
    d. loss of function

Q2. How are infections fought at tissue level?

    a. reduced blood flow to the area
    b. red blood cells enter the tissues
    c. antitoxins enter the tissues
    d. granulation tissue forms

Q3. What is the difference between acute and chronic inflammation?

    a. acute inflammation occurs over a long time
    b. acute inflammation occurs suddenly
    c. acute inflammation is very painful
    d. chronic inflammation is very painful

How well did you do?
    A1.a,c,d   A2.c,d   A3.b,c

PATHOLOGY

-ology=the study of

Pathology is the study of disease. Disease can change the structure (anatomy) and function (physiology) of tissues and organs. We recognise (diagnose) various diseases by noting (examining) these changes. This then enables us to treat the conditions either by surgery or medicine.

TYPES OF PATHOLOGY

While reading the text answer the following;

Q1. What is infection?

Q2. What is an ulcer?

Q3. What is a cyst?

Q4. What is a tumour?

Q5. Name two types of tumour.

Q6. What is the difference between a congenital and a genetic defect?

Q7. What are the symptoms of an allergic reaction?

INFECTION

Infection is the invasion of the body by microscopic organisms such as bacteria, viruses or fungi. During dental procedures, the clinical team wears gloves, masks and glasses to protect themselves from the microbes present in the patient's blood and saliva. The microbes can enter your body through cuts in the skin, your airway or your eyes. The sterilisation of dental equipment after every treatment prevents infection spreading from patient to patient.

ULCER

An ulcer is a shallow breach of the skin or mucosa. The base of an ulcer can often be painful and bleed. Ulcers may be caused in a variety of ways such as trauma (e.g. a chipped tooth rubbing the tongue), infection (e.g. herpetic ulcers) or cancer.

CYSTS

A cyst is an abnormal fluid filled sac. Cysts become troublesome when they grow too large and displace or destroy nearby structures. Cysts within the jaws can move the teeth or weaken the jaw to cause a pathological fracture.

TUMOUR

A tumour is excessive and uncontrolled division of cells. Tumours often present as a lump. There are two types; benign and malignant.

Benign tumours stay as a lump of cells that grow bigger, displacing or destroying adjacent tissue.

Malignant tumours not only grow bigger to cause local problems, but some of the cells break away to form secondary growths elsewhere in the body. The malignant cells may travel through the body in the blood or lymphatic systems. Malignant tumours are commonly known as cancer.

CONGENITAL DEFECTS

A congenital defect is an unusual condition which was present at birth e.g. cleft palate, heart murmur.

GENETIC DISORDERS

These disorders are passed down from generation to generation by the genes e.g. haemophilia, Down's syndrome.

ALLERGY

An allergic reaction is an over reaction of our immune system to a specific substance (allergen). For example many people suffer from hay fever which is an over reaction to pollen. In most cases allergens cause relatively mild reactions such as sneezing, itching, streaming eyes and nose, skin rashes or mouth ulcers. However the allergic response may be far more severe resulting in sudden death due to anaphylactic shock. Common examples of potential allergens within the dental surgery are latex gloves and penicillin.

Q1. What is an infection?

    a. shallow breach in the skin
    b. the invasion of the body by microbes
    c. an abnormal proliferation of cells
    d. a fluid filled sac

Q2. What is an ulcer?

    a. shallow breach in the skin
    b. the invasion of the body by microbes
    c. an abnormal proliferation of cells
    d. a fluid filled sac

Q3. What is a cyst?

    a. shallow breach in the skin
    b. the invasion of the body by microbes
    c. an abnormal proliferation of cells
    d. a fluid filled sac

Q4. What is a tumour?

    a. shallow breach in the skin
    b. the invasion of the body by microbes
    c. an abnormal proliferation of cells
    d. a fluid filled sac

Q5. Which of the following are types of tumour.

    a. benign
    b. malignant
    c. cancer
    d. cyst

Q6. A congenital defect is hereditary and a genetic defect is present at birth. True or false?

Q7. What are the symptoms of an allergic reaction?

    a. rash
    b. anaphylactic shock
    c. cancer
    d. sneezing

How well did you do?
    A1.b   A2.a   A3.d   A4.c
    A5.a,b,c   A6.False   A7.a,b,d

IMMUNITY

While reading the text answer the following;

Q1. What is immunity?

Q2. Name the two types of immunity.

Immunity is the body's ability to resist disease. White blood cells fight infection by releasing antibodies and antitoxins into the plasma. Anything that causes white blood cells to respond in this matter is called an antigen. An antigen may be a micro-organism, a toxin or a foreign substance for example an incompatible blood transfusion or organ transplant.

We can have two different types of immunity;

1. NATURAL IMMUNITY

Natural immunity is present from birth. It is non-specific (acts on many organisms) and does not become more efficient on subsequent exposure to the same organisms.

2. ACQUIRED IMMUNITY

Acquired immunity occurs in response to an infection. Following recovery from an infection by a specific micro-organism the patient will never develop that same infection again because they are protected against that specific micro-organism. Acquired immunity may be gained actively or passively.

Active immunity is achieved by recovering from an infection or being vaccinated against the infection.

Passive immunity is achieved by the transfer of antibodies from an immune person. For example an unborn baby will receive passive immunity from the mother which will continue to protect the baby for the first few months after birth.

A vaccine is usually made from dead microbes. The dead microbes cannot produce disease but the body recognises them as being foreign. The dead microbes are antigens and so the body will produce specific antibodies to fight them. At a later date if the vaccinated person is exposed again to the same disease the body recognises the micro-organisms immediately and the antibodies are already present to fight the infection before it takes hold.

All dental nurses should be vaccinated against diptheria, hepatitis B, pertussis, poliomyelitis, rubella, tetanus and tuberculosis. You will have received all of these during childhood except for hepatitis B.

Q1. Immunity is the body's ability to resist disease. True or false?

Q2. Which of the following are types of immunity.

    a. natural immunity
    b. acquired immunity
    c. active immunity
    d. impassive immunity

How well did you do?
    A1.True   A2.a,b,c

Medical History

"First do no harm."

SO WHY DO WE TAKE A MEDICAL HISTORY?

A medical history is always taken before every examination so that the patient's whole health is taken into account before making any treatment plans. The general health of the patient influences their dental treatment. In your practice you will have seen the medical histories of numerous patients. In this chapter you will learn the relevance of these questions and how they affect the way we treat and monitor patients. As a dental nurse you may be asked to help the patients complete their medical history forms. The patients may ask you questions such as "What is hepatitis?" or "Why do you need to know about my arthritis?" You will feel foolish if you don't know the answers and the patients will be annoyed at answering so called "irrelevant" questions, unless you can give them a valid reason.
If a patient has a disorder, e.g. diabetes, ask them how this effects them. Patients know their own disorders better than anyone and their information can be useful and should be recorded clearly on their notes.

HEART DISEASE

While reading the text answer the following;

Q1. Adrenaline should be avoided in which patients?

Q2. Which equipment should not be used in patients with pacemakers?

Q3. Which arteries are partially blocked in angina patients?

As you have learnt, the heart is responsible for pumping blood around the body so that oxygen is carried to every single cell.

HIGH BLOOD PRESSURE (BP)

- Many patients are permanently on medication to keep their BP at a normal level. Will their medication react with any dental prescriptions?
- A competent nurse is great at relaxing the patient by being attentive and reassuring. This will help keep the patient's BP stable.
- Local anaesthetic with adrenaline should be avoided as adrenaline stimulates the heart.

PACEMAKERS

- As you know, the heart has a natural pacemaker which regulates the heart beat. When this does not work properly the heart becomes inefficient at pumping blood as the heart muscle does not contract in a co-ordinated fashion. The problem may be rectified with an artificial pacemaker. A small electronic pacemaker is inserted either under the skin or ribs to regulate the heart beat.
- Ultrasonic scalers and electro-surgery should NOT be used on these patients as the high frequency and electronic pulses can affect the pacemaker.

ANGINA

- You have learn that the first branches of the aorta supply the actual heart muscle. These are called the coronary arteries. If these arteries are partial blocked, the patient may experience angina during exercise or emotional stress. During exercise or stress the heart beats faster and so the heart muscle requires more oxygen/blood. If these arteries cannot supply this extra blood the patient experiences chest pain. This is angina.

- Again the nurse should always provide a relaxed and reassuring manner so that the patient remains calm during any treatment.
- Adrenaline should not be used in local anaesthetic as this can make the heart beat faster.
- If an angina attack occurs the patient should immediately receive glycerol trinitrate tablets or spray and oxygen. The nurse should have both ready before stress inducing treatments such as extractions. Medical histories allow you to think ahead. Forewarned is forearmed!

Q1. Adrenaline should be avoided in which patients?

    a. patients with diabetes
    b. patients with angina
    c. patients with high blood pressure
    d. patients with asthma

Q2. Which equipment should not be used in patients with pacemakers?

    a. high speed handpiece
    b. ultrasonic scaler
    c. blue light
    d. electro-surgery

Q3. Which arteries are partially blocked in angina patients?

    a. coronary arteries
    b. aorta
    c. carotid
    d. hepatic

How well did you do?
    A1.b,c   A2.b,d   A3.a

LIVER DISEASE

While reading the text answer the following;

Q1. What can adversely affect the liver?

Q2. Which respiratory problem could mimic dental pain?

Q3. What common allergens are found in the dental surgery?

The liver is a large organ with many functions. It processes many substances and will breakdown waste products before sending them to the kidneys via the bloodstream. The kidneys then filter out the waste products and excess water to form urine which can be passed out of the body.

- The liver processes many drugs. A diseased liver cannot do this efficiently. This affects what medicine can be prescribed and also the dose.
- Paracetamol should be avoided in patients with liver disease and alternative painkillers should be used.
- Alcoholism damages the liver. It causes inflammation and cirrhosis limiting the liver's ability to process various chemicals.
- Hepatitis is liver inflammation which may be caused by the hepatitis A, B or C virus. The virus may cause permanent liver damage in severe cases. Most importantly hepatitis B and C are highly virulent and can be passed to others through blood and saliva. As a dental nurse you must be immunised against hepatitis B. There is no vaccine for C but it is less common.

LUNGS AND RESPIRATORY PROBLEMS

ASTHMA

- Encourage asthmatic patients to bring their inhalers to every dental appointment.
- Anxiety or running to a dental appointment can trigger an asthmatic attack.
- Ask the patient how often do they get an asthmatic attack? What triggers their asthma?

BRONCHITIS

- Long term antibiotics for chest infections can mask dental abscesses and infections.
- Any breathing difficulty will make dental procedures difficult. It is best to treat patients when they have recovered if possible.

SINUSITIS

- Referred pain from the maxillary sinus can present as toothache and visa versa. Nasal sprays rather than root treatment may be required!

ALLERGIES

- Patients can be sensitive to a variety of things. Common allergies which affect dentistry include allergies to antibiotics especially penicillin, painkillers such as aspirin, materials such as eugenol and latex gloves. Indeed as a nurse you may develop a latex allergy yourself. Vinyl gloves are a safe alternative.
- Patients who suffer from hay fever, eczema and asthma are more likely to become allergic to other substances such as penicillin. They are also more likely to suffer the severe reaction of anaphylactic shock if they come in contact with an allergen.

Q1. Which of the following can adversely affect the liver?

    a. alcohol
    b. hepatitis C virus
    c. cancer
    d. paracetamol

Q2. Which respiratory problem could mimic dental pain?

    a. asthma
    b. bronchitis
    c. sinusitis
    d. choking

Q3. Which common allergens are found in the dental surgery?

    a. latex gloves
    b. penicillin
    c. grass
    d. eugenol

How well did you do?
    A1.a,b,c,d   A2.c   A3.a,b,d

BLOOD DISORDERS

While reading the text answer the following;

Q1. Name two drugs which increase clotting time.

Q2. Name the blood disorder that has unusual haemoglobin.

Q3. List the infectious diseases that are carried in the blood.

BLEEDING DISORDERS

- Patients may have rare but serious clotting/bleeding disorders such as haemophilia. Dental treatment of patients with these serious bleeding disorders should always be done in hospital.
- More commonly many patients regularly take medication to "thin the blood" e.g. warferin or aspirin. This medicine prevents the blood clotting abnormally within the body. They are used for certain heart conditions and for people who have suffered strokes from blood clots.
- Patients on anticoagulants often carry a medical warning card. Their doctor should be informed about the proposed dental treatment especially if deep scaling or extractions are involved. In these cases the doctor and dentist may decide to temporarily alter the drug regime or to keep it as it is and accept a longer clotting time.
- A history of prolonged bleeding after extractions should be recorded even if the patient is otherwise healthy.

SICKLE ANAEMIA AND SICKLE CELL TRAIT

- Sickle cell anaemia and sickle cell trait are inherited conditions.
- These patients have sickle haemoglobin which causes the red blood cells to become sickle shaped when they release oxygen. This makes the red blood cells stick together and they have difficulty passing through capillaries.
- Patients with sickle cell trait have normal red blood cells as well as sickle shaped ones. Unlike those with sickle cell anaemia, these patients are usually fine under normal conditions. However both conditions are exasperated under general anaesthetic.

Q1. Which drugs increase clotting time?

    a. aspirin
    b. paracetamol
    c. warferin
    d. penicillin

Q2. Which blood disorders have unusual haemoglobin.

    a. haemophilia
    b. sickle cell anaemia
    c. regular anaemia
    d. sickle cell trait

Q3. Which diseases have pathogens in the blood?

    a. AIDS
    b. hepatitis B
    c. anaemia
    d. haemophilia

How well did you do?
    A1.a,c   A2.b,d   A3.a,b

DIABETES

While reading the text answer the following;

Q1. When a diabetic suddenly collapses in the surgery what is the most likely cause?

Q2. What drug should be avoided in patients with hyperthyroidism?

Q3. What questions would you ask a patient with epilepsy?

- Appointment times should fit in with a diabetic patient's eating habits. It is best to treat a diabetic just after a meal.
- Any infections should be treated rapidly and vigorously.

- Diabetics should understand the importance of looking after their gums as they are more vulnerable to periodontitis.
- Interestingly the same diet that causes diabetes causes dental decay i.e. frequent, high sugar snacks.
- Collapse in the surgery is usually due to hypoglycaemia.
- If a patient is diabetic it is useful to know whether it is controlled by insulin or diet alone. How well controlled is their diabetes? Has the diabetes effected other organs such as the kidneys?

THYROID PROBLEMS

- Hyperthyroidism is a condition whereby too much thyroxin is secreted. These patients have a racing metabolism. Their pulse rate is high, even at rest, and they loose weight even though they are eating well.
- Patients with hyperthyroidism should avoid adrenaline in local anaesthetics.
- Patients with thyroid problems often take thyroxin tablets. Ask the patients if their condition is well controlled.

EPILEPSEY

- Some anticonvulsant drugs cause overgrowth of the gums. Good oral hygiene can prevent this.
- Patients suffering from epilepsy may have a convulsion in the chair.
- Ask the patient when they last had a fit. Is their condition stable i.e. is their medication is keeping them fit free? Do they have any prior warning before a fit occurs? What triggers their fits e.g. anxiety, lights? How does the fit effect them e.g. do they vomit? Who should we call if they fit? You will be grateful that you have asked these questions if they ever have a fit in the dental chair as it will help you to monitor your patient and know what to expect!

Q1. When a diabetic suddenly collapses in the surgery what is the most likely cause?

    a. hyperglycaemia
    b. hypoglycaemia
    c. low blood glucose
    d. high blood glucose

Q2. What drug should be avoided in patients with hyperthyroidism?

    a. penicillin
    b. adrenalin
    c. felypressin
    d. local anaesthetic

Q3. What questions would you ask a patient with epilepsy?

    a. how long does your blood take to clot?
    b. when was your last fit?
    c. what triggers a fit?
    d. are your blood glucose levels under control?

How well did you do?
    A1.b,c   A2.b   A3.b,c

PREVIOUS OPERATIONS

While reading the text answer the following;

Q1. When prescribing penicillin what advise should be given to women on the contraceptive pill?

Q2. If we are sterilising the instruments why do we still need to know if a patient has HIV?

Q3. Why do patients sometimes fail to disclose the medication they are taking?

- Previous operations can tell us how the patient responded to a general anaesthetic.

- Depending on the previous operation the patient may need a quick diagnosis and treatment of oral infections, e.g. hip replacement operation.

PREGNANCY

- Pregnant women are often concerned about the effects of x-rays or medication on their unborn baby.
- Modern x-rays produce very little scatter so dental x-rays can be taken safely. However psychologically it is best to avoid these and, if a film is necessary, for the woman to wear a lead apron.

- Treating pregnant women can be problematic as they may suffer from nausea (morning sickness) especially in the first trimester and they may faint when lying down in the third trimester due to the enlarged uterus pressing on the vagal nerve.
- Pregnant women and those on oral contraceptives may be more prone to gum disorders. Diligent oral hygiene can prevent this.
- Giving penicillin to a woman on the contraceptive pill without warning her that it decreases the effectiveness of the pill could cause pregnancy!

IMMUNITY

- Patients may have a reduced immune response due to their medical conditions for example AIDS or due to the drugs they are taking such as immunosuppressant in transplant patients. Any oral infection must be treated rapidly and vigorously in these patients.
- Routine treatment should be timed when the patient is at their best and their immune system is working at its optimum.
- The dentist should consult the patient's doctor when planning treatment.

- Some local autoimmune disorders present in the mouth e.g. lichen planus.

CANCER

- Oral infections must be treated rapidly and vigorously if the patient is taking chemotherapy or radiotherapy as both may lower the patient's immune response.
- Radiation of the head and neck may decrease the flow of saliva resulting in dry mouth.
- Raised lymph vessels in the neck may indicate oral cancer or secondary cancer.

SMOKING

- The medical history should record how many cigarettes are smoked per day.
- Patients should be warned about the detrimental effects of smoking on oral tissues. Smoking causes oral cancer. Smokers take longer to heal and are more prone to gum disease.
- A high alcohol intake and smoking greatly increases the likelihood of developing oral cancer.

MEDICINES

- Every medication should be recorded in case it reacts with a dental prescription.
- Patients taking long term antibiotics or painkillers, e.g. for arthritis, may be masking oral infections and pain.
- Anti-acid tablets for conditions such as hernias will explain why the patient has eroded teeth. In this case erosion is not due to a high acid diet but acid reflux. Recommending fluoride mouth rinse will be more productive and less frustrating for the patient than giving them a lecture about their diet!

- Patients should be asked if they are taking steroids or have received steroids in the last three months. They may need a supplemental steroid injection before extractions to prevent collapse.
- Patients may not disclose all their medication for a number of reasons. They may be embarrassed or feel that it has no relevance to dentistry. They may not even regard the pills that they are taking as medicine!

All medical histories should be updated regularly. Know your patient!

Q1. When giving penicillin what advise should be given to women on the contraceptive pill?

   a. keep taking the pill but also use another form of birth control for the rest of that monthly cycle.
   b. the combination of the pill and the penicillin will make their gums bleed
   c. women taking penicillin should not smoke
   d. penicillin has no effect on the contraceptive pill

Q2. We need to know if a patient has HIV so that we can treat them when their immune system is at it's best. True or false?

Q3. Why do patients sometimes fail to disclose the medication they are taking?

   a. they forget
   b. they are embarrassed
   c. they have been taking the tablets for so long that they no longer think of them as medicine
   d. because they think it's none of our business

How well did you do?
   A1.a   A2.True   A3.a,b,c,d

Pharmacology

Various medications are used in dentistry. All medicine undergoes strict research and clinical trials. It is important for a dentist to correctly diagnose an illness and prescribe the precise medicine in the exact dose and relay this information to the patient to get the optimum result. Furthermore patients can be allergic to certain drugs or be taking other medicine which could interact with the dentist's prescription. Pregnant women should avoid any medicine due to possible unknown effects on the developing foetus. Yet again the wisdom of taking a thorough medical history can be seen. Sometimes some patients feel more comfortable disclosing personal information to the nurse. Important information such as illness or medication regimes must be passed on to the dentist so that the patient can be treated safely and efficiently.

PRESCRIPTIONS

While reading the text answer the following;

Q1. How can drugs be named?

Q2. How should prescriptions be written?

Q3. What drugs may be kept in stock?

Q4. What security measures should be taken with drugs?

Most drugs have different names. The first is their generic name or recommended international non-proprietary name (rINN). The second is their brand name. For example Dispirin is a brand name for aspirin. Prescriptions are usually written in generic form.
Most drugs require a prescription from a doctor or dentist.

SURGERY DRUGS STOCK

A dental practice normally stocks a small supply of prescription drugs for two reasons;

1. Every practice must have an emergency drugs kit. This contains prescription drugs for medical emergencies.
2. A practice may keep a small supply of antibiotics, painkillers or sedatives. Antibiotics and painkillers are useful to have at hand when treating emergency patients out of office hours. Sedatives are used for conscious sedation. They are controlled drugs and must be kept locked away. Surgery drugs should be stored safely according to the manufacturer's instructions. They are best kept in the manufacture's packaging as they must be labelled with the strength and type of drug. Drugs should not be kept beyond their expiry date.

DISPENSING

Drugs that are given to the patient by the dentist from the surgery stock must;

* Include the manufacturer's instructions. So they must be labelled with the date, dose, quantity and name of the drug and have directions and precautions for use.
* Have the patient's name and address.
* Have the dentist's name and address. It is good practice to have a stock drugs' book. Every time stock drugs are handed to a patient the date, dose, quantity, type of drug, patient's name and dentist's signature should be recorded.

SECURITY

* Drugs, needles and prescription pads should be kept out of view.
* Controlled drugs must be kept in a locked cupboard and the dentist should keep the key.
* Prescription pads should not be stamped or signed until handed to the patient.

DISPOSAL OF DRUGS

Unused drugs or out of date drugs should be returned to the pharmacy for disposal.

Q1. How can drugs be named?

    a. generic name
    b. brand name
    c. recommended international non-proprietary name
    d. stock name

Q2. How should prescriptions be written?

    a. in pencil
    b. signed by the dental nurse
    c. signed by the dentist
    d. with the patient's name

Q3. What drugs may be kept in stock?

    a. emergency drugs
    b. sedatives
    c. antibiotics
    d. painkillers

Q4. What security measures should be taken with drugs?

    a. prescription pads should be pre-stamped
    b. needles should be on display
    c. controlled drugs should be locked away
    d. prescription pads should be kept out of view

How well did you do?
    A1.a,b,c   A2.c,d   A3.a,b,c,d
    A4.c,d

TYPES OF MEDICINE

While reading the text answer the following;

Q1. What are antibiotics used to treat?

Q2. How can penicillin effect oral contraceptives?

Q3. Which patients may need antibiotic cover?

Q4. What are the alternative antibiotics to penicillin?

Q5. What instructions should be given with metronidazole?

ANTIBIOTICS

Antibiotics are used to fight bacteria. They are useless against viral infections e.g. colds or flu.
All bacterial infections of the mouth have to be treated "surgically". For example decayed dentine has to be removed from the tooth and a filling placed. Likewise gum disease involves removing bacterial plaque and scaling calculus from the roots. Antibiotics reduce acute infections to a level whereby the dentist can then comfortably treat the patient by removing the cause. It is important for the patient to understand this. So, for example, if they are given antibiotics for a periapical abscess, they must make an appointment to return for a root filling otherwise the infection will return within weeks. Dentists do not like to over prescribe antibiotics as this can lead to resistant strains of bacteria, making infections harder to treat. Furthermore patients can develop allergies to antibiotics preventing their future use.

PENICILLIN

Any drug ending with -cillin is a member of the penicillin family. This is a very useful antibiotic and you will probably have seen your dentist prescribe amoxicillin capsules. Amoxicillin is known as a broad spectrum antibiotic as it can kill a wide variety of bacteria. It is useful in cases of acute periapical abscesses. Penicillin V is often used in severe cases of pericoronitis.

PENICILLIN ALLERGY

A significant number of patients develop allergies to penicillin. An allergy usually presents as a raised red skin rash. Patients sometimes say that they are allergic to a medicine if it gives them an upset stomach. However this is not a true allergy. Antibiotics not only kill the bacteria causing the oral infection but also disrupt the normal (healthy) bacteria in the gut. Because these bacteria have been disrupted the patient may feel nauseas and/or suffer from diarrhoea.

Taking bio-yogurts (yogurt which contains live friendly bacteria) can help to restore the gut flora. If a patient is allergic to one type of penicillin they will be allergic to all members of the penicillin family.

So, for example, if a patient is allergic to amoxicillin they also must never be given ampicillin.

PENICILLIN AND ORAL CONTRACEPTIVES

Penicillin can decrease the effectiveness of oral contraceptives. Often female patients fail to disclose that they are taking the contraceptive pill as many people do not regard this as a medicine. When the dentist prescribes penicillin to a female of reproductive age they must always inform her that penicillin effects the contraceptive pill and the patient should continue to take the pill but use some other form of contraceptive as well for that cycle. It should be expressed in
general terms to avoid offence e.g. when prescribing penicillin to teenagers. Diplomacy is paramount!

ANTIBIOTIC COVER

Before certain oral surgery procedures such as implant placement, prophylactic antibiotics are given. This is called antibiotic cover. It helps to prevent post operative infections. A high dose of amoxicillin is given one hour before treatment. This means that the antibiotic is already in the patient's blood stream and ready to kill the bacteria immediately as they enter, by the time the dental treatment begins. Three grams of amoxicillin (Amoxil™) is given by dissolving the powder in a little water.

Do not dissolve the powder in an entire cup full of water as the patient might find it hard to swallow so much liquid. (Some patients do not like the taste!) You may be asked to watch the patient taking their amoxicillin and to monitor them for a while as patients should take this in the presence of another adult as there is always the possibility that anaphylactic shock may result.

ERYTHROMYCIN

Erythromycin is a useful alternative to amoxicillin for patients who are allergic to penicillin. These tablets often irritate the stomach and so the patient must be warned to take them after food.

CLINDAMYCIN

Again clindamycin is a good alternative to amoxicillin especially when a high dose needs to be given as in antibiotic cover.

METRONIDAZOLE

Metronidazole (Flagyl) is the drug of choice for gum infections. Periodontal disease is caused by spirochetes and fusiform bacteria. Metronidazole is good at attacking these type of bacteria. The patient usually only needs a short course of treatment for three days. The patient must return to have the underlying problems of poor oral hygiene and plaque and calculus build-up removed. If the patient does not return the gums usually flare up within a month if not sooner. Metronidazole reacts badly with alcohol. Every patient prescribed metronidazole tablets must be warned to avoid all alcohol.

When an infection is severe, especially when it involves both a periapical abscess and periodontitis (gum disease) then a course of amoxicillin and metronidazole may be used together.

Q1. What are antibiotics used to treat?

    a. viral infections
    b. bacterial infections
    c. fungal infections
    d. anaphylaxis

Q2. How can penicillin effect oral contraceptives?

    a. make them more effective
    b. make them less effective
    c. have no effect
    d. increase the chance of allergy

Q3. Which patients may need antibiotic cover?

    a. those with a history of rheumatic fever
    b. those with heart murmurs
    c. those with artificial heart valves
    d. those with a pacemaker

Q4. What are the alternative antibiotics to penicillin?

   a. amoxicillin
   b. metronidazole
   c. clindamycin
   d. erythromycin

Q5. What instructions should be given with metronidazole?

   a. drink plenty of water
   b. abstain from alcohol
   c. abstain from smoking
   d. do not take with penicillin

How well did you do?
   A1.b   A2.b   A3.none   A4.c,d   A5.b

ANTIFUNGAL DRUGS

While reading the text answer the following;

Q1. Give examples of antifungal drugs.

Q2. Give the name of an antiviral drug.

Antifungal drugs are used to treat Candida albicans infections. These infections are found in debilitated patients, patients with poor oral hygiene and patients who continually wear their dentures. Useful antifungal drugs are nystatin and amphotericin. They come as pastilles and lozenges as the patient must suck the medicine slowly to kill the fungus. If the patient has denture stomatitis they must of course be instructed to suck the lozenge with their dentures out!
Some patients get Candida infections at the corner of their mouth. This is called angular chelitis. Miconazole (Daktarin™) gel is applied topically to the corners.

ANTIVIRAL DRUGS

Viral infections of the mouth are normally caused by the herpes simplex virus. They present as cold sores or mouth ulcers and can be treated with acyclovir.
Acyclovir cream is used topically for cold sores. Acyclovir tablets are used systemically for mouth ulcers. (Topical means that the medicine is placed on the surface and acts directly. Systemic means that the medicine is swallowed or injected so that it enters the circulation and is carried around the body.) Cold sores tingle before the blisters form. Acyclovir is far more effective if treatment begins early at the tingling stage.

Q1. Which of the following are antifungal drugs?

   a. acyclovir
   b. nystatin
   c. clindamycin
   d. miconazole

Q2. Which of the following are antiviral drugs?

   a. acyclovir
   b. nystatin
   c. clindamycin
   d. miconazole

How well did you do?
   A1.b,d   A2.a

PAINKILLERS/ANALGESICS

While reading the text answer the following;

Q1. Which painkillers should not be given to asthmatics?

Q2. Which patients should not take paracetamol?

Many painkillers can be brought over the counter and so the patient will usually take them as soon as any dental pain starts. Patients who are taking daily painkillers for other reasons, e.g. severe arthritis, may mask toothache, making diagnosis more difficult.

NON-STEROIDAL ANTI-INFLAMMATORY DRUGS (NSAID)

Most dental pain is due to inflammation. So the best painkillers for tooth ache are anti-inflammatory as well as analgesic. This group of drugs is called non-steroidal anti-inflammatory drugs (NSAID). Unfortunately NSAID cannot be used on patients with peptic ulcers or asthma. The most common ones used in dentistry are aspirin and ibuprofen.

1.   ASPIRIN

- Many people take a low daily dose of aspirin to prevent heart attacks and strokes. During extractions these patients may bleed for longer than usual.
- Aspirin is particularly corrosive and so, like other NSAID, must not be given to patients with peptic ulcers (stomach ulcers) as it will cause their stomachs to bleed. All patients should be advised to swallow aspirin with plenty of water.
- Aspirin must not be given to children as it may cause a rare but fatal brain disease (Reye's syndrome). Also aspirin should not be given to pregnant women.

2. IBUPROFEN

- Like aspirin, ibuprofen should not be given to patients with peptic ulcers or asthma.
- Ibuprofen is safe with children.

PARACETAMOL

- Paracetamol is an analgesic but has no anti-inflammatory properties.
- It is a good alternative to aspirin and ibuprofen.
- It can not be used in patients with liver damage. In fact overdoses of paracetamol may cause liver failure a few days later in otherwise healthy patients.
- Interestingly paracetamol is good at helping to overcome colds and flu.
- Junior paracetamol is available for children.

Q1. Which painkillers should not be given to asthmatics?

    a. aspirin
    b. ibuprofen
    c. paracetamol
    d. NSAID

Q2. Which patients should not take paracetamol?

    a. children
    b. alcoholics
    c. asthmatics
    d. patients with peptic ulcers

How well did you do?
    A1.a,b,d   A2.b

CORTICOSTEROIDS

While reading the text answer the following;

Q1. What are the dental uses of corticosteroids?

Q2. Name two oral sedatives.

Corticosteroids are anti-inflammatory drugs. In dentistry they have two main uses;

1. Topical steroids are used to heal mouth ulcers, e.g. Adcortyl in Orabase™ (This is fiddly for the patient to use as the mucosa must be dry for it to stick.)
2. Corticosteroid paste may be used within the tooth in endodontics as a temporary dressing e.g. Ledermix™.

ORAL SEDATION

Patients who are very anxious about dental procedures can be given oral sedation. These drugs are known as tranquillisers. They make the patient less anxious without sending them to sleep. However the patients are often drowsy. These patients should be driven to and from the surgery by a responsible adult. They are forbidden to work, drive, operate machinery, take alcohol or sign legal papers for up to 24 hours by which time the tranquilliser has worn off.

Oral sedation does not relieve pain so local anaesthetic is still required.

Tranquillisers can also be given intravenously for conscious sedation.

Example of oral sedatives are;

- Diazepam (Valium™) which is started the night before.
- Temazepam which is given 1 hour before treatment.

Q1. What are the dental uses of corticosteroids?

    a. to relieve mouth ulcers
    b. used as an antibiotic
    c. to anaesthetise teeth
    d. as a temporary dressing

Q2. Which of the following are oral sedatives?

    a. diazepam
    b. ibuprofen
    c. temazepam
    d. miconazole

How well did you do?
    A1.a,d   A2.a,c

LOCAL ANAESTHETIC

Local anaesthetic e.g. lignocaine is used daily in dentistry to abolish pain during dental procedures. Local anaesthetic may be used alone or with a vasoconstrictor. The vasoconstrictor decreases the diameter of the blood vessels and so prevents the anaesthetic from being carried away too quickly in the blood stream. This gives the dentist a longer operating time.

TOPICAL ANAESTHETIC

Topical anaesthetic is applied to the gum to anaesthetise the mucosa before an injection e.g. benzocaine.

HAEMOSTATIC AGENTS

Haemostatic agents are used to stop local bleeding. They often contain the vasoconstrictor adrenaline and may come as absorbable packs. Haemostatic packs can be placed in the socket after an extraction to stop the bleeding and encourage clotting. Likewise, retraction cord soaked in a haemostatic agent is used to stop gingival bleeding before taking an impression.

EMERGENCY DRUGS BOX

The emergency drugs box must contain the following medicines;

1. Adrenaline injection (1:1000, 1mg/ml)
2. Aspirin dispersible (300mg)
3. Glucagon injection (1mg)
4. Glyceryl tinitrate (GTN) spray (400mg/dose)

5. Midazolam (5mg/ml or 10mg/ml intranasal)
6. Glucose solution (oral)
7. Oxygen (size D cylinder)
8. Salbutamol inhaler (100mg/dose)

It is also useful to have the following;

1. Piriton injection (10mg)
2. Hydrocortisone injection (100mg)

The medical emergency kit should be easily accessible to all members of the dental team in the advent of an emergency but it should be stored away from public access. It must be checked monthly to ensure that all the medication is in date. Ideally this should be done on a rota basis by all members of the dental team so that everyone is familiar with the drugs.

SPECIAL PRECAUTIONS

While reading the text answer the following;

Q1. What precautions should be taken when prescribing for children and the elderly?

ADVERSE REACTIONS

Any adverse reaction to any drug must be recorded on the patient's records. These drugs should be avoided in the future as a mild reaction to a drug may result in a life threatening one next time. A comprehensive medical history is needed as the patient may be allergic to the drug or it may be interacting with other medication that they are already taking. For a number of reasons some patients do not fully disclose their medical history or they may be on a complicated drug regime. In these cases the dentist should consult the patient's doctor.

CHILDREN

Generally young children need a lower dose of medicine than adults. Also many children will not swallow tablets and must be given the medicine in its liquid form. Most medicines are now available in a sugar free form as prolonged medication of sugary syrups may cause extensive decay.

ELDERLY

Elderly patients may need lower doses as they may have some kidney or liver impairment. They may also be on several medicines already. Some elderly patients may be forgetful or have difficulty reading the instructions or opening childproof bottles.

PREGNANCY AND BREAST FEEDING

As a general rule all drugs are best avoided in breast feeding and pregnant women. However there are local anaesthetics and antibiotics which have been used for decades with no adverse effect on the foetus. If dental treatment cannot be postponed the patient should be reassured of this.

If in any doubt with any patient the dentist will refer to the Dental Practitioners' Formulary (DPF), the Monthly Index of Medical Specialities (MIMS) or phone the patient's doctor.

Q1. What precautions should be taken when prescribing for the elderly?

a. lower doses may be required due to liver impairment.
b. higher doses may be required due to liver impairment
c. prescriptions may interact with other medication
d. the elderly may have difficulty opening childproof bottles

How well did you do?
A1.a,c,d

5. Dental Anatomy and Physiology

Tooth Structure

While reading the text answer the following;

Q1. What is the hardest layer of the tooth?

Q2. What are enamel prisms?

Q3. Which cells produce dentine?

Q4. What is found in the pulp chamber?

Q5. What is the function of cementum?

THE TOOTH

ENAMEL

- This is the tough outer layer of the crown of a tooth.
- Enamel is the hardest part of the body. Harder than bone. It is the "armoured coating" of the crown.
- Enamel is composed of long parallel hydroxyapatite crystals organised in bundles called prisms.
- The prisms lie at right angles to the surface.
- It has no nerves or blood vessels so it does not feel pain and is not alive.
- Enamel cannot repair itself as it is non living.
- However if the enamel becomes porous (demineralises) it can re-harden (re-mineralise).
- Enamel becomes even tougher when it incorporates fluoride. The fluoride forms fluorapatite crystals.
- Enamel has a translucent, glass-like appearance.
- It is brittle.

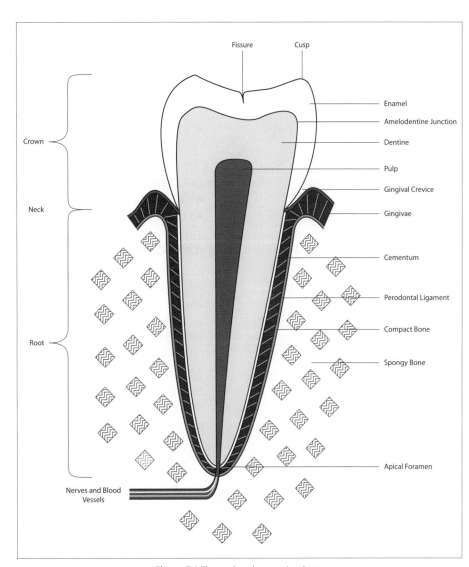

Figure 5.1 The tooth and supporting tissues.

DENTINE

- Dentine is the hard layer found between the enamel and pulp. It forms the bulk of the tooth.
- Dentine is yellow and gives the tooth its colour.
- It has tubules running through it radiating out from the pulp.
- Because the tubules are hollow decay spreads rapidly through dentine.
- The tubules are mineralised but inside are living dentinal fibrils.
- This is why dentine is sensitive to pain.
- Dentine is produced by odontoblasts.
- Dentine is slightly elastic.

PULP

- The pulp is the soft centre of the tooth.
- The pulp occupies the pulp chamber and root canals.
- It has blood vessels and nerves which enter the apex through the apical foramen. The nerves make the pulp highly sensitive to pain.
- The outermost layer of the pulp lies next to the dentine and consists of specialised cells called odontoblasts.
- Odontoblasts lay down new dentine, called secondary dentine, in response to damage.

- Odontoblasts have dentinal fibrils which project into the dentine tubules. This is why dentine can feel pain, temperature and pressure.
- Even in the absence of damage the odontoblasts slowly lay down dentine causing the pulp chamber to shrink with age.

CEMENTUM

- This is found on the root surface only.
- The cementum attaches the periodontal ligament to the root.

Q1. What is the hardest layer of the tooth?

a. enamel
b. dentine
c. cementum
d. fluoride

Q2. What are enamel prisms?
a. crystals which run parallel to the enamel surface
b. crystals which run at right angles to the enamel surface
c. translucent crystals
d. hard mineralised layer

Q3. Which cells produce dentine?

a. odontophils
b. odontoblasts
c. haemophils
d. haemoblasts

Q4. What is found in the pulp chamber?

a. nerves
b. soft tissue
c. blood vessels
d. cementum

Q5. What is the function of cementum?

a. it provides the teeth with nutrients
b. it provides the teeth with oxygen
c. it anchors the periodontal ligaments to the root
d. it anchors the periodontal ligaments to the bone

How well did you do?
A1.a   A2.b,c,d   A3.b   A4.a,b,c A5.c

THE PERIODONTIUM

While reading the text answer the following;

Q1. What is the gingival crevice?

Q2. What are the interdentally papillae?

Q3. In which direction do the fibres of the periodontal ligament run?

Q4. What is alveolar bone?

The periodontium is the name given to the supporting structures of the teeth.

GINGIVEA

- The gingivea are the gums. The gingivae is firmly attached to the underlying alveolar bone.
- There is a slight crevice between the gum and the tooth and this is called the gingival crevice. The depth of the gingival crevice can be measured. When there is gum disease it becomes deeper.
- Healthy gums form a scalloped edge around the teeth. In between the teeth the gum is raised and known as the interdental papillae.
- Healthy gums have a pink stippled appearance.

PERIODONTAL LIGAMENT

- The periodontal ligament is composed of fibrous tissue. The fibres run obliquely from the bone to the cementum.
- The periodontal ligament firmly attaches the tooth to the bone and acts as a shock absorber.
- When the periodontal ligament becomes damaged the tooth loosens for example after trauma and during periodontal disease.
- At the neck of the tooth the fibres attach the cementum to the surrounding gum and neighbouring teeth.
- Nerves within the periodontal ligament detect pressure for example high spots on fillings. This results in pain which warns the patient that the tooth is under too much pressure.

ALVEOLAR BONE

- The alveolar process is the name given to the part of the jaw that supports the teeth.
- When teeth are extracted the alveolar bone resorbs.
- The alveolar process consists of a strong outer layer of compact bone and a softer interior of spongy bone.
- The teeth sit within bony sockets which are also lined with compact bone.

Q1. What is the gingival crevice?

a. it is the crevice between the gum and the tooth
b. it is the scalloped gum margin
c. it is the raised gum between the teeth
d. it is the amount of gum which shows when you smile

Q2. What are the interdentally papillae?

    a. it is the crevice between the gum and the tooth
    b. it is the scalloped gum margin
    c. it is the raised gum between the teeth
    d. it is the amount of gum which shows when you smile

Q3. In which direction do the fibres of the periodontal ligament run?

    a. parallel to the root surface
    b. at right angles to the root surface
    c. obliquely to the root surface
    d. in a loop around the root surface

Q4. The function of the alveolar bone is to support the teeth. True or false?

How well did you do?
    A1.a   A2.c   A3.c   A4.True

CLASSIFICATION OF PERMANENT TEETH

While reading the text answer the following;

Q1. What is the shape of an incisor?

Q2. Which tooth has the longest root?

Q3. Which premolar has two roots?

Q4. What is the difference between upper and lower molars?

INCISORS

- These teeth nibble and cut food and so are blade-like.
- The upper central incisors are larger than the upper lateral incisors. The lower incisors are all of similar size and smaller than the uppers.
- Incisors have one root.
- On the palatal/lingual surfaces the incisors are bulbous. This is called the cingulum.

CANINES

- These teeth are for piercing food and so are pointed.
- Palatal/lingual surfaces have a cingulum.
- Each canine has one long root.
- Upper canines have the longest roots of all the dentition.

PREMOLARS

- Both premolars and molars are used for grinding and chewing food.
- The upper first premolar has two roots but the other premolars only have one.
- All premolars have at least two cusps; one buccal, one palatal/lingual.

MOLARS

- Molars chew and grind food and have a large occlusal surface for this.
- Molars have four to five cusps.
- Separating the cusps are fissures (which can collect plaque).
- Upper molars have three roots; two buccal and one palatal.
- Lower molars have two roots, one mesial and one distal.
- The roots of the third molar (wisdom tooth) may be fused together.

Q1. What is the shape of an incisor?

    a. flat, blade-like
    b. pointed
    c. multi-cusped
    d. they have a palatal cingulum

Q2. Which tooth has the longest root?

    a. wisdom
    b. lower canine
    c. upper canine
    d. upper molar

Q3. Which premolar has two roots?

    a. upper first premolar
    b. upper second premolar
    c. lower first premolar
    d. lower second premolar

Q4. Upper molars have two roots and lower molars have three.
True or false?

How well did you do?
    A1.a,d   A2.c   A3.a   A4.False

PERMANENT TOOTH ERUPTION

While reading the text answer the following;

Q1. When do permanent teeth erupt?

The permanent teeth start to develop within the bone at birth but only start to erupt at 6 years. The first permanent teeth to erupt are the first molars. These erupt behind the primary dentition without the need for any baby teeth to fall out.
This is important as often the parents are unaware that their child has new teeth and so they risk being neglected. This is one reason why the first molars are prone to decay.

AGE OF PERMANENT TOOTH ERUPTION

1 central incisor	=	7 years
2 lateral incisor	=	8 years
3 canine	=	9 years (lower), 11 years (upper)
4 first premolar	=	10 years (lower), 9 years (upper)
5 second premolar	=	11 years (lower), 10 years (upper)
6 first molar	=	6 years
7 second molar	=	12 years
8 third molar	=	18+ years

- The primary incisors and canines are replaced by the permanent incisors and canines.
- The primary molars are replaced by the permanent premolars.
- The permanent molars erupt as the jaws grow and lengthen.

The deciduous teeth become loose and eventually fall out as their permanent successors erupt. The baby teeth loosen due to the resorption of their roots.

Q1. Write down the eruption times of the following permanent teeth;

    a. upper canine
    b. upper first molar
    c. lower central incisors
    d. lower first premolar

How well did you do?
    A1.a = 11 years, b = 6 years,
    c = 7 years, d = 10 years

Charting Teeth

TOOTH NOTATIONS

There are two methods of charting teeth;

1. PALMER SYSTEM

As you have learnt the mouth is divided into four quadrants;

upper right quadrant	(URQ)
upper left quadrant	(ULQ)
lower right quadrant	(LLQ)
lower left quadrant	(LLQ)

The permanent teeth are designated numbers 1 to 8, starting from the central incisor to the wisdom tooth. So for example the upper right first molar can be recorded as UR6.

2. INTERNATIONAL DENTAL FEDERATION (FDI) SYSTEM

This system is a two digit system.
It replaces the quadrant symbol with a number.

quadrant 1	quadrant 2
quadrant 4	quadrant 3

However the tooth numbers remain the same. So for example the upper right first molar can be recorded as 16.

CHARTING TREATMENTS

You know how to chart fillings and extractions. However it is possible to chart all the other types of dental treatment by using the following codes;

Am	amalgam filling
A	artificial tooth
BA	bridge abutment
BP	bridge pontic
Cm	composite filling
FGC	full gold crown
F/S	fissure sealant
GI	gold inlay
GIC	glass ionomer filling (glass ionomer cement)
PBC	porcelain bonded crown
PI	porcelain inlay
PV	porcelain veneer
RCT	root canal treated
Tm	temporary filling
#	fracture
+	retained root
<->	tooth missing and space closed

Q1. Give the FDI equivalent to the following Palmer tooth codes;

    a. UR5
    b. UL7
    c. LL2
    d. LR3

Q2. Give the Palmer tooth notation to the following FDI codes;

    a. 18
    b. 23
    c. 33
    d. 46

Q3. Give both the Palmer and FDI codes to the following teeth.

    a. upper right canine
    b. upper left first premolar
    c. lower left lateral incisor
    d. lower right second molar

Q4. Give the charting notation for the following;

    gold inlay, porcelain veneer, glass ionomer filling, fracture, retained root

How well did you do?
    A1. a.15 b.27 c.32 d.43
    A2. a.UR8 b.UL3 c.LL3 d.LR6
    A3. a.UR3, 13 b.UL4, 24
    c.LL2, 32 d.LR7, 47
    A4. GI, PV, GIC, #, +

The Skull

While reading the text answer the following;

Q1. What is the main function of the cranium?

Q2. What are the names of the bones which make up the cranium?

Q3. What cavities are found in the maxilla?

Q4. What is the name of the arch which forms the "cheek bone"?

Q5. What is the name of the bone which supports the teeth?

The skull consists of a hard hollow housing for the brain and a lower wedged shaped portion which forms the face and jaws.

THE CRANIUM

The main function of the cranium is to house and protect the brain. The living brain is very soft (the consistency of thick custard). The cranium consists of six plates of bone fused together.

- One frontal bone
- Two parietal bones
- Two temporal bones
- One occipital bone

At the base of the cranium, holes called foramen run through the bones to allow blood vessels and nerves to pass through. The largest foramen is the foramen magnum in the occipital bone and this allows the spinal cord to pass through.

THE MAXILLA

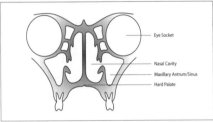

Figure 5.2 A cross-section of the maxilla.

The maxilla consists of two bones fused together to form the face. The maxilla is fused to the skull and is immovable. It supports the eyes, air sinuses, nose, cheeks and upper teeth. The base of the maxilla forms the hard palate. This is the roof of the mouth and separates the mouth (oral cavity) from the nose (nasal cavity).
In an arch around the hard palate is the alveolar bone which supports the upper teeth. On either side behind the last teeth the alveolar bone bulges to form the tuberosities of the maxilla.
The main body of the maxilla is hollow. In the centre is the nasal cavity and either side are the maxillary sinuses (antrum). The sinus lies above the posterior teeth. When the sinus is inflamed the condition is called

sinusitis. This is painful and the pain may be referred to the back teeth and present as toothache. The reverse is also true. The dentist has to correctly diagnose whether the patient has toothache or sinusitis. Sometimes the roots of the posterior teeth extend up into the sinus. If they are extracted the sockets can connect the mouth with the nose until the area heals. The zygomatic arch forms the "cheek bone". The cheek bone is actually made from three different bones. The front part of the zygomatic arch is made from the maxilla.

THE MANDIBLE

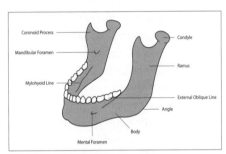

Figure 5.3 *The mandible.*

The lower jaw is called the mandible. It is connected to the base of the scull by a unique movable joint. When we eat and speak the upper jaw remains stationary while the lower jaw moves. Like the maxilla, the mandible is actually made of two bones which are fused together along the midline. (This happens as the foetus is forming in the womb). The mandible is shaped like a horseshoe in the horizontal plane and rises up at each end to form the ramus. The horizontal part is called the body of the mandible and carries the lower teeth in the alveolar bone. Along the inside of the mandible is a ridge of bone called the mylohyoid ridge. The mylohyoid muscle attaches to the mylohyoid ridge and forms the floor of the mouth.
The top of the ramus ends in a rounded piece of bone called the condyle.
The condyle forms part of the temporomandibular joint.

THE TEMPOROMANDIBULAR JOINT

While reading the text answer the following;

Q1. Where is the TMJ found?

Q2. How can the mandible become dislocated?

Q3. What is nocturnal bruxism?

Q4. What are the functions of a bite guard?

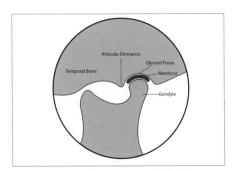

Figure 5.4 *The temporomandibular joint.*

The temporomandibular joint (TMJ) is the joint between the temporal bone of the scull and the mandible. This allows the lower jaw to open and close and move from side to side. The condyle of the mandible fits into a groove in the temporal bone called the glenoid fossa. The condyle and the glenoid fossa are separated by a pad of cartilage so that the two bones do not grate against each other. In front of the joint is a bony ridge called the articular eminence. This prevents the condyle from slipping out of the fossa and dislocating.

DISLOCATED MANDIBLE

Sometimes the articular eminence is not very prominent and the patient is prone to dislocating their lower jaw. If the condyle slips too far forward during mouth opening, it can pop over the articular eminence and become stuck. The lower jaw is now dislocated and the alarmed patient cannot close their mouth. To relocate the jaw the dentist needs to push down on the molars and then backwards to slip the condyle back into the fossa.

BRUXISM/GRINDING

A much more common complaint is pain in the TMJs due to tooth grinding. This often happens at night when the patient is asleep and is called nocturnal bruxism. Subconsciously the patient grinds their teeth causing their teeth to wear down. This tooth wear can be see at routine examinations. The patients often wake up with sore TMJs and tension in their jaw muscles. Often the muscles on one side are in spasm and the mouth no longer opens along the midline but deviates to the right or left. The dentist may provide jaw exercises for the patient to rectify this. Bruxism is connected with stress in many cases so relaxing before going to sleep and not having any caffeine from 5pm can help this complaint. High fillings or tooth movement (from a tooth tilting into the space left by a previous extraction) can cause bruxism. As tooth grinding is a subconscious action the patient cannot control it. Often the dentist has to make a bite guard for the patient to wear at night. These are made of either soft or hard acrylic and are also known as occlusal splints. There are many different types but they all help in three ways;

1. The bite guard evens out any discrepancies in the bite and may stop the grinding as the mind is no longer trying to "smooth" the teeth.

2. If the grinding continues (often because the underlying stress continues e.g. work, relationship or financial problems) the bite guard will wear down instead of the teeth. It is much easier to replace a bite guard than rebuild an entire set of teeth!

3. The plastic of the bite guard has more "give" than enamel (which is like rock) and so decreases the jarring effect that grinding has on the temporomandibular joints.

CLENCHING

Another condition of the temporomandibular joints is tooth clenching. Here the patient does not grind but clenches their teeth tightly building up enormous pressure in the TMJs. The teeth do not necessarily wear however a bite guard will reduce the pressure being transmitted to the joints. Again a common factor seems to be stress. The patients who clench are recognisable as soon as they walk in to the surgery as their cheek muscles are abnormally large due to this "weight training" of the jaws.

Both grinders and clenchers may or may not be aware of their habit. Often it is the partners of the nocturnal grinders who are aware, as the sound of their partner's tooth grinding keeps them awake!

Q1. Where is the TMJ found?

   a. between the temporal bone and the mandible

   b. between the temporal bone and the condyle

   c. between the temporal bone and the articular eminence

   d. between the maxilla and the mandible

Q2. How can the mandible become dislocated?

    a. when the condyle pops over the articular eminence
    b. when the ramus pops over the articular eminence
    c. when the maxilla pops over the articular eminence
    d. when the condyle pops over the ramus eminence

Q3. What is bruxism?

    a. tooth grinding
    b. dislocation of the maxilla
    c. dislocation of the mandible
    d. tooth decay

Q4. What are the functions of a bite guard?

    a. to prevent tooth wear
    b. to prevent grinding
    c. to prevent bruxism
    d. to prevent joint pain

How well did you do?
    A1.a,b   A2.a   A3.a   A4.a,b,c,d

The Muscles of the Mouth

While reading the text answer the following;

Q1. List the muscles of mastication.

Q2. What is the function of the facial muscles.

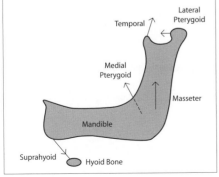

Figure 5.5 *Muscles of mastication and the suprahyoid muscle.*

THE MUSCLES OF MASTICATION

These muscles extend from skull to the mandible and allow the lower jaw to chew from side to side and to close. There are four main pairs of muscles of mastication.

1.   Temporal muscles
2.   Masseter muscles
3.   Medial pterygoid muscles
4.   Lateral pterygoid muscles

The temporal, masseter and medial pterygoid muscles close the mouth. When both lateral pterygoid muscles contract the mandible moves forward. When only one contracts the lower jaw moves to the opposite side.

SUPRAHYOID MUSCLES

The hyoid bone is found in the front of the neck. The suprahyoid (supra=above, hyoid=hyoid bone) muscles extend from the chin down to the hyoid bone and allow the mouth to open.

BUCCINATOR

The buccinator muscle forms the cheek.

MUSCLES OF FACIAL EXPRESSION

These muscles are found beneath the skin and allow us to change the expression on our face.

Q1. Which of the following are muscles of mastication.

    a. suprahyoid
    b. masseter
    c. temporal
    d. distal pterygoid

Q2. The function of the facial muscles is to allow us to make facial expressions. True or false?

How well did you do?
    A1.b,c   A2.True

The Nerve Supply of the Mouth

While reading the text answer the following;

Q1. What are the three types of nerve?

Q2. What is the name of the fifth cranial nerve?

Q3. What are the three divisions of the trigeminal?

Q4. Through which gland does the facial nerve pass?

Q5. Name two nerves which innervate the tongue.

Q6. Which blood vessels supply the face and jaws?

The twelve pairs of cranial nerves supply the head. The cranial nerves branch off from the brain whereas the nerves supplying the body branch off from the spinal cord. The fifth, seventh, ninth and twelfth cranial nerves are relevant to dentistry.

There are three different types of nerve.

1.   Sensory nerves which feel sensation such as temperature, pain and pressure.
2.   Motor nerves which supply glands and muscles.
3.   Mixed nerves which contain both sensory and motor fibres.

TRIGEMINAL NERVE / FIFTH CRANIAL NERVE

This is the most important nerve in dentistry as it is the branches of this nerve that we numb every day to produce painless dentistry. It is described in detail later on but basically the trigeminal nerve has three divisions; the ophthalmic, maxillary and mandibular divisions.

The maxillary division has a sensory supply to the upper teeth, maxilla and the middle third of the face.

The mandibular division has a sensory supply to the lower teeth, mandible and lower third of the face. The mandibular division also has a motor branch which supplies the muscles of mastication.

FACIAL NERVE / SEVENTH CRANIAL NERVE

The facial nerve is a mixed nerve. The motor branches innervates the muscles of facial expression. The facial nerve passes through the parotid gland. If this nerve was inadvertently numbed during an inferior dental block then that side of the face would be paralysed for as long as it took the anaesthetic to wear off! Other motor branches supply the submandibular and sublingual salivary glands.

The sensory branches of the facial nerve allow us to taste as they supply the anterior two thirds of the tongue.

GLOSSOPHARYNGEAL NERVE / NINTH CRANIAL NERVE

The ninth cranial nerve is a mixed nerve and supplies the throat muscles, parotid glands and the posterior third of the tongue.

HYPOGLOSSAL NERVE / TWELFTH CRANIAL NERVE

This motor nerve supplies the muscles of the anterior two thirds of the tongue. (glossal=tongue)

The Blood Supply

Branches of the external carotid artery supply the face, teeth and jaws. The blood returns to the heart via the superior vena cava. The blood vessels travel beside the nerves to form neurovascular bundles. The blood vessels usually have the same name as the nerve they are running alongside. For example the inferior dental artery runs alongside the inferior dental nerve and becomes the mental artery when it passes through the mental foramen.

Q1. What are the three types of nerve?

    a. mixed
    b. motor
    c. sensory
    d. sensitive

Q2. What is the name of the fifth cranial nerve?

    a. facial
    b. trigeminal
    c. hypoglossal
    d. glossopharyngeal

Q3. What are the three divisions of the trigeminal?

    a. facial
    b. maxillary
    c. mandibular
    d. ophthalmic

Q4. Through which gland does the facial nerve pass?

    a. submandibular
    b. sublingual
    c. parotid
    d. thyroid

Q5. Name two nerves which innervate the tongue muscle.

    a. facial
    b. trigeminal
    c. hypoglossal
    d. glossopharyngeal

Q6. Which blood vessels supply the face and jaws?

    a. vena cava
    b. carotid
    c. external carotid
    d. internal carotid

How well did you do?
    A1.a,b,c A2.b A3.b,c,d A4.c
    A5.c,d A6.c

The Salivary Glands

While reading the text answer the following;

Q1. List three pairs of major salivary glands.
Q2. Which childhood infection inflames the parotid?
Q3. Which gland is most likely to produce salivary stones?
Q4. Which major salivary glands lie in the floor of the mouth?

Saliva is produced by minor and major salivary glands. There are many minor salivary glands found within the lips and cheeks. There are three pairs of major salivary glands; the parotid, submandibular and sublingual. The glands produce the saliva which then passes through ducts into the mouth.

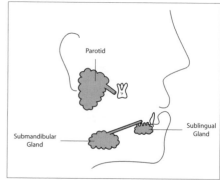

Figure5.6 Position of the major salivary glands.

PAROTID GLAND

This is the largest of all the salivary glands. It lies in front of the ear around the ramus of the mandible. Its duct opens opposite the upper second molar. You may have noticed that the dentist often places a cotton wool roll or dry guard™ in the upper buccal sulcus. This is to cover the entrance of the duct to maintain moisture control. The facial nerve passes through this gland. When a child has mumps the virus causes acute inflammation of the parotid gland which is very painful. The parotid is also the salivary gland which is most likely to get a tumour whether benign or cancerous.

SUBMANDIBULAR GLAND

The submandibular glands lie in the floor of the mouth. They each have a long duct which travels forward and opens either side of the midline. This is where you often place the saliva ejector to remove the saliva as it flows into the mouth. You can see the entrances of the ducts either side of the lingual fraenum and sometimes saliva shoots out! The saliva from the submandibular glands coats the lower anterior teeth which leads to the build up of calculus in this region. The submandibular glands are most likely to suffer from salivary stones which block the long ducts. The classic symptom of a blocked salivary gland is that it swells up during eating or on anticipating food. This is because saliva is being formed but cannot be released. The stones need to be removed surgically.

SUBLINGUAL GLAND

The sublingual glands also lie under the tongue in the floor of the mouth. They have many ducts which open up into the floor of the mouth.

Q1. Which of the following are major salivary glands?

    a. thyroid
    b. parotid
    c. mandibular
    d. submandibular

Q2. Which childhood infection inflames the parotid?

    a. mumps
    b. bumps
    c. chicken pox
    d. measles

Q3. Which gland is most likely to produce salivary stones?

    a. thyroid
    b. parotid
    c. sublingual
    d. submandibular

Q4. Which major salivary glands lie in the floor of the mouth?

    a. thyroid
    b. parotid
    c. sublingual
    d. submandibular

How well did you do?
    A1.b,d   A2.a   A3.d   A4.c,d

SALIVA

While reading the text answer the following;

Q1. What are the functions of saliva?

Q2. What are the problems associated with a dry mouth?

Q3. What causes dry mouth?

The soft tissue of the mouth are continually bathed in saliva.

FUNCTIONS OF SALIVA

1.   It lubricates the mouth.
    Saliva mainly consists of water and so moistens the mucosa. This allows easy movement of the tongue and lips enabling eating and speaking.

2.   It cleanses the mouth.
    Saliva production is increased even by the thought of food. The increase in saliva not only helps swallowing but also dislodges food from the teeth and sulcus.

3.   Digestion.
    Saliva contains the enzyme salivary amylase which starts to digest carbohydrates.

4.   Enhances taste.
    Saliva dissolves the food which allows our taste buds in the tongue to sense the taste of food.

5.   Saliva neutralises acids. The acids produced by the oral bacteria demineralise the teeth (makes them porous). Saliva neutralizes this acid. Calcium and phosphate ions in the saliva buffer (neutralise) the acid. (Incidentally, these ions also mineralise plaque to produce calculus.)

6.   Saliva defends the body against bacteria.
    Saliva contains antibodies which attack oral infections.

REDUCTION OF SALIVA

Normally we all take saliva for granted. However certain illnesses result in a decreased flow of saliva. This may greatly decrease the patients' enjoyment of life. They are more prone to the following;

- Ulceration of the mucosa due to lack of lubrication making eating and speaking painful.
- Increased decay rate. Food may clog around the teeth for many hours as they are not being cleansed by saliva. There are less ions produced to buffer the acid.
- Also as there is less saliva there are less antibodies to fight infections. This results in bad breath (halitosis) and gum disease.
- The enjoyment of food decreases as it is harder to taste since the food cannot dissolve.
- Denture wearers suffer poor retention due to the lack of a saliva film between the denture and mucosa. Poor lubrication leads to ulcers.

Conditions that cause xerostomia (dry mouth) include;

- Natural old age.
- Radiation to the head and neck.
- Autoimmune disorders for example Sjogren's syndrome.
- Some drugs e.g. antidepressants and diuretics

Patients with a reduced salivary flow often increase the amount of saliva in their mouth by sucking boiled sweets. This can be disastrous leading to wide spread decay. It is better to chew sugar free gum for short periods. The patients should be encouraged to sip water throughout the day and to always keep a glass of water by their bed at night. Naturally our saliva flow decreases at night and these patients can wake up very dry indeed. There are artificial saliva sprays available on the market e.g. Glandosane™. They can be plain or flavoured e.g. citrus or mint.

Q1. What are the functions of saliva?

    a. lubricating
    b. digests protein
    c. neutralises acid
    d. attacks bacteria

Q2. What are the problems associated with a dry mouth?

    a. oral ulcers
    b. poor denture retention
    c. caries
    d. gum disease

Q3. What causes dry mouth?

    a. head and neck radiation
    b. some autoimmune disorders
    c. ageing process
    d. some medicines

How well did you do?
    A1.a,c,d   A2.a,b,c,d   A3.a,b,c,d

6. Local Anaesthetic

So what's used and how?

> Anaesthetic = complete loss of feeling
> Analgesic = loss of pain only

Before we begin I should explain that local anaesthetic is a misnomer. The term should really be local analgesia. Anaesthesia means the complete loss of all feeling i.e. pain, pressure and movement. Analgesia is the loss of pain alone. When we "numb up" teeth we are taking away the sensation of pain but patients can still feel pressure and movement.

However the term "local anaesthetic" has been in use for decades so this is the term we will use.

As you know dentine and pulps are very sensitive so we need effective anaesthesia to treat patients painlessly.

LOCAL ANAESTHETIC DRUGS

While reading the text answer the following;

Q1. What are the contents of a local aesthetic cartridge?

Q2. What care should be taken with vasoconstrictors?

Q3. What is the quantity of adrenaline used in local anaesthetics?

Local anaesthetics come in a cartridge. The cartridge is made of glass with a rubber bung at one end and a rubber diaphragm at the other. The cartridge is labelled with its contents, the expiry date and batch number.

The contents of a cartridge are;

1. ANAESTHETIC SOLUTION
Anaesthetic is a non addictive derivative of the cocaine family so anaesthetics tend to end with -caine e.g. 2% lignocaine, 3% prilocaine

2. VASOCONSTRICTOR
Vasoconstrictors prevent the anaesthetic being carried away too quickly from the injection site by the blood. Vasoconstrictors restrict the blood flow by constricting the blood vessels in this region. This gives the dentist a longer working time which is particularly useful with extensive treatments. The main vasoconstrictors used are adrenaline and felypressin. Adrenaline is used in tiny quantities of 1:80 000. However even a small amount of adrenaline if inadvertently injected into a blood vessel can stimulate the heart and cause it to race. This is alarming to the patient. Adrenaline should be avoided in patients with heart problems, high blood pressure, hyperthyroidism or the elderly on various medications. (See the wisdom of taking a medical history. Know your patient!) The safe alternative is felypressin. However felypressin should not be used on pregnant women as it may cause premature labour. Cartridges of anaesthetic without vasoconstrictors are available.

3. STERILE WATER
This is the biggest component of the cartridge.

4. BUFFERING AGENT
This reduces the acidity and so decreases the pain of the injection.

5. PRESERVATIVE
Increases the shelf life.

Q1. The following are constituents of a local anaesthetic cartridge;

   a. buffering agent
   b. tap water
   c. preservative
   d. anaesthetic solution

Q2. The vasoconstrictor adrenaline should not be used on;

   a. pregnant women
   b. high blood pressure patients
   c. people with heart disease
   d. people with arthritis

Q3. The quantity of adrenaline in local anaesthetic is;

   a. 1:8000
   b. 1:80 000
   c. 1:1000
   d. 1:10 000

How well did you do?
   A1. a,c,d   A2. b,c   A3. b

TOPICAL ANAESTHETIC

These are gels that are placed on the mucosa to numb the surface to allow a painless injection. They may also be used before lancing a soft tissue abscess. e.g. benzocaine.

TYPES OF INJECTION

While reading the text answer the following;

Q1. Name three types of injection.

Q2. What is a self aspirating syringe?

By now you will have seen many injections. There are three main types of injection used in dentistry.

1. **LOCAL INFILTRATION**
   This is the usual method for anaesthetising upper teeth. From your dental anatomy you will remember that the nerves enter the tooth through the apex. When the dentist wishes to numb an upper tooth the dentist inserts the needle into the mucosa lying directly over the apex of the tooth. The anaesthetic spreads through the mucosa and bone to the tip of the root and numbs the nerve. Local infiltration can be used where the bone is relatively thin and porous. It is largely ineffective in the lower jaw as the bone is too dense for the anaesthetic to infiltrate. A short needle is used.

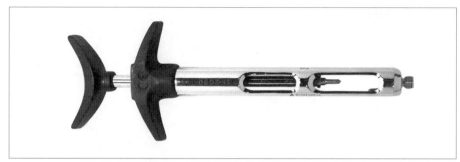

Figure 6.1 A self aspirating syringe. (Courtesy of Minerva.)

2. **NERVE BLOCK**
   When the bone is too dense a nerve block is necessary. Here the nerve is numbed before it enters the bone and a block of teeth and gum are anaesthetised by one injection.
   You will have seen the inferior dental block many times and know that this numbs half the lower jaw. Any tooth on that side of the mandible can be operated on painlessly. The inferior dental nerve runs within the bone of the mandible. It enters the jaw through the mandibular foramen which is found on the inside of the ramus. This is the site that the dentist inserts the needle. When that side of the lower lip feels numb work on the teeth can begin. In practice, when the dentist gives an inferior dental block the dentist also numbs the nearby lingual nerve so the side of the tongue tingles too.
   Blocks are deep injections so a long needle is used. It is possible for the dentist to accidentally inject into a blood vessel while giving an inferior dental block. To prevent this a self aspirating syringe is used. With this syringe, blood will flow back into the cartridge if the needle is in a blood vessel. The dentist can then simply reposition the needle before continuing the injection.

3. **INTRA-LIGAMENTARY INJECTION**
   This is an injection within the periodontal ligament. The needle is inserted into the gingival crevice using an extra short fine needle and a special intra-ligamentory syringe. (inter=between, intra=within) The periodontal space is a very small area which does not have a lot of "give". The intra-ligamentary syringe allows the anaesthetic to be deposited safely under pressure. A plastic sheath surrounds the cartridge so that if the cartridge shatters the fragments are contained within the sheath and do not fall into the patient's mouth. The advantage of this injection is that the tooth is anaesthetised immediately. The disadvantage is that it can traumatise the ligaments at the site of the injection. This method of injection is useful for teeth which are going to be extracted where damage to the ligament is irrelevant.
   If a tooth has become hypersensitive it may not respond to a local infiltration or a block. In order to be able to remove the pulp an intra-ligamentary injection may be necessary. This is acceptable in these cases as it is better for the patient to be out of pain.

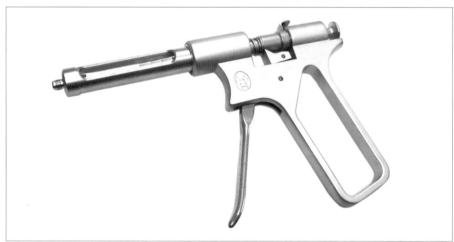

Figure 6.2 An intra-ligamentary syringe. (Courtesy of Minerva.)

NEEDLE GUARDS

Needle guards are devises that are placed over the cap of a needle. They prevent the clinical staff accidentally pricking themselves when recapping the needle. This prevents cross infection from the patient to the staff.

Figure 6.3 Needle guard. (Courtesy of Minerva.)

Q1. The 3 most common types of dental injection are;

    a. local infiltration
    b. nerve block
    c. inter-ligamentary injection
    d. intra-ligamentary injection

Q2. A self aspirating syringe shows the dentist if the needle is in a blood vessel. True or false?

How well did you do?
    A1. a.b.d A2. True

Now that you know the different types of injection let us discuss the nerve supply so that you understand which type of injection is used for each tooth.

NERVES

As you know there are three types of nerves;

1.   Sensory nerves.
    These detect pain, pressure, touch, temperature
2.   Motor nerves.
    These innervate muscles allowing us to move.

3.   Mixed nerves
    These nerves contain both sensory and motor branches.

To treat a patient comfortably we need to anaesthetise the sensory nerves which detect pain. It is best to try to avoid numbing any motor nerves so that the patients can still move their muscles. This is not always possible as you may have witnessed.

TRIGEMINAL NERVE

While reading the text answer the following;

Q1. Name the three branches of the trigeminal nerve.

As you know the teeth are innervated by the fifth cranial nerve called the trigeminal nerve. This nerve has three divisions (branches);

1.   OPTHALMIC
•   Supplies the forehead.

2.   MAXILLARY
•   The maxillary division is purely sensory.
•   It supplies the upper jaw, upper teeth and upper half of the face.

3.   MANDIBULAR
•   This is a mixed nerve.
•   The sensory branches supplies the lower jaw, lower teeth and lower half of the face.
•   The motor branches supply the muscles of mastication.

The sensory branches of the maxillary and mandibular nerves are anaesthetised to enable the dentist to work painlessly.

Q1. The following are branches of the trigeminal nerve.

    a. mandibular
    b. ophthalmic
    c. hypoglossal
    d. facial

How well did you do?
    A1. a,b

Foramen are holes within the skull and bone that allow nerves and blood vessels to pass through.

anterior	=	front
posterior	=	back
superior	=	upper
inferior	=	lower

MAXILLARY BRANCH OF THE TRIGEMINAL

The maxillary nerve divides into five smaller branches:

A. Naso-palatine nerve
B. Greater palatine nerve
C. Anterior superior dental nerve
D. Middle superior dental nerve
E. Posterior superior dental nerve

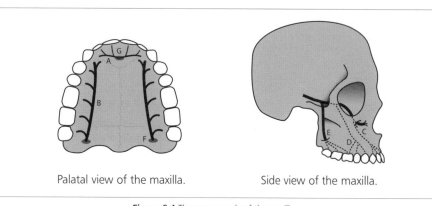

Palatal view of the maxilla.   Side view of the maxilla.

Figure 6.4 The nerve supply of the maxilla.

The greater palatine foramen (F) allows the greater palatine nerve to pass through the palate and supply the palatal gum of the posterior teeth.
The incisive foramen (G) is found opposite the upper incisors and allows the naso-palatine nerve to supply the palatal gum of the anterior teeth.

The superior dental nerve innervates all the upper teeth and their corresponding buccal gum. It splits into three branches; the posterior superior dental nerve, the middle superior dental nerve and the anterior superior dental nerve.

Remember because the maxillary bone is thinner anaesthetic can be achieved by local infiltration. If the upper teeth are being restored a buccal infiltration will suffice as the superior dental nerves supply these teeth. However if an upper tooth is being extracted then both a buccal and palatal infiltration are necessary so that the tooth and all its surrounding bone and gum are numb.

MANDIBULAR BRANCH OF THE TRIGEMINAL

The mandibular nerve divides into three smaller branches: the mandibular, inferior dental and long buccal nerves.

A. Mandibular nerve
B. Inferior dental nerve
C. Long buccal nerve
D. Lingual nerve
E. Mental nerve

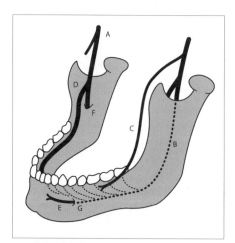

Figure 6.5 The nerve supply of the mandible.

The mandibular nerve branches into the inferior dental, lingual and long buccal nerves.
The inferior dental nerve supplies all the lower teeth. It enters the lower jaw through the mandibular foramen (F). Then it passes under the posterior teeth to emerge on the buccal side from the mental foramen (G). This lies between the lower premolars. From here on the nerve is called the mental nerve. The mental nerve supplies the buccal gum of the incisors,

canines and premolars and the lower lip and chin.
The lingual nerve runs along the inside of the mandible and supplies the tongue and lingual gum.
The long buccal innervates the buccal mucosa of the lower molars.
Before starting work the dentist asks the patient "Is the side of your lower lip numb?" If it is the dentist knows that the inferior dental block has worked and the teeth can be drilled painlessly. The patient may reply "No but the side of my tongue is numb." This means that another block is required as the inferior dental nerve is not anaesthetised only the lingual.

SO WHERE DO I FIT IN?

ROLE OF THE DENTAL NURSE

While reading the text answer the following;

Q1. How does the nurse assist the dentist when administering local anaesthetic?

1. Both the nurse and dentist check the medical history of the patient before starting any treatment.
2. The nurse gives the dentist topical anaesthetic gel on a cotton wool roll.
3. The nurse makes sure that there is mouth wash for the patient to rinse.
4. The nurse prepares the correct anaesthetic in the correct syringe with the correct needle plus needle guard under instructions from the dentist. The dentist double checks this before injecting. The nurse should never ask "Do you want a long or short needle?" as the response "Long." can heighten the patient's anxiety. It is kinder to ask the dentist "Is this a block or infiltration?"
5. While waiting to pass the syringe hold it firmly with the palm of your hand encompassing the cartridge to warm it. Better still always have a few cartridges warming in a babies bottle warmer. It is more comfortable for the patient if the local is at body temperature.

6. Discreetly and safely pass the syringe to the dentist behind the patient's head. Always pass the syringe handle first, never needle first (even if it is capped).
7. Monitor and reassure the patient during the injection. The dentist is concentrating on the injection so you must concentrate on the patient. This is the most likely time that a patient will faint or collapse during treatment. (This is why the patient is always laid flat for injections.)
8. The needle is resheathed by the dentist and placed in the nurse's working area in case further anaesthetic is required.
9. At the end of treatment the needle and empty cartridge are disposed in the sharps bin by the dentist and the syringe is scrubbed and sterilised by the nurse.

Q1. The role of the nurse during anaesthesia is;

    a. to set up the anaesthetic without instruction from the dentist
    b. to pass the syringe safely and discreetly
    c. to leave the room to load the autoclave
    d. to dispose of the used needle in the clinical waste bag

How well did you do?
    A1. b

WHAT DOES THE PATIENT NEED TO KNOW?

PATIENT ADVICE AFTER LOCAL ANAESTHETIC

This may be given by the dental nurse. The patient should be warned that they will be numb for approximately 2 to 5 hours. They should take care not to inadvertently bite their tongue or cheek. It is best not to eat for a while for this reason. It is especially important to warn patients who have never had local anaesthetic before. In the case of children both they and the accompany adult should be warned and the adult

should be asked to keep an eye on young children who may be tempted to nibble their lip during this stage.

WHAT DO I NEED TO KNOW?

NEEDLESTICK INJURY

While reading the text answer the following;

Q1. What are the steps to take with a non sterile needle stick injury?

Q2. Why is a knowledge of the medical history of a patient important?

Q3. How can you prevent a needle stick injury?

Here we are concerned with injuries caused from a used needle or sharp instrument. (If the needle is unused, i.e. sterile, wash and dress the lesion and report the incident in the accident book).
However a needle stick injury from a used needle is potentially dangerous, although the majority of cases prove harmless.

1. Immediately squeeze the wound to encourage bleeding and continue to squeeze under running water.
2. Inform the dentist.
3. Disinfect the wound. Then dry and apply a waterproof dressing.
4. Check the medical history of the patient.
5. Record the accident, the date and the name of the patient.
6. Get your blood tested by your doctor depending on the status of the patient.

If the patient's medical history is clear the wound should heal without complications. However if the patient has a blood borne disease or is in a high risk group the nurse must go for a blood test.

Remember that all nurses should be vaccinated against hepatitis B. There is no vaccine for hepatitis C but this is fortunately less common. There is also no vaccine for HIV. However a needle stick injury is unlikely to transmit AIDS as HIV has a low infectivity.

To prevent needle stick injuries always take great care when handling needles and passing syringes. Always use a needle guard. The dentist should recap the needle as soon as it has been used to avoid passing a contaminated unsheathed needle.

Q1. If a nurse gets scratched by a dirty needle the nurse should;

    a. squeeze the wound immediately.
    b. squeeze the wound after they have finished assisting the dentist.
    c. check the medical history of the patient.
    d. record the accident.

Q2. If the medical history shows that the patient is a hepatitis carrier the nurse should go for a blood test.
True or false?

Q3. To prevent a needle stick injury;

    a. always wear gloves
    b. take care when handling needles
    c. use a needle guard
    d. leave needles uncapped for quick use

How well did you do?
    A1. a,c,d   A2. True   A3. b,c

WASTE DISPOSAL

Empty glass cartridges and needles are placed in the sharps bin. This is made of strong plastic which cannot be pierced. It has a self locking lid and should be sealed when it is two thirds full. It is then collected for incineration.

7. Extractions and Minor Oral Surgery

By now you will have seen a few extractions. Most nurses enjoy this part of dentistry. Most patients do not! This is when patients are most anxious and your calm, friendly, competent support is most appreciated.

SO WHY DO WE EXTRACT TEETH?

REASONS FOR EXTRACTING TEETH

While reading the text answer the following;

Q1. List eight reasons to extract teeth.

1. Pain
2. Infection
   - e.g. Periapical abscesses.
3. Extensive decay
   - When the decay is so extensive the tooth cannot be restored.
4. Advanced periodontal disease
   - When the gum disease is so advanced that the tooth is too mobile and infected to save.
5. Impacted teeth
   - e.g. Impacted wisdom teeth that cause repeated episodes of pain or infection.
   - e.g. Impacted teeth that prevent orthodontics such as an unerupted canine.
6. Orthodontics
   - To create space to straighten crowded teeth.
   - The early extraction of deciduous teeth to influence the eruption of the permanent successors.
7. Trauma
   - e.g. Root fractures.
8. Medical reasons
   - e.g. When preparing a patient for cardiac surgery or head/neck radiation it may be necessary to extract teeth which could cause infections in the immuno-compromised patient.

Q1. Which of the following are reasons for extracting teeth?

a. periapical abscess
b. recurrent infection in an impacted tooth
c. minor caries
d. treatable periodontal disease

How well did you do?
   A1. a,b

WHAT DO WE USE TO EXTRACT TEETH?

THE INSTRUMENTS

You have seen an array of forceps and elevators used to extract teeth. One of your roles is to set up these instruments.

FORCEPS

While reading the text answer the following;

1. List three upper forceps.
2. How can you tell the upper right molar forceps from the left?
3. List two lower forceps.

Forceps consist of a handle and blades. The blades fit the anatomy of the teeth they are used to extract. By knowing the shape of the different teeth you can use your knowledge to select the correct forceps. The blades are shaped to fit around the curves of the root surface so visualise the roots.

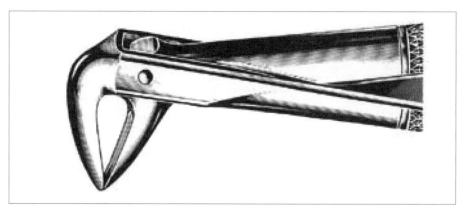
Figure 7.1 All lower forceps have the blades at right angles to the handle. (Courtesy of Minerva.)

Figure 7.2 Upper forceps have their blades roughly inline with the handle. (Courtesy of Minerva.)

Most forceps are available in smaller sizes for deciduous teeth while others have narrow blades to extract roots.

UPPER FORCEPS

1. UPPER STRAIGHT FORCEPS
These are used to extract upper
incisors and canines. As the name
implies the blade and handle lie in a
straight line.

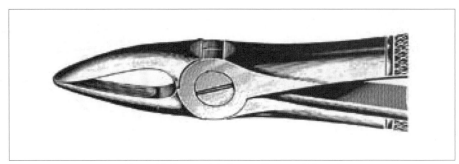

Figure 7.3 *Upper straight forceps. (Courtesy of Minerva.)*

2. UPPER ROOT FORCEPS
Upper root forceps are used to extract
upper premolars. The blades curve
slightly upwards.

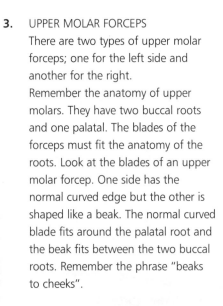

Figure 7.4 *Upper root forceps. (Courtesy of Minerva.)*

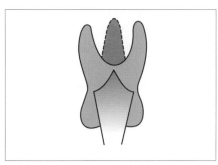

Figure 7.5 *Buccal (cheek) view*

3. UPPER MOLAR FORCEPS
There are two types of upper molar
forceps; one for the left side and
another for the right.
Remember the anatomy of upper
molars. They have two buccal roots
and one palatal. The blades of the
forceps must fit the anatomy of the
roots. Look at the blades of an upper
molar forcep. One side has the
normal curved edge but the other is
shaped like a beak. The normal curved
blade fits around the palatal root and
the beak fits between the two buccal
roots. Remember the phrase "beaks
to cheeks".

Figure 7.6 *Palatal view*

Place the forceps on the table so that the
blades curve gently upwards and then
imagine the patient is facing you. If the
beak is on the patient's left the you have
the upper left molar forceps. If it's on the
patient's right you have the upper right
molar forceps.

upper right molar
forceps

upper left molar
forceps

Figure 7.7 *Selecting upper molar forceps.*

LOWER FORCEPS

1. LOWER ROOT FORCEPS
Lower root forceps are used to extract lower incisors, canines and premolars.

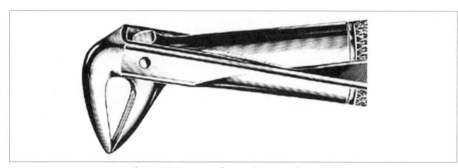

Figure 7.8 Lower root forceps. (Courtesy of Minerva.)

2. LOWER MOLAR FORCEPS

As lower molars have only two roots they have two identical beaks to fit into the bifurcation area.

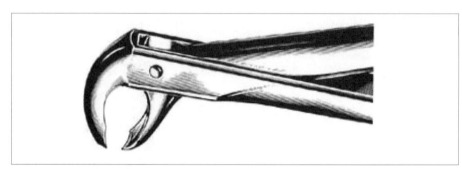

Figure 7.9 Lower molar forceps. (Courtesy of Minerva.)

These are the basic forceps. There are various other designs available and every dentist has their particular favourites.

Q1. The handle of the upper forceps are always at right angles to the blades. True or false?

Q2. The beaks of the upper molar forceps fit between the two buccal roots. True or false?

Q3. There are right and left lower molar forceps. True or false?

How well did you do?
A1.False   A2.True   A3.False

ELEVATORS

While reading the text answer the following;

Q1. Name four types of elevator.

1. COUPLAND CHISEL
A coupland chisel has a blunt end which fits between the root and the bone. It dilates (widens) the socket.

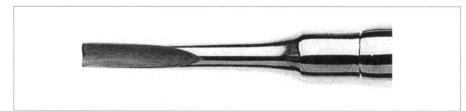

Figure 7.10 Coupland chisal. (Courtesy of Minerva.)

68

2. WARWICK JAMES' ELEVATOR
There are three types of Warwick James' elevators; straight, left and right.

Figure 7.11 Warwick James elevators. (Courtesy of Minerva.)

3. CRYER ELEVATOR
The working end of a Cryer's elevator is triangular in shape. There are two types; right and left.

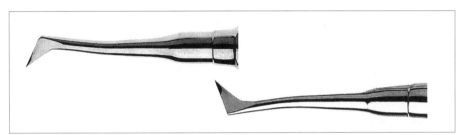

Figure 7.12 Cryer elevators. (Courtesy of Minerva.)

4. WINTER'S ELEVATOR
A Winter's elevator has a triangular end but a corkscrew handle for more leverage. They come as right and left.

LUXATORS AND ROOT TIP EJECTORS

At first glance the luxator looks similar to the Couplands. However the end of a luxator is curved whereas a Couplands is straight. The tip of the luxator is placed between the root and the bone. The luxator is then rotated around it's own axis. The curved sharp end penetrates deeper than a Coupland chisel and cuts the periodontal ligament as it goes as well as dilating the socket. This makes the extraction less traumatic for the bone and for the patient!

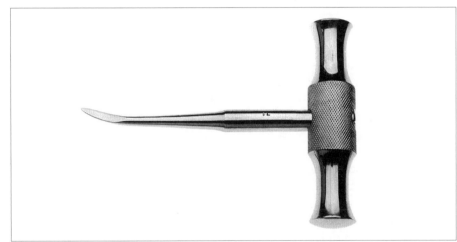

Figure 7.13 Winter's elevator. (Courtesy of Minerva.)

Root tip ejectors have thin, sharp, flexible blades. They sever the periodontal fibres around a tooth making it easier to remove. They are useful for retrieving fractured roots.

Q1. A molar forcep and Warwick James are both types of elevator. True or false?

How well did you do?
A1.False

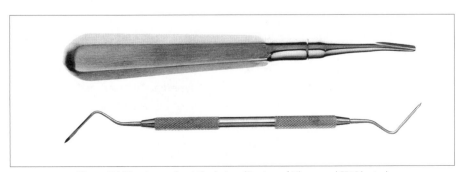

Figure 7.14 Luxators and root tip ejectors. (Courtesy of Minerva and SDI Director.)

SO WHERE DO I FIT IN?

THE NURSES ROLE

While reading the text answer the following;

Q1. What is the nurses role during extractions and minor oral surgery?

Q2. What does haemostasis mean?

1. Have the patients notes ready and the radiographs in the film viewer. Read the medical history.
2. Have the necessary sterilised instruments and local anaesthetic ready and out of sight.
3. Maintain a relaxed and reassuring manner throughout. Most patients will be nervous.
4. Provide the patient with a bib, mouthwash and tissue. Ask the patient if they have eaten. If they have not eaten for several hours give them a sugary drink.
5. While waiting for the patient to numb, it is good practice to ask the patient to swill chlorhexidine mouth rinse for 30 seconds. This reduces the number of oral bacteria.
6. Discretely hand the correct instruments to the dentist.
7. Support the patient's head during extraction.
8. Do the suction and tissue retraction as required.
9. Have bite packs ready for the patient to bite on after the extraction.
   Also have haemostatic cubes and the suturing pack ready if required. Have a scissors ready to cut the sutures.
10. Clean the patient's face with a warm wet tissue.
11. Give post operative instructions to the patient.
    The patient can leave once the dentist has checked for haemostasis.
    (Haemo=blood, stasis=still)
12. Remove and sterilise the instruments. Disinfect the surgery.

Q1. Some of the duties of the nurse during extractions are to;

    a. set up the sterilised instruments
    b. support the patient's head
    c. give post operative instructions
    d. check for haemostasis

Q2. The process whereby blood clots is called;

    a. haemophilia
    b. haemostasis
    c. haemoglobin
    d. halitosis

How well did you do?
    A1.a,b,c   A2.b

WHAT DOES THE PATIENT WANT TO KNOW?

PREOPERATIVE INSTRUCTIONS

While reading the text answer the following;

Q1. What does the patient need to know before an extraction?

These instructions are useful for both routine extractions and minor oral surgery.

1. Reassure the patient they will not feel pain as the tooth will be completely numb.
2. The patient should eat some food a couple of hours before an extraction under local anaesthetic. (This prevents fainting. These instructions are not applicable for general anaesthetic.)
3. The patient's usual medication should be taken as normal unless instructed otherwise by the dentist.
4. Children and nervous adults should be accompanied by a responsible adult. (Again if the patient is having the extraction under sedation they must be accompanied by an adult who can drive them home. The patient must not drive, operate machinery or sign legal documents for 24 hours.)

5. If antibiotic cover is required this is prescribed by the dentist and should be taken as instructed.
6. If the patient is having surgery stitches will be placed. These will either dissolve or be removed by the dentist a week later.

Q1. Before an extraction the patient should;

    a. fast for 4 hours
    b. stop taking all medication except for their antibiotic cover
    c. ask a friend to accompany them as they are having sedation
    d. double their medication

How well did you do?
A1.c

POST OPERATIVE INSTRUCTION

While reading the text answer the following;

Q1. What does a patient need to know following an extraction?

These instructions are useful for both routine extractions and minor oral surgery. They should be written as well as verbal.

1. An appropriate analgesic can be taken before the local wears off e.g. paracetamol, Neurophen™.
2. For the first 24 hours the patient should avoid drinking hot liquid and alcohol. They should also be discouraged from mouth rinsing or putting their tongue or finger into the socket. They must not do strenuous exercise.
   If bleeding does occur, the patient should take a clean tissue, roll it into a small ball, wet it slightly under the tap and then bite on it for 15 minutes.

3. The next day the patient should start taking hot salt water mouth washes. A teaspoon of salt is dissolved in a cup of warm water. The patient should take a mouthful and hold it steady over the socket. They should not swill. When the heat goes out, they should spit it out and take another mouthful. This should be repeated three times a day for a week. The salt helps to keep the area clean and the heat encourages healing.

4. If there is prolonged bleeding or pain the patient should return to the surgery. An emergency "out of office hours" telephone number should be available.

5. If sutures have been placed the patient should be informed and reviewed in a week to remove the stitches.

6. If antibiotics have been prescribed the patient is reminded to follow the dentist's instructions.

Q1. Following an extraction a patient should;

   a. start taking hot salt water mouth rinses immediately

   b. start taking hot salt water mouth rinses 24 hours later

   c. start taking hot salt water mouth rinses 1 week later

   d. rinse vigorously with salt water

How well did you do?
   A1.b

WHAT TO LOOK OUT FOR.

COMPLICATIONS DURING EXTRACTIONS

While reading the text answer the following;

Q1. When can you leave a fractured root?

Q2. What is an ora-antral fistula?

Q3. When would a patient need a chest x ray?

1. FRACTURED ROOT
This is more likely if the tooth is grossly decayed or heavily filled. The patient and nurse should both be warned of the possibility by the dentist prior to the extraction. If it occurs the nurse should have a root tip ejector ready to retrieve the root and failing that, all the instruments ready to go straight into a surgical extraction.
Sometimes just the tip of the root fractures. This can be left in situ if it is small and not infected. The patient must be told. The fragment will either stay within the bone or it will migrate to the surface over time to be shed or extracted later.

2. PERFORATION OF THE MAXILLARY SINUS
As can be seen on periapical x-rays the bone separating the roots of the molar teeth from the maxillary sinus can be very thin. When an upper posterior tooth is extracted it may leave a direct channel from the mouth (oral cavity) to the maxillary sinus (antrum) and an ora-antral fistula is formed. This can be demonstrated by air bubbles appearing in the socket as the patient breaths. If the patient rinses, fluid may go into the nose. For large perforations (fistula) the dentist will suture the socket.
If a fistula is present the patient should be warned not to blow their nose hard during healing.
Sometimes when trying to extract a root tip the root can be inadvertently pushed into the sinus. The patient must be informed and referred to an oral surgeon to retrieve it.

3. LOSS OF A TOOTH
If the tooth inadvertently slips out of the forceps during extraction it may be inhaled or ingested. The patient may swallow, cough or be totally unaware that anything untoward has happened. Immediately search the mouth, surrounding area and aspirator for the tooth. If it cannot be found the patient must be sent immediately for a chest x ray. If the tooth has been ingested it will pass through the alimentary tract without problems and the patient can be reassured. If it is in the respiratory tract there is a risk of serious respiratory infections and the tooth must be removed immediately. If it is in the main bronchi it can be removed with a bronchoscope but if it is within the lung the patient will need an extensive operation. A patient is more likely to inhale a tooth if the extraction is under general anaesthetic as they have no reflex response. Under general anaesthetic a throat pack is always used to protect the airway. The nurse must keep and account for every tooth extracted.

Q1. A fractured root can be left in situ if;

   a. you do not tell the patient
   b. it is infected
   c. it is a large fragment
   d. it is just the apex

Q2. An ora-antral fistula

   a. is a channel from the mouth to the antrum
   b. is a channel from the mouth to the sinus
   c. is a channel from the mouth to the nose
   d. can be detected by air bubbles in the socket

Q3. If a tooth is lost during extraction you should

   a. check the aspirator
   b. send the patient for a chest x ray
   c. reassure the patient that it will not cause problems.
   d. search the surrounding area

How well did you do?
   A1.d   A2.a,b,d   A3.a,b,d

COMPLICATIONS AFTER EXTRACTIONS

While reading the text answer the following;

Q1. What is dry socket?

Q2. What are the different types of haemorrhage?

Q3. How is bleeding treated?

1.   DRY SOCKET
   Dry socket is a very painful condition which may develop a couple of days after the extraction. For a socket to heal normally a blood clot must form and protect the site. When the blood clot does not form, is lost or becomes infected dry socket occurs and the bone lining the socket becomes inflamed. This is called osteitis. (osteo=bone, itis=inflammation) Patients who are prone to dry socket include those with poor oral hygiene, smokers, those who had difficult extractions or patients who have washed the clot away by vigorous mouth rinsing too soon after the extraction. To treat dry socket the dentist irrigates the socket with a warm saline solution or antiseptic solution. This removes the bacteria. A sedative dressing is then placed within the socket e.g. Alvogyl™. The patient can use anti-inflammatory analgesics for pain relief. If the infection is severe the antibiotic metronidazole is prescribed.

The post operative instructions are given again. The patient is asked to keep the area clean and to aid healing by using warm salt water mouth rinses which are to be held gently over the socket.

2.   BLEEDING / HAEMORRHAGE
   Bleeding is called haemorrhage. (haemo=blood, rrhage-think "rage") During extractions bleeding will always occur as blood vessels are cut or torn. Clotting is the body's way of sealing these vessels. As soon as blood is exposed to air a complex clotting mechanism is triggered, a clot is formed and the bleeding naturally stops. Our treatment of bleeding encourages the clotting mechanism.

There are three types of haemorrhage; primary, reactionary and secondary.

PRIMARY HAEMORRHAGE

This is natural and always occurs during an operation when blood vessels are cut. The bleeding is stopped by the dentist first squeezing together the sides of the socket and then the patient biting on a pack for several minutes. When the dentist is satisfied that a clot has formed the patient can go home.
With certain medical conditions there is prolonged bleeding or the clot does not form. For example the patient may be taking anticoagulation medicine such as aspirin or warfarin or may be a haemophiliac. This should always be assessed at the examination. If the patient is on anticoagulation therapy their doctor should be consulted and the treatment discussed. Haemophiliacs must be treated in hospital.

REACTIONARY HAEMORRHAGE

This can occur a few hours after the extraction and is due to the clot being disturbed. Often the patient has not followed the post operative instructions. This type of bleeding is not uncommon but can be alarming to the patient as a little bit of blood mixed with a pool of saliva looks worse than it is. Any activity that increases blood pressure such as exercise or alcohol consumption can disturb the clot. Vigorous mouth rinsing on the day of extraction will dislodge the clot, as will increasing the flow of blood to the area with hot drinks. To stop the bleeding the patient should bite on a clean wet tissue for 15 minutes. They should be reminded about the post operative instructions. If they are still concerned they can return to the surgery where a haemostatic dressing may be placed in the socket or the socket sutured. Haemostatic dressings are absorbable packs impregnated with adrenalin. These are placed in the socket and pressure is applied. Alternatively local anaesthetic can be given and sutures used to draw the edges of the wound together. In the rare case of continued bleeding hospitalisation may be necessary.

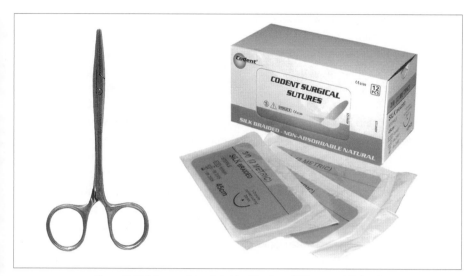

Figure 7.15 *Sutures and needle holder. (Courtesy of Minerva and Codent.)*

Instruments required for suturing include mirror, tweezers, swab, suction, haemostatic pack, local anaesthetic, suture needle, needle holder, dissecting forceps and scissors.

SECONDARY HAEMORRHAGE

This occurs over 24 hours later.
The blood clot is lost and the socket becomes infected. The dentist irrigates the socket, dresses it and may prescribe antibiotics.

Q1. Dry socket is a form of osteitis. True or false?

Q2. The different types of bleeding are;

  a. primary
  b. secondary
  c. tertiary
  d. reactionary

Q3. Haemorrhage can be treated by;

  a. having a hot drink
  b. applying pressure by biting on a pack
  c. suturing
  d. applying a haemostatic dressing

How well did you do?
  A1.True   A2.a,b,d   A3.b,c,d

Minor Oral Surgery

COMMON EXAMPLES OF MINOR ORAL SURGERY

While reading the text answer the following;

Q1. Name nine examples of minor oral surgery.

Q2. What is the main risk of extracting impacted lower wisdom teeth?

SURGICAL EXTRACTIONS

Sometimes routine extractions are impossible because the crown is too decayed to be grasped with forceps or the tooth is only partially through due to impaction. In these cases surgical extractions are necessary. This involves raising the gum and removing bone to allow the access of instruments to elevate the roots or tooth. Some surgical extractions can be preformed under local anaesthetic but conscious sedation or even general anaesthetic may be required.

IMPACTED TEETH

The most commonly impacted teeth are wisdom teeth. Impaction occurs where the jaw is too small to accommodate all the teeth so that some teeth get jammed within the bone. If the surgical extraction is particularly difficult the patient is referred to hospital to have it removed by an oral surgeon under general anaesthetic. The main risk of having an impacted lower wisdom tooth removed is that the roots are often wrapped around the inferior dental nerve and this or the lingual nerve may be damaged during the extraction. If this happens that side of the lower lip or jaw may suffer temporary or permanent numbness. Patients should be warned of this before the procedure. For this reason, if the tooth is asymptomatic (a=without, symptomatic=symptoms) i.e. not causing pain or infection it can be left in situ. Patients should also understand that they may have post operative pain, bruising or swelling for a few days or limited mouth opening (trismus). This again is temporary but inconvenient as it makes eating and speaking difficult.

CYSTS

A cyst is a fluid filled sac. (Think of a balloon filled with water.) Different types of cyst are found all over the body. In the mouth they are often seen within the bone associated with a tooth. For example you may have already seen x-rays of periapical cysts around the roots of non vital teeth. Another example are follicular cysts which are found around the crowns of unerupted teeth. Cysts need to be surgically removed with all of their soft lining. If they are left they will continue to grow and displace other structures such as teeth or they may even cause a pathological fracture of the jaw.

ALVEOLECTOMY

This is usually carried out during multiple extractions. Bone rongeurs or a surgical handpiece and burs are used to smooth the bone after the teeth have been extracted. This stops spinicles of bone remaining and causing a lumpy ridge which would make denture wearing uncomfortable.

FRENECTOMY

A frenectomy is the complete removal of a fraenum. A frenum is a fibrous flap of tissue covered with mucosa. If you peal back your upper lip you can see your labial fraenum along the midline.
In the upper jaw if the labial frenum starts between the two central incisors it can produce a midline diastema or gap. The labial frenum should be removed if the gap is to close.
In the lower jaw the lingual frenum can cause restrictive movement of the tongue commonly known as a tongue tie.

APICECTOMY

An apicectomy is the complete removal of the apex of the root. Apicectomies may be preformed on teeth with failed root fillings. This procedure is described in detail in Chapter 16 Endodontics.

GINGIVECTOMY

A gingivectomy is the removal of part of the gum or gingivae. This is described in detail in Chapter 14 Periodontal Disease. A gingivectomy is used to remove overgrown gums.

A localised gingivectomy is useful to treat pericoronitis around partially erupted wisdom teeth. If food and debris gets trapped underneath the flap of gum covering the partially erupted tooth, bacteria can thrive and the gum can become inflamed and infected. This is called pericoronitis. (peri=around, coro=coronal (but think crown) and itis=inflammation) As the gum is swollen the patient tends to bite on it, further increasing the inflammation.
The overlying gum can be removed by electro-surgery. Removal makes the distal aspect of the partially erupted wisdom tooth easier to clean avoiding future pericoronitis. The wound is cut and cauterised at the same time so no sutures are required. The nurse's role is to set up the electro-surgery equipment. This involves placing a pad between the patient's back and chair to ground the patient. You can place the pad when the patient leans forward to rinse their mouth. During electro-surgery there is an unpleasant smell of which the patient should be warned. Have the wide bore suction on high to minimise this odour and to keep the area absolutely dry. Remember saliva and metal instruments can transmit electricity. Plastic instruments should be used to avoid burning the cheek or tongue so remember to provide a plastic mirror on the dentist's bracket table. Because of the electrical pulses this treatment cannot be used on patients with pace makers. In these cases the overlying gum is removed with a scalpel and the bleeding controlled with haemostatic agents.

Non surgical treatment of pericoronitis involves irrigating under the flap with disinfectant and encouraging good oral hygiene and hot salt water mouth rinses. Antibiotics may be necessary.

BIOPSY

A biopsy is the removal of a piece of tissue from a patient so that it can be examined under a microscope in a laboratory. A biopsy is often taken to confirm the dentist's diagnosis. If the lesion is small it may be totally removed along with a margin of healthy tissue during the biopsy. If the lesion is larger, the most pathological section is removed along with it's edge of healthy tissue. After the tissue is removed the wound will require sutures so have the suture kit ready and the suction. The biopsy tissue is placed in a specimen container which has the appropriate preserver. This container is labelled with the date, patient's name and the test required. A corresponding laboratory sheet is also filled with the same information plus the dentist's name and address and any relevant information about the tissue sample. The patient is given a date for their biopsy result and removal of the sutures and post operative instructions.

IMPLANTS

Placing implants is a surgical procedure which is discussed in full in Chapter 21 Implants.

Q1. Which of the following are examples of oral surgery?

   a. frenectomy
   b. frenum
   c. gingivae
   d. gingivectomy

How well did you do?
   A1.a.d

SO WHAT DO WE USE FOR MINOR ORAL SURGERY?

INSTRUMENTS FOR MINOR ORAL SURGERY

While reading the text answer the following;

Q1. List the instruments required for minor oral surgery such as a surgical extraction.

Q2. What is the dental nurse's role during minor oral surgery?

One of the most notable differences between a routine and surgical extractions are the number of instruments involved.

1. Bib, glasses and mouth rinse
2. Mirror, tweezers and probe
3. Syringe, needle and cartridge for LA
4. Suction; wide bore and also fine bore for precision
5. Scalpel; disposable handles help to avoid accidental injuries
6. Periosteal elevator
7. Disposable water syringe
8. Retractors; Austin and Kilner retractors
9. Surgical handpiece and bone burs
10. Forceps and elevators
11. Bone rongeurs
12. Tissue dissecting forceps
13. Suture needle with silk or resorbable suture, needle holder and scissors

GENERAL PROCEDURE FOR MINOR ORAL SURGERY

The surgical extraction of a lower impacted wisdom tooth will be taken as an example of a minor oral surgery procedure.

PREPARATION OF THE OPERATING FIELD

In order to extract the tooth it will be necessary to "raise a flap" and remove the overlying bone. A sterile operating field is required. The dental nurse should cover any surface or hosing with disposable plastic film. This includes the dental unit's operating switches, overhead light handles, bracket tray handles, hosing for the handpieces, 3-in-1 syringes and suction. Sterile surgical instruments are placed on a disposable plastic tray on the bracket table. A disposable bib and glasses are put on the patient.
The patient should be asked to rinse their mouth with chlorhexidene for 30 seconds prior to surgery.

PROCEDURE

The patient may require sedation or general anaesthetic. For this example the tooth will be removed under local anaesthetic alone. The dental nurse should monitor the patient in a reassuring manner throughout the procedure.

1. The local anaesthetic is administered. The dentist may specifically ask for one with a vasoconstrictor to minimise the amount of bleeding and facilitate visual access.
2. The nurse hands the dentist the scalpel, handle first, and an incision is made as the nurse provides the suction.
3. The total thickness of gum is prised away from the bone using a periosteal elevator. The flap is held to one side with a suture or a tissue retractor.

Scalpels.

Periosteal elevator

Austin retractor

Bone rongeurs.

Tissue dissecting forceps.

Figures 7.16, 7.17, 7.18, 7.19, 7.20.

4. The overlying bone is removed with a surgical handpiece and bone bur. The nurse must continually aspirate to keep a clear field. The nurse may also be required to hold the retractor in position.

5. The exposed tooth is now elevated and/or removed with forceps. Any sharp edges of bone are removed with bone rongeurs. The socket is irrigated with sterile saline to remove all debris.

6. The gum flap is laid back in position and sutured into place using a half circle needle, dissecting forceps and a needle holder. The nurse cuts the end of the sutures with a fine scissors.

7. Written and verbal post operative instructions are given to the patient.

8. The nurse removes the instruments to be scrubbed and sterilised. The anaesthetic needle, cartridge and suture needle are disposed in the sharps by the dentist. All the plastic coverings must be removed for disposal before seeing the next patient and the surgery is disinfected.

Q1. Which of the following instruments are needed for a surgical extraction?

a. periosteal elevator
b. tissue retractor
c. bone rongeurs
d. dental mirror

Q2. During minor oral surgery the dental nurse has which of the following roles?

a. to maintain a clear operating field with efficient suction
b. to elevate the tooth
c. to monitor and reassure the patient
d. to place the sutures

How well did you do?
A1.a,b,c,d   A2.a,c

8. Medical Emergancies

This chapter was written in conjunction with Dr Yusof (Joe) Omar MBBCh, DA, MRCA

While reading the text answer the following;

Q1. In your practice do you need to dial an outside line before dialling the emergency services?

Q2. What is the difference between signs and symptoms?

Q3. What is the medical emergency protocol of your practice?

Q4. After an emergency why is it useful to have a staff meeting?

Most chapters in this book refer back to the patient's medical status. The relevance of this is highlighted in this chapter. However even a patient with a previously clear medical history may collapse unexpectedly in the dental surgery. It is the responsibility of the practice that the whole dental team (yes, that includes the receptionist!) can respond effectively and efficiently to every medical emergency. Every staff member should receive regular tuition in basic life support. Everyone should know their role in an emergency situation. They should know where the oxygen and emergency drugs kit are located and be familiar with all the various medications. They should also know how to call 999, ask for an ambulance and give the practice location. **Some practices need to dial an outside line then 999. Does yours?**

COLLAPSE OF A PATIENT

When a patient collapses any delay in the response of the dental team may be catastrophic for the patient. Knowing the patient's medical history is extremely useful. But we also have to look for signs and symptoms to arrive at a diagnosis.

> Symptoms are warnings noticed by the patient.
> Signs are noticed by the dental team.

Studies show that the dentist is more likely to notice signs that the patient is unwell. This is no longer acceptable. The dental nurse must monitor patients as closely as the dentist. With the use of loops, dentists have a greatly restricted field of vision and may not see vital signs such as a change in the patient's skin colour or sweating. The nurse is expected to monitor the general well being of the patient throughout any dental procedure and immediately notify the dentist of any problems.

GENERAL EMERGENCY PROTOCOL

Every practice should have an emergency protocol so that the members of staff work efficiently as a team. The whole team needs to focus on the collapsed patient. Every other activity within the practice must stop. For example if the receptionist needs to call an ambulance they may have to cut short an existing telephone conversation with a quick explanation so that the person on the other end of the line hangs up as well.

The following protocol is based on a practice with a dentist, dental nurse and receptionist. This protocol should be adapted to suit the number of staff and needs of your practice.

FIRST PERSON

This is the person who first notices the emergency. It could be the dentist, dental nurse or receptionist (if the patient collapses in the waiting room).
They must immediately shout for help and then return to the patient and ensure that there is an open airway.

SECOND PERSON

This is the second person on the scene and their job is to assist the first. This involves shouting for a third person to help and then returning to the patient.

THIRD PERSON

This person responds by bring the oxygen and emergency drugs to the patient. They will phone for an ambulance if required and will then go back to the others to record on paper the times and actions taken to help the patient. This is often the receptionist.

It is important to write up a detailed account of the event as it unfolds. Note down the time of critical events such as the time the patient collapsed, the time the ambulance was called and times and doses of any medication given.

At the next staff meeting it is useful to discuss what happened, how it was managed and if any improvements could be made to improve the team's response or even if the emergency could be prevented in future. This is called an audit.

If the dentist has to see a patient out of office hours and a second member of staff is unavailable the patient must bring an escort. If there is a medical emergency the escort becomes the second person. The dentist will instruct them to call 999 and to assist.

Q1. Regardless of whether you need to dial for an outside line or not, if you just press 999 you will always get through to the emergency services. True or false?

Q2. The symptoms of an illness are those noticed by the dental team. True or false?

Q3. Who is the first person in a medical emergency?

    a. this is always the dentist
    b. this is always the nurse
    c. this is possibly the receptionist
    d. this is the first person to notice the emergency

Q4. After an emergency why is it useful to have a staff meeting?

    a. for a good old gossip
    b. to discuss the response of the dental team
    c. to see if the emergency could have been prevented
    d. to discuss overtime

How well did you do?
    A1.False   A2.False   A3.c,d
    A4.b,c

COMMON CAUSES OF COLLAPSE

1.   FAINTING AND VASOVAGAL ATTACKS

While reading the text answer the following;

Q1. What is the cause of fainting?

Q2. How does it present?

Q3. What should you do if the patient faints?

Q4. How can you prevent fainting?

FAINTING

This is the most common cause of collapse in the dental surgery. It is usually due to anxiety and often occurs after the injection when the patient is sat up to rinse. Fainting is a loss of consciousness due to a lack of blood to the brain. Other contributing factors include fatigue, pain, fasting, tight clothing, dehydration and a hot stuffy room. The patient turns very pale and clammy and may complain of feeling sick and light headed or dizzy. They will have a weak rapid pulse. A normal pulse is between 60 to 90 beats/minute.

TREATMENT

Laying the patient down increases the flow of blood to the brain and allows the patient to recover within a few seconds. Let in fresh air if the surgery is too hot. Loosen tight clothing such as a tie but inform the patient what you are doing to avoid embarrassment and misunderstanding. Oxygen can be given but is often unnecessary as the patient usually recovers quickly (in about 30 to 60 seconds). Patients can feel faint after having an injection when they are sat up afterwards to rinse. As the dental nurse you are often the first to notice the patient faint as you are responsible for monitoring all patients. You must inform the dentist immediately while putting the chair back flat. Know how to do this. Most dental units have chair controls on both sides-learn how to use yours. The dentist will determine when the patient has recovered. Patients can be sat up when they are no longer clammy. Many people feel foolish when they faint and rush to get up. Be reassuring. Also update their medical history e.g. "prone to fainting on injection" so that you are forewarned in future. Reassure the patient that you can cope with their fainting.

PREVENTION

Patients attending for an extraction under local anaesthetic should be given glucose or a sugary drink if they have not already eaten to prevent light headedness and fainting.

Pregnant women in their third trimester may feel faint when lying down if the enlarged uterus presses on the inferior vena cava. They should be treated with a cushion placed under one of their hips to prevent this.

Some patients will collapse if they stand up too quickly after lying in the dental chair. This is called postural hypotension. The elderly are often susceptible to this. After any patient has been lying for a while, sit them up for a few minutes before allowing them to stand.

VASOVAGAL ATTACK

A vasovagal attack is the over stimulation of the vagus nerve. It differs from a faint in two main ways;

- The pulse is slow in a vasovagal attack whereas it is rapid in a patient who has fainted.
- A patient who has fainted recovers quickly whereas in a vasovagal attack the recovery may be very slow or the patient faints repeatedly.

It is useful to take the patient's pulse at the initial examination and record this in the patient's notes. If the patient faints at a later appointment it is easy to assess how their pulse has changed.

If the patient has a vasovagal attack they should be sent to hospital. An intramuscular injection of 0.6mg of atropine may be given. However atropine should not be given to patients with glaucoma. Atropine is a vagal blocker and will stop the attack quickly.

Q1. What can cause a patient to faint?

  a. anxiety
  b. lack of carbon dioxide to the brain
  c. the uterus pressing on the uterine
     artery
  d. fasting

Q2. How does fainting present?

  a. patient goes bright red
  b. patient feels clammy
  c. patient feels sick
  d. patient has a strong pulse

Q3. What should you do if the patient faints?

  a. ignore it-they are attention seeking
  b. lay the patient down
  c. hold the patient up so that they do
     not fall over
  d. inform the dentist

Q4. How can you prevent a patient from fainting?

  a. if the patient has not eaten give
     them glucose before treatment
  b. have a well ventilated surgery
  c. tease the patient by showing them
     the needle before an injection
  d. be reassuring and monitor the
     patient throughout the treatment

How well did you do?
  A1.a,d   A2.b,c   A3.b,d
  A4.a,b,d

2. RESPIRATORY OBSTRUCTION

While reading the text answer the following;

Q1. What can cause respiratory obstruction?

Q2. How does respiratory obstruction present?

Q3. What should you do if the patient has difficulty breathing?

Q4. How can you prevent obstruction?

Patients must be protected from inadvertently inhaling foreign objects. The nurse plays an important part by keeping the suction close to the relevant tooth. For example it is better for a crown to go up the suction where it can easily be retrieved than into the patient's lung. Rubber dam provides the best airway protection.

If a patient has a **partial obstruction** they will cough and splutter and try to sit up. They should be helped to sit up immediately and lent forward. If there is a **mild airway obstruction** the patient will cough effectively and relieve the obstruction. However, if there is a **severe obstruction** the cough will be ineffective and sound more gasping than a normal cough. If the patient is **conscious** five solid back blows should be given with the patient leaning forward. If the obstruction does not

dislodge five abdominal thrusts, the Heimlich manoeuvre, should be given. Swing the patient around so that their feet are on the floor but they are still sitting in the chair. You stand behind them and wrap your arms around them with one hand clenched in a fist and the other cupping the top of it. Your fist should point upwards and inwards under the sternum. As the patient coughs you squeeze suddenly pulling your hands upwards and inwards under the ribcage. This extra force, in time with the cough, should expel the obstruction. This should not be preformed on pregnant women and children under one year of age. Small children are best held head down over your leg as you slap them on the back.

If the patient becomes **unconscious** due to severe airway obstruction call 999 and start basic life support immediately. Basic life support will keep the blood circulating. Also, when unconscious the throat muscles relax and may allow some air in and out around the obstruction.

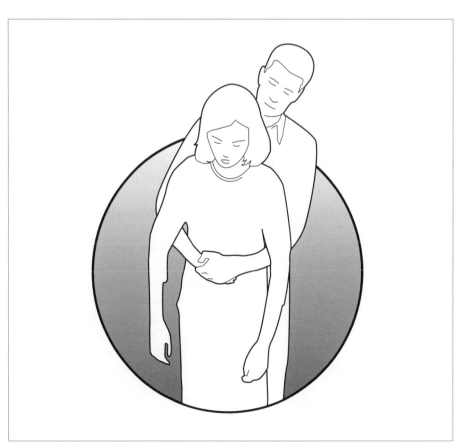

Figure 8.1 *Heimlich manoeuvre.*

If there is a **total obstruction** the patient will put their hand to their throat but will not make a sound. They will make strong respiratory efforts to no avail. They rapidly become unconscious. Within minutes if nothing is done their heart will stop. Call 999 and start basic life support.

It is possible for a small instrument or object to be inhaled right down into the lungs. If this happens the patient may continue to breath normally. If a crown or an extracted tooth, for example, is lost there should be an immediate search of the mouth, surrounding area and suction filter. If it is not found then there is a possibility that it has been swallowed or inhaled into the lung. The patient must be sent for a chest x-ray. If it is in the lung it needs to be removed by urgent bronchoscopy to prevent pneumonia or a collapsed lung. If it has been swallowed it will pass through the body naturally so no treatment is required and the patient can be reassured.

Q1. What can cause respiratory obstruction?

    a. inhaling an instrument
    b. the suction tip touching the back of the tongue
    c. inhaling a tooth
    d. hepatitis

Q2. How does respiratory obstruction present?

    a. patient coughs
    b. patient wants to lie down
    c. patient wants to sit up
    d. patient may stop breathing

Q3. What should you do if the patient has difficulty breathing?

    a. thump them on the back
    b. Heimlich manoeuvre
    c. lay them flat
    d. make them a nice cup of tea

Q4. How can you prevent obstruction?

    a. maintain good airway protection during treatment
    b. use of the rubber dam
    c. slapping the patient on the back periodically during treatment
    d. good use of the suction

How well did you do?
    A1.a,c   A2.a,c,d   A3.a,b
    A4.a,b,d

3.   ANAPHYLAXIS AND ANAPHYLACTIC SHOCK

While reading the text answer the following;

Q1. What are common allergens?

Q2. How does anaphylactic shock present?

Q3. What should you do if it occurs?

Q4. How can you prevent anaphylaxis?

Anaphylaxis is a severe life threatening reaction to an allergen. When the anaphylaxis is so severe that the patient's blood pressure decreases dramatically and the patient looses consciousness it is called anaphylactic shock. An allergen is a substance which causes an allergic reaction. Possible allergens include any medicine (especially penicillin), latex gloves or any dental material. Previously the patient may not have been allergic to the substance. (Indeed they may have been exposed to it for years without any ill effect!) However patients who have a history of asthma, eczema, hay fever or other allergies are more prone to anaphylaxis. They are called atopic patients. Fortunately most allergic reactions are relatively mild resulting in a raised red itchy skin rash and can be treated with antihistamines e.g. Piriton™.

During anaphylaxis histamine is released. If you see a raised red itchy rash developing you can stop the anaphylaxis cascade with the antihistamine Piriton. 10mg of Piriton is injected intramuscularly. The patient should then take 1 tablet of Piriton three times a day for two days and be referred to their doctor. However if the raised red itchy rash returns they should immediately go to hospital.

However the reaction of anaphylactic shock is RAPID, SEVERE AND POTENTIALLY FATAL. The patient may develop a red raised itchy rash, swell and have difficulty breathing. Patients may feel as though they are suffocating. They may vomit. This is nature's way of expelling an ingested allergen. They have a weak rapid pulse, low blood pressure and go pale. Loss of consciousness soon follows.

During an allergic reaction histamine is released and sets off a cascade of complex chemical reactions. This causes peripheral vasodilation. This leads to a fall in blood pressure and loss of consciousness. The body is now in shock.

Call 999. An intramuscular injection of 0.5mls 1:1000 adrenalin is needed to save them. Inject through the clothes in the top of the arm or leg. Resuscitation may be necessary. The effects of adrenaline wear off quickly within five to fifteen minutes. The patient needs help for longer than this. It takes hydrocortisone about 15 minutes to work. By giving 100mg injection of hydrocortisone after the adrenaline the patient has the immediate and long term help required. The adrenaline may need to be repeated every 5 to 10 minutes.

Some patients know that they are susceptible to anaphylaxis and carry Epipen™, a user friendly dose of adrenaline. If a patient has this it is good practice for you to place it in easy reach on your work station during treatment rather than let it remain buried deep in the patient's bag or personal belongings. Of course you must remember to return it at the end of treatment. Epipen has a single dose of only 0.3mls of adrenaline. The Epipen needs to be held against the body for 10 seconds for the whole dose to be administered.

Dental nurses often are in charge of ordering stock. Tip: do not order Epipen for your emergency drugs kit as it is a low single dose of adrenaline and the drug expires quickly in this form. It is also expensive. Order the ampoules as this allows you to give a second dose of adrenaline if required. There is 1mg of 1:1000 adrenaline in every ampoule. During anaphylaxis you need 0.5mg or half an ampoule.

Q1. What are common allergens?

   a. dentists
   b. latex gloves
   c. penicillin
   d. pollen

Q2. How does anaphylactic shock present?

   a. slowly
   b. red rash
   c. swelling
   d. breathing difficulties

Q3. What should you do if anaphylaxis occurs?

   a. panic
   b. call the emergency services
   c. give 1:1000 adrenaline
   d. give 1:10000 adrenaline

Q4. How can you prevent anaphylaxis?

   a. never give penicillin to hay fever sufferers
   b. avoid treating asthmatics
   c. give amoxicillin to patients who are allergic to penicillin
   d. wear vinyl gloves if the patient is allergic to latex

How well did you do?
   **A1.b,c,d A2.b,c,d A3.b,c
   A4.d**

---

4.   DIABETES AND HYPOGLYCAEMIA

While reading the text answer the following;

Q1. What is the cause of hypoglycaemia?

Q2. How does hypoglycaemia present?

Q3. What should you do if the patient collapses?

Q4. How can you prevent hypoglycaemia?

During hypoglycaemia the patient collapses due to a low level of glucose in the blood. The pancreas secrets glucagon and insulin. Glucagon raises the level of glucose in the blood while insulin lowers it. In diabetes this mechanism does not function properly. All diabetics need to control their diet and some have to take insulin daily.
When taking the medical history record how the patient's diabetes is regulated. The receptionist should aim to make a diabetic's appointments **first** in the morning or **first** in the afternoon. Basically dental appointments should be held soon after eating to avoid mistiming meals. Before treating a diabetic it is helpful to ask if they have eaten.
The nurse or receptionist should ask if they have taken their insulin. If they have not they are fine to treat. If they have you need to know when they last ate. Remember insulin lowers the blood sugar level. If they have not eaten recently their blood sugar levels will be even lower. Anxiety, agitation, running to an appointment and the use of adrenaline in the local anaesthetic will all use more glucose. Under these circumstances the risk of hypoglycaemia is now high.
It is also useful for the receptionist to tell the patient how long their dental appointment will be. Write this on their appointment card.

Hypoglycaemia is characterised by the onset of profuse sweating, restlessness, disorientation, slurred speech and an excitable aggressive attitude followed by drowsiness, twitching, convulsions and loss of consciousness. (Rather like a drunk!) If the patient is conscious and co-operative quickly give them glucose or glucose syrup (e.g. Hypostop™ or treacle) before their condition deteriorates. Glucose is immediately absorbed and will prevent the patient from becoming unconscious. This must be followed by bread or biscuits for a longer sustained release of glucose.
If they loose consciousness they need a 1mg intramuscular injection of glucagon. The glucagon will release glucose from the cells into the blood. When the patient regains consciousness give them glucose and bread so that they have a sustained source of glucose. The patient should then be hospitalised. Glucagon comes in two ampoules. With a syringe and needle draw up the water and inject this into the powder ampoule. Shake it to dissolve the powder and then draw up the solution to inject into the patient.

Q1. What is the cause of hypoglycaemia?

   a. a high blood glucose level
   b. a low blood glucose level
   c. missing a meal
   d. anxiety

Q2. How does hypoglycaemia present?

   a. sweating
   b. restlessness
   c. slurred speech
   d. aggressive behaviour

Q3. What should you do if the patient collapses?

   a. give glucagon if the patient is unconscious
   b. give adrenaline if the patient is unconscious
   c. give the conscious patient something sweet like treacle
   d. make them fast

Q4. How can you prevent hypoglycaemia?

    a. make sure the appointments are just before the patient's mealtimes

    b. make sure the appointments are just after the patient's mealtimes

    c. keep them waiting

    d. be reassuring

How well did you do?

    A1.b,c,d   A2.a,b,c,d   A3.a,c A4.b,d

5.   GRAND MAL EPILEPSY

While reading the text answer the following;

Q1. How does epilepsy present?

Q2. What should you do if the patient fits?

Epilepsy is characterised by loss of consciousness and fitting. There are two main types; petit mal and grand mal. With petit mal the patient (often a child) will go into a trace-like state for a short while and then come to. No intervention is required. Grand mal involves the patient fitting and requires our assistance.

STAGES OF GRAND MAL

1.   AURA

A person with epilepsy often knows when they are about to fit. They may hear ringing, change mood, have visual disturbances or a headache. They may warn you that they are about to fit. At home, if they have sufficient warning they will go to a place where they can fall and fit in safety. In the surgery move the bracket table and overhead light away.

2.   SPASM

If the patient is standing they will fall, cry out and their back will arch. This is when they are most likely to bite their tongue. The spasm is over in seconds.

3.   CONVULSION

This is when the patient shakes. Make sure that all instruments and equipment is moved away from the patient. Do not restrain the patient as this will only harm them. The power of the convulsions are so strong that if you try to restrain their limbs it may result in severe injury to arms and legs. However the head rests of dental chairs are very small and you must **support the patient's head**. If their head falls off the chair it may result in serious neck injury. Normally the convulsions last for up to 5 minutes only. Time this.

As well as fitting during a seizure the patient may froth at the mouth, go blue or urinate. If the patient urinates switch off the electrical supply to the chair. The urine may short circuit the chair and cause the chair to go up and down repeatedly!

4.   FLACCID STAGE

The patient slumps and may be unconscious for a while. You must maintain the airway with the head tilt and chin lift.

After the fit the patient is placed in the recovery position if they fit in the reception. If they fit in the dental chair turn their head towards the suction (this is normally on the left) and support the patient's opposite shoulder (normally the right) with something bulky like a folded coat. This ensures that the larynx is higher than the oesophagus and the patient will not inhale vomit should this occur. It is important that the patient does not inhale vomit as it is highly acidic and will burn the lungs leading to inhalation pneumonia and death. By turning the patient towards the suction they are in an accessible position for its use. A portable suction is required if the electrics have been switched off.

The patient is monitored until they regain consciousness and their nearest relative is called to collect them. No other treatment is required. The patient will be disorientated and tired when they come to.

If the patient has attended the surgery with an escort, as soon as you diagnose the convulsion call in their friend/relative from the waiting room. It is important for the escort to witness the fit as they will tell you if this convulsion is normal for them. Indeed when taking the medical history it is useful to ask the person with epilepsy what normally happens and to record this. For example if the patient normally vomits during a fit this should be noted.

A rare but serious condition is status epilepticus. Here the convulsions either continue for more than 5 minutes or there are two or more short fits. These are dangerous as prolonged fitting continually increases the intracranial pressure which may result in an intracranial bleed and death. This is treated with midazolam (Hypnoval™). 2.5mg of Hypnoval™ is placed up each nostril where it is readily absorbed. Use a needle and syringe to draw up 5mg in 1ml of Hypnoval™. Remove the needle and squirt half the syringe up one nostril and the rest up the other.

The patient should then be hospitalised.

Q1. How does grand mal epilepsy present?

    a. fitting

    b. frothing at the mouth

    c. may urinate

    d. aggressive behaviour

Q2. What should you do if the patient fits?

    a. hold them down

    b. move instruments out of the way

    c. call their relative

    d. call an ambulance if the fits continue

How well did you do?

    A1.a,b,c   A2.b,c,d

6. ASTHMA

While reading the text answer the following;

Q1. What is the cause of asthma?

Q2. How does it present?

Q3. What should you do if the patient has an asthmatic attack?

Q4. How can you prevent an attack?

Asthma is a common breathing problem. With asthma, recurrent bronchial spasm makes breathing difficult. An attack can be brought on by exercise, anxiety or an allergen. An asthmatic attack causes the patient to wheeze and gasp noisily for air. Before any dental treatment begins the patient should be asked if they have their inhaler with them. At the examination they should be encouraged to bring their inhaler to any subsequent dental appointments. Patients are better and calmer using their own medication as it is familiar to them.
A couple of puffs of salbutamol (Ventolin™) relaxes the bronchial muscles and allows the breathing to return to normal.
If the patient is a known asthmatic a spacer device is used. Attach their inhaler to one end of the device and the patient inhales from the other end. The inhaler is puffed twice into the spacer and the patient inhales this "air". During an asthmatic attack the patient may have difficulty inhaling two puffs in one go so much of the medicine may be wasted. By using a spacer they are able to inhale the two puffs over several breaths and get the benefit of the entire dose.
If the patient is having an asthmatic attack for the first time they will not have used inhalers before. Refer the patient to their doctor or if severe call 999.

If the attack is severe oxygen is also given and an ambulance called. If the patient is conscious do not lay them flat. Take their pulse. A normal pulse is between 60 to 90 beats /minute. If their pulse is over 110 beats/minute this is particularly dangerous. If the patient looses consciousness lay them flat and start basic life support.

Q1. Asthma is caused by a recurrent bronchial spasm. True or false?

Q2. How does it present?

    a. wheezing
    b. gasping for air
    c. fitting
    d. collapse

Q3. What should you do if the patient has an asthmatic attack?

    a. give them salbutamol
    b. give them glucagon
    c. give them Ventolin™
    d. give them oxygen

Q4. How can you help to prevent an attack?

    a. make the patient exercise
    b. be reassuring
    c. lay the patient flat as soon as they have breathing difficulties
    d. expose them to allergens

How well did you do?
    A1.True   A2.a,b,d   A3.a,c,d
    A4.b

7. ANGINA

While reading the text answer the following;

Q1. What is the cause of angina?

Q2. How does it present?

Q3. What should you do if the patient has an angina attack?

Q4. How can you prevent angina?

Angina consists of chest pains caused when the heart muscle does not receive enough blood and hence oxygen. It is triggered by exercise or anxiety. As soon as they feel the onset of angina the patient can quickly remedy it by spraying one or two doses of glyceryl trinitrate under the tongue. This causes the blood vessels to dilate increasing the flow of blood to the heart muscle. This increases the oxygenation of the heart muscles. The patient will also benefit from breathing oxygen, so get the oxygen cylinder ready. If symptoms do not subside within 5 to 10 minutes treat as a coronary thrombosis. Consider an angina attack as a heart attack waiting to happen.
Angina patients should always be asked if they are carrying their glyceryl trinitrate (GTN) spray or tablets before dental treatment begins. Otherwise the glyceryl trinitrate spray from the drugs kit should be on stand-by for procedures which may produce anxiety such as extractions. The spray is easier to use than the tablets which need to be held in the buccal sulcus.
Remember to use felypressin not adrenalin as the vasoconstrictor in local anaesthetics, as adrenaline can cause palpitations (rapid heart beats) which may overwhelm the blood supply.

Q1. What causes or triggers angina?

    a. lack of blood to the heart
    b. lack of oxygen to the heart
    c. anxiety
    d. exercise

Q2. How does it present?

    a. severe chest pain
    b. aggression
    c. slurred speech
    d. dizziness

Q3. What should you do if the patient has an angina attack?

    a. give glyceryl trinitrate spray
    b. glyceryl trinitrate injection
    c. glyceryl trinitrate tablets
    d. GTN spray

Q4. How can you help prevent angina?

    a. be calm and reassuring
    b. give the patient sugar
    c. use adrenalin in local anaesthetics
    d. use felypressin in local anaesthetics

How well did you do?
    A1.a,b,c,d   A2.a   A3.a,c,d
    A4.a,d

8.   CARDIAC ARREST/HEART ATTACK

Q1. What is the cause of coronary thrombosis?

Q2. How does it present?

Q3. What should you do if the patient collapses?

Coronary thrombosis is the blockage of a coronary artery which may lead to a myocardial infarction. Myocardial infarction is the death of a segment of heart muscle. This quickly causes a cardiac arrest. This is a heart attack.

The patient may have a history of angina or it may occur suddenly without warning. Cardiac arrest is more common in winter when there are more chest infections. Diabetics are more prone to heart attacks.

Classically the patient has crushing chest pain which may radiate upwards, backwards, down the left arm or to the lower jaw. The pain may mimic indigestion if the attack occurs slowly over time. The pain lasts longer than angina. It can last for several minutes or hours. The patient will show signs of shock; feel cold, clammy and have low blood pressure. They will have arrhythmia, shortness of breath and may vomit. The skin is grey and ashen.

Call 999 immediately. Maintain the patient in a comfortable posture. This is often in the semi-prone position. Let the patient decide. Reassure the patient that the ambulance is coming. Give them two sprays of glycerol trinitrate onto the tongue. This dilates the coronary blood vessels. Ask the patient if they are allergic or sensitive to aspirin. If they are not, give one aspirin 300mg tablet to thin the blood. This will stop any blood clot within the coronary arteries from increasing in size. (If the patient is already taking anticoagulants aspirin is not necessary.) Give oxygen at 4 litres/minute if the patient is breathing spontaneously or 10 litres / minute if the patient needs to be ventilated with an Ambu-bag™.

Q1. What is the cause of coronary thrombosis?

    a. blockage of a coronary artery
    b. angina
    c. low blood sugar levels
    d. inhalation of a dental instrument

Q2. How does it present?

    a. slurred speech
    b. dizziness
    c. severe chest pain
    d. cold and clammy patient

Q3. What should you do if the patient collapses?

    a. call 999 after giving the patient aspirin 300mg
    b. call 999 after giving the patient oxygen
    c. call 999 after placing the patient in the semi prone position
    d. call 999 immediately

How well did you do?
    A1.a,b   A2.c,d   A3.d

9.   STROKE

While reading the text answer the following;

Q1. What is the cause of a stroke?

Q2. How does a stroke present?

Q3. What should you do if the patient has a stroke?

A stroke occurs when there is a bleed or a clot in a blood vessel supplying the brain. This results in a lack of oxygen to that part of the brain. There may be a gradual or sudden loss of consciousness. Patients may have a headache and be confused with slurred speech. They can have paralysis or weakness down one side of their body. They may also be incontinent. This is serious and requires immediate hospitalisation. The patient should be laid flat, the airway must be clear and oxygen given while waiting for the ambulance. Basic life support may be necessary.

Q1. What is the cause of a stroke?

    a. a bleed from a vessel in the brain
    b. a clot in a vessel in the brain
    c. a bleed from a vessel in the body
    d. a clot in a vessel in the body

Q2. How does a stroke present?

    a. one-sided weakness
    b. aggression
    c. incontinence
    d. confusion

Q3. What should you do if the patient has a stroke?

    a. call 999
    b. give carbon dioxide
    c. give oxygen
    d. maintain the airway

How well did you do?
    A1.a,b   A2.a,c,d   A3.a,c,d

10. ADRENAL INSUFFICIENCY

    While reading the text answer the following;

Q1. What is adrenal insufficiency?

Q2. How does it present?

Q3. What should you do if the patient collapses?

Q4. How can you prevent adrenal insufficiency?

This medical emergency is very rare. Patients who are on steroids are unable to react to stress and may collapse during stressful procedures due to adrenal insufficiency. This is also true of patients who have taken steroids three months previously. These patients with a past or present history of corticosteroids should carry a steroid therapy card from their doctor.
Adrenal insufficiency results in the patient turning very pale and clammy and they complain of feeling light headed, sick or dizzy before loosing consciousness (similar to fainting). They have a weak rapid pulse and falling blood pressure. Call 999.
Lay the patient flat and give them oxygen and an intramuscular injection of hydrocortisone.

Collapse is prevented in these patients by giving them 100mg intramuscular hydrocortisone injection before any stress inducing treatment or, if they are still taking steroids, they can take an additional dose of their steroid 1 hour before their dental treatment.

Q1. Adrenal insufficiency is when a patient, who has been or is on steroid therapy, is unable to react to stress and may collapse in stressful conditions. True or false?

Q2. How do the signs and symptoms present?

    a. similar to fainting
    b. similar to a heart attack
    c. similar to a diabetic coma
    d. similar to a stroke

Q3. What should you do if the patient collapses?

    a. give adrenaline
    b. give glucagon
    c. give oxygen
    d. give hydrocortisone

Q4. How can you prevent adrenal insufficiency?

    a. give adrenaline
    b. give glucagon
    c. give oxygen
    d. give hydrocortisone

How well did you do?
    A1.True   A2.a   A3.c,d   A4.d

11. PANIC ATTACK/HYPERVENTILATION

Q1. What is the cause of hyperventilation?

Q2. How does it present?

Q3. What should you do if the patient hyperventilates?

During normal breathing we take 8 to 20 breaths/minute. During hyperventilation that increases to well over 20 breaths / minute. Patients who are very nervous may hyperventilate. Hyperventilation is rapid breathing. Calm the patient and instruct them on breathing normally. Breathing in and out of a paper bag will help or asking the patient to cup both of their hands in front of their nose and mouth and to breath into this space. Both methods increase the amount of carbon dioxide inhaled. The patient may stop breathing for several seconds but will resume naturally as the level of carbon dioxide in the blood rises. There is no need to give oxygen. Patients sometimes hyperventilate at the start of a faint.

Q1. What is the cause of hyperventilation?

    a. anxiety
    b. epilepsy
    c. diabetes
    d. allergens

Q2. How does it present?

    a. slow breathing
    b. rapid breathing
    c. ashen completion
    d. paralysis

Q3. What should you do if the patient hyperventilates?

    a. slap them
    b. reassure them
    c. give oxygen
    d. get the patient to breath into a paper bag

How well did you do?
    A1.a   A2.b   A3.b,d

EMERGENCY DRUGS KIT

While reading the text answer the following;

Q1. How should the emergencies drugs kit be organised?

Q2. What drugs are used for various emergencies?

It is useful to separate the drugs into individual bags which contain the necessary drugs and syringes for a specific condition. These should be clearly labelled with the following;

1. Name of the emergency.
2. Signs and symptoms.
3. Exact treatment required.

Organising the emergency drugs kit allows you to familiarise yourself with the exact drugs and doses required for any medical emergency when you are not under pressure.

In a medical emergency time is precious and your heart will be racing! You do not want to waste precious time fumbling through a jumbled box of drugs. You may panic and rely on the other members of the team without playing your role. This is detrimental to the patient. All the drugs must be stored together in a box labelled "emergency drugs".

Here are examples of how the bags of drugs should be labelled;

SEVERE FAINT

- Dizzy, light headed, nauseous, slow weak pulse, low BP, rapid loss of consciousness which is prolonged
- Lie flat and give atropine 0.6mg in 1 ml intramuscular injection or send the patient to hospital.

ALLERGIC REACTION

- Raised itchy rash and swelling
- Piriton 10mg intramuscular injection + Chlorpenamine (Piriton) tablets take one three times a day for two days

ANAPHYLACTIC SHOCK

- Raised itchy rash, swelling, breathing difficulties, low BP, collapse
- Call 999 + lay flat + 1:1000 adrenalin 0.5ml (half ampoule) intramuscular injection + hydrocortisone 100mg intramuscular injection + Piriton 10mg intramuscular injection

DIABETIC HYPOGLYCAEMIA

- Sudden onset, confusion, pallor, aggression, coma
- Conscious = oral glucose then bread/biscuits
- Unconscious = call 999 + glucagon 1mg intramuscular injection

STATUS EPILEPTICUS

- Continuous convulsions or two or more fits
- Call 999 + midazolam 5-10mg intramuscular injection or intranasal.

ASTHMA

- Wheezing and gasping for air
- Call 999 + two puffs salbutamol inhaler with spacer + oxygen
- DO NOT LAY FLAT

ANGINA

- Chest pains
- 1-2 puffs of Glyceryl trinitrate spray on tongue + oxygen 4 litres/minute + sit semi upright
- If pain is not relived within 5 to 10 minutes treat as a heart attack

HEART ATTACK

- Severe lasting chest pain radiating to left arm and neck, pale, clammy, low BP, weak pulse, difficulty in breathing, may vomit, grey and ashen
- Call 999 (defibrillator) + oxygen 4 litres/minute + 300mg aspirin + puff of glyceryl trinitrate
- Conscious = SIT SEMI-RECLINED
- Unconscious = lie flat and start basic life support + increase oxygen to 10 litres/minute if ventilation is required

ADRENAL INSUFFICIENCY

- History of steroids + collapse
- Call 999 + lay patient flat + oxygen + hydrocortisone 100mg intramuscular injection

Emergency intravenous injections should not be given by dental staff. When patients are in shock it is hard to get a vein and so this is best left to the paramedics. All injections are given intramuscularly using a 2ml syringe with a blue or green needle. Intramuscular injections are given in the upper outer arm or the thigh (in the position where our hands fall when we are standing) as there are no major nerves or blood vessels here. In an emergency inject through the patient's clothing to save time.

Only a doctor or a dentist can prescribe drugs. So receptionists, dental nurses and hygienists cannot prescribe any emergency drugs but they can administer them under instruction. So if the dentist is out of the building you can either use the patient's own medication as this has already been prescribed by a doctor or phone the dentist explain the emergency and get their verbal prescription of the recommended drug.

Q1. How should the drugs kit be organised?

    a. drugs thrown into a box-I will work it out if there's an emergency
    b. drugs in alphabetical order
    c. in separate bags clearly labelled with the condition, signs and symptoms and treatment required.
    d. don't know-it's not my responsibility

Q2. Match the correct drugs to the conditions in the following lists:

Allergic reaction	1:1000 adrenaline
Anaphylaxis	hydrocortisone
Hypoglycaemia	glyceryl trinitrate
Asthma	Piriton
Angina	salbutamol
Adrenal insufficiency	glucagon

How well did you do?
    A1.c

A2.
Allergic reactio	Piriton
Anaphylaxis	1:1000 adrenaline
Hypoglycaemia	glucagon
Asthma	salbutamol
Angina	glycerol trinitrate
Adrenal insufficiency	hydrocortisone

EMERGENCY EQUIPMENT

While reading the text answer the following;

Q1. What emergency equipment should a surgery possess?

Q2. Why should the oxygen cylinder be regularly checked?

Q3. How is an oropharyngeal airway inserted?

Q4. What further equipment is recommended for medical emergencies?

REQUIRED EMERGENCY EQUIPMENT

The emergency drugs kit and equipment should be kept together in a holdall. Every member of staff should know where the holdall is kept. It must be accessible to dental staff but not to the public. All practices should have;

1. Portable emergency oxygen, face masks and tubing.

2. Ambu-bag™ which must be latex free.

3. Emergency drugs kit.

4. Portable hand operated suction to clear a blocked airway.

5. Oropharyngeal (Guedel) airways 1 to 5 to maintain the airway.

8.2 Emergency resuscitation kit.

8.4 Portable hand operated suction.

8.3 Resus bag with mask.

8.5 Guedel airways.

8.6 Pocket mask.

Figure 8.2. 8.3, 8.4, 8.5, 8.6 (Courtesy of Minerva.)

The emergency drugs kit should be checked monthly to ensure that none of the medicines are out of date. It is useful to have a practice rota so that every staff member takes turns at doing this and are therefore familiar with the drugs and know where the kit and oxygen are kept. Out of date ampoules can be used for practice at opening ampoules correctly, loading syringes and injecting into oranges or sponges.

The oxygen cylinder should also be checked regularly as their valves can stick or, if left open, can leak, emptying all the oxygen. They must be serviced every 5 years as they are a pressurised cylinder. A self inflating bag, valve and mask devise (Ambu-bag™) should be kept with the oxygen cylinder. The cylinder must be size D or E. A size D cylinder contains enough oxygen to flow at a rate of 10 litres/minute for 34 minutes. In a large practice two cylinders should be considered. Patients who can breathe spontaneously are given oxygen at 4 litres/minute, those who need ventilating should be given oxygen at 10 litres/minute. Each surgery within the practice should have their own pocket mask. These should be kept in an accessible place within each surgery.

Guedel airways are oropharyngeal plastic tubes which are used to maintain a patent airway. They come in different sizes 1 to 5. (Size 3 usually fits an adult woman and size 4 fits a man.) The size/length of the airway used should be the same length as the distance between the angle of the mouth to the tip of the patient's ear. The Guedel airway should be inverted when inserted into the mouth. It is then rotated 180° as it passes below the palate into the oropharynx.
If your dentist does a lot of oral surgery, nasal airways should also be kept as bleeding under the floor of the mouth will raise the tongue making an oropharyngeal airway difficult to place.

It is useful to remember that patients with chronic obstructive airway disease need to be reminded to breath when given oxygen. Their respiration stimulus is low oxygen and they will not breath unless told when having oxygen. (Our respiration stimulus is high carbon dioxide levels. This is why we get hyperventilating patients to re-breath their expired air.)

RECOMMENDED EQUIPMENT

Dental surgeries are not obliged to have the following equipment but it is recommended.

1. Spacer device.
   To attach to inhalers as previously described

2. Automated glucose measuring devise. Many diabetics have these at home. The practice can test this machine on themselves. (Be forewarned, there are many people who have undiagnosed diabetes-one of them could be you!) Use the "pen" on the side of the end of your finger to prick the skin. Place a drop of blood on the stick provided and pop this in the machine to get a reading. A normal reading is between 3.5 to 5.5.

3. AED (automated external defibrillator). These are very simple to use. You must expose the patient's chest. If their chest is very hairy you may need to quickly shave it to ensure good contact between the skin and the pads. Switch on the machine. It will immediately start to give you instructions. You firmly stick the pads (electrodes) either side of the heart as shown on the diagram on the machine. It will diagnose the patient's rhythm. If the AED recognises ventricular fibrillation it will then start to charge. The machine will only shock the patient when you press the red button. It is your responsibility to command everyone to step back. No one, including yourself, must be touching the patient when you press the red button to prevent others being shocked. This is your responsibility. The machine will continue to give you commands and periodically assess the heart rhythm. AED machines need to be maintained. Their batteries and electrodes need to be replaced every 2 to 5 years depending on the make and model of the AED.

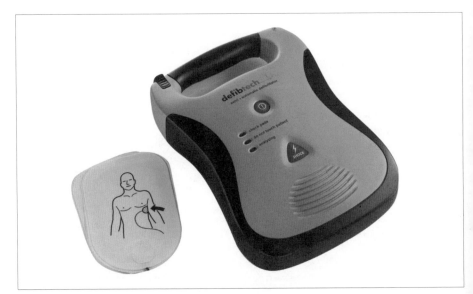

Figure 8.7 *Automated external defibrillator. (Courtesy of Minerva and Martek.)*

Q1. What emergency equipment should a surgery possess?

    a. portable oxygen
    b. portable hand operated suction
    c. oropharyngeal airway
    d. self inflating bag and valve

Q2. The oxygen cylinder should be regularly checked to make sure it is full and the valves have not stuck? True or false?

Q3. How is an oropharyngeal airway inserted?

    a. inverted when inserted into the nose
    b. inverted when inserted into the mouth
    c. rotated through 90° when it passes below the palate
    d. rotated through 180° when it passes below the palate

Q4. What further equipment is **recommended** for medical emergencies in dental practice?

    a. AED
    b. space device
    c. airway
    d. oxygen

How well did you do?
    A1.a,b,c,d   A2.True   A3.b,d
    A4.a,b

TAKING THE PULSE

While reading the text answer the following;

Q1. Name two areas where you can take a pulse.

1. RADIAL PULSE

Take your index and middle fingers and place them in the groove in the wrist that lies beneath the thumb. Move your fingers back and forth gently until you can feel a slight pulsation. This is the pulse of the radial artery which delivers blood to the hand.

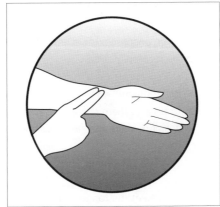

Figure 8.8 *Taking the carotid pulse.*

2.   CAROTID PULSE
    This is the best pulse to take. The carotid arteries supply the blood to the head and neck. Again take two fingers-the index and middle-and run them along the outer edge of your trachea (windpipe) below the angle of the mandible. You will be able to feel the common carotid artery.
    Do not press both sides of your neck at the same time-you may faint!

Figure 8.9 *Taking the carotid pulse.*

Q1. Name two areas where you can take a pulse.

    a. radial
    b. ulna
    c. palate
    d. carotid

How well did you do?
    A1.a,d

THE RECOVERY POSITION

While reading the text answer the following;

Q1. Why are unconscious patients placed in the recovery position?

If the patient collapses in the waiting room and is unconscious but still breathing they can be placed in the traditional recovery position. This is where the patient is carefully rolled onto their side. In this position the airway is maintained. The patient will not inhale their own vomit should this occur and the tongue cannot flop backwards to obstruct the airway. Also the position prevents them rolling.

THE RECOVERY POSITION

1. Kneel beside the patient. (The patient is on their back with their legs straight.)
2. Place the arm which is closest to you at a right angle to the patient's body with the palm facing up.
3. Place the hand furthest from you across the patient's chest and hold the back of the hand against the opposite cheek.
4. With your free hand, pull up the patient's far leg just above the knee, keeping their foot on the ground.
5. Pull the knee towards you rolling the patient onto their side. The patient's upper leg should be bent at right angles at both the hip and knee.
6. Tilt the head back to maintain the airway.
7. Check the breathing and pulse regularly until help arrives.

THE MODIFIED RECOVERY POSITION IN THE DENTAL CHAIR

1. Turn the patient's head towards the suction.
2. Support and raise the patient's opposite shoulder with something bulky like a folded coat
3. Tilt the head back to maintain the airway
4. Leave the legs straight

Q1. Why are unconscious patients placed in the recovery position?

    a. to maintain the airway
    b. to prevent them rolling into a position where the airway will be compromised
    c. to prevent them inhaling their own vomit
    d. to prevent the tongue blocking the airway

How well did you do?
A1.a,b,c,d

BASIC LIFE SUPPORT

While reading the text answer the following;

Q1. If the patient is unresponsive what should you do?

Q2. How do you check for breathing?

Q3. When should you start chest compressions?

Q4. What is the ratio of breaths to compressions?

If a patient looses consciousness in the surgery our job is to keep them alive until medical help arrives. The dental team has a duty to do this through basic life support.

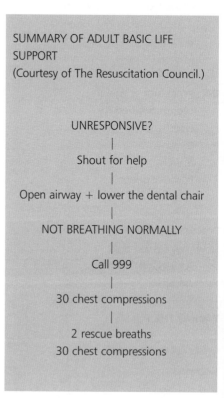

SUMMARY OF ADULT BASIC LIFE SUPPORT
(Courtesy of The Resuscitation Council.)

UNRESPONSIVE?
|
Shout for help
|
Open airway + lower the dental chair
|
NOT BREATHING NORMALLY
|
Call 999
|
30 chest compressions
|
2 rescue breaths
30 chest compressions

90

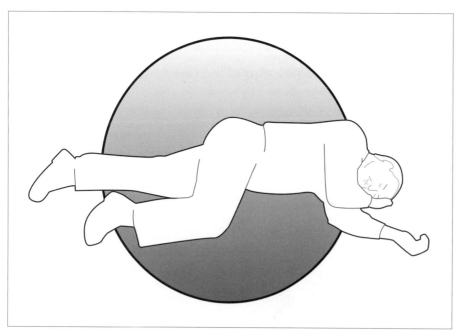

Figure 8.10 *The recovery position.*

BASIC LIFE SUPPORT IN DETAIL AT THE
DENTAL PRACTICE

ASSESS THE PATIENT

- See if they are responsive by shaking
  their shoulders and ask loudly " Are
  you all right?"

IF THE PATIENT RESPONDS;

- Monitor them.
- Leave the patient where they are and
  get help if required.

IF THE PATIENT DOES NOT RESPOND;

- Shout for help.
- Open the airway - tilt the head back
  and lift the chin. Tilt the head back
  using your hand on the patient's
  forehead. Support the chin with two
  fingers underneath the tip of the chin.
- Adjust the dental chair into the most
  appropriate position. This is usually
  lying down.
- Loosen tight clothing around the
  patient's neck.
- Remove any obvious obstruction from
  the mouth. Turn the patient's head
  sideways (preferably towards the
  suction) and scoop out or aspirate the
  obstruction. Leave well fitting
  dentures in place as these will help to
  maintain a mouth seal if ventilation is
  required.

LOOK, LISTEN AND FEEL FOR
BREATHING

- Look. Are there chest movements?
  Are there signs of life e.g. eyelash
  flutter, pink skin?
- Listen close to the patient's mouth.
  Can you hear breathing sounds?
- Feel with your cheek. Can you feel the
  breath?
- Look, listen and feel for no more than
  10 seconds to decide if the patient is
  breathing.

In the first few minutes after the cardiac
arrest the patient may be barely breathing
or taking noisy, infrequent gasps. This is
not normal.

IF THEY ARE BREATHING NORMALLY

- Monitor until the patient has
  recovered or medical help arrives.
- If the patient is in the dental chair
  leave them there but turn their head
  towards the suction, raise and
  support the opposite shoulder. If the
  patient is on the floor place them in
  the conventional recovery position.

IF THEY ARE NOT BREATHING OR IF YOU
HAVE ANY DOUBT WHETHER BREATHING
IS NORMAL

- Call an ambulance immediately. As
  the nurse you must phone the
  emergency services yourself if there is
  no receptionist or call the receptionist
  to do this so that you can go back
  and assist the dentist.

START CHEST COMPRESSIONS

- Stand by the side of the patient if
  they are in the chair and lower or
  raise the chair to a comfortable
  height for you. Kneel by them if they
  are on the floor.
- Place the heal of one hand in the
  centre of the patient's chest and the
  other on top of the first hand and
  interlock your fingers.
- Lean over the patient and with your
  arms straight, press **vertically
  down** on the sternum 4 to 5cms
  then release the pressure **without
  losing contact** between your hands
  and the sternum.
- Repeat this at a rate of 100
  compressions/minute (just under two
  compressions per second).
- Compression and release should take
  the same amount of time. Allow the
  chest to **recoil completely** after
  each compression.

- You are now making the heart pump
  blood around the body artificially. This
  is called external cardiac compression.
  It is exhausting but help will arrive
  soon. If you are working along side
  the dentist you should take over
  compressions (with a minimum of
  delay) about every two minutes to
  prevent fatigue and maintain the
  quality of performance.

COMBINE CHEST COMPRESSIONS WITH
RESCUE BREATHS

- While the dentist gives 30
  compressions apply the pocket mask
  over the patient's nose and mouth.
  You should be positioned at the
  patient's head facing the length of
  their body. The mask is triangular with
  the apex over the top of the nose and
  the lower edge on the chin. Press
  with the full length of your thumbs
  along the cushioned edge of the
  mask to get a seal but keeping the
  head tilted and chin up with your
  fingers.
- Inflate the lungs with one full, steady
  breath through the one-way mask
  valve port. This should take 1 second.
- Take your mouth away from the mask
  while the patient exhales. Watch the
  chest inflate and then fall passively.
  Take another breath and inflate the
  lungs a second time.
- The dentist should keep their hands
  lightly resting on the chest to give you
  feedback on the chest movements. If
  your rescue breaths do not make the
  patient's chest rise recheck the head
  tilt and chin lift. Do not attempt more
  than two breaths each time before
  returning to the chest compressions.

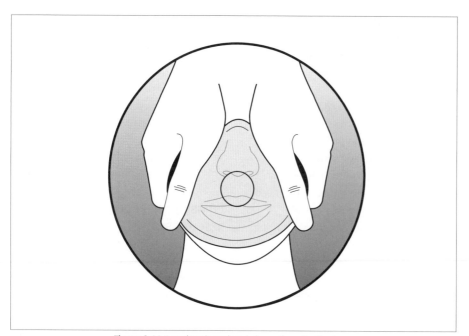

Figure 8.11 A pocket air mask sealed over the patient's airway.

- Continue with chest compressions and rescue breaths in the ratio of 30:2.
- Only stop to recheck the patient if they start breathing normally. Otherwise do not interrupt the resuscitation.

If you use an Ambu-bag attached to the oxygen cylinder you will be able to give the patient 20% to 100% oxygen. With mask or mouth alone they will only receive 16%.

Q1. If the patient is unresponsive what should you do?

    a. shout for help
    b. open the airway
    c. remove obvious airway obstructions
    d. loosen tight clothing

Q2. How do you check for breathing?

    a. look for chest movements
    b. feel the pulse
    c. listen for breathing sounds
    d. feel the breath

Q3. When should you start chest compressions?

    a. if there is no breathing
    b. if there is no pulse
    c. if the patient is unconscious
    d. if the breathing is not normal

Q4. What is the ratio of breaths to compressions?

    a. 30 to 2
    b. 2 to 30
    c. 15 to 1
    d. 1 to 15

How well did you do?
A1.a,b,c,d   A2.a,c,d   A3.a,b,d
A4.b

BASIC LIFE SUPPORT FOR CHILDREN
(Courtesy of The Resuscitation Council.)

Children go blue very quickly as they have no respiratory reserve.

UNRESPONSIVE?
|
Shout for help
|
Open airway + lower the dental chair
|
NOT BREATHING NORMALLY?
|
5 rescue breaths
|
STILL UNRESPONSIVE?
Look for signs of circulation.
|
30 chest compressions
2 rescue breaths

When compressing a child's chest use one hand only or if they are very young just your fingers. Their chest should be compressed by one third of it's depth.

After 1 minute call 999 and continue basic life support.

This is basic life support. Traditionally it consists of ventilating the lungs and external cardiac compression. When the ambulance arrives the paramedics will take over to give advanced life support. This involves the administration of stimulant drugs and the use of a defibrillator. However with user friendly AEDs now available the dental team may defibrillate the patient.
Any medical emergency must be written up in detail in the patient's dental records.

9. Plaque and Caries

While reading the text answer the following;

Q1. How is dental decay caused?

Q2. What is plaque?

Q3. Where does plaque collect?

CAUSE OF DENTAL DECAY

Caries is another term for tooth decay. It is caused by bacteria in the plaque converting sugars from the diet into lactic acid. First the acid demineralises the enamel and then the dentine. The demineralisation of these hard tissues allows the bacteria to enter the inside of the tooth and destroy the soft organic tissue in the dentine and finally the pulp.

PLAQUE

Plaque is a translucent or cream coloured sticky film which is difficult to see against the tooth. It must be removed twice a day to prevent dental decay. Plaque consists of a mixture of food debris and bacteria. If the plaque is not removed these bacteria flourish and multiply to form large colonies. Some of the bacteria, such as Streptococcus mutans and lactobacilli, can turn sugar into lactic acid. The lactic acid dissolves the underlying enamel and dentine which leads to demineralisation and decay.

Plaque tends to collect in stagnation areas. The most common stagnation areas are occlusal fissures and interproximal areas between the teeth. It is unsurprising that these are the first tooth surfaces to decay!

Q1. Dental decay is caused by bacteria producing acid which demineralises the enamel and dentine allowing the bacteria to destroy the inner organic matter. True or false?

Q2. What is plaque?

    a. plaque is a collection of bacteria and food debris
    b. plaque is soft, sticky and translucent or cream coloured
    c. plaque is hard and needs to be scaled by a hygienist
    d. plaque contains bacteria such as Streptococcus mutans and lactobacilli.

Q3. Where does plaque normally collect?

    a. fissures
    b. interproximal areas
    c. cusps
    d. any stagnation area

How well did you do?
    A1.True   A2.a,b,d   A3.a,b,d

THE DIET AND DENTAL DECAY

While reading the text answer the following;

Q1. How does sugar cause decay?

Q2. How does acid effect teeth?

Q3. What is the critical pH for demineralisation?

Q4. What two factors favour demineralisation?

Two types of food greatly increase the risk of decay;

1. SUGARS

As you know, our diet consists of carbohydrates, protein, fats, minerals and vitamins. Of these different groups only carbohydrates can be turned into acid and cause dental decay. There are two main groups of carbohydrates; sugar carbohydrates and starchy fibrous carbohydrates. The group of carbohydrates that causes dental decay is sugar, especially refined sugar. Oral bacteria can convert refined sugar into acid and decay the teeth. Refined sugars are often added to processed food. Examples of refined sugars are glucose and sucrose. They are called the non-milk extrinsic sugars (NMESs). Glucose and sucrose can be found in sweets, cakes, breakfast cereals, ice cream, chocolate and soft drinks. Naturally occurring sugar found in fruit (fructose) and milk (lactose) normally do not cause a significant amount of decay.

Starchy fibrous carbohydrates such as potatoes, rice, pasta and beans do not cause decay. However it is wise to be aware of "hidden" sugars added to processed savoury food. For example sugar is often added to canned baked beans and tomato sauce. Parents need to be advised to read the packaging of these foods especially as they are often marketed to children.

2. ACID

Some food may be acidic itself without bacteria acting on it. For example fizzy drinks are made of phosphoric acid and fruit juices naturally contain citric acid. All acids will demineralise enamel and dentine, however phosphoric acid is a strong acid and is particularly damaging to the teeth.

DEMINERALISATION, REMINERALISATION AND pH

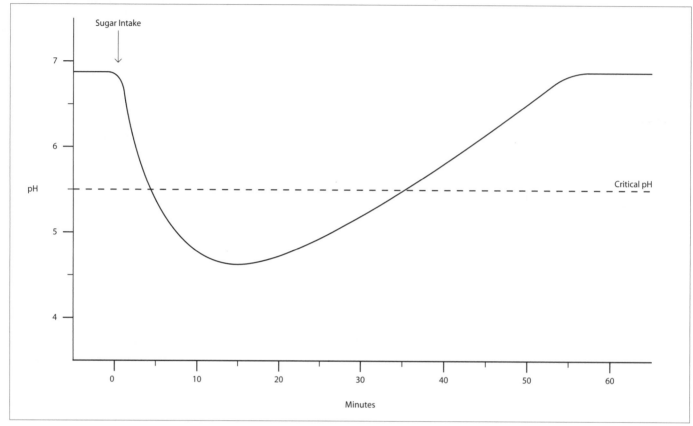

Figure 9.1 *The Stephen curve.*

When sugar is ingested the oral bacteria quickly turn it into acid. This acid attacks the enamel under the plaque making it porous. This is called demineralisation. Saliva has a neutral pH. On a scale of 1 to 14 saliva is pH7. This means that it is neither an acid or an alkaline. Acids have a pH value less than 7 and alkalines have a pH greater than 7. So as the mouth becomes more acidic the pH value falls. A pH of 5.5 or lower is needed to demineralise enamel. It takes 1 to 2 hours for saliva to neutralise the acid and bring the pH back up to 7. This can be shown on the Stephen curve.

The Saliva contains minerals such as calcium and phosphate and will try to repair the damaged tooth with these minerals. This is called remineralisation. This can only occur at a pH higher than 5.5. So as the pH of the mouth fluctuates there is a balance between demineralisation (damage) and remineralisation (repair). If more demineralisation takes place than repair decay is inevitable.

Two factors that favour demineralisation are the ability of the sugary food to stick to the teeth and the frequency of the sugary snacks.

1. Sticky sugary food such as toffee will hang around the teeth longer than non sticky sugar such as tea with sugar.

2. Frequent sugary snacks ensure the teeth are constantly bathed in acid and do not have the chance to repair. Acid attacks are less destructive if the patient routinely brushes with fluoride toothpaste which strengthens the teeth making them harder to dissolve. The level of acid in the mouth can be reduced by chewing sugar free gum to increase the salivary flow or eating alkaline food such as cheese.

ASSESSING THE PATIENT'S DIET

Sometimes it is advisable to assess the patient's diet. This is useful if the patient has obvious dental problems such as a high caries rate or erosion or they are embarking a long treatment plan which could increase plaque retention such as orthodontic treatment.

A convenient way to analyse the diet is to ask the patient to write down everything they eat and the time it was eaten over a 24 hour period. It is useful to review this diet sheet with the patient and the parents if the patient is a child. Highlight areas that contribute to demineralisation, decay and erosion and readjust the patient's eating habits where necessary.

Q1. Which of the following food can cause decay?

   a. diet fizzy drinks
   b. citric acid
   c. phosphoric acid
   d. refined sugars

Q2. How does acid effect teeth?

   a. toughens them
   b. makes them porous
   c. mineralises them
   d. demineralises them

Q3. What is the critical pH for demineralisation?

   a. pH7
   b. pH5
   c. pH5.5
   d. pH7.5

Q4. What factors favour demineralisation?

   a. eating lots of sugar
   b. eating potatoes
   c. having several sugary snacks
   d. eating toffee

How well did you do?
   A1.a,b,c,d   **A2.b,d**   **A3.c**
   A4.a,c,d

CARIES FORMATION

While reading the text answer the following;

Q1. Name four factors necessary for decay to occur?

Q2. How does caries progress?

For decay to occur you need the following factors;

1. Bacteria found in plaque.
2. A tooth surface where plaque can stagnate.
3. Sucrose and glucose from the diet.
4. Time.

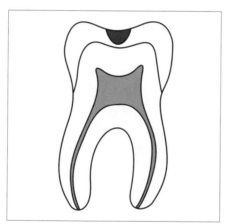

Figure 9.2 Demineralised enamel.

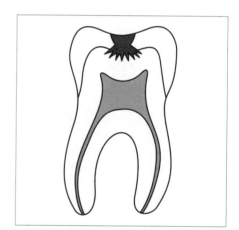

Figure 9.3 The decay "ballooning" through the softer dentine.

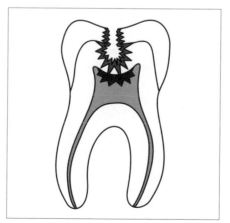

Figure 9.4 Cavitation of the enamel and pulpitis.

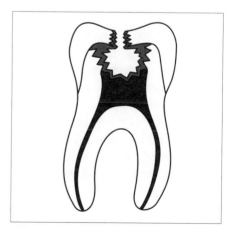

Figure 9.5 Irreversible pulpitis resulting in the death of the pulp and abscess.

If a patient has an unrestricted diet of sugar there will be an abundance of acid producing bacteria colonising in plaque stagnation sites.

1. The acid causes demineralisation of the underlying enamel. Due to the frequency of sugary snacks the enamel does not get the chance to remineralise. The enamel has no nerves so this is painless.
2. The enamel is breached and the underlying dentine becomes demineralised. The bacteria start to damage the organic tissue. The decay "balloons" out under the enamel within the softer dentine. Pain is only felt when the decay has extended quite a way into the dentine and begins to irritate the dentine fibrils. The tooth experiences sensitivity. This is usually described by the patient as short sharp pain especially to cold. This pain only lasts for seconds at a time.
3. The odontoblasts react to this bacterial attack by laying down secondary dentine to protect the underlying pulp in that part of the tooth.
4. The overlying enamel has no support and caves in resulting in a cavity.
5. As the decay approaches the pulp, pain occurs when eating hot, cold or sweet foods. This pain lasts longer.
6. The pain becomes more severe when the pulp becomes involved. The bacteria and acid causes the pulp to become inflamed. This is pulpitis and is very painful.
7. At first the pulpitis is reversible. This means that with the appropriate treatment the pulp could recover. However if it is left irreversible pulpitis occurs. The tooth throbs especially at night when the patient is lying flat or eating hot food as both increase the blood flow to the tooth.
8. As the pulp dies there tends to be a long lasting dull ache. The bacteria in the dead pulp form a periapical abscess (alveolar abscess). The pain no longer arises from the tooth itself but from the bacterial infection of the bone. The pain can be diffuse at first but then becomes localised around the dead tooth. It is tender to bite on as the biting force is transmitted through the dead tooth to the now inflamed alveolar bone.

Q1. Which factors are necessary for decay to occur?

a. bacteria
b. sugar
c. tooth
d. time

Q2. How does caries progress?

a. demineralisation, cavity, pulpitis, periapical abscess
b. cavity, demineralisation, pulpitis, remineralisation
c. demineralisation, pulpitis, cavity, periapical abscess
d. demineralisation, cavity, periapical abscess, pulpitis

How well did you do?
A1.a,b,c,d   A2.a

While reading the text answer the following;

Q1. Why is pulpitis painful?

Q2. How can the pulp die during pulpitis?

Q3. What is the difference between an acute and chronic periodontal abscess?

PULPITIS

When the pulp becomes inflamed there is an increase in blood flow through the apical foramen. However the pulp cannot swell as it is surrounded by hard tissue. This results in severe pain as the increased blood volume presses on the nerves. This pressure also compresses the blood vessels passing through the fine apical foramen. This cuts off the blood supply resulting in the death of the tooth. The severe pain stops abruptly until the periapical abscess forms.

PERIAPICAL ABSCESS

1. ACUTE PERIAPICAL ABSCESS
As the dead pulp decomposes infected matter passes through the apical foramen. This leads to inflammation of the surrounding alveolar bone. Pus forms at the apex to produce a very painful acute periapical abscess. The tooth may feel loose or further out of the socket than normal. It is extremely painful to the slightest touch. That side of the face may be swollen and the patient may have a raised temperature. The surrounding gum is red and swollen and there is a continual throbbing pain.

2. CHRONIC PERIAPICAL ABSCESS
If treatment is not sought a chronic periapical abscess will form. The infection and pus spreads through the bone dispersing the pressure and pain felt by the patient. The alveolar bone around the apex of the root is gradually destroyed. The infection makes a tunnel from the root apex through the bone to the surface of the gum. This is called a sinus and appears as a red gum boil. Because the pus is being released there is no build up of pressure within the bone and so the pain disappears.
However a chronic abscess can suddenly flare up into a painful acute abscess if the sinus becomes blocked or the patient is "run down".

Q1. During pulpitis the pulp cannot swell as it is encased in hard tissue. This causes pressure on the nerves which leads to severe pain. True or false?

Q2. Why does the pulp die during pulpitis?

   a. pressure on the nerves
   b. pressure on the dentine
   c. pressure on the enamel
   d. pressure on the blood vessels

Q3. A chronic periodontal abscess is very painful to the slightest touch whereas an acute abscess is characterised by a sinus. True or false?

How well did you do?
   A1.True   A2.d   A3.False

DIAGNOSIS OF CARIES

While reading the text answer the following;

Q1. List five methods of diagnosing decay.

1. ORAL EXAMINATION
Demineralised enamel appears chalky. More detail can be seen with loops and a good light source. Caries is seen as a brown discolouration or shadow beneath the enamel. Extensive decay presents as a cavity where the overlying enamel has collapsed.
2. PROBE
A blunt straight or sickle probe can detect occlusal decay. A Briault or sickle probe is useful in detecting interproximal caries. Care must be taken not to perforate enamel which is only demineralised and not decayed.
3. RADIOGRAPHS
Bitewings are so accurate that they will detect interproximal demineralisation of the enamel as well as frank decay.
4. TRANSILLUMINATION
When a bright fibre-optic light is placed against the crowns of anterior teeth, decay can be seen as a shadow.
5. DYES
Dyes can be used within cavities to help detect any residual decay. However demineralised dentine as well as carious dentine retains the stain.

Q1. Which of the following are methods of diagnosing decay.

   a. transillumination
   b. bitewings
   c. Briault probe
   d. caries dye

How well did you do?
   A1.a,b,c,d

TREATMENT OF DENTAL CARIES

While reading the text answer the following;

Q1. How is caries treated?

Q2. List four ways to prevent decay.

If the decay has not encroached on the pulp a simple filling will suffice. If the decay has destroyed most of the enamel or dentine but the pulp is still healthy a crown will be required.
However if there is irreversible pulpitis or a non vital pulp a root filling will be needed to save the tooth, otherwise the tooth has to be extracted.

Regular dental examinations and bitewings lead to early detection of demineralisation and decay. In the case of demineralisation the patient can be warned and preventative action can be taken. Early decay can be treated simply, conservatively and relatively cheaply.

PREVENTION OF CARIES

1. DIET
- Decrease the quantity of sugar in the diet.
- Decrease the frequency of sugary snacks. Sugar-free snacks such as nuts and cheese can be eaten between meals.
- Decrease sticky sugary foods that stay around the teeth for a long time.
- Limit sugar consumption to mealtimes.
- Be aware that sugar-free fizzy drinks are acidic and will erode the enamel.

2. ORAL HYGIENE
- The regular and effective removal of plaque.

3. FLUORIDE
- This toughens the enamel making it harder to demineralise.
- Fluoride encourages remineralisation of porous enamel.

4. FISSURE SEALANTS
- This forms a physical barrier over pits and fissures preventing decay. Fissures not only provide a stagnation area for plaque but the occlusal enamel is very thin in the depth of a fissure. It does not take long for the bacteria to reach the amelodentine junction under the fissures.
- Fissure sealants do not protect the remaining surfaces of the tooth and the patient should be informed of this.

5. REGULAR DENTAL EXAMINATIONS
- Enables the detection of demineralisation and early decay allowing it to be arrested by non intrusive methods such as fluoride applications or minimal restorations to conserve the remaining enamel and dentine.

6. PATIENT EDUCATION

Q1. How can caries be treated when the pulp is healthy?

    a. composite fillings
    b. amalgam fillings
    c. root canal treatment
    d. crown

Q2. Which of the following prevent decay?

    a. tooth brushing
    b. fluoride mouth rinse
    c. fissure sealants
    d. high sugar diet

How well did you do?
    A1.a,b,d   A2.a,b,c

10. Oral Hygiene Education

While reading the text answer the following;

Q1. What is the minimum length of time needed to clean your teeth?

Q2. What are the advantages of an electric toothbrush?

Q3. What are the advantages of interdental brushes compared to floss?

Q4. How do specialist toothpastes eliminate bad breath?

Before teaching a patient about oral hygiene or giving them dietary advise ask them about their existing routine and knowledge. It is important not to insult the patient. Their existing habits may only require a few modifications.
It is important that every member of the practice is consistent with the information they provide to avoid confusing patients. Remember, some patients will be involved in educating others, for example midwives, nursery teachers and parents, so your information may be passed on to others. You are responsible at ensuring that your information is consistent and correct.

Patients can be motivated to improve their eating habits and oral hygiene by explaining the benefits of healthier teeth, a nicer smile and fresh breath. When teaching a patient new skills, demonstrate the skill on a model first to allow the patient to see the demonstration clearly and ask questions. You can then demonstrate on the patient themselves to show that what you are asking is achievable. However do not expect too much too soon. It is better to set achievable goals to prevent the patient from becoming despondent. Observe the patient repeating your demonstration on themselves. This shows that the patient has understood and is capable of following your technique. If there are any difficulties these can be remedied. Monitor the patient's progress at subsequent appointments. By praising positive progress the patient's skills will develop over time.

Patients can be motivated by showing them their achievements by using disclosing tablets and periodontal examination scores.

TOOTH BRUSHING AND TONGUE BRUSHING

The teeth should be brushed twice a day for a minimum of 2 minutes. (Time yourself this feels longer than it is!) Tooth brushing is recommended after breakfast and last thing at night before going to bed. It is important to establish how effective the patient is at removing plaque and to make sure that they are not causing damage by brushing too hard. If their tooth brushing is over vigorous there will be gum recession and cervical abrasion cavities. The patient may also report that the bristles on their toothbrush splay after a short while. The bristles should still be upright after three months use.

Figure 10.1 The Bass Technique.

The Bass method of tooth brushing is recommended. The bristles of the toothbrush are placed at an angle of 45° towards the gum and gently rotated in a small circular motion. However if the patient's own tooth brushing method is effective and not causing damage there is no need to change their technique to the Bass method.
Patients should choose a toothbrush to suit their mouth. The size of the brush head should only aim to cover one to two teeth at a time. Children need smaller, softer tooth brushes than adults.

Electric toothbrushes are very efficient at removing plaque. They are particularly useful for people with reduced manual dexterity e.g. arthritic patients, and their chunky handles are easier to grip. When using an electric tooth brush the patient should hold the bristles gently against their teeth and allow the toothbrush to do the work. There is no need to make any circular movements. The disadvantage of electric toothbrushes is their cost. However, most models have interchangeable heads so the whole family can use the same machine.
Patients who are prone to periodontal disease may also need to brush their tongues to decrease the number of bacteria found there. Tongue brushes are now widely available and some are incorporated into the standard toothbrush.

INTERDENTAL BRUSHING

Interdental brushing is an alternative to dental floss. Patients often find interdental brushes much easier to use than floss which means that they are more likely to integrate them into their oral hygiene routine. The interdental brushes come in a range of different sizes and can be matched precisely to the size of the patient's interdental spaces. They are shaped like minute bottle brushes and the patient uses them as they would a toothpick. However they remove far more debris than any toothpick. The interdental area is brushed gently by inserting the interdental brush between the teeth and the gum level. For front teeth the brush is used straight and for the back teeth the brush is curved.

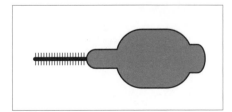

Figure 10.2 Interdental brush.

FLOSSING

Figure 10.3 *Flossing.*

Dental tape or floss is recommended every evening after tooth brushing. Floss is circular in cross section whereas tape is flat. Tape removes more interdental plaque than floss. Waxed floss is useful for teeth with tight contacts.

The patient is shown how to wrap a length of floss around their middle fingers and use their index fingers to control and manipulate the floss in a C shape around the teeth. The disadvantage of flossing is that the patient needs to be dextrous. Flossing is also time consuming so patients can get disheartened very quickly. However floss is now sold on holders to make it more user friendly.

TOOTHPASTES

Toothpastes contain fluoride to strengthen the teeth. The fluoride becomes incorporated into the enamel surface as it demineralises. The fluoride replaces the lost calcium and phosphates to become fluorapatite. This makes the outer surface of the enamel more resistant to future acid attacks. The amount of fluoride in toothpastes varies. Children's toothpastes usually contain 600ppm (parts per million) and adult's 1000ppm.

Periodontal patients often have exposed roots which may be sensitive. Certain toothpastes such as Sensodyne™ and Duraphat 2800™ will desensitise the root surface. Care must be taken with the Duraphat 2800™ toothpaste as it has a very high concentration of fluoride and must be kept out of reach of small children.

When brushing with any toothpaste only a pea-size amount of paste should be used. Parents/guardians should supervise children so that they rinse and do not swallow the paste. Too much fluoride is toxic and can be fatal if taken in high doses especially in small children. Children should not be allowed to run around with toothbrushes in their mouths as this may cause injury should they fall.

Patients suffering from sinusitis and periodontal disease often complain of bad breath or a bad taste in their mouth. Most toothpastes and mouthwashes just mask this problem. However Retardex™ toothpaste and mouthwash will solve the condition by chemically eliminating volatile sulphur compounds (VSC) which cause halitosis. However the underlying cause of the problem should not be ignored.

Q1. What is the minimum length of time needed to clean your teeth?

    a. 2 seconds
    b. 20 seconds
    c. 2 minutes
    d. 20 minutes

Q2. What are the characteristics of an electric tooth brush?

    a. high level of manual dexterity is needed
    b. chunky handle is easy to grip
    c. more plaque is left on the teeth
    d. only half the time is needed with an electric tooth brush

Q3. What are the advantages of interdental brushes compared to floss?

    a. different sizes available
    b. harder to use
    c. patients are more likely to use the brushes
    d. the brushes are quick and efficient

Q4. How does Retardex™ eliminate bad breath?

    a. by masking the smell
    b. by eliminating volatile sulphur compounds
    c. by eliminating volatile fluoride compounds
    d. by eliminating volatile nitrous compounds

How well did you do?
    A1.c   A2.b   A3.a,c,d   A4.b

MOUTHWASHES

Q1. What is the disadvantage of chlorhexidine?

Q2. What is the nurse's role when disclosing a patient's teeth?

Q3. What is the ideal amount of fluoride to have in drinking water?

Fluoride can also be provided topically by mouthwashes. A child needs to be old enough to rinse and spit out. For this reason mouthwashes are used for people who are 6 years old or over. Fluoride mouthwashes are useful during the mixed dentition stage to toughen the teeth as they erupt, especially as the permanent teeth are often crowded at first making tooth brushing challenging. Mouth rinsing should not replace tooth brushing. Fluoride mouth rinse is useful for patients who have a low salivary flow and are more prone to decay. It is also useful for people with acid reflux for example those with peptic ulcers, hernias or bulimia. Patients are instructed to take the rinse after their nightly tooth brushing. The patient should rinse the toothpaste away with water then take a mouthful of fluoride mouthwash and swill it around their mouth for 30 seconds before spitting out. Afterwards they should not rinse their mouth with water or eat or drink but should go straight to sleep. This allows the fluoride to soak into the enamel when the salivary flow is at it's lowest.

Figure 10.4 Fluoride mouthwash.
(Courtesy of Minerva and Colgate.)

Antibacterial mouthwashes reduce the number of microbes in the mouth. They are particularly useful in the short term to help get an acute infection under control or after surgery when the gums are too tender to brush. They are not an alternative to routine tooth brushing. The most effective antibacterial mouthwashes contain chlorhexidine. Unfortunately chlorhexidine stains the teeth. This stain is extrinsic and can be removed by the hygienist.

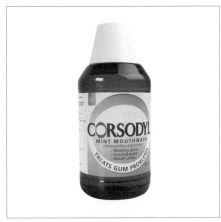

Figure 10.5 Chlorhexidine mouthwash.
(Courtesy of Minerva and GSK.)

A soothing mouth rinse for patients with ulcers and sore mucosa is Aloclair™. This coats the ulcer providing pain relief.

DISCLOSING AGENTS

Figure 10.6 Plaque disclosers. *(Courtesy of Minerva.)*

As plaque is tooth coloured it is good to dye the plaque so that it can be clearly seen by the patient. This is achieved with disclosing solution or tablets. It is often surprising for the patient when they realise how much plaque has collected around their teeth. It also demonstrates how only gentle but thorough tooth brushing can remove it.

Before using a disclosing agent make sure that the patient is not allergic to colorants. Always put petroleum jelly on the patient's lips before you start so that they do not leave the surgery with dyed lips. Warn the patient that the dye will temporarily stain their tongue. A bib is necessary as these dyes will stain clothes. Patients can be given disclosing tablets to use at home however two tone disclosing solutions are very useful in the surgery. The solution is wiped over the teeth with a cotton wool bud. Then the patient carefully rinses to remove excess dye. Recent plaque is stained one colour and old plaque another. This educates the patient in the colonisation of plaque. It shows them that their hurried tooth brushing is not an isolated incident but an ingrained habit which will soon result in dental disease.

SYSTEMIC FLUORIDES

Toothpaste, fluoride mouthwash and fluoride varnishes are all examples of topical fluorides. They strengthen the outer layer of the enamel. Fluoride can be ingested. This is called systemic fluoride and it has the ability to strengthen the full thickness of enamel when given during tooth development. Fluoride tablets or drops can be given from the age of 6 months to 5 years by which time the crowns of all the permanent teeth, except the wisdom teeth, have formed. However it is important that the child does not have too much fluoride from other sources such as toothpaste. Too much fluoride will result in unsightly marks on the teeth. This is fluorosis. These marks usually present as white speckles but can appear as dark orange/brown patches. If the parents / guardian decides to give fluoride supplements to their children they must understand the long term commitment.

They should also be advised never to double the dose if they forget to give the supplement one day. Often the children who least need fluoride supplements receive them and the ones who are most in need do not.

In some areas fluoride is added to the water supply at a level of 1ppm (part per million). This is the optimum level to prevent decay. It is also the best way to give systemic fluoride as people drink water throughout the day as opposed to getting a full dose once a day. It also improves the oral health of those in lower socioeconomic groups and those who do not visit the dentist. It strengthens bones and teeth preventing toothache and decay. However many people do not like this concept as they feel that it is mass medication and it infringes individual rights to choose. They also argue that it reduces people's incentive to look after their own dental care. It is important to know if fluoride has been added to your water supply and to modify your oral health education accordingly.

Q1. What are the disadvantages of chlorhexidine?

   a. foul taste
   b. stains teeth
   c. it is not an alternative to tooth brushing
   d. stains the tongue pink

Q2. What is the nurse's role when disclosing a patient's teeth?

   a. put the bib on the patient
   b. put petroleum jelly on the patient's lips
   c. make sure the patient is not allergic to food dyes after disclosing
   d. explain the results of the procedure

Q3. What is the ideal amount of fluoride to have in drinking water?

   a. 0.1ppm
   b. 1ppm
   c. 10ppm
   d. 600ppm

How well did you do?
   A1.b,c   A2.a,b,d   A3.b

ABRASION, EROSION AND ATTRITION

While reading the text answer the following;

Q1. What is the difference between abrasion, erosion and attrition?

Enamel and dentine can be destroyed by dental caries. However the tooth surface can also be lost by other means such as abrasion, erosion and attrition.

ABRASION

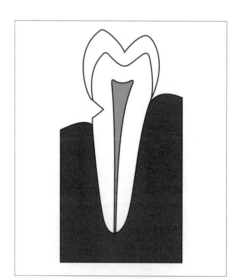

Figure 10.7 *A tooth with an abrasion cavity.*

Abrasion is caused by using too much pressure during tooth brushing. It is seen as gum recession and non carious cervical cavities. If a patient is in the habit of scrubbing the teeth the gums recede exposing the root surface. The root surface is softer as it is not protected by enamel so as the habit continues the patient wears a groove in the side of their root. This usually occurs on the buccal/labial surfaces.

EROSION

Acids dissolve the teeth. The acid may be dietary such as fizzy drinks or from the stomach for example due to reflux. Acids initially make the enamel more porous which causes sensitivity. Continued exposure to acid results in the enamel dissolving away and the fillings are left sitting proud of the tooth. Further erosion may be prevented with dietary advise or overcoming the underlying medical problem. Asking the patient to cleanse the mouth with water followed by a fluoride mouth rinse will assist remineralization after gastric reflux.

ATTRITION

Attrition is the wearing away of the biting surfaces of the teeth by fibrous food or, more commonly, tooth grinding. The occlusal surfaces of the posterior teeth and the palatal surfaces of the upper anterior teeth are the most common surfaces to be effected. Patients may be unaware that they grind their teeth as it tends to occur during sleep. Sleeping with an occlusal mouth guard is often required.

Q1. Which of the following causes erosion?

   a. vigorous tooth brushing
   b. gastric reflux
   c. nocturnal grinding
   d. fizzy drinks

How well did you do?
   A1.b,d

11. Fillings

Fillings are direct restorations. By now you have assisted in placing many fillings. You have practical experience of many restorative materials and the equipment needed to conserve teeth. As you work in the surgery think of the reasons why the dentist has chosen a particular filling material and what the alternatives are.

WHY DO I NEED A FILLING?

REASONS FOR FILLINGS

While reading the text answer the following;

Q1. Give 5 reasons why fillings are necessary?

Fillings replace the dentine and enamel that have been destroyed by decay or trauma.
They prevent decay spreading further, prevent pain, maintain the tooth's vitality, restore function and can restore appearance.

Q1. Which of the following are reasons to fill?

    a. to stop the decay spreading further
    b. to keep the tooth alive
    c. to restore function
    d. to restore appearance

How well did you do?
    A1.a,b,c,d

SO WHERE DO I FIT IN?

NURSE'S ROLE

1. Have the patient's notes and radiographs present. Check the medical history. Note any "red flags" such as needle phobia.
2. Have all the equipment and instruments sterilised and ready. Cover the instruments on the dentist's bracket table with a tissue. (Instruments on display may heighten patient's anxiety.)
3. Greet and seat the patient. Place the bib and glasses once they have had a chance to speak to the dentist.
4. Monitor and reassure the patient throughout the process and especially during the injection.
5. Anticipate the dentist's needs when handing instruments and materials. Have a tissue ready to wipe the end of the instruments as the dentist works. Every dentist works differently and even experienced nurses take a little while before they know what a new dentist needs.
6. Provide good moisture control by suction.
7. Know the correct way to mix and handle the materials you use.
8. Clear away the used instruments and scrub them thoroughly ready for sterilising. Oil the handpieces. Bin disposables in the correct containers.
9. Clear and disinfect all the work surfaces.
10. Remove paper records and x-rays once they have been completed by the dentist.

WHAT DO I NEED?

INSTRUMENTS REQUIRED FOR THE PLACEMENT OF FILLINGS

While reading the text answer the following;

Q1. List the hand instruments required for fillings.

Q2. What are the differences between high and slow handpieces?

Q3. Name three ways in which burs can be defined.

Q4. List three types of retention.

By reading the treatment plan in the patient's records and by knowing what your dentist requires for a certain procedure, you will be able to get the trays ready in advance. Always plan ahead as this saves time and allows the day to flow.

HAND INSTRUMENTS

1. Mouth mirror, college tweezers, probe.

2. Excavators.
- These are spoon like to scoop out soft decay.

Figure 11.1 *Excavator.*
(Courtesy of Minerva and Densply.)

3. Plugger.

Figure 11.2 Plugger.
(Courtesy of Minerva and Densply.)

- They press filling materials into the cavity eliminating air spaces.
- Removes excess mercury from amalgam.

4. Burnisher.

Figure 11.3 Burnisher.
(Courtesy of Minerva and Densply.)

- Ball, pear or inverted cone shaped.
- Adapts the filling to the cavity walls eliminating spaces.

5. Flat plastic instrument.

Figure 11.4 Flat plastic.
(Courtesy of Minerva and Densply.)

- Flat, curved ends.
- Adapts the filling material to the cavity walls.

6. Carvers.

Figure 11.5 Hollenbach carver.
(Courtesy of Minerva and Densply.)

- e.g. Ward's carver, half Hollenback carver
- Shapes the filling.

MISCELLANEOUS

1. Amalgam carrier and pot.

Figure 11.6 Amalgam holder and pot.
(Courtesy of Minerva.)

2. Matrix retainer, matrix strips.

- e.g. Siqveland, Tofflemire, sectional matrices
- This gives the interproximal shape to the restoration.

3. Articulation paper and holder.

Figure 11.7 Miller forceps.
(Courtesy of Minerva.)

- e.g. Miller forceps
- Reveals high spots.

4. Moore's mandrel and pop on mandrel.

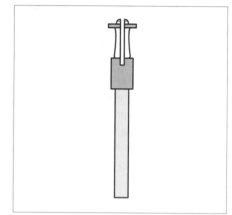

Figure 11.8 Moore's mandrel.

- Holds the polishing discs; course to fine grade.

5. Plastic wedges and wooden wedges.
- These are placed between the teeth after the placing of the matrix band to hold the band against the tooth to prevent an overhanging restoration.

6. Moisture control equipment.
- e.g. rubber dam kit, dry guards, cotton wool rolls

HANDPIECES

The handpiece is the drill. There are 3 types;

1. HIGH SPEED HANDPIECE

Figure 11.9 High speed handpiece.
(Courtesy of Minerva and Kavo.)

- Run at very high speeds of 400,000 revolutions per minute. Remember the nurse must protect the soft tissues with the suction because these drills cut through anything.
- Unfortunately they make a high pitched noise. Patients need reassurance as most people find this sound unsettling.
- They need friction grip burs i.e. burs with a short, smooth shank.
- Contra angled to use in the mouth.
- Always have water spray to keep the tooth cool. The pulp is easily damaged by excessive heat.
- May have fibre-optic light.
- Available in small sizes for small mouths and awkward areas.

2. SLOW SPEED HANDPIECE

Figure 11.10 *Slow speed handpiece.*
(Courtesy of Minerva and Kavo.)

- These run at lower speeds but vibrate. Forewarn the patients that they "tickle".
- They need latch grip burs i.e. burs with a short, notched shank.
- Contra angled to use in the mouth.
- May have water spray to keep the tooth cool.
- May have fibre-optic light.

3. STRAIGHT HANDPIECE

Figure 11.11 *Straight handpiece.*
(Courtesy of Minerva and Kavo.)

- Use friction grip burs (i.e. burs with a long, smooth shank).
- Straight to use outside the mouth for example on dentures or in the laboratory.

BURS

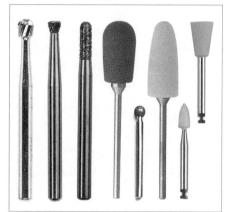

Figure 11.12 *Various burs.*
(Courtesy of Minerva.)

These are the cutting parts of the drill. They are defined in many ways all of which are logical.

1. What they are made of. e.g. diamond, tungsten carbide, stainless steel or acrylic.
2. Which handpiece they fit. e.g. friction grip, latch grip or straight handpiece.
3. The shape e.g. round, pear, flame, inverted cone, flat fissure, tapered fissure or bud.

So for example you may be asked for a "tapered fissure, tungsten carbide, friction grip bur"!

RETENTION

The filling needs to be held within the tooth so that it does not fall out. This is called retention. There are three main methods of retention.

1. **MECHANICAL RETENTION**
   Mechanical retention is achieved by making undercuts in the cavity. Dovetails, slots, pits and grooves are made into the cavity walls and floor. This allows non adhesive filling materials to be used.

2. **BONDS**
   Bonds are used to "glue" the filling to the enamel and dentine. This enables the dentist to keep the size of the cavity to a minimum. Before a bond can be used the enamel should be etched and the dentine should be primed.

3. **PINS**
   Some teeth are so broken down that in extreme cases pins may be required. Pins are made of steel or titanium. The pin hole is made with the appropriate sized bur in the slow speed handpiece. Then the same sized pin is placed in the hole. The pin is part of a plastic latch grip bur. It rotates into the pinhole and the pin self-shears from the plastic base which is then discarded.
   However with the various bonds now available the need for pins has greatly diminished. Pins may cause post operative sensitivity in the tooth. Also, there is a risk of perforating the pulp or periodontal ligament during the placement of pins.

Q1. Which of the following hand instruments are required for fillings?

    a. flat plastic instrument
    b. burnisher
    c. luxator
    d. plugger

Q2. Which of the following are features of the high speed handpiece?

    a. it always has a water spray
    b. it may have fibre optic light
    c. it uses latch grip burs
    d. it is straight

Q3. Burs may be clinically defined in which of the following ways?

    a. colour
    b. the handpiece used
    c. shape
    d. price

Q4. Pins have which of the following disadvantages?

    a. pins may perforate the maxillary sinus
    b. pins may perforate the periodontal ligament
    c. pins may perforate the inferior dental nerve
    d. pins may perforate the pulp

How well did you do?
    A1.a,b,d   A2.a,b   A3.b,c
    A4.b,d

MOISTURE CONTROL

While reading the text answer the following;

Q1. Why is moisture control necessary?

Q2. Name nine methods of controlling moisture.

Q3. List the equipment in a rubber dam kit.

WHY USE MOISTURE CONTROL?

1. It makes the patient more comfortable, less claustrophobic and anxious as water does not collect near the patient's airway.
2. Waste is removed along with the water e.g. amalgam and acid etchant.
3. Most restorative materials are affected by moist conditions.

METHODS

1. High speed aspiration.
2. Low speed aspiration i.e. saliva ejector.
3. Rubber dam.
4. Dry guard™. This is placed over the parotid duct and can absorb large amounts of moisture.
5. Cotton wool rolls. They are cheap but they get saturated very quickly.
6. Cotton wool pledgets can dry cavities.
7. 3-in-1 syringe blows out compressed air to dry the cavity.
8. Astringent. This will stop any gingival bleeding. It is often used with retraction cord.
9. It is often best to treat all periodontal disease before placing permanent fillings. Even with rubber dam bleeding gums may risk contaminating deep interproximal cavities.

RUBBER DAM

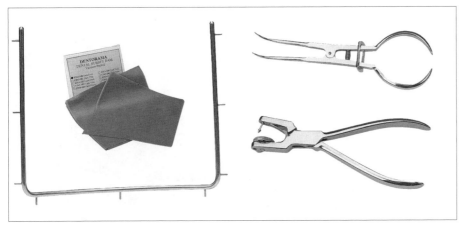

Figure 11.13 Rubber dam kit.. (Courtesy of Minerva.)

This is the most comprehensive way of isolating a tooth. A sheet of rubber is fitted over a frame. A hole is punched through the centre of the rubber with a rubber dam punch. A winged rubber dam clamp is positioned through the hole. Then by using clamp forceps both the clamp and rubber dam are placed as one over the tooth to be isolated. If several teeth need to be isolated the same number of holes are made in an arch in the rubber sheet. Only one clamp is required as the nurse uses dental floss to work the rubber between the teeth to hold the dam in position. Some rubber dams are anatomically shaped for easier use and patient comfort.

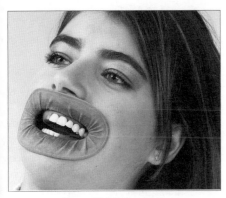

Figure 11.14 Optradam™.

As well as controlling moisture the rubber dam prevents the patient inhaling small instruments such as root canal files. It prevents water collecting in the back of the mouth making procedures more comfortable for the patient. It also retracts the soft tissues allowing better visual access. The rubber dam helps cross infection control by limiting the amount of bacteria caught up in the spray from the handpieces. It is particularly useful for placing composites and root canal treatment.

Remember the rubber dam is made from latex. Conventional rubber dams should not be used on patients with a latex allergy.

Q1. Moisture control is necessary for which of the following reasons?

    a. patient comfort
    b. collect the waste
    c. allow fillings to harden and stick
    d. save water

Q2. Methods of controlling moisture include which of the following?

    a. rubber dam
    b. asking the patient to swallow
    c. dry guards™
    d. saliva ejector

Q3. Which of the following are found in a rubber dam kit?

    a. clamps
    b. frame
    c. hole punch
    d. clamp forceps

How well did you do?
    A1.a,b,c   A2.a,c,d   A3.a,b,c,d

MATRIX BANDS

While reading the text answer the following;

Q1. What are the functions of a matrix band?

Q2. What are the advantages of sectional matrix bands?

Q3. What are the disadvantages of reusable Siqveland and Tofflemire matrix retainers?

Matrix bands are required when the interproximal surface of a tooth is being filled. They form a cuff around the tooth which prevents the filling material being pushed down the gingival crevice to form an overhang. They also allow a contact point to be made between the filling and the adjacent tooth

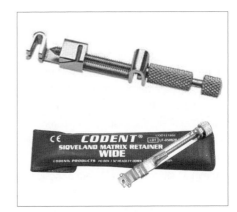

Figure 11.15 Siqveland and Tofflemire matrix retainers. (Courtesy of Minerva.)

The traditional matrix retainers and bands such as the Siqveland and Tofflemire are steadily being replaced by separation rings and sectional matrices.

The Siqveland retainers and bands come in two sizes; narrow and wide. As a rule of thumb the narrow bands are used for premolars and the wide for molars. Practice setting up both the Siqveland and Tofflemire retainers as they are complicated and the bands must be replaced between each patient. Both retainers must be scrubbed thoroughly before autoclaving as both have intricate areas which can harbour debris and microbes. Entirely disposable matrix systems based on the traditional matrix retainer system are available to combat this problem.

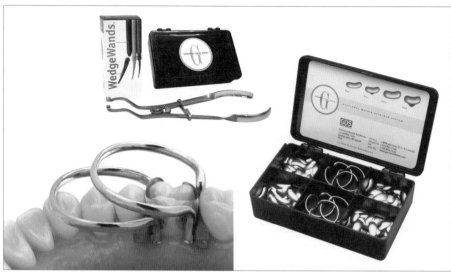

Figure 11.16 *Sectional matrices, separation rings, wedges and forceps. (Courtesy of Minerva and Garrison.)*

Sectional matrices are generally kidney shaped. They are disposable. These matrices provide a better placed contact point between the filling and adjacent tooth. Sectional matrices are held in place with wedges and/or separation rings. The separation ring is placed with sectional matrix forceps. If a rubber dam has not been placed it is wise to tie floss around the separation ring before placing, in case it is accidentally dropped and inhaled. Due to their simple design the separation rings are easily scrubbed and autoclaved and are considered more hygienic than reusable Siqveland and Tofflemire retainers.

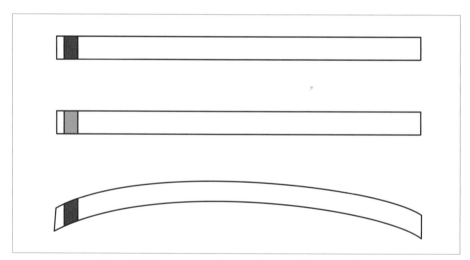

Figure 11.17 *Transparent matrix stripes. (Courtesy of Minerva and Kerr.)*

Siqveland, Tofflemire and sectional matrices are used for fillings in posterior teeth. Transparent matrix strips are used for anterior teeth. These may be curved or straight and are disposable. Transparent matrix strips are held in place with wedges. Wedges are either wooden or plastic and come in a variety of sizes. All are disposable.

They ensure that the matrix is adapted to the tooth eliminating the possibility of an overhang.

Q1. What are the functions of a matrix band?

  a. to make a contact point between the new filling and the adjacent tooth
  b. to form a cuff around the tooth to prevent an overhanging margin
  c. to help form the interproximal part of the filling
  d. to help form the base of a filling

Q2. What are the advantages of sectional matrices and separation rings?

  a. sectional matrices place the contact point in the correct position
  b. separation rings are easily scrubbed and sterilised
  c. due to their complicated design, separation rings can harbour microbes
  d. these small matrices and rings are impossible to inhale

Q3. What are the disadvantages of reusable Siqveland and Tofflemire matrix retainers?

    a. their complicated designs can harbour microbes
    b. they are difficult to scrub and sterilise
    c. the contact point is often in the incorrect position
    d. they require forceps to place them correctly

How well did you do?
    A1.a,b,c   A2.a,b   A3.a,b,c

WHAT'S IN A FILLING?

RESTORATIVE MATERIALS

PERMANENT RESTORATIONS

While reading the text answer the following;

Q1. What are the ideal properties of a permanent restorative material?

These are the characteristics of an ideal filling material. Permanent restorations should be strong enough to allow the patient to bite down hard. Biologically they must be compatible so they do not irritate the pulp or surrounding soft tissues. They should also last a number of years and ideally have the same wear as enamel so that they do not wear down too fast or wear the opposing teeth. All fillings should seal the cavity to prevent recontamination. It is also preferable for a filling to be tooth coloured.

Q1. Which of the following are ideal properties of permanent filling materials?

    a. biological compatible
    b. tooth coloured
    c. strong enough to wear the opposing teeth
    d. must last a couple of years

How well did you do?
    A1.a,b

Composites

While reading the text answer the following;

Q1. What are the three types of light cured composite.

Q2. What are the advantages of composite?

Q3. What are the disadvantages of composites?

These are tooth coloured restorations. They contain inorganic particles of silica suspended in resin. The particles of silica vary in size. Small particles alone are used in **microfine** composites. This enables them to be polished to a high sheen and have good aesthetics. Microfine composites are used for anterior fillings. However fillings in posterior teeth need to be stronger and harder wearing. **Hybrid** composites have a high content of particles of various sizes which makes them strong and durable. These are used for posterior fillings or composite cores.

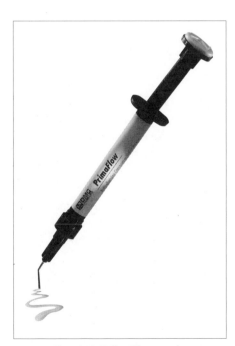

Figure 11.18 *Flowable composite.*
(Courtesy of Minerva and DMG.)

Flowable composites are mainly composed of resin. A single layer is used to line the cavity before placing a microfine or hybrid composite. They ensure that there are no voids between the bond and the composite filling and help to eliminate micro leakage. Flowable composites come in syringes. (The old chemically cured, two paste systems have been superseded by light cured composites and are rarely used now.)

ADVANTAGES OF COMPOSITES

1.   Great aesthetics which the patients like.
2.   Bonded composites adhere to the tooth so they seal the cavity.
3.   Light cured so the dentist controls the working time.
4.   Composites are at full strength after curing i.e. within seconds.
5.   Strong enough for back teeth even in large restorations.
6.   As composites are bonded to the tooth only minimal cavities are needed so sound tooth tissue is conserved. Usually there is no need for extensions or dovetails.
7.   Useful for restoring worn teeth without taking further tooth tissue away.
8.   The dentine bonds desensitise the teeth.
9.   As they are thermally nonconductive they do not need a base even in deep cavities.
10. Composites do not contain metal including mercury. Again most patients prefer this.

DISADVANTAGES OF COMPOSITES

1.   Technique sensitive and they require excellent moisture control.
2.   More expensive than amalgam.
3.   Care is needed with the etchant and curing light. But this is not complicated.

Q1. Microfine composites contain particles of various sizes. True or false?

Q2. Which of the following are advantages of composites?

    a. there are tooth coloured.
    b. they adhere to the tooth.
    c. they are at full strength by the end of the appointment.
    d. the dentist controls the working time.

Q3. Which of the following are disadvantages of composites?

    a. the tooth must be protected against thermal shock.
    b. they are technique sensitive.
    c. they irritate the pulp.
    d. they are more expensive than amalgam.

How well did you do?

    A1.False   A2.a,b,c,d   A3.b,d

ACID ETCH TECHNIQUE

While reading the text answer the following;

Q1. Describe the acid etch technique.

Q2. How do we use dentine primer and bonds?

Composite alone does not bond to enamel. At first the enamel surface needs to be specially prepared before the composite can be "glued" to it with a bond. Composite and bonds are moisture sensitive so good moisture control is required. The best moisture control is by rubber dam otherwise an array of dry guards, cotton wool rolls, saliva ejectors and the high speed suction are required.

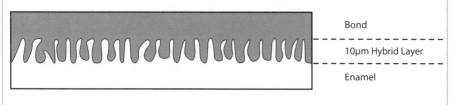

Figure 11.19 The bond between composite and etched enamel.

The enamel surface is prepared using the acid etch technique. An etchant of 33% phosphoric acid is placed on dry enamel for up to 30 seconds. It is precisely placed with an applicator or directly using a syringe. The aim is to partially demineralise the outer 10 micrometers of enamel. The enamel must not be over etched. The dentist may ask the nurse to time this part of the procedure so that they can concentrate on the tooth. (All surgery wall clocks should have a third hand to measure seconds.) This makes the outer layer of enamel porous. The enamel must be thoroughly washed with the 3-in-1 syringe for 1 minute to remove all the etchant. Again the nurse may have to time this part of the procedure as well as providing the suction. The tooth is then lightly dried for 5

seconds. The etched enamel appears frosty. The tooth is not over dried as this would decimate this delicate etched layer. The enamel bond is now placed on the tooth using a fibre tipped applicator or brush. When the bond is placed tags are formed within the porous enamel layer to form a solid layer of enamel and bond. This is called the hybrid layer and provides the adhesion.

Figure 11.20 Curing lights..
(Courtesy of Minerva, Kerr and SDI.)

The dentist cures the bond with the blue curing light while the nurse protects their eyes with the orange light screen.

DENTINE BONDS

Again dentine bonds are moisture sensitive so good moisture control is required. The best moisture control is of course rubber dam.

Figure 11.21 Dentine primer and bond. (Courtesy of Minerva and Kuraray.)

Dentine bonds often come in two bottles; the dentine primer and the dentine bond. The primer is self etching. This is placed all over the cavity both on the dentine and the freshly cut enamel. It is not washed off.

There is no post operative pain with dentine bonds as the tooth cannot be over etched.

In fact dentine bonds are often good desensitisers. The dentine primer is placed with a fibre tipped applicator or brush and is gently agitated within the cavity. After the required time, usually at least 20 seconds, the cavity is gently air dried. A thin layer of bond is placed with a fibre tipped applicator or brush and is light cured for 10 seconds with the nurse holding the orange light shield.

Every bonding system is different so both the dentist and nurse must read the manufacturer's instructions for the brand that they use. Every second is important. Some dentine bonds now come in one bottle as the primer and bond have been combined.

Dentine primers will etch dentine and newly cut enamel. However they will not etch uncut enamel. Uncut enamel must be etched with phosphoric acid first. Sometimes the dentist will etch the enamel, wash the tooth, dry it and then apply the dentine primer and bond, especially if there is very little remaining tooth so good adhesion is paramount.

Tip; Very little primer and bond is required per tooth. If no mixing is involved, it is better if the nurse drops the primer and bond directly from their bottles onto the clean applicator tips. Placing the primer and bond into dappen dishes first, wastes material. Also, the primer and bonds will evaporate from the dappen dishes changing the constituency. Always replace bottle caps immediately again to prevent evaporation.

Q1. During the acid etch technique which of the follow apply;

　　a. 22% phosphoric acid is used
　　b. 33% phosphoric acid is used
　　c. the etchant is placed on the enamel only
　　d. the etchant is placed on the enamel and dentine

Q2. Freshly drilled enamel does not need to be etched. Dentine primer and bond can be used instead and applied to both the dentine and enamel. True or false?

How well did you do?
　　A1.b,c　　**A2.True**

PLACEMENT OF COMPOSITES

1. The patient is anaesthetised.
2. The rubber dam is placed. Some dentists place this before preparing the cavity while others place it after cutting the cavity but before placing the filling. If a dam is not used a dry guard™ must be used for posterior teeth as cotton wool rolls are not enough. Again some dentists place this at the beginning while others place the dry guard™ just before filling the cavity.
3. All the decay is removed using the air turbine and friction grip diamond or tungsten carbide burs. The slow handpiece with latch grip round head burs and hand instruments such as excavators may have also been used.
4. The cavity is checked for retention and then disinfected. Even though composites are adhesive mechanical retention is thought to increase the lifespan of larger fillings.
5. The nurse places the saliva ejector in the patient's mouth. The cavity is washed and dried with the nurse assisting using the high power suction.
6. Matrix bands/stripes are placed if the restoration involves an interproximal surface and wedges are placed.
7. The enamel may be etched, washed and dried first if required. Dentine primer and bond are placed with applicators following the manufacture's instructions and light cured. The nurse protects their eyes with the orange light shield.
8. Next the flowable composite is handed to the dentist and a single layer is placed around the cavity. This is cured with the blue curing light. Again the orange light shield is used. Sometimes it is not necessary to use the flowable composite.

9. The stiff composite is placed in increments and cured between each increment. The nurse passes the composite gun and hand instruments back and forth to the dentist. Have a clean, dry tissue ready to wipe the end of the instruments. Some dentists use bond as a separator so that the composite does not stick to their instruments. The dental nurse should dim the overhead light so that the composite does not set prematurely.

10. The composite is placed and shaped with the flat plastic, burnishers and carvers.

11. The matrix band and rubber dam is removed and the final shape finished with polishing burs. The bite is checked with articulation paper / occlusal indicator paper. The filling may be polished with composite polishing discs, burs and paste.

SANDWICH TECHNIQUE

Some dentists like to place a base of glass ionomer in deep cavities. Calcium hydroxide liner is placed first to protect the pulp. The second layer is a thick base of glass ionomer. Then the enamel is etched and bond is applied and a third layer of composite is placed. This is called the sandwich technique. The glass ionomer should be light curable. It may be advantageous to use a resin modified glass ionomer to provide a bond between the glass ionomer and composite.

Amalgam

While reading the text answer the following;

Q1. What are the constituents of amalgam?

Q2. What are the advantages of amalgam?

Q3. What are the disadvantages of amalgam?

Amalgam has been in use for over 150 years. Amalgam consists of liquid mercury and a powder alloy which when mixed together form a solid mass. The alloy powder consists of approximately 40 to 70% silver, usually 20 to 30% copper and tin and zinc.

The mercury and alloy are mixed together in an amalgamator. The mercury and alloy are placed in their respective reservoirs and the machine mixes the required amount, called spools. Alternatively the amalgam comes pre-packed in capsules of varying amounts/spools. The capsules consist of compatible portions of mercury and alloy separated by a rubber membrane. As the amalgamator shakes the capsule, the rubber ruptures allowing the two to mix. This is the safer method of mixing amalgam as there is no risk of mercury spillage. Always take care to place the capsule firmly into the amalgamator and to close the lid before pressing the start button.

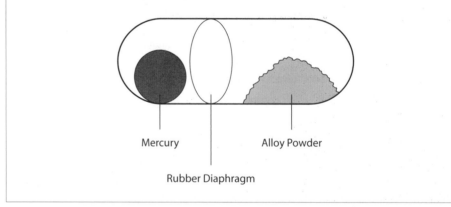

Figure 11.22 *Amalgamator and an amalgam capsule. (Courtesy of Minerva and Kerr.)*

Amalgam does not adhere to the tooth. For most fillings this is fine. However if retention is critical for example for a crown core when little tooth remains, the amalgam can be bonded to the tooth using a metal to tooth bonding system such as Panavia™.

ADVANTAGES OF AMALGAM

1. Cheap.
2. Technically easy to use.
3. Long lasting.
4. It is a well established filling material with decades of research.

DISADVANTAGES OF AMALGAM

1. Poor aesthetics.
2. Mercury is toxic. Care is needed when handling mercury and amalgam. Gloves must be worn. Sandals should not be worn.
3. Many patients to not like amalgam because of reasons 1 and 2 and also because of the negative press it has received in the media.
4. Amalgam often requires fairly extensive cavities. It is non adhesive so cavities need mechanical retention such as undercuts which involves the loss of sound tooth tissue.
5. Amalgam takes approximately 20 minutes to set and hours to achieve its top strength so patients have to take care of their amalgam fillings to prevent fracture on the day they are placed. Amalgams cannot be polished at the filling appointment for this reason.
6. Amalgam is metallic so liners and bases are needed to protect the pulp from thermal shock.
7. Waste mercury and amalgam need to be collected and disposed separately to other waste. The dental unit requires special filters to prevent waste amalgam entering the national water systems.

Q1. Which of the following are constituents of amalgam?

   a. tin
   b. silver
   c. lead
   d. copper

Q2. Which of the following are advantages of amalgam?

   a. it adheres to the tooth
   b. contains mercury
   c. cheap
   d. tooth coloured

Q3. Which of the following are disadvantages of amalgam?

   a. it is non adhesive to the tooth
   b. contains mercury
   c. must be lined
   d. takes hours to reach maximum strength

How well did you do?
   A1.a,b,d   A2.c   A3.a,b,c,d

LINERS AND BASES FOR AMALGAM FILLINGS

While reading the text answer the following;

Q1. What is the function of a liner or base?

Q2. What are the properties of calcium hydroxide?

Q3. What is the best way to mix cements?

Q4. What are the properties of zinc oxide and eugenol?

Liners and bases are important in protecting the living pulp from fillings which may chemically irritate the pulp or metal fillings which transmit temperatures causing thermal shock.

CALCIUM HYDROXIDE

Calcium hydroxide should be placed as a thin layer under all amalgam fillings. Calcium hydroxide encourages the growth of secondary dentine and so helps the dentine to repair. As it is also highly alkaline it kills any bacteria present. However calcium hydroxide is not strong and can only be used in a thin layer so in deep cavities a further base is required to prevent thermal shock.
Calcium hydroxide comes as two pastes; a base and a catalyst. Equal quantities are mixed on a paper pad with a metal applicator for 10 seconds. The colour should be uniform and streak free.

ZINC OXIDE AND EUGENOL

Zinc oxide and eugenol is used as a base for deep cavities. The cavity is dried and lined with calcium hydroxide and then a thick base of zinc oxide and eugenol is laid. When this is set the amalgam is placed on top.
The advantage of zinc oxide and eugenol is that it is sedative to the pulp. The disadvantage is that it cannot be used with composites as it stops them setting. Also some people are allergic to eugenol.
It comes as zinc oxide powder and eugenol (oil of cloves) liquid. These are mixed together on a glass slab with a metal spatula. Zinc oxide and eugenol is also useful as a temporary filling. A thick mix is required for a base or temporary.

GENERAL PRINCIPLES FOR MIXING MATERIALS

All material have;

1. A mixing time. This is the length of time that you have to mix the material. This may only be seconds.
2. A working time. This is the time the dentist has to place the material.
3. A setting time. This is the time the material takes to become hard. This time is important to the patient as they cannot bite on a filling until it has set.

A few general tips in mixing materials;

1. Read the instructions of any unfamiliar materials and follow them precisely.
2. Most materials set quicker in warmer weather.
3. If the material comes as two pastes put equal lengths of each. Mix until there are no streaks but only uniform colour.
4. If using a liquid the bottle should be completely inverted to get the correct droplet size.
5. When using powders shake the bottle before opening as some constituents may have settled.

6. If you are half way through mixing and need more powder use the other end of the spatula to dip into the bottle. Never contaminate a bottle.

7. Mix in the centre of the pad to prevent the powder flying everywhere.

8. For temporaries and bases a thick mix is required. For liners the same materials should be mixed to a "double cream" consistency.

9. Replace lids on bottles promptly to prevent evaporation.

10. Wipe the spatula immediately after mixing and clean the glass slab as soon as possible. Dried material is hard to remove!

Q1. The function of a liner or base is to protect the living pulp from thermal shock and chemical irritation from the permanent restoration. True or false?

Q2. Calcium hydroxide has which of the following properties?

    a. acidic
    b. kills bacteria
    c. alkaline
    d. encourages secondary dentine growth

Q3. The correct way to mix cements include which of the following?

    a. following the manufacturer's instructions
    b. shaking the bottle of powder first
    c. mixing two pastes until they are streaky in colour
    d. mixing liners to a "double cream" consistency

Q4. Zinc oxide and eugenol has which of the following properties?

    a. irritant
    b. can be used under composites
    c. can only be used in shallow cavities
    d. sedative

How well did you do?
A1.True   A2.b,c,d
A3.a.b.d   A4.d

WHAT DO I NEED TO KNOW?

SAFETY PRECAUTIONS REQUIRED WHEN USING AMALGAM

While reading the text answer the following;

Q1. How is mercury toxic?

Q2. List seven precautions that should be taken when handling amalgam.

Q3. What are the constituents of a mercury spillage kit?

Mercury is toxic. Mercury vapour is released at room temperature. This vapour is invisible and odourless and so it can be inhaled without knowing. More vapour is released at higher temperatures. Mercury can also be absorbed by the skin especially the nail cuticles. When using amalgam follow these safety precautions;

1. The surgery should be well ventilated.
2. Always use gloves, mask and safety glasses.
3. Use capsules rather than bottles of liquid mercury.
4. Use effective high speed suction when removing old amalgams.
5. Wear closed shoes not sandals (even in summer-sorry!)
6. Have a mercury spillage kit in the surgery and then handle mercury and amalgam so well that you never need to use it!
7. Dispose of waste amalgam in the special waste containers stored away from heat sources such as autoclaves and radiators. The special waste containers have chemicals which absorb the vapour.

MERCURY SPILLAGE

Figure 11.23 *Mercury spillage kit. (Courtesy of Minerva.)*

1. Immediately tell the dentist.
2. Always wear disposable gloves.
3. Globules of mercury can be drawn up with an intravenous syringe (without a needle) then placed in the amalgam waste container.
4. Waste amalgam is collected up in damp paper towels and then placed in the amalgam waste container.
5. Large spills can be rendered safe with a mercury spillage kit. This consists of equal parts of calcium hydroxide and flowers of sulphur which are mixed with water. Cover the contaminated area with the paste and wait for it to dry. This is then mopped up with damp paper towels and placed in the waste container.
6. For larger spillages or if you suspect mercury contamination contact the environmental health department to test for mercury vapour. Urine tests can detect any mercury within the body.

Early symptoms of mercury poisoning include fatigue, headaches, irritability, nausea and diarrhoea. These develop into hand tremors, visual disturbances, kidney failure and mental disturbances. (Remember the phrase "as mad as a hatter". In the olden days hat makers used mercury and subsequently went mad.)

Q1. Mercury can be absorbed through the skin and its vapour can be inhaled. True or false?

Q2. Which of the following precautions should be taken when handling amalgam?

a. always wear sandals
b. use the high speed suction when removing old amalgams
c. capsules are the safer way to mix amalgam
d. waste amalgam containers have chemicals which absorb mercury vapour

Q3. A mercury spillage kit contains flowers of calcium. True or false?

How well did you do?
A1.True   A2.b,c,d   A3.False

PLACEMENT OF AMALGAMS

While reading the text answer the following;

Q1. What liner and base are often used under amalgams?

Q2. How is amalgam mixed?

1. All decay is removed using the air turbine and friction grip diamond or tungsten burs. The slow handpiece with latch grip round head burs and hand instruments such as excavators may have also been used.
2. The cavity is checked for mechanical retention.
3. The nurse places the saliva ejector in the patient's mouth. The cavity is washed and dried with the nurse assisting using the high power suction.
4. If the cavity extends interproximally a matrix band is placed around the tooth and wedges are used.

5. Calcium hydroxide liner is mixed to a cream and placed with an applicator. If the cavity is very deep a zinc oxide eugenol base is placed. The nurse mixes this until it can be rolled. This allows the dentist to pack it, removing any voids. It will also set quicker.
6. The nurse mixes the amalgam in the amalgamator, places it in a pot and scoops it up into the amalgam carrier. The nurse then places the amalgam carrier into the dentist's hand. After the dentist has deposited it in the cavity the nurse takes back the carrier and hands over an amalgam plugger to condense the material. This continues back and forth until the cavity is full.
7. The filling is shaped with amalgam carvers and burnishers as it is setting until the anatomy of the tooth is restored. The dental nurse removes the saliva ejector and uses the wide bore suction to remove the excess amalgam.
8. The wedges and matrix band are carefully removed by the dentist and the filling is checked for overhangs.
9. The occlusion is checked and any high spots are removed.
10. The patient is warned not to chew on the tooth for several hours.

Q1. A good liner for amalgam is calcium hydroxide and if the cavity is deep a base of zinc oxide and eugenol is often added. True or false?

Q2. In which of the following is amalgam mixed?

a. rubber glove
b. amalgamator
c. dappen pot
d. agitator

How well did you do?
A1.True   A2.b

Glass Ionomer

While reading the text answer the following;

Q1. What is glass ionomer?

Q2. When is it used?

Q3. What are the advantages of glass ionomer?

Q4. What are the disadvantages of glass ionomer?

Q5. How are glass ionomers placed?

Glass ionomer is comprised of powdered glass and polyacrylic acid powder mixed with water. It also comes in compoules which are mechanically mixed and then inserted into the cavity with an injection gun.

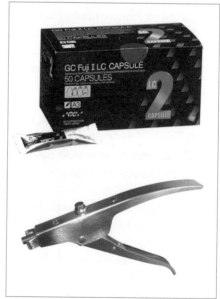

Figure 11.24 *Glass ionomer capsules and injection gun. (Courtesy of Minerva.)*

USES OF GLASS IONOMERS

1. They may be used in abrasion cavities in adult teeth as they bond to dentine. Abrasion cavities are also known as cervical cavities or Black's class 5 cavities.

2. Deciduous fillings. Minimum preparation is required as they bond to the tooth and the fluoride released helps to prevent secondary decay. As deciduous teeth have a limited lifespan the lack of strength and durability is not critical.
3. Base in deep cavities. It is usually placed over a layer of calcium hydroxide to protect the pulp from its acid content.
4. Temporary fillings.
5. Adhesive for orthodontic bands.

ADVANTAGES OF GLASS IONOMERS

1. Glass ionomers are adhesive to enamel and dentine.
2. They release fluoride in the first few months of placing making them cariostatic during this period.
3. They are tooth coloured.
4. Both light and chemically cured brands are available.
5. Glass ionomers can be strengthened by the addition of metal powder. These are called **cermets** e.g. Ketac silver™. They have also been combined with composites. These are called **compomers** e.g. Dyract™.

DISADVANTAGES OF GLASS IONOMERS

1. Glass ionomers are weak so they cannot be used for large cavities or on the biting surface of adult teeth. If the patient does not correct their brushing technique they can wear away cervical fillings very quickly.
2. They are sensitive to moisture during placement and setting. Chemical setting glass ionomers need to be protected with a coat of varnish or light cured resin.
3. Glass ionomers have a short life expectancy compared to amalgams and composites.

4. They stain easily so they can look tatty quite quickly. Polishing cannot take place until it has completely set (after several hours) unless a light cured glass ionomer has been used.
5. Critical mixing is necessary. The wrong texture quickly leads to failure.
6. Glass ionomer sticks to instruments.
7. Even though they are tooth coloured, they are quite opaque and often look unnatural.

Dentine bonds and composite are a good alternative to glass ionomer for restoring cervical cavities.

PLACEMENT OF GLASS IONOMERS

1. Often abrasion cavities are free from decay and no drilling is required. If there is decay this is removed in the normal manner with high and low speed handpieces and the appropriate burs.
2. The cavity is washed and dried.
3. The nurse places the saliva ejector while the dentist isolates the area with cotton wool rolls.
4. Polyacrylic acid conditioner is applied with an applicator for 10 seconds.
5. The conditioner is washed off and dried with the 3 in 1 syringe. The nurse assists with the high speed suction.
6. The nurse mixes the glass ionomer using the exact measure of water to powder.
7. The dentist places it in the cavity with a flat plastic. The nurse is ready with a wet tissue to wipe the instruments.
8. A cervical matrix foil can be used to provide a smooth finish.
9. Excess material is removed with hand instruments only. It cannot be polished that day.
10. The restoration is coated with varnished, petroleum jelly or light cured resin to protect it from moisture.

Q1. Glass ionomer is composed of which of the following?

    a. powdered glass
    b. polyacetic acid
    c. polyacrylic acid
    d. polycarboxylate

Q2. Glass ionomer is used in which of the following circumstances?

    a. cervical cavities
    b. deciduous teeth
    c. as a base
    d. Black's class 5 cavity

Q3. Which of the following are advantages of glass ionomers?

    a. they are adhesive to teeth
    b. they release fluoride
    c. they look better than composites
    d. they are very strong

Q4. Which of the following are disadvantages of glass ionomers?

    a. they are sensitive to moisture
    b. they stain easily
    c. they are not very strong
    d. they can wear down the opposing teeth

Q5. When placing glass ionomers which of the following apply?

    a. polyacrylic acid conditioner is applied
    b. polycarboxylate conditioner is applied
    c. a cervical matrix foil can be used
    d. it can be polished immediately

How well did you do?
    A1.a,c   A2.a,b,c,d   A3.a,b
    A4.a,b,c   A5.a,c

Temporary Restorations

While reading the text answer the following;

Q1. When are temporary fillings used?

Q2. What are the properties of zinc oxide eugenol?

TEMPORARY FILLINGS

Temporary fillings are often placed at emergency appointments or if the restoration of the tooth involves more than one appointment. In an emergency the patient may arrive at the surgery without an appointment and there may be insufficient time to place a permanent restoration. A temporary filling can be quickly placed on a fractured or carious tooth. Temporaries provide a physical barrier against extremes of temperature and prevent food, debris and further bacteria from entering the cavity. Some temporary filling materials contain eugenol and so provide a sedative effect on the pulp reducing pain.

Some temporaries come pre-mixed in a paste or putty form. These are simply placed in a dry cavity with a flat plastic and harden with time under the influence of mouth temperature. They are easy and quick to apply and adhere to the tooth. However they have little strength and should be replaced with a permanent restoration as soon as possible. Other temporary dressings come as a powder and liquid and must be mixed by the dental nurse. This is true of zinc oxide and eugenol temporaries. They should be mixed to a sticky putty-like consistency. These temporaries are harder than premixed ones and last longer. However all temporary restoratives are much softer than permanent filling materials. The larger the temporary the more likely it is to fall out if the patient does not return quickly. If a temporary is lost on a root filled tooth leakage will occur and bacteria will enter the root and may compromise the endodontic restoration.

TEMPORARY CEMENTS

When a patient has an indirect restoration a temporary crown, bridge or inlay must be placed while the permanent restoration is being constructed. The temporary crown, bridge or inlay is placed with a temporary cement so that it can easily be removed. Again these may or may not be eugenol based. They are mixed to a creamy consistency.

Q1. Temporary restorations are used for which of the following reasons?

    a. between root canal therapy appointments.
    b. they are used to protect fractured teeth at an emergency appointment
    c. to sedate a sore tooth
    d. to maintain the structure of a tooth to avoid food traps

Q2. Zinc oxide and eugenol has which of the following properties?

    a. irritant
    b. can be used under composites
    c. can only be used in shallow cavities
    d. sedative

How well did you do?
    A1.a,b,c,d   A2.d

12. Radiology

Dental radiography uses x-ray beams to produce an image of the teeth and jaws. The x-rays are produced by the x-ray set. They exit the set through the collimator which aims the beam and prevents scatter. These rays pass through the teeth and on to the radiographic film.

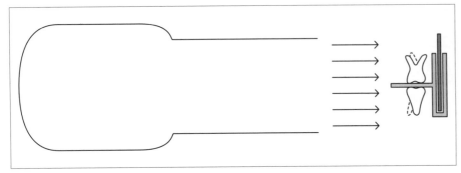

Figure 12.1 *Taking an x-ray.*

X-rays easily pass through soft tissue which look dark on film. However the beam cannot pass so easily through hard tissue which appears blank/white. The denser the tissue the lighter it looks on film. So enamel and metal look blank/white, dentine and bone appear grey and the pulp looks black. Decay involves a softening or demineralisation of the enamel and dentine and periodontal disease involves demineralisation of bone. This is why diseased tissue appears darker than healthy tissue. Dentists often describe this diseased tissue as "a shadow on the x-ray". For example a periapical abscess appears as a dark circle within the bone around the root apex.

WHY TAKE X-RAYS?

TYPES OF RADIOGRAPHS AND THEIR USES

While you work pay attention to the different types of radiographs and why they are taken. Try to anticipate which films will be required.

While reading the text answer the following;

Q1. List 6 types of dental radiograph.

Q2. When would each be used?

INTRA-ORAL FILM

Intra-oral film is placed inside the patient's mouth.

1. Bitewing radiograph.
- Used for the early detection of interproximal decay and deminerlisation.
- Also shows occlusal and recurrent decay.
- Detects overhangs and marginal deficiencies of existing restorations.
- Shows the bone levels.

2. Periapical radiograph.
- Detects periapical abscesses.
- Detects periodontal disease.
- Taken preoperative to extractions to reveal the shape and size of roots.
- Taken before crowning or bridging teeth to check that the roots and surrounding bone are adequate and healthy.
- May detect root fractures.
- Root treatment.

3. Occlusal radiograph.
- Detects unerupted teeth.
- Detects cysts.

4. Digital radiograph.
- Same uses as for bitewings and periapicals.

EXTRA-ORAL FILM

Extra-oral film is held outside the patient's mouth.

1. Panoramic radiograph.
- Overall view of both jaws which is useful for screening.
- Reveals impacted wisdom teeth.
- Orthodontics - shows developing jaws, unerupted teeth and retained roots.
- Bone pathology such as cysts, bone diseases, cancer.
- View the sinuses.
- Examine the TMJ (temperomandibular joint).
- Jaw fractures.
- Taken before implant surgery.

2. Lateral oblique.
- Children's dentistry to show unerupted teeth.

3. Cephalometric radiograph.
   For example frontal or lateral views of the skull. Used for;
- Orthodontics.
- Jaw surgery.

Q1. Which of the following are types of intra-oral radiographs?

   a. bitewing
   b. frontal view
   c. periapical
   d. panoramic

Q2. A bitewing is used to detect;

   a. periapical abscesses
   b. retained roots
   c. jaw fractures
   d. interproximal decay

How well did you do?
   A1.a,c A2.d

X-RAY FILM

While reading the text answer the following;

Q1. What are the components of a radiographic film packet?

Q2. What is an intensifier screen?

Q3. How should films be stored?

1. INTRA-ORAL FILM
Intra-oral films are used to take detailed pictures of small areas of the mouth. The standard size for periapicals and bitewings is 3 x 4cm. A smaller size is available for children and a larger one for occlusal views.

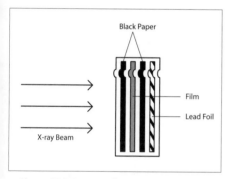

Figure 12.2 Contents of an intra-oral film packet.

The X-ray film is basically a black and white photographic film wrapped on both sides with black paper. This protects it from any light which would fog/darken the film. On the side furthest away from the x-ray tube is a piece of lead foil. This absorbs scattered radiation. All of this is wrapped in a sealed plastic envelope to protect it from moisture and light. On one corner of the sealed film is a pimple. This points outwards on the side that faces the x-ray tube.

2. EXTRA-ORAL FILM

Figure 12.3 Extra-oral film cassette. *(Courtesy of Minerva.)*

The unwrapped extra-oral films come together in a large packet that should only be opened in a dark room. The film is then placed in a metal cassette. The cassette is light proof when shut. On each inside cover of the cassette is an intensifier screen. These screens fluoresce on exposure to x-rays intensifying the image onto the screen. This greatly reduces the exposure time for the patient.
It is the nurse's role to load the cassettes and store the x-ray films. All films must be used within their expiry date and should be stored in dry conditions away from heat and the x-ray set.

Q1. The layers of a film packet in order from the collimator tube are;

    a. paper, lead, paper, film
    b. paper, film, paper, lead
    c. paper, lead, film, paper
    d. lead, paper, film, paper

Q2. The intensifying screens do which of the following?

    a. fluoresce on exposure to x-rays
    b. reduce exposure time
    c. increase exposure time
    d. decrease the dose of radiation required

Q3. Films should be stored in dry conditions away from heat and the x-ray set. True or false?

How well did you do?
    A1.b   A2.a,b,d   A3.True

119

TAKING INTRA-ORAL RADIOGRAPHS

While reading the text answer the following;

Q1. What is the paralleling technique?

Q2. What is the bisecting angle technique?

Dental nurses are not allowed to take x-rays unless they have had advanced dental nurse training in this subject. The x-ray set is switched on. The dentist decides the exposure time depending on the speed of the film used and the part of the mouth being x-rayed. The nurse places the film in the appropriate holder with the pimple facing the teeth. The dentist then places the film in the patient's mouth and the patient bites together on the holder and is asked to stay still. The x-ray tube/collimator is lined up with the x-ray holder and the dentist takes the x-ray. This is called the paralleling technique. The exposed film is removed from the mouth and holder and alcohol wiped. It is usually processed immediately but if not the patient's name and the date should be written on it. The x-ray set is switched off as soon as the radiographs have been taken as a safety precaution against possible radiation leakage from a faulty machine.

Before the paralleling technique was devised the patient had to hold the film in their mouth with their finger. The dentist then estimated the correct angle to place the tube using the bisecting angle technique. The dentist had to guess the angle of the teeth to the film, halve it and then aim the beam at 90° to this imaginary line. This was not accurate and lead to many distorted periapicals. The paralleling technique should be used whenever possible to achieve consistently good results.

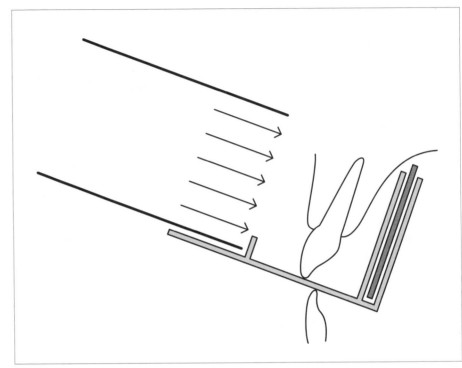

Figure 12.4 *Paralleling technique using a film holder.*

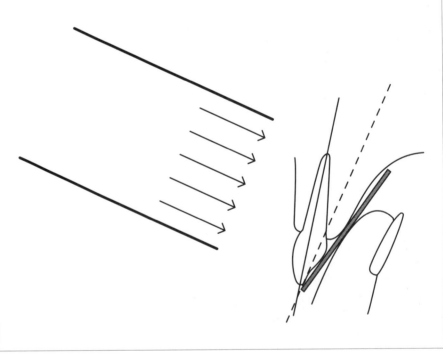

Figure 12.5 *Bisecting angle technique using the patient's finger.*

120

Q1. Which of the following are true of the paralleling technique?

  a. involves the patient holding the film with their finger
  b. should only be used after the bisecting angle technique has failed
  c. produces good consistent results
  d. involves the patient biting on the film holder

Q2. With the bisecting angle technique the collimator is placed at right angles to an imaginary line bisecting the angle between the long axis of the tooth and the film. True or false?

How well did you do?
  A1.c,d   A2.True

TYPICAL TYPES OF FILM HOLDERS

The dental nurse is often expected to preload the film holders for efficiency. The film envelope must always have the pimple pointing outwards towards the patient's teeth to ensure that the film comes before the lead. Bitewing holders should be loaded with a standard sized periapical film.

Figure 12.6 Bitewing holder.
(Courtesy of Minerva and Kerr.)

There are two types of periapical holder; one for the posterior teeth and one for the anterior. When loading the posterior holder a standard sized periapical film is used. The pimple should face towards the teeth and lie at the fixed end of the holder. If the pimple lies at the free end it may cover the apex of the tooth in the developed film distorting the image in this important region.

Figure 12.7 Posterior periapical holder.
(Courtesy of Minerva and Kerr.)

The anterior holder accepts the smaller periapical film. Again the pimple must face the teeth and lie at the fixed end of the holder.

Figure 12.8 Anterior periapical holder.
(Courtesy of Minerva and Kerr.)

TAKING EXTRA-ORAL RADIOGRAPHS

While reading the text answer the following;

Q1. What is the difference between panoramics and cephalometrics?

PANORAMICS

This requires a special x-ray set. Panoramics show the complete upper and lower jaws and sinuses. However it does not give the fine detail that an intra-oral film provides. The film was called an orthopantomograph (OPG) and is now called a dental panoramic tomography (DPT) or simply a panoramic. All terms are in wide use. The film is 13 x 31cm and placed in a cassette.
The patient stands upright and their head is gently held in the correct position by supports and by the patient themselves biting on a fixed peg. The patient's head must be in the centre of the machine so that the midline of the face corresponds to the midline of the radiograph. The motor driven tube and cassette sweeps around their head in an arc while taking the x-ray. The exposure time is approximately 15 seconds. The cassette is removed from the DPT machine and taken to the dark room to be opened and then processed in the same manner as an intra-oral film.

CEPHALOMETRICS

Again a special set called a cephalostat can be required but most DPT machines also take these films. Cephalostats take both frontal and lateral views of the skull. The patient's head is placed precisely using locating posts which fit into the ears and the film is taken. It measures the spatula relationship between the jaws, skull and teeth. This is useful in monitoring the orthodontic development of a child and in oral surgery when the jaw relationship is to be altered.

Q1. Panoramics show the jaws and sinuses whereas cephalometrics show either the front or side of the skull. True or false?

How well did you do?
A1.true

TAKING DIGITALS RADIOGRAPHS

While reading the text answer the following;

Q1. What are the advantages of digital radiography?

All the techniques discussed so far have involved using a chemical process to produce a radiograph. Now it is possible to get an intra-oral image within seconds using digital radiography. Instead of a film a reusable intra-oral sensor plate is placed in the mouth. The x-ray is taken with the same set but the image is not processed in the traditional manner. The exposed sensor plate is placed into a laser scanner connected to a computer. It then appears on the computer screen. The electronic sensor is so sensitive that only a fraction of the radiation dose is required. Also, as there is no chemical processing, there are no processing faults. Images can be sent immediately to other professionals who have computerised systems via email. The disadvantage of digital radiographs compared with traditional radiographs is that some of the details in the image may be lost. This is usually unimportant but in a few case can prove critical. Also the sensor plate is larger and so perhaps more uncomfortable for the patient than a standard periapical film.

Q1. Which of the following are the advantages of digital radiography?

a. a disposable sensor plate is used
b. the radiation dose is greatly reduced
c. an image is produced very quickly
d. the processing chemicals need to be changed frequently

How well did you do?
A1.b,c

WHERE DO I FIT IN?

PROCESSING RADIOGRAPHS

While reading the text answer the following;

Q1. In what order are the processing tanks?

Q2. Why are the tanks covered?

Q3. What is the optimum temperature for processing films?

Q4. What are the advantages of automated processing compared to manual?

Q5. How are films mounted?

X-ray film must not be exposed to light before it is fully processed. Processing occurs in a dark room using a red safelight or in a dark box looking through a light filtering window. Most modern practices use an automatic processor as the results are more consistent than manual processing. The dental nurse is responsible for developing the film and cleaning out the chemical tanks regardless of the method used. The nurse should always wear gloves as the chemicals are irritant. A dental tunic, a plastic apron, mask and glasses should also be worn to protect against splashes.

MANUAL FILM PROCESSING

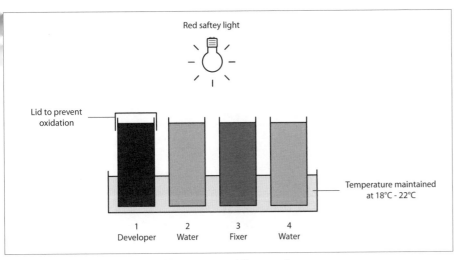

Red saftey light

Lid to prevent oxidation

Temperature maintained at 18°C - 22°C

1 Developer 2 Water 3 Fixer 4 Water

Figure 12.9 Manual film processing.

The film envelope is opened in the dark and the film is attached to a hanger. It is then dipped in succession into four different tanks. These tanks are covered to prevent oxidation of the solutions. First the film is lowered into the developer tank and then into the water to be washed. The film is then lowered into the fixer and then into the final water tank to be washed again. The film hanger is hung up to allow the film to dry naturally. The developer produces the image and the fixer fixes it onto the film.

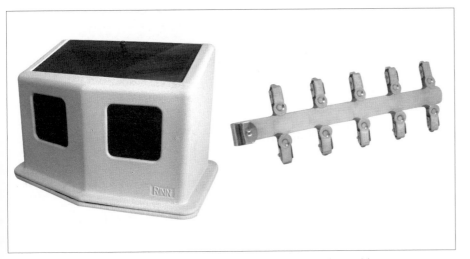

Figure 12.10 Dark box and hanger. (Courtesy of Minerva and Dentsply.)

If you do this manually you must follow the manufacturer's instructions to the letter. The temperature of the chemicals should be between 18°C to 22°C and the amount of time the film stays in the chemicals is critical and must be timed precisely. The manufacturer usually provides a table giving the correct times for developing and fixing at various temperatures. The film must be thoroughly washed between each step.

AUTOMATED FILM PROCESSING

Machine processing takes the uncertainty away. It heats up to the optimum temperature before allowing you to process the film. During automated processing the film goes along a conveyor belt which dips it into the four containers for the correct amount of time and then dries the film automatically. This method is a lot cleaner during film processing as the chemicals cannot splash your clothes. It also allows the dental nurse to continue assisting the dentist while the films are automatically being developed.

Whether manual or automated processing is used, the dental nurse must maintain these systems. It is the nurses role to change the chemicals when they deplete and to make sure that the four tanks are always full.

The films come out of the automatic processor dry so they can be mounted in a transparent plastic cover and the patient's name and the date taken recorded immediately. This decreases the possibility of lost films. Manually processed films are left to dry on their hanger first. The nurse must take care not to confuse different patient's x-rays while they are drying.

Films are best mounted in plastic covers as this protects them from damp hands and fingerprints. Always hold the film by the edge until they are mounted to avoid fingerprints. When mounting films the pimple should point upwards. They are mounted as they would appear on the charting. The radiographs are now ready to be viewed on an illuminated view screen. A magnifying glass can be used to view small details.

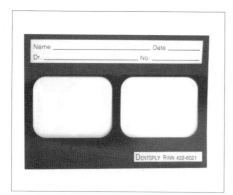

Figure 12.11 *Plastic film cover.*
(Courtesy of Minerva and Dentsply.)

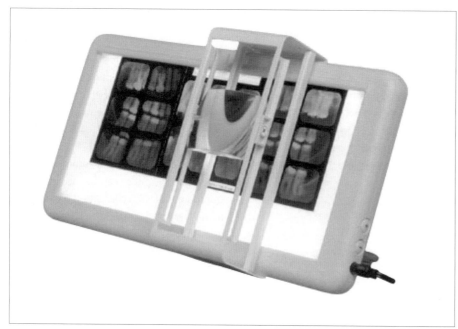

Figure 12.12 *X-ray viewer. (Courtesy of Minerva and Dentsply.)*

Q1. When processing films they are placed in tanks in the following order;

  a. water, developer, water, fixer
  b. fixer, water, developer, water
  c. water, developer, water, fixer
  d. developer, water, fixer, water

Q2. The tanks are covered to prevent oxidation. True or false?

Q3. The optimum temperature for developing films is;

  a. 18°C
  b. 18°C to 20°C
  c. 20°C to 22°C
  d. 18°C to 22°C

Q4. The advantages of automatic processing are;

  a. the machine keeps the chemicals at the optimum temperature
  b. the nurse is free to continue assisting the dentist
  c. the films come out dry
  d. the whole process is quicker manually

Q5. When mounting films which of the following apply?;

  a. the pimple should point upwards, towards you
  b. the pimple should point downwards, away from you
  c. the label should state the date the radiograph was taken
  d. the label should state the date the radiograph was developed

How well did you do?
**A1.d   A2.True   A3.d
A4.a,b,c   A5.a,c**

IT'S JUST TAKING A PICTURE-WHAT CAN GO WRONG?

FAULTS ON TAKING A FILM

While reading the text answer the following;

Q1. Give seven faults that can occur when taking a radiograph.

Q2. How can these faults be avoided?

Every time an x-ray is taken the patient is being irradiated. The law requires the dentist to have a good clinical reason for taking a picture in the first place. Any faults whether made during the taking or processing of a film are taken seriously. The reason why it happened must be noted and lessons learnt. This is called an audit.

1. BLANK FILM
* The cone was incorrectly placed or the patient moved so that the film was outside the x-ray beam. The dentist should ensure that the film is correctly placed and the patient is given clear instructions not to move.
* No film was placed in the cassette. Always replace an exposed film with a new one at the time of processing.

2. PARTIALLY BLANK FILM (CONING)
* Inaccurate aim of the tube by the dentist or the patient moved slightly before the film was taken. This shows as a curved or straight section depending on the cross section of the tube.
* Again care is taken placing the film. This is greatly helped by using a film holder. Clear instructions are given to the patient to keep still.

3. BLURRED FILM
* The patient moved during exposure.
* Clear instructions needed.

4. DISTORTION OR OVERLAPPING OF THE TEETH
* Incorrect angulation of tube to patient can produce foreshortening (where the teeth appear shortened), elongation (where the teeth appear to be stretched) or overlapping of the teeth.
* Again correctly align the tube to patient using film holders. Correct use of the head guides when taking panoramics and clear instructions to the patient to hold still are required.

5. DARK FILM
* Overexposure.
* Reduce the exposure time.

6. FAINT IMAGE
* Underexposure.
* Increase the exposure time.

7. FOGGED FILM
* The film has passed it's expiry date.
* Check before taking the film. Have an efficient stock taking method.

Q1. Which of the following faults can occur when taking a radiograph?

    a. coning
    b. blurred film
    c. foreshortening of the teeth
    d. elongation of the teeth

Q2. If the film is too dark it is;

    a. overexposed and needs the exposure time reduced
    b. overexposed and needs the exposure time increased
    c. underexposed and needs the exposure time reduced
    d. underexposed and needs the exposure time increased

How well did you do?
    A1.a,b,c,d   A2.a

SO WHAT PITFALLS SHOULD I LOOK OUT FOR?

FAULTS ON PROCESSING

While reading the text answer the following;

Q1. List 11 faults that can occur when processing a film.

Q2. How can these processing faults be avoided?

Processing is normally the dental nurse's role so you are directly responsible for these mistakes. Avoid them!

1. BLANK FILM
* No developer in the tank or the film was placed in the fixer before the developer.
* Care in refilling the tanks and placing them in the correct order.

2. PARTIALLY BLANK FILM
* Incomplete immersion of the film in the developer.
* Attach the film to the lower clips on the hanger and make sure that the tanks are full.

3. BLACK FILM
* Film was exposed to the light before processing.
* Check for light leakage in the dark room/box.

4. DARK IMAGE
* The film is over developed because it has spent too long in the developer or the developer was too strong or too warm.
* Follow the manufacturer's instructions.

5. FAINT IMAGE
- The film is under developed because it has spent too little time in the developer or the developer was too weak or too cold.
- Follow the manufacturer's instructions. The developer may need changing.

6. FADING IMAGE
- Insufficient time spent in the fixer.
- Follow the manufacture's instructions.

7. BLANK SPOTS
- Splashes of fix on the undeveloped film leaves transparent spots.
- Take care in processing.

8. BROWN OR GREEN STAINS
- The film is incompletely fixed.
- Make sure that the fixer is not old (change it regularly) and that you do not contaminate it with an unwashed hanger.

9. FILMS STUCK TOGETHER
- Films stuck to one another or the black paper.
- Take care to identify all the components especially when processing double films. (This is where two films are present in one envelope. This is useful when one film is to be sent off with a referral letter. The practice can keep the remaining copy.)

10. SCRATCHES OR FINGERPRINTS
- This is poor handling.
- Hold the film by the edges.

11. WHITE CRYSTALS
- This is due to inadequate washing after fixing.
- Wash well.

126

Q1. Which of the following faults can occur in processing a film?

    a. brown or green stains
    b. blank spots
    c. dark image
    d. overlapping teeth

Q2. A faint image can be due to;

    a. underexposure
    b. weak developer
    c. too little time in the developer
    d. the developer is too cold

How well did you do?
    A1.a,b,c   A2.a,b,c,d

AREN'T X-RAYS DANGEROUS?

HEALTH AND SAFETY

While reading the text answer the following;

Q1. What precautions are taken when using ionising radiation?

Q2. Name the three appointments required by law for practices using ionising radiation.

Q3. When are dental staff legally required to wear a dosemeter?

Q4. Who can take dental x-rays?

As x-rays cannot be seen, heard or felt it is easy to forget how dangerous they can be. Strict laws are in place to protect all members of staff working with radiation. Dental radiographs require low doses of radiation so patients should never receive an overdose. However it is the dentists and nurses who take the x-rays who are potentially most at risk as these small doses are repeated over a working lifetime.

1. All radiographs must be clinically justified.
2. Only suitably qualified staff may take x-rays.
3. The controlled area where x-rays are exposed should be clearly identified.
4. All x-ray machines must be regularly serviced and checked for radiation leakage. Automatic processors must be maintained and serviced.
5. The fastest films and/or intensifier screens should always be used to reduce exposure.
6. The smallest aperture for the film size should be used so that the surrounding tissues are not irradiated unnecessarily.
7. Film holders and the paralleling technique should be used in preference to the bisecting angle technique.
8. Only the patient should be in the radiation field when taking x-rays. The operators should be at least 2 meters away or behind a screen. The operators should never stand in the beam of the x-ray.
9. Ideally monitoring badges should be worn by staff. These are called personal monitoring dosemeters and are supplied and processed by the National Radiological Protection Board (NRPB).
10. Avoid repeating the same radiographs. All equipment should be well maintained and any faults reported to the dentist immediately. Ensure that there is no light leakage in automatic processors or light boxes.
Replenish chemicals regularly. Label films immediately to avoid lost x-rays.
11. X-ray machines should be switched off when not in use.
12. A quality assurance programme should be followed to ensure that no unnecessary exposure occurs because of poor technique or lack of training.
13. A risk assessment of the use of ionising within the practice must be reviewed every 5 years.

IONISING RADIATION LEGISLATION

The legal requirements to ensure the safe use of ionising radiation are governed by the following regulations;

- Ionising Radiation Regulations 1999 (IRR99)
- Ionising Radiation (Medical Exposure) Regulations 2000 (IRR(ME)2000)
  The Health and Safety Executive must be notified by the dental practice when x-ray equipment is first installed, if the practice moves to new premises or if there is a change of ownership of the practice.

FORMAL APPOINTMENTS AND IRR99

By law all dental practices must make the following formal appointments;

1. LEGAL PERSON
- The legal person is usually a senior dentist.
- Their job is to ensure that all members of staff comply with both sets of regulations.

2. RADIATION PROTECTION ADVISOR
- This is usually the company responsible for routine radiation surveys.
- The advisor is appointed in writing and offers advise for IRR99.

3. RADIATION PROTECTION SUPERVISOR
- The supervisor is usually a dentist.
- The supervisor understands the importance of complying with IRR99.
- They assess the risks of radiation and ensure these are kept to a minimum by implementing the correct procedures and precautions.

PATIENT PROCEDURES AND IRR(ME)2000
- The patient who needs a specific radiograph must be correctly identified before the exposure. This is authorised by the dentist.
- This procedure safe guards against patient identity mix-ups.

STAFF
- Dose levels should be kept below 1mSv (millisievert) per year for every member of staff.
- Personal dosemeters can monitor staff exposure.
- Dosemeters are legally required if more than 50 panoramic or 100 intra-oral exposures occur weekly.
- Pregnant staff should not be exposed to radiation.

PATIENTS
- Every exposure must be justified and doses should be kept as low as possible.
- A clinical audit should be carried out every 12 months to monitor this.
- To amass information for the audit, every film taken and processed should be recorded and a simple comment made on the quality and usefulness of the film. This book can be kept near the developer. This provides information for quality assurance.

WHO CAN TAKE X-RAYS
- All dentists can take and process x-rays.
- Suitably trained dental nurses may;

1. Process films.

2. Assist in the quality assurance program.

3. Press the exposure button, **in the presence and under the guidance of the dentist**.

- A dental nurse with a Certificate in Dental Radiography may also;

4. Select the exposure times and doses.

5. Position the patient and machine for the exposure.

Q1. What precautions are taken when using ionising radiation?

   a. dentists and nurses may stand in the beam if they are 2 meters away from the patient
   b. all radiographs must be justified
   c. x-rays should be taken in a designated area which people can walk through at any time
   d. a quality assurance program should be followed by every member of staff

Q2. Which of the following are appointments required by law for practices using ionising radiation?

   a. legal person
   b. radiation protection advisor
   c. radiation prevention supervisor
   d. radiation protection lawyer

Q3. When are dental staff legally required to wear a dosemeter?

   a. when they are pregnant
   b. when they take more than 50 intra-oral x-rays per week
   c. when they take more than 100 intra-oral x-rays per week
   d. when they take more than 50 panoramic x-rays per week

Q4. Who can take dental x-rays?

   a. student dental nurse
   b. a dental nurse with a Certificate in Dental Radiography
   c. a dentist
   d. a receptionist under the supervision of a qualified dental nurse

How well did you do?
   A1.b,d   A2.a,b   A3.c,d   A4.b,c

13. Periodontal Disease

" You don't have to brush your teeth - just the ones you want to keep".

While reading the text answer the following;

Q1. What does the periodontium comprise of?

Q2. What is the difference between periodontitis and gingivitis?

Periodontal disease is the disease of the supporting tissues of the teeth. The supporting tissues are the gums, periodontal ligament and alveolar bone. These are known collectively as the periodontium.
Periodontitis is inflammation of all the supporting tissues. (perio=periphery, dont=tooth, itis=inflammation)
Gingivitis is inflammation of the gums alone. (gingiv=gingivae=gums, itis=inflammation)

Periodontal disease is one of the commonest diseases of mankind. Periodontal disease starts early in life but takes longer to progress than caries. This means that whereas decay is often found in children and young adults, periodontal disease generally tends to become more obvious in older patients. It also tends to go through phases where it is more active than at other times. Any condition that lowers the immune system will allow periodontal disease to flourish.

Q1. The periodontium comprises of which of the following?

    a. periodontal ligament
    b. tooth
    c. alveolar bone
    d. gingivae

2. Periodontitis is the inflammation of the periodontal ligament, bone and gums. True or false?

How well did you do?
    A1.a,c,d   A2.True

SO WHAT DOES GUM DISEASE LOOK LIKE?

THE APPEARANCE OF PERIODONTAL DISEASE

While reading the text answer the following;

Q1. What are the main features of a healthy periodontium?

Q2. What are the main features of gingivitis?

Q3. What are the main features of periodontitis?

HEALTHY PERIODONTIUM

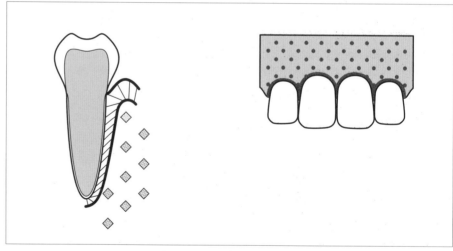

Figure 13.1 *Healthy periodontium.*

1. The gums are pink, dull and stippled (like orange peal).
2. There is a tight gingival cuff around the tooth with a gingival crevice of 2mm or less. This is called a normal pocket.
3. There are "knife-edge" papillae between the teeth.
4. The gums do not bleed on probing.
5. The mouth is virtually free from plaque because it is removed thoroughly twice a day.

GINGIVITIS

1. The gingivae appear red, swollen and shiny.
2. There are false pockets. These are apparently deep but are actually due to the swelling of the gums.
3. The gums bleed on probing and brushing.
4. Plaque is visible at the gingival margins.
5. Supra-gingival calculus may be present.
6. Start of halitosis (bad breath).

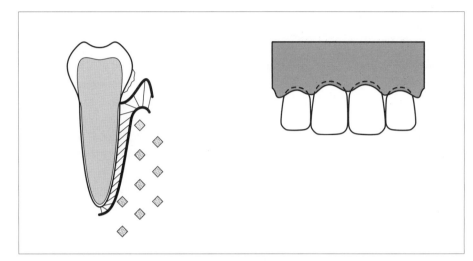

Figure 13.2 Gingivitis.

CHRONIC PERIODONTITIS

1. The gingival may be inflamed or may appear normal as the active disease is happening deep down in the depths of the pockets.
2. True pockets have formed which become deeper as the disease progresses. These pockets are due to bone loss.
3. The gums bleed on probing.
4. Supragingival and subgingival calculus are present.
5. New and old plaque are present in large amounts. (This can be demonstrated with a two tone disclosing solution.)
6. The teeth become mobile.
7. Periapical x-rays reveal bone loss.
8. Recession is present and may even expose furcation areas.
9. Pus may be extruded from lateral periodontal abscesses that may be present. In severe cases it may even flow spontaneously.
10. Halitosis.

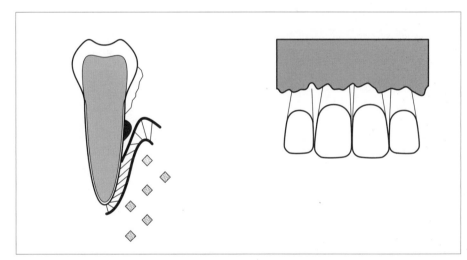

Figure 13.3 Chronic periodontitis.

Q1. What are the main features of a healthy periodontium?

    a. red gums
    b. pockets of 2mm or less
    c. bleeding only on probing
    d. knife-edge papillae

Q2. What are the main features of gingivitis?

    a. pink gums
    b. swollen gums
    c. true pockets
    d. bleeding on brushing

Q3. What are the main features of periodontitis?

    a. false pockets
    b. normal pockets
    c. true pockets
    d. mobile teeth

How well did you do?
A1.b,d   A2.b,d   A3.c,d

CAUSE OF PERIODONTAL DISEASE

While reading the text answer the following;

Q1. What is the sole cause of periodontal disease?

Q2. What factors increase plaque retention?

Q3. What factors exasperate gum disease?

The sole cause of periodontal disease is the build up of plaque. Periodontal disease can not occur if the plaque is regularly removed. This means that the patient has to actively participate in their treatment for lasting success. The dental nurse may have to explain the cause of gum disease to the patient. The nurse needs to be able to explain what will happen if it continues unheeded. Often the patient has no pain and is unaware of the situation. The nurse needs to be able to motivate patients into caring for their teeth and gums.

However any factor that encourages the retention of plaque should be eliminated if possible. These include the following;

1. Poor dentistry.
    The dentist has a responsibility to produce fillings with flush margins and good contact points. Food traps develop from overhanging fillings and ill designed prostheses which allow stagnation areas to facilitate the build up of plaque.
2. Crooked teeth.
    Young patients with crowded teeth should be diagnosed early during their routine check ups and offered orthodontic treatment not only to improve the appearance and bite but also to remove stagnation areas and so facilitate their oral hygiene.

Once present, periodontal disease can be exacerbated by any of the following factors;

1. Smoking.
2. Hormonal changes such as pregnancy, puberty and the contraceptive pill.
3. Dry mouths. Mouth breathers and people with incompetent lip seal tend to dry out the gingivae. Saliva washes away plaque and contains antibodies which help protect us against the bacteria found in plaque. So when the gums are dry they are more prone to periodontal disease.
4. Certain medical conditions such as diabetes, leukaemia, AIDS, stress and vitamin C deficiency.
5. Certain medicine such as some immunosuppressant, epilepsy and hypertension drugs.

Q1. What is the sole cause of periodontal disease?

    a. calculus
    b. deep pockets
    c. plaque
    d. flossing

Q2. What factors increase plaque retention?

    a. smoking
    b. diabetes
    c. overhanging fillings
    d. immunosuppressant

Q3. What factors exasperate gum disease?

    a. stress
    b. faulty heart valves
    c. epilepsy medication
    d. smoking

How well did you do?
    A1.c   A2.c   A3.a,c,d

HOW DO WE KNOW IF THE PATIENT HAS GUM DISEASE?

PERIODONTAL ASSESSMENT

While reading the text answer the following;

Q1. In the BPE how is the mouth divided?

Q2. How is the score per sextant obtained?

Q3. What do the values from 0 to 4 mean in a BPE?

Q4. What is the difference in accuracy between the BPE and a full periodontal pocket chart?

Q5. Which probe is required for a full charting?

PERIODONTAL PROBES

These are blunt ended probes with graduations to measure periodontal pocket depths.

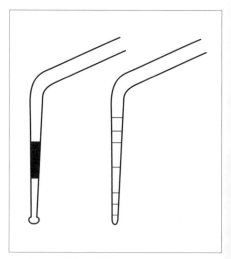

Figure 13.4 *BPE (CPITN or WHO) probe and pocket measuring probe.*

PERIODONTAL RECORD CHARTS

Periodontal disease is often painless. The first sign of gum problems is bleeding on brushing but this is often dismissed by the patient as unimportant. For these reasons periodontal disease would progress unchecked and undetected until late in the disease process but for the dentist examining the gums at routine check ups. The main way in which the periodontium is monitored is by probing. The state of the gums is recorded on periodontal charts.

1. BASIC PERIODONTAL EXAMINATION (BPE)
   Here the mouth is divided into six segments and the teeth are probed with the BPE probe.

upper right molars & premolars	upper canines & incisors	upper left molars & premolars
lower right molars & premolars	lower canines & incisors	lower left molars & premolars

The BPE probe has a broad band on the centre. The teeth in each sextant are quickly probed and the deepest measurement for that sextant is recorded as a single numerical score as follows;

0 = Normal pockets, no bleeding, no treatment required.

1 = The band is visible but there is bleeding on probing (BOP). No calculus present. Oral hygiene instructions (OHI) are needed.

2 = The band is visible but there is BOP and calculus. A routine scale and OHI are required.

3 = The band is partially covered. A full assessment is required as periodontitis is present.

4 = The band is fully covered. A full assessment is required as advanced periodontitis is present.

* = Furcation involvement or recession.

As the name implies this is a basic examination of the gums and if a score of 3 or 4 is reached in any sextant a full pocket charting is required in that sextant.

2. FULL PERIODONTAL CHART
   This records six pocket readings around every tooth using the pocket measuring probe. It is very precise! The dentist and hygienist can pin point the exact problem areas and treat and monitor them closely. The actual pocket depths are recorded and so the numbers correspond to this depth in millimetres. (The numbers are not a code.) If you are recording these numbers on a computer it usually also spontaneously provides you with a diagram of the gum. This is a good visual aid to show the patient when explaining the extent of the problem as it is so visual. Electronic probes will record the depth and relay them to the computer without the need for a nurse!

Q1. In the BPE the mouth is divided into how many areas?

   a. 2
   b. 4
   c. 6
   d. 8

Q2. In the BPE the deepest pocket reading in the sextant is recorded as a single numerical code from 0 to 4. True or False?

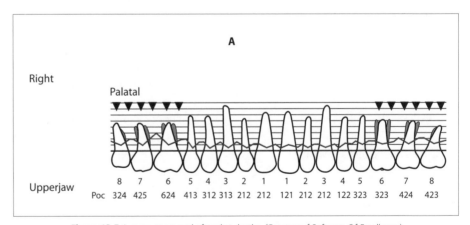

Figure 13.5 A computer record of pocket depths. (Courtesy of Software Of Excellence.)

Q3. In the BPE what does the value 2 mean?

    a. there is bleeding on probing, calculus present and on probing the band is totally covered

    b. there is bleeding on probing, calculus present and on probing the band is partially covered

    c. there is bleeding on probing and calculus present but on probing the band remains uncovered

    d. the halitosis is so bad two masks must be worn

Q4. The BPE gives one overall value for up to 6 teeth whereas a full periodontal chart gives 6 actual pocket depths for each tooth. True or false?

Q5. Which probe is required for a full charting?

    a. straight probe

    b. CPITN probe

    c. pocket measuring probe

    d. BPE probe

How well did you do?

    A1.c A2.True A3.c A4.True A5.c

3.   RECESSION CHART

While reading the text answer the following;

Q1. What is the advantage of recording the recession on a computer screen?

Q2. What does a bleeding chart record?

Q3. How is mobility graded?

Q4. What level of plaque is acceptable in the mouth?

If the recession is pronounced a full recession chart is taken at the same time as the full pocket chart using the pocket measuring probe. Again computers will record this both numerically in millimetres and visually. The computer spontaneously adapts the visual pocket depth to the recession line to give an accurate picture of how much (or little!) bone is supporting the teeth.

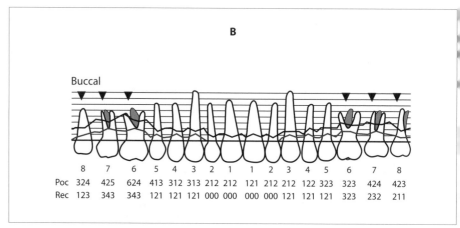

Figure 13.6 *A computer record of pocket depths and recession. (Courtesy of Software Of* Excellence.)

4.   MOBILITY

The mobility of a tooth is graded as follows;

1 = The tooth moves from side to side by less than 2mm.

2 = The tooth moves from side to side by more than 2mm.

3 = There is also vertical movement.

5.   BLEEDING CHART

This simple records whether there was bleeding at the site probed. Bleeding is a sign of active disease. Periodontal disease progresses at different rates which often correspond to the general health of the patient. If the patient is "run down" the periodontal disease will flourish.

6. PLAQUE SCORES

Plaque is recorded as present or not on a chart with four surfaces (mesial, distal, buccal/labial and lingual / palatal) for each tooth. At the end this is totalled and an overall score of less than 10% is considered satisfactory.

$$\frac{\text{Total number of surfaces with plaque}}{\text{Total number of teeth} \times 4} \times 100 = \text{The percentage of plaque present.}$$

Dental computers work this out automatically saving time.

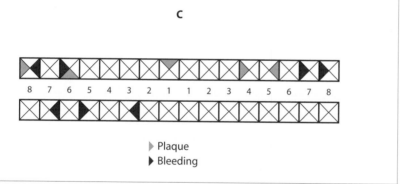

Figure 13.7 *A computer record of plaque and bleeding scores. (Courtesy of Software Of Excellence.)*

Q1. The advantage of recording the recession on a computer screen is that it gives a visual picture of the loss of bone which is a good teaching aid for the patient. True or false?

Q2. What does a bleeding chart record?

a. the severity of the bleeding
b. the time it takes for the gums to start bleeding
c. simply whether a site bled or not when probed
d. whether the patient is a haemophiliac

Q3. What does a mobility of grade 2 mean?

a. the tooth moves from side to side by 2mm
b. the tooth moves up and down by 2mm
c. the tooth moves from side to side by more than 2mm
d. the tooth moves from side to side by less than 2mm

Q4. What level of plaque is acceptable in the mouth?

a. None
b. 8%
c. 1%
d. 4%

How well did you do?
A1.True   A2.c   A3.c   A4.a,b,c,d

THE PROGRESSION OF PERIODONTAL DISEASE

While reading the text answer the following;

Q1. How does the bacteria found in plaque irritate the gums?

Q2. Why do gums bleed?

Q3. What is calculus composed of?

Q4. Why do teeth become mobile?

Q5. Which diseases are associated with periodontitis?

GINGIVITIS

1. Plaque is not removed and starts to build up around the gingival margins.
2. Because the mouth is warm, moist and receives a regular food supply the bacteria in the plaque multiply to form colonies.
3. The bacteria in the outer surface of the plaque breathe aerobically (with oxygen). However the bacteria in the inner layers of the plaque do not have access to oxygen and breathe anaerobically (without oxygen). These anaerobic bacteria produce acid and toxic by-products.

4. These irritate the gingivae, initially causing acute (short term) gingivitis which progresses to chronic (long term) gingivitis. The gums become shiny, red and swollen producing false pockets. They bleed easily due to micro-ulceration of the gingival crevice. The patient may notice this when they brush their teeth.

5. The patients get halitosis (bad breath) which becomes more and more pronounced as the disease progresses. Unfortunately it is other people and seldom the patients themselves who notices this.

6. Saliva contains minerals which become incorporated within the plaque to form supragingival calculus (tartar).This is a creamy yellow colour.

7. The rough surface of the calculus further facilitates plaque formation.

8. This is chronic gingivitis and is completely reversible at this stage if treated.

PERIODONTITIS

1. However when left untreated the whole periodontium becomes involved. Toxins and bacteria enter the underlying tissues through microscopic ulcers which have formed deep in the gingival crevice forming true pockets.

2. The bacteria destroy the periodontal ligaments, working their way down the root surface. When this happens the periodontal pockets become too deep for the patient to clean.

3. Due to the build up of subgingival plaque, subgingival calculus develops which is black/brown in colour due to the incorporation of blood products.

4. Eventually the alveolar bone becomes involved.

5. The destruction of the ligaments and bone leads to mobile teeth. Periodontitis is not usually painful so the patient may present at this stage because their anterior teeth are splayed (due to drifting) or are wobbly.

6. The gums recede exposing the root surface.

7. There may be periodontal abscesses where pus is weeping from the deep pockets. This places a load on the patient's immune system.

8. The oral bacteria continually enter the systemic blood system which can potentially lead to an increased risk of stroke and heart disease.

9. Teeth with grossly diseased periodontium tend to extrude from their sockets as the body tries to shed them.

Gingivitis can occur in less than 48 hours. (Stop cleaning your teeth and they will soon feel furry as the plaque builds up. Brush and floss just a day later and you will see blood on rinsing!) However periodontal disease progresses from start to finish over many years.

Q1. Bacteria found in plaque irritate the gums by producing toxins? True or false?

Q2. Gums bleed because the bacteria in the plaque cause tiny gingival ulcers. True or false?

Q3. From which of the following is calculus composed?

a. plaque
b. minerals
c. blood products
d. bacteria

Q4. Why do teeth become mobile?

a. loss of the periodontal ligament
b. loss of alveolar bone
c. loss of enamel
d. loss of fluoride

Q5. Which diseases are associated with periodontitis?

a. stroke
b. heart disease
c. in-growing toe nails
d. conjunctivitis

How well did you do?
**A1.True   A2.True   A3.a,b,c,d
A4.a,b   A5.a,b**

TREATMENT OF PERIODONTAL DISEASE

1. ORAL HYGIENE INSTRUCTIONS (OHI)

Periodontal disease is directly caused by the retention of plaque. As our mouths are moist, warm and naturally harbour bacteria we continually produce plaque. Every individual must effectively remove this plaque twice daily to maintain good oral health. It is up to the dental team to explain this and motivate the patient. Most people do brush twice a day but are not cleaning their teeth effectively and tend to rush this chore. This needs to be diplomatically put to them. It is important to "win the patient over" and not to be condescending. All periodontal treatment will be ineffective unless the patient is persuaded to clean their mouths effectively. It is our job to find a method that fits in with the patient's lifestyle and ability.

Effective removal of plaque is achieved by the following methods;

TOOTH BRUSHING AND TONGUE BRUSHING

- The teeth should be brushed twice a day.
- A minimum of 2 minutes is needed to brush all the teeth.
- The Bass method is recommended.
- Patients who are prone to periodontal disease may also need to brush their tongues to decrease the flora found there. Tongue brushes are now widely available.
- Electric toothbrushes when correctly used often remove more plaque than manual brushes. They are particularly useful for people with reduced manual dexterity, for example arthritic patients, and their chunky handles are easier to grip.

INTERDENTAL BRUSHING

- Patients generally find interdental brushes much easier to use than floss which means that they are more likely to integrate them into their oral hygiene routine.
- The interdental brushes come in a range of different sizes and can be matched precisely to the size of the patient's interdental spaces.
- They are quick and efficient to use.

FLOSSING

- Tape removes more interdental plaque than floss.
- Waxed floss is useful for tight contacts.
- The disadvantage of flossing is that the patient needs to be dextrous. Flossing is also time consuming so patients can get disheartened very quickly.
- Floss is now sold on holders to make it more user friendly.

TOOTHPASTES

- Periodontal patients often have exposed roots which may be sensitive. Certain toothpastes such as Sensodyne™ and Duraphat 2800™ will desensitise the root surface. Care must be taken with toothpaste containing a high concentration of fluoride. They must be stored out of reach of small children.
- Periodontal patients often complain of bad breath or a bad taste in their mouth. Most toothpastes and mouthwashes just mask this problem. However Retardex™ toothpaste and mouthwash will solve the condition by chemically eliminating volatile sulphur compounds (VSC) which cause halitosis.

MOUTHWASHES

- Antibacterial mouthwashes may be used in the short term to help get an acute infection under control or after periodontal surgery when the gums are tender. They are definitively not an alternative to efficient tooth brushing and interdental cleaning. The most effective antibacterial mouth washes contain chlorhexidine. Unfortunately this stains the teeth.
- A soothing mouth rinse for patients with ulcers and sore mucosa is Aloclair™. This coats the ulcer providing pain relief.

2. SCALING

While reading the text answer the following;

Q1. How can supragingival calculus be removed?

Q2. How does an ultrasonic scaler work?

Q3. What caution should be taken with an ultrasonic scaler?

SUPRAGINGIVAL SCALING AND POLISHING

Calculus cannot be removed by the patient as it is a hard mineralised deposit. It must be removed by the dentist or hygienist with hand instruments or an ultrasonic scaler. The working edges of hand instruments need to be kept sharp either using a sharpening stone or sending them to a professional sharpener.

Fine supragingival calculus can be difficult to remove between crowded lower incisors. The Prophyflex™ can remove this. It should not be used on patients with lung complaints such as asthma. The Prophyflex™ is best described as a "miniature sandblaster" as it sprays a mixture of water and aluminium oxide powder onto the teeth removing fine supragingival deposits from the nooks and crannies. It cannot be used subgingivally.

After scaling the teeth are polished with prophylactic paste and a brush or polishing cup in the slow handpiece. A smooth tooth surface prevents plaque build up and allows the patient to experience and remember how a clean mouth should feel.

Ultrasonic scalers vibrate at very high frequencies and shatter the calculus deposits. They are very efficient at removing mineralised substances. They need to be water cooled as the vibration quickly generates heat. Suction is always needed to remove the water and calculus chips. The ultrasonic scaler cannot be used on patients with artificial pacemakers as it may disrupt the heart rhythm. Also hearing aids should be switched off. The ultrasonic scaler emits a high pitched noise and all patients should be warned of this and reassured that it is not a drill. Patients' comfort levels vary enormously during subgingival scaling. All patients should be given the option of local anaesthetic during treatment. This may mean that they need two appointments as only half the mouth is anaesthetised at any time.

Q1. How can supragingival calculus be removed?

    a. drill
    b. hand scalers
    c. Prophyflex
    d. ultrasonic scaler

Q2. An ultrasonic scaler works by vibrating at a high frequency shattering the calculus. True or false?

Q3. Which of the following patients need to avoid the ultrasonic scaler?

    a. those with heart murmurs
    b. prosthetic heart valves
    c. rheumatic fever
    d. pacemaker

How well did you do?
    A1.b,c,d   A2.True   A3.d

136

Figure 13.8 Prophyflex.
(Courtesy of Minerva and Kavo.)

SUBGINGIVAL SCALING

Subgingival calculus is particularly hard and can be difficult to remove. There are various designs of hand scalers and ultrasonic tips. All are shaped to contour the root surface as every bit of calculus must be removed. Often the cementum is removed as well. With periodontitis any bone loss is permanent but the periodontal ligament will reattach if the calculus is totally removed and good oral hygiene is maintained. As the ligaments heal the junctional epithelium also reattaches and the depth of the periodontal pockets return to normal. This may result in recession and exposure of the root surface and patients should be pre-warned of this. Subgingival instruments tend to be finer than supragingival instruments. They have longer shanks as they must access deep pockets.

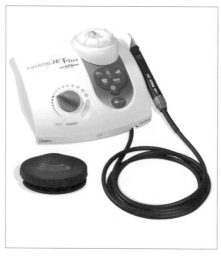

Figure 13.9 Ultrasonic scaler.
(Courtesy of Minerva and Dentsply.)

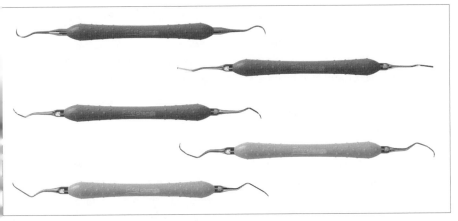

Figure 13.10 *Hand instruments. (Courtesy of Minerva and Dentsply.)*

WHAT DOES THE PATIENT NEED TO KNOW?

PREOPERATIVE INSTRUCTIONS FOR SCALING

While reading the text answer the following;

Q1. How can patients help with the treatment of their periodontal disease?

- Patients must be committed to improving their oral hygiene to overcome their gum disease.
- Local anaesthetic is available if required.
- The teeth may be sensitive for a few days after treatment especially if there is recession. This can be reduced with fluoride varnishes, desensitising toothpastes and fluoride mouthwashes.
- After treatment the pockets will reduce and the resulting shallow pockets may be easily cleaned by the patient. However regular hygiene appointments are recommended to remove newly formed calculus and to keep the patient motivated. These may be required every 3 months.

- Smoking encourages gum disease and delays healing. The patient should consider giving up smoking. One incentive is that the teeth will be free from tobacco stains at the end of the treatment.
- Treatment for advanced periodontal disease may result in recession exposing root surfaces which may be unsightly and require cosmetic treatment in extreme cases.
- If shallow, maintainable pockets cannot be achieved by scaling alone periodontal surgery may be necessary. (This is a good motivator for patients to improve their oral hygiene!)

Q1. How can patients help with the treatment of their periodontal disease?

    a. stop smoking
    b. brush more efficiently
    c. regularly visit the hygienist
    d. rely solely on antibiotics

How well did you do?
    A1.a,b,c

3. ANTIBIOTICS

While reading the text answer the following;

Q1. What antibiotic is used for gum disease?

Q2. What are the various forms of metronidazole?

A short course of systemic antibiotics may be used to treat an acute periodontal infection. The antibiotic of choice is metronidazole. The patient takes a short three day course of metronidazole tablets. They must be warned not to take any alcohol as it will react with the metronidazole making the patient nauseous and sick. These antibiotics reduce the inflammation enough to allow the dentist or hygienist to comfortably scale the patient's teeth. Antibiotics alone will not cure gum disease. If the patient does not return for further treatment and does not improve their oral hygiene the infection will quickly return.

Instead of prescribing systemic antibiotics, the dentist may place topical metronidazole into deep pockets after scaling them thoroughly. This topical metronidazole may be in the form of a gel (in a syringe) or a chip. Some brands need to be stored in the fridge to prolong their shelf life. The dental nurse should remove the topical metronidazole from the fridge at the beginning of the appointment. By the time scaling has been completed the gel will have reached room temperature and the dentist will be able to place it in the depths of the pocket.

Q1. What antibiotic is normally used for gum disease?

    a. penicillin
    b. amoxicillin
    c. acyclovir
    d. metronidazole

Q2. What are the various forms of metronidazole?

    a. gel
    b. chips
    c. tablets
    d. lozenges

How well did you do?
    A1.d   A2.a,b,c

4.   PERIODONTAL SURGERY

While reading the text answer the following;

Q1. What is a gingivectomy?

Q2. How is the area dressed after a gingivectomy?

Q3. When is flap surgery necessary?

Q4. What instruments are required?

GINGIVECTOMY

This is the removal of persistent false pockets which are often caused by drugs used to treat epilepsy and high blood pressure or suppress the immune system. The overgrowth of the gum is called gingival hyperplasia. The excess gum may be removed with a Blake's gingivectomy knife. The blade is at right angles to the handle making it easier to contour the gums.

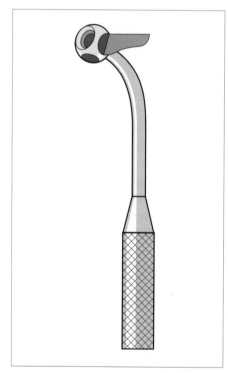

Figure 13.11 *Blake's gingivectomy knife.*

After use the blade is removed from the handle using a needle holder to prevent "needle stick injury" and immediately disposed in the sharps bin. After the gingival hyperplasia is removed the resulting raw wound is dressed with a zinc oxide and eugenol dressing. Some dressings such as Coe-pak™ do not contain eugenol. Coe-pak™ comes in two pastes or in automix cartridges. If mixing manually, equal lengths of paste are mixed on a large pad or glass slab. They should be mixed rapidly until no streaks remain.

After healing the gingivectomy allows the patient to thoroughly clean their teeth. However, if their oral hygiene slips and plaque starts to accumulate, the gum overgrowth will return.

FLAP SURGERY

Most periodontal disease is treated successfully by scaling and improving the oral hygiene. However in some cases persistent deep periodontal pockets may need to be eliminated and the gum recontoured by flap surgery. Local anaesthetic containing a vasoconstrictor is administered. The vasoconstrictor reduces bleeding allowing a clearer operating field. A flap is raised using a scalpel and periosteal elevator. The flap is held aside with a periosteal tissue retractor exposing the bone. This allows direct access to the pockets. These can be thoroughly cleaned and all contaminated cementum and subgingival calculus are removed with hand scalers. The nurse aspirates to maintain a clear visual field. Any granulation tissue is also removed. The bone may even be contoured but care is taken to preserve as much bone as possible. The flap is then sutured back into place in a more apical position to eliminate the deep pockets. Suturing involves using dissecting forceps, needle holder, suture needles and scissors. The patient returns to have the sutures removed. There will be noticeable root exposure after surgery of which the patient should be forewarned. After healing the patient will find the area far easier to maintain.

Q1. A gingivectomy is the removal of excess gum. True or false?

Q2. How is Coe-pak™ mixed?

    a. until it is streaky
    b. two equal measures of paste
    c. on a small pad
    d. on a glass slab

Q3. Flap surgery may be necessary for persistent deep pockets which are impossible to clean. True or false?

Q4. What instruments are required for periodontal surgery?

    a. periosteal elevator
    b. retractor
    c. scalpel
    d. suturing kit

How well did you do?
A1.True   A2.b,d   A3.True
A4.a,b,c,d

SPECIFIC TYPES OF PERIODONTAL DISEASE AND MUCOSA CONDITIONS

While reading the text answer the following;

Q1. What is pericoronitis?

Q2. How is acute herpatic gingivitis treated?

Q3. How does Lichen Planus present?

Q4. How is Lichen Planus treated?

Q5. What causes ANUG?

Q6. How is ANUG treated?

Q7. How is a lateral periodontal abscess treated?

PERICORONITIS

Pericoronitis is inflammation of the gum overlying a partially erupted tooth. It is most common in impacted lower wisdom teeth. Because the tooth is trapped in the partially erupted position, the gum flap persists. It is hard for the patient to clean under the gum so plaque accumulates until there is an acute flare up resulting in painful pericoronitis. Treatment involves irrigating debris from under the gum with saline or chlohexidine. Antibiotics are prescribed in severe cases. Recurrence is prevented by removing the gum flap or extracting the wisdom tooth.

ACUTE HERPETIC GINGIVITIS

Unlike other cases of gingivitis this is not caused by bacteria or poor oral hygiene. It is caused by the herpes simplex virus and usually affects infants. The oral mucosa as well as the gingivae may be involved. They are covered in tiny ulcers which are very painful. The condition is short lived. However the antiviral drug, acyclovir, will further shorten the illness if started early. The patient may not be able to eat much but should have plenty of fluids, a soft diet and plenty of rest. It is highly contagious. After the mouth has returned to normal the virus will remain in a dormant state. It can be reactivated at a later stage and present as a cold sore or new mouth ulcers. Reactivation can occur with strong sunlight or colds and flu.

LICHEN PLANUS

Lichen planus is an autoimmune disorder. It can present on the oral mucosa or skin. In its mild form this condition can be seen as lacy white lines on the attached mucosa and causes little problems and requires no treatment. However it can present as gingivitis with the gums swollen, red and fragile. Areas of mucosa slough off leaving painful ulcers. Lichen planus may be initiated by stress. Sometimes a short course of steroids is needed. The oral hygiene should be maintained to a high level as any plaque or calculus will further aggravate the condition. A soothing mouthwash such as Aloclair™ which coats the ulcers can provide some pain relief.

ACUTE NECROTISING ULCERATIVE GINGIVITIS (ANUG)

This is caused by poor oral hygiene and often occurs in teenagers and young adults. The attack may be precipitated by a lowering of the patient's immune system from stress or a systemic infection such as a cold or flu. It occurs suddenly and presents as red, swollen ulcerated gingival with yellowish necrotising areas. ANUG is characterised by pain and halitosis. The infection is caused by spirochaetes and fusiform bacteria. It is treated initially with a three day course of metronidazole. Chlorhexidine mouthwash can be used during this period. Both of these kill the bacteria and so reduce the pain and inflammation. The patient is then recalled for scaling and oral hygiene instructions to prevent recurrence.

ACUTE LATERAL PERIODONTAL ABSCESS

This occurs when an acute abscess forms in an existing (chronic) periodontal pocket down the side of a vital tooth. Treatment involves draining the pus, scaling the area and then placing metronidazole deep into the pocket. Oral hygiene instructions are reiterated and regular hygiene appointments are recommended. If the pocket is too deep to maintain, periodontal surgery is an option or extraction.

Q1. Pericoronitis is inflammation of the gum covering a partially erupted tooth. True or false?

Q2. How is acute herpatic gingivitis treated?

   a. antibiotics
   b. acyclovir
   c. antiviral drug
   d. antifungal drug

Q3. How does Lichen Planus present in the mouth?

   a. lacy white lines
   b. swollen red gums
   c. mucosa sloughs off
   d. ulceration of the mucosa

Q4. How is Lichen Planus treated?

   a. antibiotics
   b. antiviral drugs
   c. steroids
   d. antifungal drugs

Q5. What causes ANUG?

   a. poor oral hygiene
   b. poor immune system
   c. heart disease
   d. spirochaetes

Q6. How is ANUG treated?

   a. improve the patient's oral hygiene
   b. give penicillin
   c. give metronidazole
   d. scale

Q7. How is a lateral periodontal abscess treated?

   a. drain the pus
   b. scaling
   c. metronidazole
   d. improve oral hygiene

How well did you do?
   A1.True   A2.b,c   A3.a,b,c,d
   A4.c   A5.a,b,d   A6.a,c,d
   A7.a,b,c,d

14. Crowns, Bridges and Inlays

DIRECT AND INDIRECT RESTORATIONS

While reading the text answer the following;

Q1. What is the difference between a direct and non direct restoration?

INDIRECT RESTORATIONS

Inlays, crowns and bridges are all examples of indirect restorations. They involve the final restoration being constructed outside the mouth. They are usually made in a laboratory by a dental technician but can be made in-surgery using a ceramic machine. Indirect restorations are rigid and so the tooth must be prepared without any undercuts so that the finished restoration can be fitted. Cements or bonds are used to keep these restorations permanently in place. They often require two appointments; the first to prepare the tooth and the second to fit the final restoration.

DIRECT RESTORATIONS

Direct restorations are made entirely within the mouth without the use of impressions. Plastic filling materials such as composite and amalgam are often used. These materials flow into the undercuts before setting hard. Direct restorations are normally completed in one appointment.

Q1. Which of the following are indirect restorations?

    a. amalgam filling
    b. composite inlay
    c. gold inlay
    d. composite filling

How well did you do?
    A1.b,c

IMPRESSION MATERIALS USED FOR INDIRECT RESTORATIONS

While reading the text answer the following;

Q1. Name two types of "rubber" impression material.

Q2. What are the properties of rubber impression materials?

Q3. How are rubber impression materials disinfected?

Q4. Name the main types of tray used to take impressions of prepared teeth.

Q5. How is the bite recorded?

Every impression material used to record the prepared teeth must be very accurate to show every minute detail and stable so that it will not distort during transit between leaving the surgery and being cast up at in the laboratory. They must also be elastic so that they do not tear on removal from the mouth. These impression materials have a rubber like consistency when set and so are commonly referred to as rubber impressions. There are two main types; addition silicone and polyether.
Unlike alginate, they do not dry out and do not need to be sent wrapped in wet tissue. However they should be carefully rinsed in cold water and placed in 1% sodium hypochlorite (bleach) solution. They are then rinsed again with cold water, dried thoroughly with the 3-in-1 syringe and carefully wrapped before dispatching to the laboratory.
Alginate is often used to record the opposing teeth but is not accurate enough to record the prepared teeth.

IMPRESSION TRAYS

It is recommended that an impression of at least half an arch is taken in each tray. A full arch will give the technician even more information.

There are two main types of stock tray in use:

1.   FIRM, DISPOSABLE, PERFORATED PLASTIC TRAYS

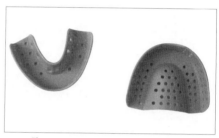

Figure 14.1 *Upper and lower stock trays. (Courtesy of Minerva and Codent.)*

These are single-use, non flexible trays of perforated plastic. An alternative to these are reusable perforated metal trays. When using these trays three impressions are required;

1.   A rubber impression of the prepared teeth.
2.   An opposing impression in alginate.
3.   The bite.

The bite is recorded with wax or mousse in centric occlusion. A big disadvantage of wax is that it can easily distort especially with heat. Mousse is reliable and stable. The dentist will require a scalpel to trim a mousse bite to eliminate any soft tissue recordings as only the occlusal recording should be handed to the technician.

The upper and lower impressions are cast up individually by the technician. The bite is then used to articulate the separate upper and lower models into centric occlusion. Centric occlusion is where the teeth interdigitate the most.

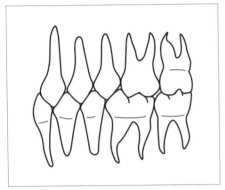

Figure 14.2 *Teeth in centric occlusion.*

2. BITE REGISTRATION TRAYS

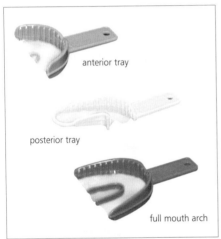

anterior tray

posterior tray

full mouth arch

Figure 14.3 *Bite registration trays.*
(Courtesy of Minerva and Perfection Plus.)

These trays record the prepared teeth, the opposing teeth and the bite all at the same time.
Rubber impression material is the only impression material used in these trays.
These trays provide a time-saving, accurate impression. The technician casts this impression up as one.

Q1. Which of the following are "rubber" impression materials?

    a. alginate
    b. addition silicone
    c. polyether
    d. composite

Q2. What are the properties of rubber impression materials?

    a. they do not tear
    b. they are dimensionally unstable
    c. they are accurate
    d. they distort

Q3. How are rubber impression materials disinfected?

    a. with alcohol
    b. with diluted bleach
    c. under running water alone
    d. with sodium hypochlorite

Q4. Name the types of tray used to take impressions of prepared teeth.

    a. flexible perforated plastic trays
    b. perforated reusable metal trays
    c. bite registration trays
    d. firm reusable plastic trays

Q5. How can the bite be recorded?

    a. with wax
    b. with composite
    c. with mousse
    d. with bite registration tray

How well did you do?
    A1.b,c A2.a,c A3.b,d
    A4.b,c,d A5.a,c,d

RETRACTION CORD

While reading the text answer the following;

Q1. What is the purpose of retraction cord?

Q2. Describe the single step impression technique.

Q3. Describe the wash impression technique.

Q4. How are polyether impression pastes mixed?

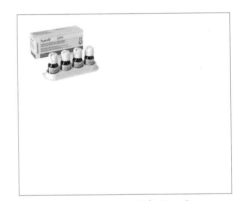

Figure 14.4 *Retraction cord of various diameters. (Courtesy of Minerva and Septodont.)*

It is important to take a detailed impression of the margins of the prepared teeth. Most margins are placed just above the gingival crevice and the margins of anterior crowns are actually placed just within it so the gingival crevice needs to be included in the impression. To get an accurate impression of the gingival crevice, this area has to be widened. This is often achieved with retraction cord.

The retraction cord is first soaked in a haemostatic agent. The soaked cord both widens the crevice and stops any bleeding. The teeth must be dry for a good impression. One or two cords may be placed around each tooth. Two cords will open the gingival crevice further. The cords are left in place for approximately 4 minutes to get maximum benefit before removing and taking the impression. It is the nurses role to cut the cord to the required length (usually about 3 centimetres) and soak them in the haemostatic agent. They are placed in a dappen dish before being placed on the dentist's bracket table. Some haemostatic agents stain so avoid splashing on clothing.

METHODS OF TAKING AN IMPRESSION

First the trays must be lightly coated with the appropriate adhesive. Different impression materials have different adhesives. The adhesive must overlap onto outer surface of the tray so that the borders of the impression are firmly fixed to the tray. In bite registration trays the mesh should not be coated.

The trays are place to one side while the impression materials are prepared.

ADDITION SILICONES

Addition silicones are used at two consistencies; heavy-bodied and light-bodied. The heavy-bodied material records the basic shape of the teeth and supports the light-bodied material which flows into every nook and cranny and so records the fine detail.

he light-bodied material is automatically mixed using a dispenser gun. The heavy-bodied material may come in a cartridge for a dispenser gun or as putty in two tubs. The disadvantage of using the putty is that the material is affected by latex gloves so the nurse has to change to vinyl gloves when mixing otherwise the material will not set properly. The dispenser gun cleanly, quickly and efficiently mixes the impression material. However before placing a new nozzle on the gun make sure that both cartridge openings are running freely as one or both can become blocked with set material. The nozzle of the gun containing the light-bodied paste can be fitted with a fine tip for greater precision.

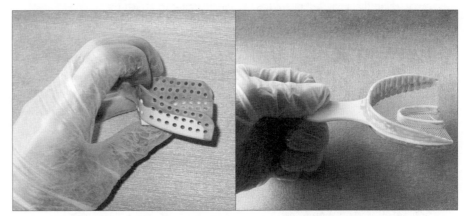

Figure 14.5   *An upper tray with adhesive.*   *A bite registration tray with adhesive.*

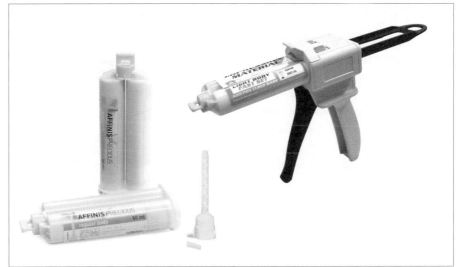

Figure 14.6 *Nozzle, fine tip and dispenser gun loaded with cartridge. (Courtesy of Minerva and Whaledent.)*

There are two methods of taking a silicone impression.

1. SINGLE STEP TECHNIQUE
   The dental nurse mixes the heavy-bodied impression material while the dentist mixes the light-bodied. The nurse places a small quantity to one side and places the remaining bulk into the tray. The dentist syringes a small quantity onto the bracket table and then the bulk of the light body around the prepared teeth. This is done simultaneously. The loaded tray is then placed in the patient's mouth and kept still in the correct position until both the light and heavy bodied materials have set. This is determined by checking the small test quantities which were placed to one side. The impression is then removed and checked by the dentist for distortion or voids.

2. WASH TECHNIQUE
   The heavy body is mixed by the nurse, a test quantity is placed to one side first and the rest is placed in the tray. Again this is handed to the dentist and placed in the patient's mouth until set. This impression is then removed from the mouth and dried. The light bodied is mixed and a thin wash is placed over the dry teeth and the set impression is immediately reinserted back into the mouth. When the wash has set the impression is removed again and checked by the dentist for distortion or voids. The disadvantage of this method is that it is more complicated, time consuming and tiring for the patient and dental team. It also relies on reseating the impression correctly. The dentist may use a scalpel to place venting grooves in the initial impression to allow the excess wash to flow out of the tray.

Tip; When using a dispenser gun always use the **first** part of the mixed impression material as the tester not the last. If both pastes did not extrude evenly at first this part of the impression material will not set correctly. It is better to have this part as the tester rather than around the crown preparations.

POLYETHERS

Polyether impression paste is traditionally used in one consistency. It is often used with a reusable syringe. However it is now available in cartridges to be mixed in automatic mixing machines.
The reusable syringe comes in three parts; the nozzle, main body and plunger. Remember to attach the nozzle to the body before you start to mix to save time. Apply the polyether adhesive to the tray. The dental nurse squeezes equal lengths of both pastes onto a large waxed paper pad. The nurse mixes the two pastes until the colour is even and no streaks remain. The reusable polyether syringe is then loaded by scooping it across the pad of paste.

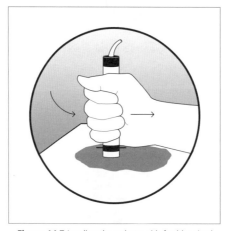

Figure 14.7 Loading the syringe with freshly mixed polyether impression material.

The dental nurse inserts the plunger and hands the syringe to the dentist to syringe around the dried prepared teeth. In the meantime the nurse scoops up the rest of the polyether with the mixing spatula and loads the tray. This is then passed to the dentist to place over the teeth. After it has set the impression is removed and the patient is sat up to rinse. Polyether is stiffer than silicones and the tray can be more difficult to remove from the mouth.
Tip; Wait for the polyether to set completely before dismantling the syringe. The set material will easily pull away from the syringe in one piece.
Disinfect the polyether impression and dry it thoroughly before sending it to the technician. These impressions may distort with moisture. Polyether is a highly accurate material but not the nurse's favourite as it is so messy to use.

Q1. What is the purpose of retraction cord soaked in haemostatic agent?

    a. to deepen the gingival crevice
    b. to widen the gingival crevice
    c. to enable a good impression of the margin to be taken
    d. to stop gingival bleeding

Q2. Which of the following describes the single step impression technique?

    a. a heavy-bodied impression is taken and when it has set a light-bodied wash is taken
    b. the heavy and light bodied impression materials are used at the same time
    c. the nurse and the dentist must mix their impression pastes at the same time
    d. the light and heavy bodied impression materials set together

Q3. The wash impression technique is a two stage technique that involves taking a light body impression of the teeth using the set heavy body impression. True or false?

Q4. What is the dental nurse's role in mixing polyether impression paste?

    a. the nurse mixes the two pastes
    b. the nurse loads the syringe
    c. the nurse loads the tray
    d. the nurse takes the impression

How well did you do?
    A1.b,c,d   A2.b,c,d   A3.True
    A4.a,b,c

CEMENTS AND BONDS USED TO FIT INDIRECT RESTORATIONS

While reading the text answer the following;

Q1. What is the difference between a luting cement and a bond?

Q2. Name the different types of dentine bonds.

Q3. What are the properties of zinc phosphate?

Q4. What are the properties of zinc polycarbonate?

Q5. What are the properties of glass ionomer?

For many decades indirect restorations were cemented on to teeth with luting cements.

These cements adhered to the dentine to various degrees but often did not adhere well to both the restoration and the tooth. The retention of the indirect restoration relied greatly on the walls of the preparation being as tall and as near parallel as possible. Often one of the main functions of a luting cement was to fill the space between the restoration and the prepared tooth. This space was kept as small as possible by taking accurate impressions.

However there are now many different bonding systems which are capable of actually bonding tooth to metal or porcelain. Dentine bonds greatly increases retention allowing teeth to be conserved that may otherwise have been extracted.

However the same principles of making the preparations as tall and near parallel as possible and taking an accurate impression still apply when using dentine bonds.

DENTINE BONDS

- Dentine bonds have been developed to bond dentine to etched porcelain, metal and composite. This improves the retention of any restoration. Dentine bonds usually come with a primer. This primer contains etchant. After 20 seconds it is lightly air dried but not washed before the bond is placed. It is impossible to over etch the tooth so there is no post operative pain. Indeed dentine bonds are desensitising. The bond is then placed and resin tags are formed in the dentine. The bond hardens when cured. There are three different ways in which a dentine bond can set; light, chemical or duel cure.

- The light cure systems require direct access to the blue curing light. These dentine bonds are used to line the cavity before placing the plastic core material. The overhead and room lights will begin to cure these bonds if they are left out in dappen dishes. This is why these bonds come in black light-proof bottles.
  Always replace the tops on these bottles immediately and put the bond straight on the applicator when it is required and not before.

- The chemical cured dentine bonds usually come as two pastes and begin to chemically bond when mixed together. They are used in areas where a curing light cannot reach. They are useful for cementing posts and the metal wings of adhesive bridges.

- Duel cured dentine bonds will set both chemically and with the curing light. This means that when a crown, bridge, inlay or post is placed with a duel cured bond, the margins can by cured by the blue curing light while the rest of the bond sets chemically underneath.

The advantage is that thedentist can control the setting of the margins which seals the restoration, protecting the rest of the bond as it chemically sets.

ZINC PHOSPHATE CEMENT

- This comes as zinc phosphate powder and phosphoric acid liquid.
- It is mixed on a cool thick glass slab with a metal spatula.
- Unlike all other materials the longer you take to mix zinc phosphate the longer the working time. So mix by adding tiny amounts of powder at a time if the dentist requires a longer working time.
- Advantages; It is adhesive to dentine and it sets very hard within a few minutes.
- Disadvantages; It does not bond to metal or porcelain used in crowns and bridges. As it is acidic it would irritate the pulp in deep cavities.
- Practical tip; Soak the glass slab in water to remove the dried cement.

ZINC POLYCARBOXYLATE CEMENT

- The powder contains zinc oxide and polyacrylic acid. The liquid is water.
- It is mixed on a glass slab or paper with a metal spatula.
- Uses; It is used as an alternative to zinc phosphate as a luting cement.
- Advantage; It is more adhesive to dentine and less irritating than zinc phosphate
- Disadvantages; It sticks to instruments.
- Practical tips; Dip the tips of your instruments in the dry cement powder first to prevent the mixed cement sticking to them. Wash the instruments in water before the cement sets.

GLASS IONOMER CEMENT

- Glass ionomer is comprised of powdered glass and polyacrylic acid powder mixed with water.
- It can be mixed by hand however it also comes in compoules which are mechanically mixed and then inserted into the crown with an injection gun.
- Uses: In adult teeth it is used as a permanent filling for cervical cavities, as a temporary filling or as a luting cement.
- Advantage; It releases fluoride initially. It also adheres to dentine, enamel and metal.
- Disadvantage; Critical mixing is necessary. The wrong texture quickly leads to failure. Glass ionomers stick to instruments. The glass ionomer margins need to be protected from moisture while it is setting.
- Practical tips; Use a wet tissue to wipe the instruments to prevent the glass ionomer sticking to them.

Q1. How are crowns made to stay fixed to the tooth?

- **a.** making the prepared tooth as short as possible
- **b.** making the sides of the prepared tooth close to parallel
- **c.** using an adhesive bond which adheres the prepared tooth to the crown
- **d.** placing undercuts in the prepared tooth

Q2. Name the different types of dentine bonds.

- **a.** light cured
- **b.** duel cured
- **c.** chemical cured
- **d.** mechanical cured

Q3. Which of the following is true of zinc phosphate?

- **a.** mix on a thick cool glass slab
- **b.** sedative
- **c.** acidic
- **d.** sets very hard within minutes

Q4. Which of the following is true of zinc polycarboxylate ?

- **a.** alternative to zinc phosphate
- **b.** adheres to the teeth and instruments
- **c.** sedative
- **d.** irritant

Q5. Which of the following is true of glass ionomer ?

- **a.** sticks to metal
- **b.** releases fluoride
- **c.** alkaline
- **d.** moisture sensitive

How well did you do?
A1.b,c   A2.a,b,c   A3.a,c,d
A4.a,b,d   A5.a,b,d

Crowns

WHEN ARE CROWNS REQUIRED?

REASONS FOR CROWNING TEETH

While reading the text answer the following;

Q1. Why are teeth crowned?

Q2. What are the three stages of making a crown?

Q3. How is a core placed in a vital tooth?

Q4. How is a preformed cast metal post made?

Q5. How is a white fibre post placed in a tooth?

Artificial crowns are required when there is little left of the natural crown of the tooth. Crowns are placed to restore the appearance and function of the tooth. When there has been a lot of decay or a large fracture, there is too little tooth left to support a routine filling. The artificial crown encases the remaining tooth providing strength and form. Root treated teeth are routinely crowned to prevent the tooth fracturing as these teeth are more brittle than vital teeth.

A full crown completely covers the tooth. A three quarters crown covers three quarters of the tooth. Often a full crown is required.

Crowns are made of ceramic (e.g. porcelain), metal (e.g. gold) or a combination of metal and porcelain.

PROCEDURE FOR MAKING A CROWN

Crowns are made in the following stages;

1. Core.
2. Crown preparation.
3. Crown fit.

From the nurse's viewpoint the procedure for making a crown or bridge is exactly the same. When making an inlay there is no core appointment.

CORE BUILD-UP

Amalgam and hybrid composites are good plastic core materials as they are strong and both can be bonded to dentine. Glass ionomer is a weak material so should only be used to block out undercuts.
The core is built up differently depending on whether the tooth is vital or root filled. Patients with vital teeth should be fore warned that crowned teeth have a 15-20% risk of becoming non vital at a later date. If this occurs a root filling can be placed by drilling through the crown. The crown is then restored with a direct filling.

VITAL TEETH

The nurse prepares a standard filling instrument tray. The tooth is anaesthetised and all the decay is removed. Mechanical retention is created by slots and grooves. When little dentine remains titanium pins may be necessary. (Pins are best avoided if possible as they tend to place stress within the dentine and may cause injury to the pulp.) The core is built up in a strong plastic material such as amalgam or composite. Bonds such as Panavia™ may be used with amalgam to increase retention by bonding it to the dentine. If composite is used the dentist can continue on to prepare the crown. However a further appointment is usually needed with amalgam cores as they may take 20 minutes to set.

NON VITAL TEETH

These teeth are root filled first. In multi rooted teeth it may be possible to avoid posts by utilising the retention from the coronal aspect of the canals and the pulp chamber for the core. However in anterior teeth a post is usually required.

There are several methods of making a post. These are two common methods in practice today;

1. PREFORMED CAST METAL POSTS

PREPARATION

- No local anaesthetic is required.
- Successively wider Gates Glidden™ burs are used to remove the coronal and middle sections of gutta percha.
- Then a preformed post system is used. Successively wider files are used to increase the diameter of the canal and give it the precise shape to fit the future post. These files (and the plastic impression posts and temporary aluminium posts) are all colour co-ordinated to precise matching sizes.

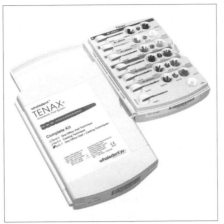

Figure 14.8 *A preformed post system of files, impression posts and temporary posts. (Courtesy of Minerva and Coltene Whaledent.)*

- When the canal is fully prepared an antirotation groove is made with a tapered crown bur and the crown margins are prepared.
- Retraction cord soaked in a haemostatic agent is placed.
- The preparation is washed and dried with the 3-in-1 syringe and large paper points. The nurse places the saliva ejector in the patient's mouth.
- The corresponding plastic impression post is placed in the canal and fully seated.
- A final rubber impression is then taken. When the impression is removed the plastic impression post will be embedded in it. This is all sent to the technician.
- The technician casts this up and from the model (known as a "die") makes a cast metal post and core and a separate crown to go over the top.

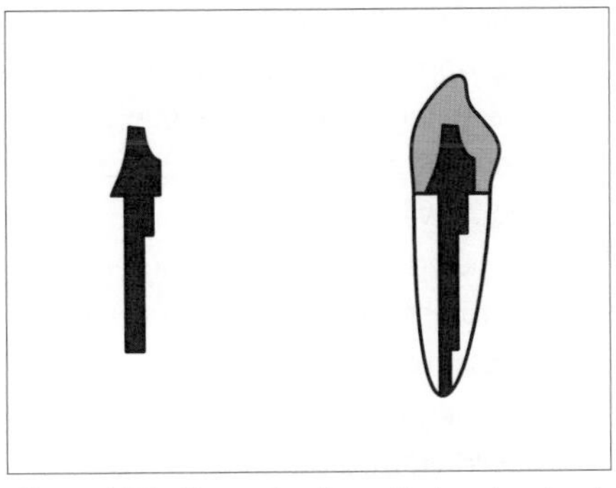

Figure 14.9 *Cast post and core. Root, cast post and core and crown.*

- The corresponding temporary aluminium post is placed in the tooth and a temporary crown is made and fitted with a temporary cement.
- Post operative instructions are given to the patient to avoid biting on the crown for that day as the temporary cement may still be soft and to return to the surgery immediately if the temporary post and crown should come out. The laboratory prescription is written with the return date marked.

FITTING THE CAST POST AND CORE

- The laboratory work returns and on the die is the crown and the post and core.
- The temporary post and core are removed with forceps or orthodontic pliers.
- The airway is protected and the permanent post and core is seated and checked for fit. The crown is placed on top and again checked for fit, contact points and appearance. If all are correct and the patient approves the appearance the post and core and crown are cemented or bonded into place.

147

2. WHITE FIBRE POSTS

White fibre posts are made from silica or fibreglass. When bonded into the tooth they evenly disperse biting forces through out the root reducing the chance of root fracture.

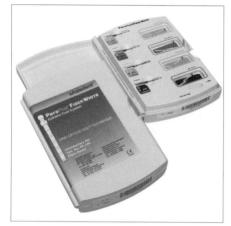

Figure 14.10 *White fibre post system. (Courtesy of Minerva and Coltene Whaledent.)*

PREPARATION AND PLACEMENT OF THE POST

- No local anaesthetic is required.
- Successively wider Gates Glidden burs are used to remove the coronal and middle sections of gutta percha.
- Then a white fibre post system is used. Successively wider files increase the diameter of the canal and give it the precise shape to fit the future white fibre post. Again the files and posts are colour coded.
- The preparation is washed and dried with the 3-in-1 syringe and large paper points. The nurse places the saliva ejector in the patient's mouth.

- A duel cure dentine bonding system such as Panavia F™ is used. The nurse mixes equal drops of liquid primer A and B and passes them to the dentist with a long brush. The dentist brushes the mixture into the canal for 30 seconds. In the meantime the dental nurse mixes equal lengths of the two Panavia F™ pastes together and dips the end of the white fibre post in this. The dentist removes excess primer from the canal with a wide paper point and seats the paste coated white fibre post into the canal. Excess bond is removed with a flat plastic and the bond is then cured with the blue curing light. The bond deep within the root cures chemically.
- The dentist then proceeds to build up the core in hybrid composite.
- The core is then prepared using tapered crown burs.
- Retraction cord soaked in a haemostatic agent is placed. A rubber impression is taken and sent to the laboratory with instructions for the crown construction. A temporary crown is placed.
- Post operative instructions are given to the patient to avoid biting on the crown for that day as the temporary cement may still be soft and to return to the surgery immediately if the temporary crown should come off.

Whichever method is used, the dental nurse assists the dentist by;

- Preparing the surgery. Setting out the equipment required and ensuring that the work is back from the laboratory.
- Reassuring the patient throughout. Providing a bib, glasses and mouthwash.
- Providing the suction, passing relevant instruments and mixing the cement or bonds.
- Cleaning the surgery afterwards and sterilising the instruments.

Q1. Why are teeth crowned?

    a. there is too little natural tooth left to support a filling
    b. the tooth has been root treated
    c. the tooth has been bleached
    d. the tooth has a chip

Q2. What are the possible stages of making a crown?

    a. the core build-up
    b. crown preparation
    c. post placement
    d. crown fit

Q3. How is a core retained in a vital tooth?

    a. by utilising the pulp chamber
    b. by utilising the coronal aspect of the root canals
    c. by using slots and grooves
    d. by using bonds

Q4. How is a preformed cast metal post made?

    a. at the chairside
    b. in the laboratory
    c. using a plastic impression post
    d. with silica

Q5. How is a white fibre post placed in a tooth?

    a. with a dentine bonding system
    b. with an enamel bonding system
    c. with a light cured resin
    d. with a duel cured resin

How well did you do?
    A1.a,b   A2.a,b,c,d   A3.c,d
    A4.b,c   A5.a,d

CROWN PREPARATION

While reading the text answer the following;

Q1. What is the nurse's role in preparing a crown?

Q2. What equipment is needed during crown preparation?

THE DENTIST'S INSTRUMENTS

- Mirror, tweezers, probe.
- Flat plastic.
- Carver and excavator.
- Slow and high speed handpieces and burs.
- Bite registration paper in Miller forceps.
- Scalpel.

PREOPERATIVE PREPARATION

- The instruments and materials are laid out. The patient's records are reviewed especially the medical history and periapical x-rays of the teeth to be prepared.
- The patient is anaesthetised if the teeth are vital.
- The patient confirms the type of crown that they would like, for example gold or porcelain. If required, the tooth shade is taken before the teeth dry out and lighten.
- A bib and glasses are placed on the patient by the nurse.
- An alginate impression is taken of the teeth to be prepared and the opposing arch if required.

CROWN PREPARATION

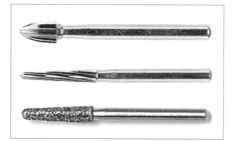

Figure 14.11 Various crown preparation burs. (Courtesy of Minerva.)

- The crown is prepared using diamond or tungsten carbide tapered crown burs in the high speed handpiece to reduce the walls of the teeth and a diamond flame shaped bur or fissure bur to reduce the occlusal surface. Different types of crowns require different types of burs to get the correct margins. (Hence the reason why the type of crown requested was confirmed with the patient at the onset.)
- The nurse aspirates remembering to protect the soft tissues and provide good access for the dentist. This is very precise work and the dentist must be able to cut the tooth at the exact angles. Good nursing and suction technique is greatly appreciated!

RETRACTION CORD

- Appropriate lengths of retraction cord are soaked in a haemostatic agent. One or two strands of retraction cord are placed around each prepared tooth. The cord and haemostatic agent gently open the gingival crevice and stop any gingival bleeding. This allows the impression material to flow into the gingival crevice and precisely record the margins of the crown. This allows the dental technician to make a well fitting crown.

MAKING THE TEMPORARY CROWN

- The top retraction cord is removed leaving the deeper one in place or the sulcus empty if only one was used. The dentist washes and dries the prepared teeth while the nurse aspirates. The nurse then places the saliva ejector into the patient's mouth.
- The nurse hands the dentist the dispenser gun containing the temporary crown material.
- While the patient is laid flat the preoperative alginate impression is loaded with the temporary crown material by the dentist and placed in the patient's mouth. When it has set it is removed and trimmed by the dentist.

IMPRESSIONS

- While the cord is still working the dentist explains to the patient that a precise impression of the prepared teeth will be taken. The dentist explains how long the tray will be in their mouth and that the patient must be as still as possible. If a triple tray is to be used the unloaded tray is placed in the mouth and the patient is asked to close together to check that they are biting naturally into centric occlusion.
- While the dentist removes the retraction cord the dental nurse lightly coats the impression tray with fixative. The nurse places the light-bodied impression gun onto the dentist's bracket table. When the dentist gives the command the nurse mixes the heavy-bodied impression material and loads the tray while the dentist simultaneously injects light-bodied impression paste around the prepared teeth.
- The dental nurse then removes the saliva ejector from the floor of the mouth and smoothly and quickly places the loaded impression tray into the dentist's hand. The dentist seats the tray in the mouth and either holds it in position or gets the patient to bite.

- When the material has set the impression is removed by the dentist. The nurse sits the patient up to rinse while the dentist inspects the impression with the overhead light.
- The nurse should be ready to quickly re-nozzle the impression guns if another impression is required.
- You will have noticed that the success of impression taking relies on the good co-ordination of the dentist and nurse. Once the teeth are dried the loaded trays or dispenser guns must be placed immediately into the dentist's hand. To ensure that the teeth remain dry the dentist will be looking at the teeth the whole time so the nurse must correctly position the tray in their hand. If there is a problem with mixing the heavy body and the material is not performing properly the nurse must inform the dentist immediately so that the impression can be aborted before it is placed in the patient's mouth.

BITE REGISTRATION

- Next a mousse bite is recorded if single impressions have been taken. The patient remains in the upright position. The teeth are dried by the dentist with the 3-in-1 syringe. The gun is smartly handed to the dentist and the dentist injects mousse over the lower occlusal surfaces and then gets the patient to bite into centric occlusion.
- After the moose has set the patient is asked to open and the bite is removed and trimmed with a scalpel. The nurse invites the patient to rinse while the dentist trims the moose bite.

FITTING THE TEMPORARY CROWN

- Under the dentist's command the nurse mixes the temporary cement, for example Tempbond™, and uses the dentist's flat plastic to put the cement around the inside edges of the temporary crown and hands the crown to the dentist on the outstretched palm of the hand.
- The dentist seats the temporary and asks the patient to bite. After the temporary bond has set the dentist uses the wiped flat plastic or carver to remove the excess cement. The bite is checked with articulating paper in a Miller forcep.
- The patient has a final rinse. The nurse hands the patient a mirror and a warm wet tissue to remove any paste from their face.
- Post operative instructions are given by the dentist or nurse. The patient should avoid biting on the temporary that day as the temporary cement may still be soft. After the first day the patient should treat the tooth as normal. If the temporary crown falls out they must return to the dentist to have it recemented as soon as possible even if the tooth does not hurt.

LABORATORY PRESCRIPTION

- The nurse is responsible for disinfecting and wrapping the impressions before they are posted to the technician. Any alginate impressions are cast up immediately or wrapped in damp tissue and an airtight plastic bag. The nurse makes sure that the dentist has filled in the type of crowns required and the shade. The dental nurse fills in the patient's name and the return date. This is usually the day before the patient's next appointment.

Q1. What is the nurse's role in preparing a crown?

   a. to lay out the instruments and materials required
   b. to provide the suction
   c. to make the temporary
   d. to disinfect and label the impressions

Q2. What equipment is needed during crown preparation?

   a. flat plastic
   b. retraction cord
   c. ultrasonic scaler
   d. temporary crown material

How well did you do?
   A1.a,b,d   A2.a,b,d

CROWN FIT

While reading the text answer the following;

Q1. What is the nurse's role during the fitting of a crown?

Q2. What equipment is required?

THE DENTIST'S INSTRUMENTS

- Mirror, tweezers and probe.
- Flat plastic.
- Carver and excavator.
- Articulation paper in Miller forceps.
- High speed handpiece and burs.

PROCEDURE

Figure 14.12 Indicator marking spray.
(Courtesy of Minerva and Pascal.)

- The dental nurse makes sure that the laboratory work is back at the beginning of the day. This allows the patient to be contacted and their appointment rescheduled if the work has not arrived, saving the patient a wasted visit.
- The required instruments and materials are laid out.
- The patient's records are reviewed. The patient is asked how the teeth have been since their last appointment.
- A bib and glasses are placed on the patient by the nurse. The patient is laid back for a local anaesthetic if required.
- The temporary crown is removed with the nurse providing the suction.
- The airway is protected with a sheet of gauze and the crown is placed on the tooth. The dentist checks the fit and contact points. The bite is checked with articulation paper held in Miller forceps. The contact points are checked with indicator marking spray. Any adjustments are made **outside the patient's mouth**. The dentist uses the water cooled high speed handpiece with the nurse collecting the water in an empty plastic beaker.

If the dentist is satisfied the patient is given a mirror to see the crown in situ. They are forewarned that the crown is not bonded so that they must look at the crown without moving or speaking, to prevent inadvertently swallowing/inhaling it. After they have seen the crown in situ, the crown and then the gauze are removed and the patient is sat up to give their views. If they approve the appearance they are laid back down for the fit.

- The tooth is washed and dried and the nurse places the saliva ejector in the mouth. The dentist isolates the tooth with cotton wool, dry guard or rubber dam. The airway is protected by dam or gauze.
- The dentist decides which cement or bond to use and the nurse mixes this.
- The nurse places the appropriate bond on the inside walls of the crown and places the crown on the palm of an outstretched hand for the dentist to take and fit.
- The patient may be asked to bite on a cotton wool roll to ensure that the crown is fully seated.
- The bond is given time to set or is light cured. Excess bond is removed with a flat plastic or carver. The contact points are flossed.
- The bite is rechecked.
- The patient is given post operative instructions.
- The nurse clears away the instruments to be scrubbed and sterilised. The dental nurse asks the dentist whether to keep the patient's models or discard them.

Q1. What is the nurse's role during the fitting of a crown?

    a. to make sure the crown has arrived from the laboratory
    b. to mix the cement or bond
    c. to place the bond in the crown
    d. to put the crown on the tooth

Q2. What equipment and materials are required to place a crown?

    a. a flat plastic
    b. alginate
    c. mousse bite
    d. temporary resin

How well did you do?
    A1.a,b,c   A2.a

TEMPORARY CROWNS

While reading the text answer the following;

Q1. Why are temporary crowns necessary?

Q2. How is a temporary crown made at the chair side?

Q3. What are preformed temporary crowns made from?

Q4. What post operative instructions are given to the patient during crown treatment?

Temporary crowns are required for the following reasons;

1. To restore the appearance.
2. To prevent pain and sensitivity between appointments.
3. To prevent over eruption and tilting of the opposing and adjacent teeth.
4. To prevent the gingivae covering the margins of the prepared teeth.

Temporary crowns can be preformed or made in the surgery.

CUSTOM MADE TEMPORARY CROWNS

The advantage of these crowns is that they are based on the patient's original teeth. It is often easier and quicker making a crown by the chairside than trying to adapt a preformed temporary crown. The material comes in a range of colours to match the patient's teeth. If several anterior crowns are being made the patient can see how a lighter shade looks.

An alginate impression of the teeth is required **before** the teeth are prepared. After the teeth are prepared, temporary crown material in a dispenser gun is injected into the alginate impression by the dentist and the impression is seated in the patient's mouth. When the material has set the impression is removed. The temporary crown is neatened with discs. The nurse mixes the temporary cement into a creamy consistency. A thin coat is placed around the sides of the crown before it is passed to the dentist on an outstretched palm. The dentist fit's the temporary onto the dried tooth.

These crowns are always a good fit and usually need to be drilled off the tooth at the next appointment. If they fall off prematurely the dentist needs to review the crown preparations and the bite in centric and excentric occlusion to make sure nothing has been overlooked in the design.

PREFORMED TEMPORARY CROWNS / CROWN FORMS

These crown forms are either tooth coloured or clear plastic, aluminium or stainless steel. They come in a range of shapes and sizes. No impressions are required. The dentist chooses the crown form which is the closest height and width of the original tooth. The crown form is adjusted using acrylic trimming burs, discs or Beebee crown sheers.

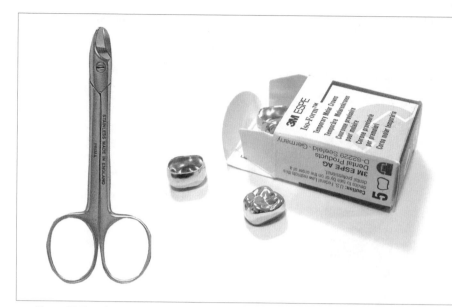

Figure 14.13 *Beebee crown sheers and preformed temporary crowns. (Courtesy of Minerva and 3M ESPE.)*

The nurse mixes zinc oxide and eugenol temporary cement into a thick sticky mix and generously loads the temporary crown. The dentist fits it onto the dried tooth. These teeth rarely match the colour of the patient's neighbouring teeth and the patient usually takes time to adjust to the often bulky contours. These crowns can usually be flicked off at the next appointment with an excavator. However they are useful when the patient presents with a lost crown.

POST-OPERATIVE INSTRUCTIONS

- If local anaesthetic has been used the patient must be careful not to bite their cheeks, tongue or lips.
- Allow several hours for temporary and permanent cements to set. Resin bonds will set immediately.
- After the local anaesthetic has worn off the tooth should be comfortable or may feel as though it has had work done but this sensation should not last longer than a day. Teeth with post-operative pain or discomfort lasting more than a day should be seen by the dentist.

- The bite should be perfect. If the patient feels that the crown is catching or high they should return to the surgery for a short appointment to get it adjusted within a couple of days.

Q1. Why are temporary crowns necessary?

  a. to avoid permanent crowns
  b. to prevent pain
  c. to prevent over eruption of the opposing teeth
  d. to restore the appearance

Q2. How is a custom made temporary crown produced at the chair side?

  a. an alginate impression is taken after the teeth have been prepared
  b. temporary crown material is placed in an alginate impression and reinserted into the patient's mouth
  c. a preformed crown is necessary
  d. no temporary cement is required

Q3. What can preformed temporary crowns be made from?

  a. gold
  b. plastic
  c. porcelain
  d. stainless steel

Q4. What post operative instructions are given to the patient during crown treatment?

a. if local anaesthetic has been used the patient must take care not to bite their lip

b. the patient should wait for the cement to set before biting on the crown

c. if the bite is high at first no treatment is required as the crown will wear down

d. the patient should expect the tooth to be uncomfortable for the first week before it settles

How well did you do?

A1.b,c,d   A2.b   A3.b,d   A4.a,b

Bridges

WHEN ARE BRIDGES REQUIRED?

REASONS FOR BRIDGING TEETH

While reading the text answer the following;

Q1. When are bridges required?

Q2. What is a pontic?

Q3. Describe four types of bridge.

Q4. How are adhesive bridges placed?

Q5. How should the patient clean the bridge?

Bridges are required when one or more teeth have been lost leaving a gap in the arch. They are an alternative to dentures or implants. The advantage of a bridge is that it is permanently fixed in place, it does not require surgery and it can be completed within a couple of weeks. Unlike a denture it does not cover an excessive amount of mucosa and is easily tolerated by people with a strong gag reflex. If the gap remained unfilled the opposing teeth may over erupt and the adjacent teeth may tilt into the space causing stagnation areas for plaque to collect and TMJ dysfunction. By placing a bridge the appearance and function is restored.

Every tooth, whether artificial or natural, involved in the bridge is called a unit. You may hear the dentist refer to a 3 or 6 unit bridge for example. The length of the bridge is called the span. So a 6 unit bridge has a greater span than a 3 unit bridge. The teeth which support the bridge are called the abutments and their crowns are called retainers. The artificial teeth are called the pontics.

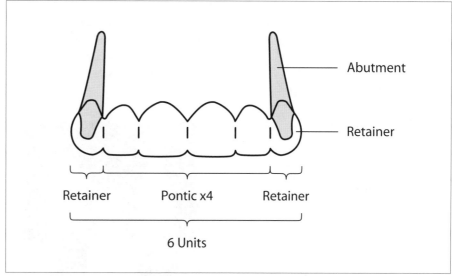

Figure 14.14 *Components of a six unit bridge.*

TYPES OF BRIDGE

FIXED-FIXED BRIDGE

A fixed-fixed bridge is made in one solid piece. They are usually made of porcelain bonded to metal. The bridge is supported by an abutment at either end.

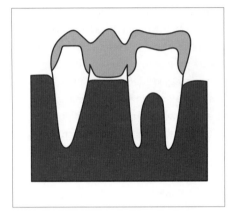

Figure 14.15 *Fixed-fixed bridge.*

FIXED-MOVEABLE BRIDGE

This bridge is made in two sections with a dovetail joint in between. This allows a small degree of flexibility. These bridges always include metal.

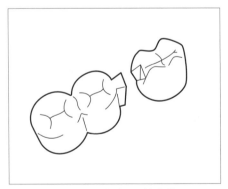

Figure 14.16 *Fixed-movable bridge.*

CANTILEVER BRIDGE

A cantilever bridge is only fixed on one side to an abutment. This is useful when only one abutment is available for example the tooth on the other side is already being used as an abutment to another bridge, to extend the arch or where the patient would like to preserve a diastema (gap).

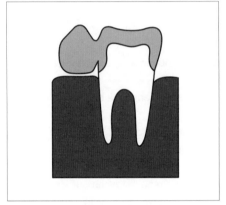

Figure 14.17 *Cantilever bridge.*

ADHESIVE BRIDGE/MARYLAND BRIDGE

This bridge consists of a porcelain pontic being held in place by one or two metal wings which are bonded to the palatal aspect of one or both teeth either side. The retention relies on the strength of the metal-enamel bond. Adhesive bridges are useful when the abutment teeth have never been restored as minimal preparation (tooth reduction) is needed.

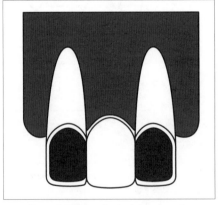

Figure 14.18 *An adhesive bridge from the palatal aspect.*

The other bridges are fitted in the same manner as fitting a crown. However an adhesive bridge is more complicated to seat.

These bridges are fitted using rubber dam to provide good moisture control which will ensure a strong bond strength. They always require a duel cure resin or a chemically cured resin. The enamel is etched, washed and dried. The nurse mixes equal amounts of the two duel cure pastes (e.g. Panavia F™) with a plastic spatula. The dental nurse then loads the dull fitting surface of the wings with the duel cure resin making sure that the entire surface is covered with an even layer.

This is passed to the dentist on the flat of an outstretched palm. The dentist seats the bridge and wipes the excess bond away. The nurse passes the curing light and the dentist cures the margins of the wings. The light cannot penetrate through the metal wing so the dentist must hold the bridge in place for a few minutes until the resin has chemically cured underneath.

If a chemically cured resin (e.g. Panavia EX™) is used, after seating the bridge and wiping away the excess resin, an oxiguard™ gel is placed over the margins. This prevents oxygen inhibiting the setting of the resin bond.

Fitting an adhesive bridge requires excellent nursing. If the dental nurse takes too long mixing the resin it will begin to set before it is placed and the bridge will not seat correctly. The nurse must also be attentive when wiping hand instruments and passing the curing light as the dentist will be concentrating on the teeth.

ORAL HYGIENE INSTRUCTIONS FOR BRIDGES

Technicians make all bridges with as little stagnation areas as possible. However the patient must be shown how to clean under the pontic where it meets the abutment as conventional floss cannot be used. The patient can be shown Superfloss™ which is stiff at one end so that it can be treaded under the pontic to clean the abutments. Many patients find interdentally brushes are easy to use either side of the abutments. These are simple to use and inexpensive. Sonic toothbrushes and water picks may also help to maintain the region.

Q1. When are bridges required?

    a. when one or more teeth have been lost
    b. as an alternative to a crown
    c. as an alternative to a denture
    d. as an alternative to a implant

Q2. What is a pontic?

    a. this is the tooth which supports the bridge
    b. this is the artificial tooth
    c. this is the retainer
    d. this is a unit of the bridge

Q3. Which of the following are types of bridge?

    a. cantilever
    b. fixed-movable
    c. fixed-fixed
    d. adhesive

Q4. How are Maryland bridges placed?

    a. with light cured resin
    b. with zinc phosphate cement
    c. with glass ionomer
    d. with chemically cured resin

Q5. How should the patient clean under their bridge?

    a. with Superfloss
    b. with floss in a holder
    c. with an interdental brush
    d. with dental tape

How well did you do?
    A1.a,c,d   **A2.**b,d   **A3.**a,b,c,d
    A4.d   **A5.**a,c

IMMEDIATE TEMPORARY BRIDGES

While reading the text answer the following;

Q1. Why is a temporary bridge necessary?

Q2. What temporary prosthesis can be used to maintain the space?

Often a permanent bridge is made to replace a denture. After preparing the teeth, temporary crowns are made for the abutments and the patient continues to wear the existing denture until the next appointment.
However there are cases where a patient needs an extraction and would eventually like a permanent bridge to fill the gap. As you know when a tooth is extracted the alveolar bone resorbs over the following 6 months. If a permanent bridge was placed straight after the extraction, within a couple of months the patient would return to complain about the gap appearing between the pontic and gum. This means that a temporary prosthesis is required to hold the gap and prevent tilting of adjacent teeth and over eruption of the opposing teeth. This can be done by;

1. Making a standard temporary acrylic denture.
This incurs a laboratory fee and an extra impression appointment before the extraction.

2. Making a one unit, removable nylon prosthesis.

Figure 14.19 *One unit nylon prosthesis.*

This is useful for posterior teeth. It is made entirely of white nylon. It is retained by clasps and by engaging the undercuts as nylon is flexible. Unfortunately there are limited shades and the prosthesis is not strong enough for a long span. Again a laboratory fee and an extra impression appointment is incurred.

3. Making a temporary bridge.
This is particularly useful for anterior teeth as the shape of the temporary will be based on the patient's present teeth. It is very useful in an emergency situation for example when there is a longitudinal fracture in a post crown requiring immediate extraction.
- The patient is anaesthetised in preparation for an extraction.
- The tooth shade is taken.
- An alginate impression is taken of the tooth to be extracted. The interdental alginate around the tooth to be extracted is removed from the impression by the dentist.
- The teeth either side of the tooth to be extracted are prepared in the normal manner for a bridge using diamond or tungsten tapered crown burs.
- The tooth is then extracted and haemostasis achieved.
- A temporary crown material of the appropriate shade is syringed into the alginate impression by the dentist. This is placed in the patient's mouth.
- After it has set the impression is removed. The temporary bridge is trimmed while the patient bites on more gauze to stem further bleeding.

- The bridge is then cemented into place with a temporary cement. After waiting 6 months for the socket to heal and the bone to remodel a permanent bridge can be made. As a precaution a rubber rather than an alginate impression can be taken at the onset and kept in the surgery in case the patient breaks their temporary and it needs to be remade. This is advised in bridges with long spans for example from maxillary canine to canine.

Q1. A permanent bridge is not placed immediately after a tooth has been extracted as bone resorption would soon ruin the appearance.
True or false?

Q2. What temporary prosthesis can be used to maintain the space?

    a. a denture
    b. a temporary crown
    c. a temporary filling
    d. a temporary bridge

How well did you do?
    A1.True   A2.a,d

Inlays

While reading the text answer the following;

Q1. What is an inlay?

An inlay can be used as an alternative to a filling. Inlays are indirect restorations which are made gold, porcelain or a composite which contains more filler than normal and so is extra strong. Inlays are used to provide stronger, longer lasting restorations than plastic filling materials.
The tooth is prepared in the same way as for a filling however there must be **no undercuts**. The technique from here on is similar to a crown preparation and fit. Rubber impressions are taken and the bite is recorded. These are sent to the laboratory where the permanent inlay is made. In the meantime the patient has a temporary placed. The temporary inlay should be able to be removed without drilling into the prepared tooth walls. At a second appointment the patient has the inlay cemented/bonded into position. Gold inlays have their margins further adapted to the wall by burnishing (pressing with a burnisher) the margins against the tooth before they are cemented in place.
The disadvantage of inlays are that they are more costly and time consuming than fillings. Inlays can be increased in size to cover the weakened cusps of teeth without preparing the full crown. These are called onlays or cuspal coverage inlays.

Q1. Which of the following is true of an inlay?

    a. an inlays relies on undercuts for retention
    b. an inlay may be extended to include cuspal coverage
    c. an inlay needs to be cemented / bonded into place
    d. an inlay can be made of gold, porcelain or composite

How well did you do?
    A1.b,c,d

15. Endodontics

While reading the text answer the following;

Q1. Define endodontics.

Q2. List the reasons for endodontics.

Q3. Why is it often necessary to crown a root filled tooth?

Q4. What are the alternatives to root fillings?

Endodontics is treatment of the pulp. It includes;

1. Pulp capping; Keeping the pulp alive.
2. Root filling; Removing all the nerve in a mature permanent tooth.
3. Pulpotomy; Removing part of the nerve in a vital but immature permanent tooth.
4. Apicectomy; Removing the infected apex of a root filled permanent tooth.

SO WHY DO WE ROOT TREAT TEETH?

REASONS FOR ENDODONTICS

Endodontics is required following injury or infection to the pulp which results in pulpitis. Pulpitis is inflammation of the pulp. This is either reversible or irreversible. Irreversible pulpitis always results in the pulp dying and a root filling is required to save the tooth. Pulpitis is caused by;

- Deep decay.
- Fracture of the crown resulting in pulpal exposure.
- Impact injury; A blow to the tooth may cut off the blood supply so the pulp dies.
- Exposure during cavity preparation.
- Thermal injury to the pulp.
- Chemical irritation of the pulp.

ALTERNATIVES TO ENDODONTICS

Most root filled teeth need to be crowned afterwards as they tend to become brittle and prone to fracture. This is particularly true of posterior teeth. The patient needs to be warned of this before embarking on root treatment. However the only alternative to root therapy is extraction and then the patient is left with a gap. The treatment options after extraction are;

1. Accept the gap and the possible consequences of tooth movement.
2. Wear a denture. Chrome dentures are healthier than acrylic but more expensive. Today patients are less willing to accept dentures.
3. Place a bridge. This is more expensive than root treating and crowning. It is also more destructive as the adjacent teeth need to be prepared.
4. Place an implant. This is the most expensive option involving surgical treatment which spans over several months.

With modern technology and improved treatment methods, root fillings are now very successful.

Q1. Endodontics includes which of the following?

    a. pulp cap
    b. night cap
    c. pulpotomy
    d. apicectomy

Q2. When may a root filling be necessary?

    a. after a blow to the tooth cutting off its blood supply
    b. after trauma resulting in pulpal exposure
    c. to treat reversible pulpitis
    d. to treat deep decay causing necrosis of the pulp

Q3. Following endodontics a tooth is crowned as root filled teeth are brittle and prone to fracture. True or false?

Q4. Which of the following are alternatives to root treatment?

    a. composite filling
    b. crown
    c. bridge
    d. denture

How well did you do?
    A1.a,c,d   A2.a,b,d   A3.True A4.c,d

HOW DO WE KNOW THE TOOTH IS DYING?

VITALITY TESTS

While reading the text answer the following;

Q1. What are the symptoms of a dying pulp?

Q2. What does a periapical abscess look like on x-ray?

Q3. What are the advantages of the electric pulp test?

Q4. What is the nurse's role when using an electric pulp tester?

Q5. What substance is used to cold vitality test teeth?

Q6. What must be applied to the teeth before heat testing them?

The deciding factor between a routine filling and endodontics or extraction is the state of the pulp. It is important to determine if it is vital or non vital. If the pulp is vital but damaged will it recover or die? Often the patients symptoms will give an indication. For example a short, sharp pain to cold indicates a healthy pulp. However a long lasting, dull ache especially to heat indicates a dying tooth particularly if it throbs at night waking the patient. An examination of the mouth can reveal a sinus (gum boil) which indicates a non vital root. Periapical x-rays reveal abscesses as a shadow around the apex of dead roots. Sometimes it is not so clear and a vitality test is needed.

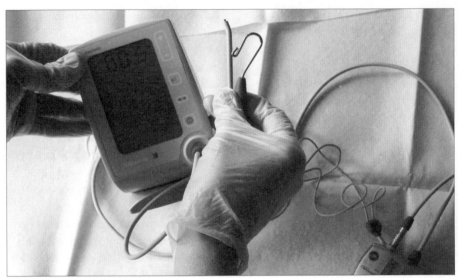

Figure 15.1 Electric pulp tester.

1. ELECTRIC PULP TEST

This is a valuable way to measure "vitality" as it measures the strength of the response to a given stimuli. This allows the dentist to monitor the pulp in its recovery or decline and decide exactly when to intervene. The nurse's role is to set up the electric pulp tester. It has a monitor screen, a working end (conductive wand) and a metal circuit connector which the nurse lightly rests over the patient's lower lip. The nurse should also place the saliva ejector in the patient's mouth as the teeth need to be dry. While the dentist dries the teeth with the 3-in-1, the nurse dips the working end of the pulp tester in toothpaste to improve conductivity and then passes it to the dentist to hold against the tooth. Slowly the voltage of electricity is increased until the patient puts up their hand to show they feel a tingle. The nurse records the final voltage. Several teeth are recorded to gain an insight into their normal response. The electric pulp test is the kindest method of determining vitality as it starts with a very low voltage which increases in fine increments. Remember these teeth are sore and need to be treated gently.

Often the electric pulp tester and the apex locator are combined into one machine. The nurse should check that the machine is on the correct setting for the function required.

2. COLD

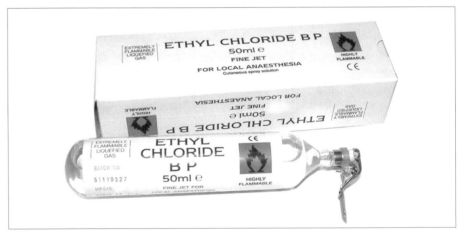

Figure 15.2 Ethyl chloride spray. (Courtesy of Minerva.)

A cotton wool pledget sprayed with ethyl chloride is applied to each tooth. The time taken for the tooth to respond is noted. Take care not to drop the glass ethyl chloride container as it will explode on impact!

3. HEAT

The teeth are coated in petroleum jelly and warm gutta percha (GP) is applied to each tooth. Remember dying teeth are highly sensitive to heat so this test can be uncomfortable. The jelly stops the GP sticking and causing prolonged pain.

Q1. A dying tooth gives a short, sharp pain to cold. True or false?

Q2. A periapical abscess appears as a shadow around the apex of the dead root on a periapical x-ray. True or false?

Q3. Which of the following are advantages of the electric pulp test?

    a. it is precise
    b. the voltage starts at a high setting
    c. the voltage is decreased in fine increments
    d. it impresses the patient

Q4. Which of the following is the nurse's role during electric pulp testing?

    a. set up the machine
    b. apply tooth paste to the conductive wand
    c. place the metal circuit connector over the patient's lip
    d. record the final voltages of the teeth

Q5. Which of the following is used as a cold vitality test?

    a. acrylic chloride
    b. ethyl chloride
    c. calcium chloride
    d. gutta-percha

Q6. Which of the following is applied to the teeth before heat testing them?

    a. gutta-percha
    b. petroleum jelly
    c. raspberry jelly
    d. toothpaste

How well did you do?
    A1.False.   A2.True.   A3.a
    A4.a,b,c,d   A5.b   A6.b

PULP CAPPING

While reading the text answer the following;

Q1. What is the aim of pulp capping a tooth?

Q2. Why is calcium hydroxide used?

When there is a pin hole exposure in a cavity free from decay it is not always necessary to proceed with a full root filling. If the exposed pulp appears healthy and has not had the symptoms of a dying tooth, the pulp can be saved. The cavity may be disinfected with a pledget of cotton wool dampened with chlorhexidene as there will have been an influx of bacteria into the pulp chamber. After 30 seconds, the dentist removes the pledget, washes the chamber with water and gently dries it. The dentist ensures that the bleeding has stopped with a dry cotton wool pledget. The exposure is lined with calcium hydroxide to promote secondary dentine formation. A permanent filling, such as composite or amalgam, is placed. If amalgam is used a base of zinc oxide and eugenol should be placed to prevent thermal shock. The patient is warned that the tooth may be sensitive to extremes of temperature for the first few weeks, so they should be kind to it!

If the pulp is exposed and cannot be saved, it is covered with calcium hydroxide or Ledermix™ and a sedative temporary dressing such as zinc oxide and eugenol is placed. The aim is to relieve pain until the tooth can be root filled.

Q1. The aim of pulp capping an exposed healthy pulp is which of the following?

    a. to save the pulp
    b. to painlessly kill the pulp
    c. to maintain the vitality of the tooth
    d. to allow future root treatment

Q2. Why is calcium hydroxide used to pulp cap a tooth?

    a. to promote secondary dentine formation
    b. to prevent thermal shock
    c. to stop the bleeding
    d. to provide a temporary filling

How well did you do?
    A1.a,c   A2.a

WHAT DO I NEED?

INSTRUMENTS AND EQUIPMENT

While reading the text answer the following;

Q1. What is the function of a speed reducing endodontic handpiece?

Q2. What is an apex locator?

Q3. What are the three functions of a rubber dam?

Q4. When are Gates Glidden™ burs used?

Q5. List the various hand instruments used in endodontics.

1. SPEED REDUCING ENDODONTIC HANDPIECE AND CORRESPONDING FILES

Figure 15.3 *Speed reducing handpiece and file. (Courtesy of Minerva and Morita.)*

These handpieces and their corresponding latch grip files have revolutionised root treatment making it quicker and more reliable. They work at greatly reduced speeds and some models automatically reverse if the file hits an obstacle. There are different systems available. All these systems shape the root canal from the coronal end first down to the apex using the step down technique. This insures that the most infected coronal tissue is removed first and bacteria are not dragged right down to the apex.

Figure 15.4 *Latch grip files. (Courtesy of Minerva and Dentsply.)*

The files shape the canal to fit a standard cone gutta percha point. An ideal taper of 0.6 is achieved in most cases. (Very fine canals may be tapered to 0.4.) The files are made of nickel titanium and are capable of flexing around severe curves. They are also strong and far less likely to fracture than those made of steel. Some handpieces also incorporate an apex locater so the dentist knows exactly where the file is within the canal.

2. APEX LOCATOR

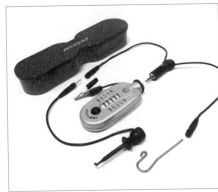

Figure 15.5 *Apex locator. (Courtesy of Minerva and Septodont.)*

This is an electronic machine that allows the dentist to precisely measure the length of the canal by accurately locating the apex. The canal is washed with water to flush out the bleach (which may give a false reading) and the pulp camber is dried. The file is inserted down the canal and relays to a screen how close to the apex the tip of the file is positioned. This is measured in millimetres or finer. The apex locator is set up by the nurse. The screen must be within reading distance of the dentist. Two lines come from the machine; one to attach to the file and the other for the nurse to hook over the patient's lower lip.

3. RUBBER DAM KIT

A rubber dam kit isolates the teeth preventing contamination of the canals. It also protects the airway from inhalation of hand instruments and the mucosa from corrosive splashes of bleach.

4. GATES-GLIDDEN™ BURS

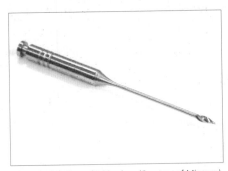

Figure 15.6 *Gates-Glidden bur. (Courtesy of Minerva.)*

Gates-Glidden™ burs are used to widen the canal. They have a pointed tip to follow the canal but the working end is "side cutting" only so that they cannot perforate the canal. In endodontics they are used to flare out the opening of the canal. This allows files and the sodium hypochlorite syringe to be introduced to fine canals. There are various sizes relating to the diameter required. The sizes are marked as grooves along the shank of the burs. Gates-Glidden™ burs are also used to remove the coronal part of existing root fillings when preparing the root for a post.

5. RULER AND RUBBER STOPS

Figure 15.7 *File measure and holder. (Courtesy of Minerva and Sybron Endo.)*

A ruler and rubber stops are used to precisely measure the files to the correct length of the root. Often latch grip files are manufactured with key measurements marked along their length. Many dentists ask the nurse to measure and mark the files. You must be precise!

6. HAND FILES

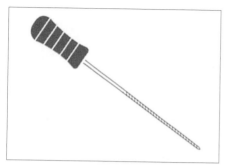

Figure 15.8 Hand file.
(Courtesy of Minerva and Dentsply.)

These files are used to widen and shape the canal and come in various sizes which are colour coded. They should be discarded after use as there is a theoretical risk of prion contamination.

7. BARBED BROACH

Figure 15.9 Barbed broach.

Barbed broaches may be used to remove the pulp from the canal. They should be discarded after use.

8. ENDODONTIC IRRIGATION SYRINGE

This is a disposable syringe with a side bevel to prevent irrigants being ejected through the apex.

9. FINGER SPREADER

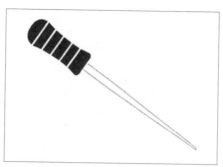

Figure 15.10 Finger spreaders.

These are used to condense the gutta percha laterally to allow more gutta percha points into the canal and prevent voids. They are colour coded to follow the ISO sizing.

10. LATERAL CONDENSER

These have the same use as a finger spreader

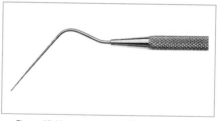

Figure 15.11 Lateral condenser. (Courtesy of Minerva.)

11. ROTARY PASTE FILLERS/SPIRAL PASTE FILLER

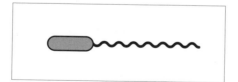

Figure 15.12 Rotary (spiral) paste filler.

These spiral paste around the walls of the canal so that they are completely covered.

12. ULTRASONICS

These are specialist instruments which are used to find extra canals. They can also be used to remove old fractured files when retreating a root filled tooth. They are best used with a microscope or illuminated loupes. Ultrasonics are also a useful means of delivering irrigant.

13. OPERATING MICROSCOPES AND LOUPES WITH ILLUMINATION

Figure 15.13 Loupes.
(Courtesy of Minerva and SJT Medical.)

These give magnification and illumination allowing the dentist to see fine details.

14. EQUIPMENT TO HEAT THE GUTTA
PERCHA

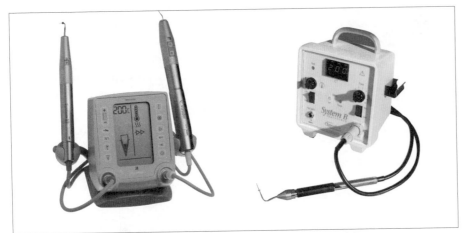

Figure 15.14 System B. (Courtesy of Minerva and Sybron Endo.)

Different systems are available, for example System B™, Obtura 2™, Touch and Heat™. Heating the gutta percha allows it to flow into voids. Often the final x-ray shows a surprisingly complicated root system. Care should be taken with hot instruments not to burn the patient or each other!

Q1. What is the function of a speed reducing endodontic handpiece and their nickel titanium files?

   a. to shape the canals
   b. to help perforate the roots
   c. to "straighten out" curved canals
   d. to make endodontics more efficient and reliable

Q2. What is the function of the apex locator?

   a. measures the bifurcation area
   b. locates the root apex
   c. helps to determine the length of the root
   d. cleans the canal

Q3. What are the functions of a rubber dam?

   a. to prevent the patient talking incessantly
   b. to prevent inhalation of instruments
   c. to prevent contamination of the canals
   d. to protect the mucosa from bleach

Q4. Gates Glidden burs are used to lengthen the canals. True or false?

Q5. Which of the following hand instruments are used in endodontics.

   a. barbed broach
   b. finger spreader
   c. root canal hand file
   d. System B

How well did you do?
   A1.a,d   A2.b,c   A3.b,c,d
   A4.False   A5.a,b,c

ISO SIZES

While reading the text answer the following;

Q1. What is the ISO system?

Widening a root canal is a very precise job. Files, paper points, gutta percha points and finger spreaders are all sized exactly using the ISO system. This is a colour coded international system that denotes the size of the tip of an instrument or point. For example;

Purple = size 10 = 0.10mm at the tip
White = size 15 = 0.15mm at the tip
Yellow = size 20 = 0.20mm at the tip
Red = size 25 = 0.25mm at the tip
Blue = size 30 = 0.30mm at the tip

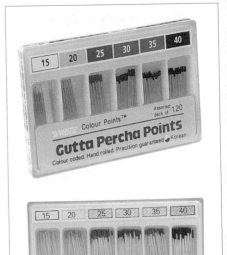

Figure 15.15 ISO coded gutta percha points and paper points. (Courtesy of Minerva and SS White.)

Files also come in different lengths as well as different diameters. As a general rule; Incisors require files which are 25mm long. Canines require files which are 30mm long. Molars and premolars require files which are 21mm long.

These correspond to the lengths of the teeth.

Q1. The ISO system is a British colour coded system denoting the size of the tip of an instrument. True or false?

How well did you do?
A1.False

WHAT MEDICAMENTS SHOULD I GET READY?

ENDODONTIC MEDICAMENTS

While reading the text answer the following;

Q1. How does bleach differ from other irrigating solutions?

Q2. Why are chelating agents used?

Q3. What is the function of calcium hydroxide?

Q4. What is the function of paste fillers?

1.   IRRIGATING SOLUTIONS
      There are several types of irrigating solutions for example sodium hypochlorite (bleach), Milton™, chlorhexidine and hydrogen peroxide. They are used to disinfect the canals from bacteria. Files shape the canal, irrigants clean the canal. However sodium hypochlorite is the best as it not only disinfects but actually dissolves all organic material within the canals. It is used between 1% to 5% concentration. The nurse is responsible for diluting the bleach to the correct concentration and placing it in a syringe.

The plastic syringe is disposable and has a side bevel to prevent solutions being injected through the apical foramen. (You can imagine how painful it would be to have bleach squirted into living bone!)

2.   CHELATING AGENTS
      Chelating agents, such as File-eze™, dissolve dentine chips within the canal system. It removes the smear layer caused by the files shaping the dentine walls. Removing the smear layer allows the bleach to penetrate the infected dentine tubules resulting in a bacteria free canal. Chelating agents are good at unblocking partially mineralised canals.

3.   CALCIUM HYDROXIDE
      Calcium hydroxide encourages secondary dentine formation. This is useful when pulp capping or performing a pulpotomy. It is also bactericidal (kills bacteria).

4. PASTE FILLERS

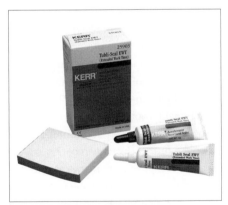

Figure 15.16 Paste filler.
(Courtesy of Minerva and Sybron Endo.)

Several types are available. They contain various ingredients such as anti-inflammatory and anti microbial agents. Paste fillers are used in conjunction with gutta percha and help to eliminate voids. Slow setting pastes are required if the gutta percha is to be warmed e.g. as with system B. Remember this when ordering supplies.

Q1. Bleach differs from other irrigating solutions in its ability to dissolve organic matter. True or false?

Q2. Why are chelating agents used?

   a. to dissolve organic matter
   b. to kill bacteria
   c. remove the smear layer
   d. dissolve dentine chips

Q3. What is the function of calcium hydroxide?

   a. to dissolve organic matter
   b. to kill bacteria
   c. encourage dentine formation
   d. dissolve dentine chips

Q4. What is the function of paste fillers?

   a. to fill voids
   b. to prevent bacterial growth
   c. to inflame the apex
   d. to be soothing

How well did you do?
   A1.True   A2.c,d   A3.b,c   A4.a,b,d

163

ENDODONTIC X-RAYS

While reading the text answer the following;

Q1. When are radiographs taken?

Q2. What are the advantages of digital x-rays?

1. TRADITIONAL PERIAPICALS
   Often a periapical radiograph is necessary to diagnose a periapical abscess and to determine if it is treatable. As the dentist is effectively working blind a periapical is taken during treatment to confirm that the file is at the apex and then another is taken at the end to check the finished root filling. Periodically, at future examinations, periapicals may be taken to monitor existing root fillings.

2. DIGITAL PERIAPICALS
   This is an extremely useful tool to help locate the apex. Digital radiography uses far less radiation than traditional x-rays and the image appears on the computer screen almost immediately making it ideal to use during endodontic treatment. The nurse does not need to leave the room to develop the x-ray. This means that the nurse can continue assisting at the chair side.
   However traditional radiography does provide a more detailed image which is sometimes required.

Q1. What are the reasons for taking endodontic x-rays?

   a. to diagnose a periapical abscess
   b. to see if root treatment is viable
   c. to determine the working length
   d. to check that the root filling is adequate

Q2. What are the advantages of digital x-rays?

   a. the images are produced quickly
   b. the radiation dose is very low
   c. the images are more detailed
   d. no radiation is involved

How well did you do?
   A1.a,b,c,d   A2.a,b

HOW DO WE ROOT TREAT A TOOTH?

THE PROCEDURE OF PLACING A ROOT FILLING

While reading the text answer the following;

Q1. In which order is the root cleaned in the step down technique?

Q2. How is the working length measured?

Q3. How are the canals dried?

Q4. Why is it important to seal the root filling?

The placement of a root filling can be a one stage or two stage procedure. Basically the first appointment involves removing the pulp, shaping the canal, cleaning the canal and placing a temporary. The second appointment involves reassessing the canal. If no infection is present it is root filled otherwise further cleaning/irrigating is required. It is possible in many cases to do both appointments in one sitting. (However in difficult cases it may take more than two appointments!)

APPOINTMENT 1;
CLEANING AND SHAPING THE CANALS

1. Local anaesthetic is given.
2. All the decay is removed and a rubber dam is placed.
3. The pulp chamber is opened and its contents removed. The chamber is washed with bleach and the entrances to the canals are located.
4. A barbed broach may be used to remove the nerve. However often the dentist does not want to risk dragging bacteria down into the depths of the canal and so proceeds straight to point 5.
5. The canal walls are systematically widened from the crown to the apex using hand files or more quickly and precisely rotary titanium instruments in a speed reducing handpiece. Basically the canal is divided into three parts; the coronal, middle and apical thirds. Rotary preparation involves a step down technique. The first file flares greatly and opens up the coronal part of the canal. This allows medicaments to be syringed into the canal. The second file is longer and finer and penetrates to within a few millimetres of the apex. The final file goes right to the apex and needs to be at least ISO size 25 to allow good irrigant penetration. Gates-Glidden burs can also be used initially to open up the canal entrances.
6. The canals are copiously irrigated throughout preferably with sodium hypochlorite/bleach to dissolve all organic matter and kill the bacteria.
7. Chelating agents are used to prevent canal blockage with dentine particles and to remove the smear layer allowing the bleach to penetrate further.
8. Endodontic ultrasonics can also be used to clean the canal.
9. The working length of the canal is determined with a apex locator or by taking a periapical radiograph of an instrument in the canal to the predicted length using the parallel technique.

10. At this stage the root filling may be completed or the canal is dried and a temporary filling placed. The temporary must seal the canals completely to prevent recontamination between appointments. (Sometimes an antiseptic such as cresophene soaked paper points are placed in the canals before temporising.) A dry cotton wool pledget is placed in the pulp camber and a temporary filling such as zinc oxide and eugenol is placed.

APPOINTMENT 2;
ROOT FILLING THE CANALS

1. The patient is asked how the tooth has been. A painless tooth with a healing sinus is good news.
2. Local anaesthetic may still be required for the patient's comfort and confidence.
3. The rubber dam is applied.
4. The temporary is removed and the canal is examined. Ideally this should be dry if it was left empty. If the canal is not dry or worse, pus or blood are present the periapical infection still persists. The canals are irrigated with bleach and chelating agent and re-filed if necessary. Missed canals are sought and if found irrigated and shaped. The tooth is then temporarized again. If the canals are clean and the tooth is symptom free it is still prudent to flush with bleach and then water.
5. The master gutta percha point of the correct ISO size is measured to the correct working length and checked in the wet canal for fit.
6. The canals are thoroughly dried with paper points.
7. The master point is then dipped in a layer of sealing cement and fitted into the canal.

8. Then either one of the following techniques is used to obliterate any remaining space within the canal. Either: Cold lateral condensation The gap between the master point and canal wall is filled by condensing successive accessory gutta percha points against the wall with a finger spreader until no space is left. Or; Vertical condensation Warmed gutta percha using System B™ and Obtura 2™ is used to seal the canal by vertical condensation. Because the gutta percha is heated it flows into every nook and cranny often revealing complicated canal systems on the final x-ray.
9. The excess gutta percha is removed with a hot hand instrument.
10. The entrance to the canals is sealed with a dentine primer, bond and flowable composite or glass ionomer as it is imperative to prevent bacteria re-entering the canal. The tooth is the permanently filled or a temporary filling such as IRM™ is placed and a future crown preparation appointment made.
11. A final periapical radiograph is taken to review the root filling.

Q1. In which order is the root cleaned in the step down technique?

   a. coronal, middle then apical third
   b. middle, coronal then apical third
   c. apical, middle then coronal third
   d. coronal, apex then middle third

Q2. How is the working length measured?

   a. by periapical using a file in the tooth and the parallel technique
   b. by guessing the length of the tooth from the pre-operative periapical
   c. using an apex locator
   d. by feel

Q3. How are the canals dried?

   a. hairdryer
   b. 3-in-1 syringe
   c. paper points
   d. gutta percha points

Q4. Why is it important to seal the root filling?

   a. to prevent new nerves forming
   b. to prevent re-infection
   c. to prevent root fracture
   d. to allow the tooth to be crowned

How well did you do?
   A1.a   A2.a,c   A3.c   A4.b

WHAT'S MY ROLE?

NURSE'S ROLE IN ENDODONTICS

Q1. What is the dental nurse's role in root filling procedures?

Q2. What procedures are taken to prevent injury to the patient and clinical team?

1. Have the patient's notes and radiographs ready and check their medical history.
2. Get the sterile instruments ready including the rubber dam. Set up any machinery required such as endodontic speed reduced handpieces, apex locators and machines for heat filling gutta-percha or a Bunsen burner.
3. Place a bib and glasses on the patient. The patient, nurse and dentist must wear glasses as they are using bleach which is corrosive and can burn mucosa, skin and eyes.
4. The nurse sets up the local anaesthetic and hands it to the dentist.

5. While the patient is numbing the nurse passes the dentist the rubber dam which has been placed on the frame. The dentist punches the hole(s) and asks for the specific clamp. The nurse has floss ready to "floss" the rubber through the contact points. The rubber dam protects the tooth from bacteria, the mucosa from bleach and the airway from hand file inhalation. The nurse places the saliva ejector under the dam.

6. The nurse operates the suction in the normal manner.

7. The nurse passes to the dentist safe ended syringes that have been preloaded with the required concentration of bleach. No instrument is passed over the patient's face.

8. The dentist may ask the nurse to measure hand files to specific lengths. The nurse is fully familiar with the international ISO colour coded sizing of files, gutta-percha points and paper points and is able to measure and mark files precisely.

9. If the apex locator is used the nurse places the metal circuit connector over the patient's lip under the dam.

10. The nurse processes working radiographs efficiently so that the dentist has the periapical radiograph within minutes.

11. The nurse is ready with temporary cements or filling pastes as required and mixes them appropriately. Just the tip of the gutta-percha points are placed in the filling paste.

12. College tweezers are used to pass points from the packet to the dentist's tweezers or tray so that cross infection control is maintained.

13. Either the nurse or dentist gives the patient post operative instructions.

14. Needles, barbed broaches and files are disposed in the sharps container. The surgery is disinfected and the remaining instruments are sterilised.

Q1. What is the nurse's role during root fillings?

   a. to make the tea during this long procedure
   b. to fill the safe ended syringes with bleach
   c. to file the canal
   d. to process radiographs

Q2. What procedures are taken to prevent injury to the patient?

   a. the patient wears glasses
   b. instruments and irrigating solutions are passed over the patient's face
   c. the rubber dam prevents bleach splashing on the mucosa
   d. the rubber dam prevents inhalation of hand instruments

How well did you do?
   A1.b,d   A2.a,c,d

WHAT SHOULD I TELL THE PATIENT?

POST OPERATIVE INSTRUCTIONS FOR ENDODONTICS

While reading the text answer the following;

Q1. What are the post operative instructions for endodontics?

1. In most cases, after the local has worn off the tooth will feel fine. However it may feel tender for the first day. This should settle. If it does not the patient should contact the surgery for the tooth to be redressed. Anti-inflammatory analgesics can be used on the first day but should be unnecessary after this initial period.

2. If the temporary breaks or falls out the patient should contact the surgery immediately even if there is no pain. It is imperative to keep to tooth free from bacteria.

3. Remind the patient again that the root filled tooth should be crowned as soon as possible to avoid fracture and make the necessary appointments.

Q1. What are the post operative instructions for endodontics?

   a. the tooth may feel tender for the first day
   b. if the temporary breaks phone the surgery to get it replaced quickly
   c. if the temporary breaks wait until your next appointment to have it replaced
   d. root treated teeth are just as strong as vital teeth

How well did you do?
   A1.a,b

ENDODONTICS IN CHILDREN

PULPOTOMY

While reading the text answer the following;

Q1. When is a pulpotomy preformed?

Q2. How is the vitality of the tooth preserved?

A pulpotomy is the treatment of choice in an exposure of a vital but immature permanent tooth. Such an exposure may occur in a playground accident. The exposed pulp must be protected from contamination in order for the tooth to remain vital and continue to mature. When a tooth erupts it takes 3 years for the apex to narrow. A wide open apex allows a good blood supply to the tooth which in turn promotes healing.

1. Local anaesthetic is administered.
2. The rubber dam is applied.
3. A small cavity is cut at the exposure site using a high speed handpiece with copious amount of waterspray to cool. A high speed is less traumatic than a slow handpiece or excavators.
4. The cavity must be cut to the level of vital healthy pulp tissue.
5. The cavity is washed with sterile saline.
6. Cotton wool pledgets are used to stop the bleeding.

7. A calcium hydroxide dressing is placed and the tooth is sealed with a layer of glass ionomer and then composite. The calcium hydroxide allows a calcific barrier to form. The filling must bond to the tooth to stop bacteria entering.

8. The tooth is monitored clinically and by radiograph periodically. The root apex should mature and close.

Q1. When is a pulpotomy performed?

a. pulpal exposure of a vital mature tooth
b. pulpal exposure of a vital immature tooth
c. pulpal exposure of a non vital mature tooth
d. pulpal exposure of a non vital immature tooth

Q2. How is the vitality of the tooth preserved?

a. by drilling without water
b. keeping the cavity clean
c. placing a calcium hydroxide liner
d. placing a zinc phosphate liner

How well did you do?
A1.b   A2.b,c

OPEN APEX ROOT FILLING

While reading the text answer the following;

Q1. What is the prognosis of root filling a dead immature tooth?

Q2. Why is the tooth repeatedly dressed with calcium hydroxide?

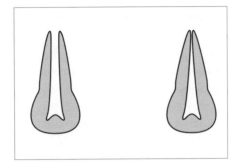
Figure 15.17 Open and closed apices.

A pulpotomy can only be preformed on a vital tooth. An immature tooth that is non vital has a poor prognosis and the patient and parents/guardians should be warned of this. It may be more practical to wait until the tooth causes problems and then extract and fit an immediate denture to be replaced with an adhesive bridge or an implant when the child is older.

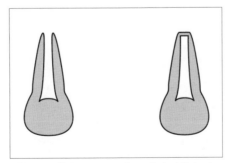
Figure 15.18 Open apex and an apical calcific barrier.

If a root filling is preformed the tooth is irrigated copiously with sodium hypochlorite to dissolve all organic matter but very little filing is done to the already thin walls of the immature root. The canal is packed with soluble calcium hydroxide and a temporary of IRM™ is placed. The calcium hydroxide is replaced every 1 to 3 months until an apical calcific barrier has formed. This may involve several appointments over several months. It is then root filled by injecting heated gutta percha with the Obtura 2 system™.

Q1. The prognosis of root filling a dead immature tooth is poor and future implants should be considered. True or false?

Q2. The tooth is repeatedly dressed with calcium hydroxide to form an apical barrier. True or false?

How well did you do?
A1.True   A2.True

APICECTOMY

While reading the text answer the following;

Q1. What is an apicectomy?

Q2. When is an apicectomy required?

Q3. List the instruments required.

An apicectomy is when the root apex and infected surrounding tissue is surgically removed. An apicectomy is required if a root filling has failed and cannot be re-root treated because the apex is now inaccessible. For example the tooth may have a post and crown which cannot be removed or a fractured instrument in the canal. An apicectomy is the last resort before extracting a tooth. It is required when a periapical infection persists.

1. Under local anaesthetic an incision is made and a periosteal flap is raised with a periosteal elevator.
2. Using the surgical slow handpiece and sterile saline irrigation a window is cut in the bone overlying the apex.
3. The apex is removed. The surrounding infected tissue is scrapped away with a curette.
4. Microsurgical instruments are used to prepare the root-ended cavity. Specialised tips can be used in the Piezon™ ultrasonic unit and these prepare the cavity and help remove bacteria.
5. Good haemostasis is achieved by placing a cotton pledget dipped in a vasoconstrictor e.g. adrenaline.
6. Root end filling material is placed e.g. MTA™ or IRM™ (reinforced zinc oxide cement). These have largely replaced amalgam.
7. The surgical site is washed with sterile saline.
8. A periapical x-ray is taken and any necessary adjustments made.
9. The periosteal flap is replaced and sutured.
10. The patient is given the routine post operative instructions.
11. Periodically the apicectomy is reviewed by radiograph.

Q1. An apicectomy is where the crown of the tooth is surgically removed.
True or false?

Q2. When is an apicectomy required?

a. failed root filling which cannot be removed
b. failed root filling which can be removed
c. blocked canal
d. patent canal

Q3. The instruments required for an apicectomy include which of the following?

a. ultrasonic unit
b. surgical slow handpiece
c. periosteal elevator
d. suture kit

How well did you do?
A1.False   A2.a,c   A3.a,b,c,d

ANTIBIOTICS AND ENDODONTICS

Before root treating a tooth it may be necessary to use antibiotics to bring down the infection. Usually amoxicillin or erythromycin are used. In severe cases metronidazole may also be prescribed.

16. Dentures

"Be true to your teeth and they will never be false to you."

While reading the text answer the following;

Q1. What is the definition of a denture?

Q2. What happens when tooth loss goes untreated?

A dental prosthesis is when artificial tooth (teeth) used to replace the one(s) missing. These can be fixed prostheses such as bridges or implants or removable prostheses such as dentures. This chapter describes removable dental prostheses.

If all the teeth in an arch are missing a full denture is needed. Likewise if some teeth remain only a partial denture is required. When no teeth remain the jaw is said to be edentulous.

EFFECT OF UNTREATED TOOTH LOSS

1. Missing front teeth result in poor aesthetics. This can lead to low self esteem. Loosing a front tooth often motivates the patient to see a dentist even if they have not seen one in several years.
2. When one tooth is lost, the biting function of two teeth is lost as the unopposed tooth has nothing to bite against. Many missing teeth limits the patient's diet to a softer diet decreasing their enjoyment of a variety of foods.
3. Missing teeth increase the load on the remaining teeth.
4. Over eruption of the opposing tooth causes food traps and may prevent future prostheses or necessitate reducing the tooth height to restore the original bite. It can also encourage bruxism which leads to TMJ problems.
5. Tilting of the adjacent teeth into the space again causes food traps and may prevent future prostheses and cause bruxism.

Q1. Dentures are removable prostheses to replace missing teeth. True or false?

Q2. When tooth loss goes untreated which of the following occurs?

    a. other teeth over erupt or tilt into the space
    b. movement of the remaining teeth can lead to bruxism
    c. self esteem improves
    d. there is a decrease in enjoyment of food

How well did you do?
    A1.True   A2.a,b,d

DISADVANTAGES OF DENTURES

It is often better to provide a bridge or implant as a denture has the following disadvantages;

- It covers a larger area of mucosa and allows plaque to collect so micro organisms tend to flourish. This makes the patient more prone to decay, Candida infections and periodontitis.
- Dentures tend to move during eating and speaking as they just rest on the gums and so require skill to wear. Denture movement is socially embarrassing.
- Denture movement can rub the gums and cause traumatic ulcers.
- Dentures should be removed at night which again can lead to social embarrassment. For this reason the patient may keep them in at night which further promotes decay, Candida and periodontal disease.

Q1. Which of the following are disadvantages of wearing dentures?

    a. the patient is more prone to certain oral infections
    b. denture wearing requires patient skill
    c. denture movement can cause ulcers
    d. removal of dentures each night can be socially embarrassing

How well did you do?
    A1.a,b,c,d

SO, WHAT DO I NEED?

INSTRUMENTS USED TO MAKE DENTURES

While reading the text answer the following;

Q1. How are the following instruments used?

1. Mirror, tweezers, probe
2. Wax knife; Heating and manipulating wax.
3. Bunsen burner; Heat source.
4. Le Cron carver; Heating and manipulating small amounts of wax.
5. Willis bite gauge; Measures the lower face height i.e. the vertical plane.
6. Fox's bite occlusal plane guide; Helps estimate where the teeth should lie in the horizontal plane with edentulous patients.
7. Pressure indicating paste; Shows high spots on the fitting surface of the denture.
8. Articulating paper in Miller forceps; Shows high spots on the occlusal surface.

Q1. A Fox's bite gauge is used to measure the lower face height. True or false?

How well did you do?
    A1.False.

THE STAGES OF ACRYLIC DENTURE CONSTRUCTION

While reading the text answer the following;

Q1. How is the patient initially assessed?

Q2. What is the nurse's role during the impression stage?

Q3. What is the nurse's role during the bite registration?

Q4. What is the nurse's role during the try-in?

Q5. What is the nurse's role during the fit?

Obviously before beginning any treatment, the patient is assessed by the dentist to see if the provision of new dentures is the most suitable treatment for that patient. This includes;

- Reviewing any existing dentures. How is the retention, wear and appearance? Can improvements be made?
- An oral examination to see how the mouth has changed. How good is the bone support? Has the ridge resorbed? Is it flabby or solid? Are the remaining teeth sound? Will the patient require surgery first, for example to augment the ridge or place implants?
- X-rays to check for retained roots and pathology such as cysts.
- Patient assessment to gauge their expectations and requirements. What type of denture would be best for them? Would a fixed prosthesis be preferable to a denture?

1. INITIAL IMPRESSIONS

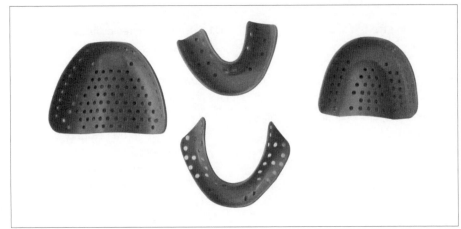

Figure 16.1 *Stock trays. (Courtesy of Minerva and Codent.)*

- In the surgery; The first impression of both the upper and lower jaws are taken with stock trays using alginate. The shade of the teeth is taken.
- Nurse's role; Get the patient's notes, mirror, probe, tweezers, shade guide and impression trays ready. If teeth are present a boxed stock tray is used. If not use an edentulous stock tray. Place a bib on the patient. Brush adhesive onto the trays. The adhesive should cover all of the inside of the tray and overlap the edges onto the outer surface. This ensures that edge of the impression stays fixed to the tray on removal from the mouth. Mix the alginate and load the impression trays. As soon as the impressions are removed from the mouth disinfect them, wrap them in wet tissue and seal them in an airtight plastic bag. This is labelled with the patient's name. The laboratory instructions are written by the dentist but the nurse must make sure the correct return date is on the docket as well as the patient's and dentist's name.
- In the laboratory; The impressions are cast in plaster and special trays are made using the models. These are made of acrylic or shellac and are perforated for retention.

2. FINAL IMPRESSIONS

- In the surgery; Secondary impressions are taken with the special trays which fit the patient's jaws precisely.
- Nurse's role; At the beginning of the day the nurse ensures that the work has returned from the laboratory. Place a bib on the patient. After the dentist has checked the special trays in the patient's mouth, the nurse covers the trays with an adhesive, mixes the alginate, loads the trays and the dentist takes the impressions. Afterwards the impressions must be disinfected, then wrapped in wet tissue and sealed in an airtight plastic bag labelled with the patient's name. Again the dental nurse is responsible for the return date. The patient is given a warm wet tissue and mirror to wipe their face.
- In the laboratory; The impressions are cast in a reinforced plaster to produce the working models and wax record blocks/rims are made on these.

3. BITE REGISTRATION/OCCLUSAL
REGISTRATION

5. FIT
- In the surgery; The dentures are fitted and any final adjustments are made. The patient is given instructions in cleaning the dentures and adjusting to the new teeth. The patient is shown how to insert and remove the dentures and must be able to demonstrate this themselves.
- Nurse's role; Have ready the patient's records, laboratory work, articulation paper in Miller forceps, pressure relief cream, cotton wool rolls and the straight handpiece with an acrylic trimming bur. The nurse should be able to give the patient the new denture instructions.

6. REVIEW

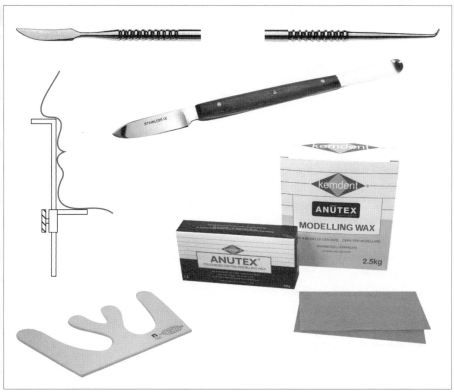

Figure 16.2 Wax knife, Le Cron, Willis bite gauge, Fox's bite occlusal plane guide and modelling wax. (Courtesy of Minerva, ALMA and Kemdent.)

Figure 16.3 Acrylic trimming bur. (Courtesy of Minerva.)

- In the surgery; The dentist records the occlusal face height using record blocks. This tells the technician how the upper and lower jaws relate to each other. The midline is marked and the type of occlusion required is stated.
- Nurse's role; The nurse makes sure the work is back and the patient's records are present. Place a bib on the patient. The nurse must also get ready the Bunsen burner, wax knife, Le Cron, sheet of modelling wax, Willis bite gauge and Fox's bite occlusal plane guide. Again the nurse is responsible for disinfecting the work and for ensuring the return date on the laboratory sheet.
- In the laboratory; Using the bite blocks the models are now mounted on an articulator. The acrylic teeth are set up in wax. This is a perfect copy of the proposed final denture.

4. TRY-IN

- In the surgery; The dentist checks the try-in for fit, occlusion and appearance. The patient is given a mirror to see how the denture looks. As the teeth are in wax they can be repositioned if necessary. The patient must approve the appearance and bite before the denture is finished.
- Nurse's role; The nurse makes sure that the patient's records and laboratory work is present. If the dentist needs to make any adjustments the nurse will set up the Bunsen burner, Le Cron, wax knife, articulation paper and sheets of modelling wax. A large hand mirror is provided for the patient. Again the nurse is responsible for disinfecting the work and for the return date.
- In the laboratory; The wax is replaced with acrylic and the finished dentures are polished.

- In the surgery; Patient and dentures are reviewed and any problems such as rubbing are sorted.
- Nurse's role; Have ready the patient's records, articulation paper, pressure relief cream and the straight handpiece with an acrylic trimming bur.

Q1. The initial assessment of the patient for dentures include which of the following?

a. radiographs
b. patient expectations
c. oral examination
d. examine existing dentures

Q2. During the impression stage the nurse's role includes which of the following?

a. mix the impression paste
b. disinfect the impressions
c. make the special trays
d. label the impressions

Q3. During the bite registration the nurse's role includes which of the following?

a. light the Bunsen burner
b. record the occlusal face height
c. set the teeth in wax
d. disinfect the work

Q4. During the try-in the nurse's role includes which of the following?

a. must approve the appearance of the denture.
b. must provide a Le Cron carver.
c. must reposition the teeth if necessary.
d. provides a hand mirror for the patient.

Q5. During the fitting of a denture the nurse's provides which of the following?

a. Le Cron carver
b. Willis bite gauge
c. Miller forceps
d. wax knife

How well did you do?
A1.a,b,c,d   A2.a,b,d   A3.a,d
A4.b,d   A5.c

WHAT SHOULD I TELL THE PATIENT?

NEW DENTURE INSTRUCTIONS

While reading the text answer the following;

Q1. List seven instructions given to patients with new dentures.

1. Even experienced denture wearers must be warned that there will be an adjustment period. They may lisp for a couple of weeks until the tongue learns the new shape of the mouth.
2. The patient should start with soft food until they are used to the new shape and bite.
3. If the dentures rub they should go back to wearing their old set. The patient should take warm salt water mouth rinses with their dentures out three times a day to promote healing of these ulcers. However on the day of their review appointment, the patient must wear the dentures for at least a couple of hours so that the dentist can see the red, rubbed areas on the mucosa. This allows the dentist to adjust the denture precisely.
4. Dentures should be cleaned at the same time as the natural teeth. They should be cleaned over a basin of water so if they are dropped the water will cushion their fall and prevent breakage. The dentures should be cleaned with a brush, soap and cold water. Very hot water is damaging and will distort the acrylic as will bleach. Care must be taken with soft liners and clasps.
5. If a commercial denture cleaner is used the patient must follow the manufacturer's instructions.
6. Dentures should be taken out at night to prevent mucosa infections such as denture stomatitis caused by Candida. When not being worn the denture must be kept in cold water as it may distort if it dries out.

7. All patients should return for regular examinations to check the fit and function of the dentures and to examine the mouth for pathology.

Q1. Which of the following are new denture instructions?

a. The patient must wear the dentures continually even if they rub.
b. Clean the dentures with a brush, soap and hot water.
c. Dentures should be taken out at night.
d. Edentulous patients do not need regular check-ups.

How well did you do?
A1.c

172

IMPRESSION MATERIALS

1.   ALGINATE

While reading the text answer the following;

Q1. How do you mix alginate?

Q2. What are the advantages of alginate?

Q3. What are the disadvantages of alginate?

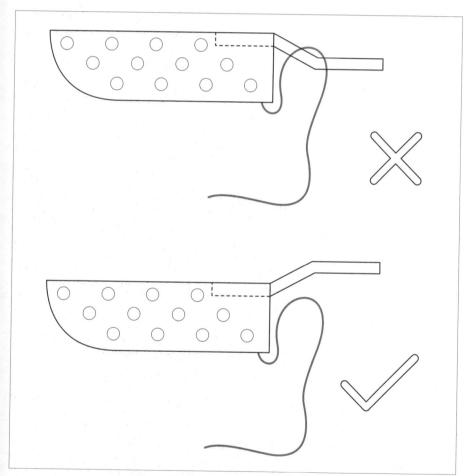

Figure 16.4 *The correct position of a tray handle.*

- Use a perforated tray and/or adhesive. Fit the handle in the tray. (Imagine the tray in the mouth, the handle has to follow the contour of the lip.)
- The thin layer of adhesive should totally cover the inside of the tray and overlap the outside edges.

- Make sure that the lid is tightly shut on the box of alginate. Shake the box, inverting it completely and then back again, to mix all the powder. Tap the box before opening. Scoop up a heaped measure of powder. Do not press it down but use the side of the spatula to remove the excess. Put the measure into the mixing bowl.

- Measure precisely the amount of water required for the number of scoops of powder. The warmer the water the quicker the alginate will set.
- When the dentist is ready mix the water with the powder in one go. Use small quick circular movements to "wet" all the powder. Then increase the circular movements, spreading the mixture onto the walls. Scoop it all up into a ball and place in the tray. Quickly pressing down the edges to remove any air spaces.
- Hand the tray to the dentist, handle first.
- After the impression has been taken it is handed back to the nurse who soaks it in sodium hypochlorite for 10 minutes. It is then wrapped in damp tissue and sealed in a labelled air tight bag.

Figure 16.5 *Alginate. (Courtesy of Minerva and Cavex.)*

ADVANTAGES OF ALGINATE

- Accurate. It records undercuts well.
- Sets within a couple of minutes and is a pleasant taste.
- Cheap.
- Alginate is the universal impression paste as it can be used in most cases.

DISADVANTAGES OF ALGINATE

- Dimensionally unstable. It can absorb moisture and expand or loose it and shrink.

Q1. When mixing alginate the water should be added in increments. True or false?

Q2. The advantages of alginate are which of the following?

    a. accurate
    b. sets quickly
    c. records undercuts
    d. pleasant tasting

Q3. The disadvantages of alginate are which of the following?

    a. inaccurate
    b. sets slowly
    c. does not record undercuts
    d. tastes unpleasant

How well did you do?
    A1.False   A2.a,b,c,d   A3.none

2.   ZINC OXIDE AND EUGENOL IMPRESSION PASTE

While reading the text answer the following;

Q1. How do you mix impression paste?

Q2. What are the advantages of zinc oxide and eugenol impression paste?

Q3. What are the disadvantages of zinc oxide and eugenol impression paste?

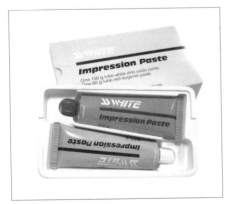

Figure 16.6 *Impression paste.*
(Courtesy of Minerva and SS White.)

This comes as two pastes; a white zinc oxide and a red eugenol paste.

- Put petroleum jelly on the patient's lips as this impression paste is very sticky.
- Dispense equal lengths of the two pastes on a mixing pad.
- Mix rapidly until there are no streaks. Keep the pink paste to the centre of the pad.
- Clean the spatula with a tissue in case there are streaks on it. Pick up some of the mix with the spatula and hand it to the dentist, handle first.

ADVANTAGES OF ZINC OXIDE AND EUGENOL

- Very useful for relining dentures.
- The impression can be improved by adding freshly mixed paste to a void in the set impression and reinserting it back into the patient's mouth.

DISADVANTAGES OF ZINC OXIDE EUGENOL

- Some patients are sensitive to eugenol.
- It may not record all the undercuts as the impression material may tear away from the tray in these areas.
- It sticks to the patient's lips and is messy to use.

Q1. Which of the following are the correct ways to mix impression paste?

    a. Put twice as much zinc oxide as eugenol on the mixing pad.
    b. Put twice as much eugenol as zinc oxide on the mixing pad.
    c. Put equal amounts of zinc oxide and eugenol on the mixing pad.
    d. Mix the two pastes until all the streaks have gone.

Q2. The impression can be improved by adding freshly mixed impression paste and reinserting it in the patient's mouth. True or false?

Q3. The disadvantages of impression paste are which of the following?

    a. Some patients are sensitive to the impression paste.
    b. It tears in deep undercuts.
    c. It tastes horrible.
    d. It is messy to use.

How well did you do?
    A1.c,d   A2.True.   A3.a,b,d

3.   ELASTOMERS

While reading the text answer the following;

Q1. When are elastomers used?

Q2. What are the advantages of elastomers?

Q3. What are the disadvantages of elastomers?

Examples of elastomers are addition silicones and polyethers.
These "rubber" impression pastes are used in acrylic special trays and give a very accurate and stable impression of the mouth. This can be useful when constructing metal dentures or over dentures with attachments. Accuracy is further increased by using a heavy body paste in the tray and a light body wash over the teeth.

ADVANTAGES OF ELASTOMERS

- Strong and elastic so the impression is unlikely to tear on removing from the mouth.
- More accurate and more dimensionally stable than alginate.

74

DISADVANTAGES OF ELASTOMERS

- Higher cost.
- Technique is more complicated.

Q1. Elastomers are used when a highly accurate impression is required. True or false?

Q2. The advantages of elastomers are which of the following?

- **a.** record undercuts
- **b.** accurate
- **c.** dimensionally stable
- **d.** tears easily

Q3. The disadvantages of elastomers are which of the following?

- **a.** expensive
- **b.** inaccurate
- **c.** dimensionally unstable
- **d.** more complicated technique

How well did you do?
A1.True.   A2.a,b,c   A3.a,d

TYPES OF DENTURES AND DENTURE PROCEDURES

1.   ACRYLIC DENTURES
While reading the text answer the following;

Q1. How do full dentures stay in place?

Q2. What are the disadvantages of acrylic dentures?

Acrylic is used to make full and partial dentures. Stainless steel clasps can be incorporated into partial acrylic dentures to aid retention. Acrylic dentures rest entirely on the mucosa. In order to stay in place they must be a good fit and engage in any available undercuts found in the bone or teeth. Upper full dentures rely on the suction of a film of saliva between the denture and palate. A little ridge of acrylic called a post dam is placed along the posterior border of the upper full denture to seal the back and maintain this suction.

ADVANTAGES

- Cheapest choice of all removable and fixed prostheses.

DISADVANTAGES

- Lower partial dentures can be "gum strippers" as they may accelerate gingival recession.
- A lot of mucosa needs to be covered with acrylic for the dentures to be useable.

Q1. How do full acrylic dentures stay in place?

- **a.** by suction from a film of saliva between the mucosa and the upper denture
- **b.** by engaging bony undercuts
- **c.** by the post dam in the lower denture
- **d.** by fitting well

Q2. Unfortunately lower partial acrylic dentures can accelerate gingival recession. True or false?

How well did you do?
A1.a,b,d   A2.True

2.   METAL DENTURES

While reading the text answer the following;

Q1. How are cobalt chrome dentures made?

Q2. What are the advantages of cobalt chrome dentures?

Metal dentures are usually made of a cobalt and chrome framework which supports the acrylic teeth. Partial dentures are often made with a metal framework. These dentures are supported by the teeth and are better tolerated by the soft tissues. Sometimes the palate of a full upper denture is made of metal if the patient has a heavy bite. In these cases an acrylic denture would fracture. Cobalt chrome dentures are made in a similar way to acrylic dentures but for the following differences;

- Occlusal rests are placed in the abutment teeth. These provide the necessary space for clasps and help to seat the denture, allowing it to rest on the teeth.
- The final impression is often taken with the highly accurate elastomer rather than alginate. The metal framework cannot be adjusted and so must fit the mouth perfectly or be remade!
- Often there are two try-ins. One with a wax-up of the teeth and another of the metal framework.
- The laboratory work involved in producing the metal framework is detailed and time consuming so you will have to give the technician more time for this part before recalling the patient.

After the denture is fitted the patient must be given the usual instructions but they should also be warned against using bleach based cleaning products as these will corrode the metal framework.

ADVANTAGES

- As metal is stronger than acrylic the dentures tend to be thinner and cover less mucosa and teeth. This is healthier for the gingivae as fewer microbes can accumulate.
- Metal is strong and can accommodate heavy bites which would fracture acrylic dentures.
- Metal dentures tend to be supported by the teeth rather than the mucosa and so are less traumatic to the soft tissues.
- Skeleton designs in upper dentures allow the palate to remain uncovered and allows the patients to feel the food in their mouths.

DISADVANTAGES

- Some patients are allergic to chrome.
- Metal dentures take slightly longer to make and are more expensive than acrylic ones.

Q1. When making cobalt chrome dentures which of the follow apply?

   a. a special tray is not required
   b. elastomer is often used for the final impression
   c. there are two try-ins
   d. occlusal rests are placed in adjacent teeth

Q2. Which of the following are advantages of cobalt chrome dentures?

   a. stronger than acrylic
   b. less bulky than acrylic
   c. more hygienic than acrylic
   d. better for the mucosa

How well did you do?
   A1.b,c,d   A2.a,b,c,d

3.   FLEXIBLE DENTURES

While reading the text answer the following;

Q1. What are flexible dentures?

Q2. What are the advantages of flexible dentures?

These dentures are made of nylon which is flexible when placed in warm water. (Warm not hot water which can permanently distort all dentures!) They are made the same way as acrylic dentures but during the final stage nylon rather than acrylic is used for the base. However the teeth are still made of acrylic. The teeth are only mechanically and not chemically held in place as nylon does not bond to acrylic.

ADVANTAGES

- Good for partial dentures where there are free end saddles (no back teeth) or the patient has only a few teeth left which are all spaced apart.
- Good for dentures with large undercuts due to tilted teeth or deep bony undercuts.
- Often a palate is not required in the upper jaw.

DISADVANTAGES

- Patient selection is important. For example the patient must have a good ridge and adequate vertical dimension (enough space for the height of the teeth).
- The patient must not grind their teeth as the acrylic teeth are not chemically bonded to the nylon base and could be lost.
- If these dentures break they are harder to mend. This means that they often take longer to mend as they are sent to a special laboratory and they are more likely to fracture again in the same position.

Q1. Flexible dentures are nylon dentures which can flex when warmed. True or false?

Q2. Which of the following are advantages of flexible dentures?

   a. They engage deep undercuts.
   b. Patient selection is unimportant.
   c. They may be good for free end saddles.
   d. Useful in bruxism.

How well did you do?
   A1.True   A2.a,c

4.   IMMEDIATE DENTURES

While reading the text answer the following;

Q1. Why are immediate dentures necessary?

Q2. How are they made?

Q3. Why do they need to be relined?

Q4. What specific instructions are given with immediate dentures?

When a tooth is extracted the bone resorbs (shrinks) and reshapes for the next six months. Ideally it would be best to extract the teeth and allow the bone and gums to heal before making a permanent denture six months later. However, understandably patients do not like to be without teeth for this length of time especially if the gap shows. In these cases an immediate denture is made. The tooth shade is recorded.

Alginate impressions are taken in stock trays and the bite is registered. All of these are sent to the laboratory. The technician casts the impressions and sets up the models on an articulator. The technician then cuts off the teeth which are due to be extracted and makes the denture from start to finish. The immediate denture is returned to the surgery. The patient is numbed and the teeth extracted and the immediate denture is fitted straight away. The dentist may have to make adjustments to the denture to fit it. Ideally the patient is reviewed the next day as they are numb when they leave the surgery so they cannot feel if the denture is pressing. Also the mucosa is swollen as anaesthetic has just been injected into the area which can make it difficult for the dentist to assess the fit.

ADVANTAGES

- The patient is never without teeth.

DISADVANTAGES

- The patient must be warned at the initial examination that in six months they will need a new denture or the immediate denture relined. An immediate denture is always made out of acrylic not metal so that it can be relined.
- The immediate denture is initially resting on a raw wound which is uncomfortable.
- The immediate denture will get progressively looser over the next six months and denture fixatives may be necessary in the interim.

POST OPERATIVE INSTRUCTIONS

These include all the post operative instructions for an extraction and for routine dentures plus the following;

- The patient should wear the immediate denture that night! They should only remove it the next day. After the first 24 hours the denture should be left out at night.

- When they have warm salt water mouth rinses this should be done with the dentures out.

Q1. Immediate dentures replace the newly extracted teeth saving the patient the embarrassment of a gap and loss of bite. True or false?

Q2. An immediate denture is made in which of the following ways?

a. The denture is made, the tooth is extracted and then that tooth is added to the denture.
b. The tooth is extracted and six months later an immediate denture is made.
c. The acrylic denture is made with the tooth to be extracted on it, the tooth is extracted and the denture fitted.
d. A metal denture is made with the tooth to be extracted on it, the tooth is extracted and the immediate denture is fitted.

Q3. Immediate dentures need to be relined as the remaining teeth tend to move changing the shape of the mouth. True or false?

Q4. Post operative instructions after fitting an immediate denture includes which of the following?

a. take warm salt water mouth rinses with the dentures in
b. the immediate denture should be taken out for the first night and then left in after that
c. do not exercise after the extraction
d. analgesics may be taken

How well did you do?
**A1.True   Q2.c   A3.False
A4.c,d**

5.   OVER DENTURES

While reading the text answer the following;

Q1. What is an over denture?

Q2. Why is it an advantage to leave the roots in situ?

Q3. How can the retention be improved?

An over denture is a denture that sits over a retained root(s) or implant(s). Bone resorbs when a tooth is extracted but does not resorb if the root is left in situ. It is sometimes advantageous to leave the roots for this reason especially in the lower jaw. The retained roots often need to be root filled. A gold cap or a small filling seals the root treatment. These leave the root surface slightly domed and flush with the gum. The denture is then prepared in the normal manner. By retaining the root and hence bone you give the denture extra stability.
Stability is the denture's ability to resist being dislodged by lateral forces. Retention is the denture's ability to resist being dislodged by vertical forces (e.g. toffee).
If it is necessary to increase the retention instead of doming the root the dentist will place an attachment in it. In these situations the root is root treated and a stud attachment is placed in the top of it. The denture is constructed with a corresponding slot made for the attachment. The principle is the same as a clothes popper. When the denture is in the mouth it is held down by the stud/popper. An alternative type of attachment uses magnets. Attachments are very useful in the lower jaw when a couple of teeth are retained either side of the midline.
When no roots remain implants placed directly in the bone can be used to support a full denture in a similar manner.

Q1. An over denture is a removable prostheses that has been made on top of a root. True or false?

Q2. Alveolar bone resorbs faster if the roots are left in situ. True or false?

Q3. The retention of an over denture can be improved in which of the following ways?

    a. place a stud attachment in the root
    b. place a stud attachment in the implant
    c. place a magnet attachment in the root
    d. root fill the retained root

How well did you do?
    A1.True   A2.False   A3.a,b,c

178

6.   RELINES

While reading the text answer the following;

Q1. Why is a denture relined?

Q2. How is the impression taken?

Q3. What are the two methods of relining dentures?

If the denture is loose but otherwise fine it is not necessary to remake the whole denture. The denture may be tightened with a reline. The patient has an early morning appointment. The dentist removes any undercuts from the existing denture with acrylic trimmer burs in a slow speed handpiece. The denture is then used as a "special tray". A wash impression is taken in the denture with impression paste. During the impression the patient must bite down in their normal occlusion. The denture is sent to the laboratory where it is processed and the impression paste is changed to acrylic. This is polished and returned to the surgery that day. The patient returns at the end of the day to have the relined denture fitted.

ADVANTAGES

- The whole denture does not have to be replaced so the process is quick and cheap.

DISADVANTAGES

- The patient is without their denture for several hours.
- It is impossible to reline a metal denture.

It is possible to reline a denture in the surgery. This is done with cold cure acrylic and is inferior to a laboratory reline as the reline is very porous. The patient's mouth is lubricated with petroleum jelly. Cold cure acrylic is mixed to a creamy consistency and placed in the fitting surface of the denture. The denture is placed in the patient's mouth. Excess material is quickly removed. The patient must be warned of the bad taste (it is aromatic) and the fact that it will warm up as it sets. The denture is removed before the acrylic sets completely. It is trimmed and polished before being fitted.

ADVANTAGES

- The patient is never without their denture.

DISADVANTAGES

- Poor quality reline which can harbour more colonies of microbes.
- Initially there is a strong lasting taste of acrylic monomer.

Q1. A loose but otherwise adequate denture can be made to fit better with a reline. True or false?

Q2. The impression is taken as a wash impression inside the denture. True or false?

Q3. Relines may be done in the surgery or via a laboratory. True or false?

How well did you do?
    A1.True   A2.True   A3.True

7.   SOFT LININGS

While reading the text answer the following;

Q1. Why is a denture lined with a soft liner?

Q2. What are the disadvantages of soft liners?

As the bone resorbs the nerves within the bone lose their bony protection. Dentures press down on the exposed nerves causing discomfit. This occurs more often in the lower jaw. Sometimes this can be relieved locally be removing acrylic in that area. Often it is best to reline the denture with a soft liner. The soft liner cushions the ridge. The fitting surface of the denture is removed with acrylic trimming burs in the straight handpiece. A wash impression is taken with the denture. This is sent to the laboratory and replaced with soft liner. The patient returns at the end of the day to have it fitted.

ADVANTAGES

- Allows the patient to wear a denture comfortably.

DISADVANTAGES

- The soft liner is harder to adjust than acrylic.
- Over time the soft liner hardens with age and periodically needs to be replaced. The patient must be warned of this and advised not to use bleach to clean their denture as this will accelerate the hardening process.
- Soft liners may peal away from the acrylic over time and again need replacing if this occurs.

Q1. A soft lining cushions the mucosa making denture wearing more comfortable. True or false?

Q2. Which of the following are disadvantages of soft liners?

    a. they can peal away from the denture
    b. they become harder with time
    c. they cannot be washed with bleach
    d. they periodically need replacing

How well did you do?
    A.True   A2.a,b,c,d

8.   TOOTH ADDITIONS

While reading the text answer the following;

Q1. Why are teeth added to existing dentures?

Q2. What are the limitations of additions?

A patient with an existing denture may need an extraction. In these cases the patient is usually seen at an early morning appointment. Two alginate impressions are taken. An alginate impression is taken with the denture in the patient's mouth and a second impression of the opposing arch. These impressions are sent to the laboratory. The technician casts up the impressions. They are articulated. The tooth to be extracted is cut off the model with the denture. An acrylic tooth is waxed on, the model is invested and the wax replaced with acrylic. The denture is polished and returned to the surgery that day. The patient returns at the end of the day. They are numbed, the tooth is extracted and their old denture, with the tooth added, is fitted.

ADVANTAGES

- The whole denture does not have to be replaced so the process is quick and cheap.

DISADVANTAGES

- The patient is without their denture for several hours.
- As with immediate dentures the addition may need relining in six months.
- It is sometimes impossible to add a tooth to a metal denture.

Q1. Teeth can be added to most existing dentures and avoid the need to remake the whole denture. True or false?

Q2. Additions can be more difficult with metal dentures and are sometimes even impossible. True or false?

How well did you do?
    A1.True   A2.True

ORAL SURGERY AND DENTURES

While reading the text answer the following;

Q1. List three types of bone surgery associated with dentures.

1.   IMPLANTS
When the ridge is edentulous implants can be placed into the bone. An attachment such as a stud or a bar is placed on the implant. These attachments fit into the overlying denture, making the denture more secure.

2.   ALVEOLECTOMY
This is often preformed immediately after the teeth are extracted. Any sharp bony ridge is smoothed to make future denture wearing more comfortable.

3.   RIDGE AUGMENTATION
This is where bone is added to a resorbed ridge to enhance stability and retention. Sometimes bone is added so that implants can be placed before making the final denture.

Q1. Which of the following involve bone surgery to help the fit of a denture?

    a. ridge augmentation
    b. implants
    c. gingivectomy
    d. alveolectomy

How well did you do?
    A1.a,b,d

ORAL MEDICINE AND DENTURES

1.   DENTURE STOMATITIS

While reading the text answer the following;

Q1. What causes denture stomatitis?

Q2. How is it treated?

If the dentures are worn continually or the oral hygiene is poor a fungal infection can occur. This results from the over proliferation of Candida albicans. The mucosa which is covered by the denture appears red and inflamed. Sometimes white strands of the fungi are seen. It is treated with the antifungal lozenges, nystatin or amphotericin, sucked slowly four times a day with the dentures out.

Q1. Denture stomatitis is caused by the proliferation of the fungi Candida albicans under a denture. True or false?

Q2. Denture stomatitis is treated with which of the following?

    a. amoxicillin
    b. nystatin
    c. penicillin
    d. amphotericin

How well did you do?
    A1.True   A2.b,d

2. DENTURE HYPERPLASIA

While reading the text answer the following;

Q1. What causes denture hyperplasia?

Q2. How is it treated?

Denture hyperplasia is seen in denture wearers who have not attended the dentist for several years. Sometimes when the bone resorbs over time instead of rubbing and ulcerating the mucosa, the denture flange gradually digs into the mucosa. The chronic (long term) irritation leads to an overgrowth of mucosa in the region. The denture flange needs to be cut back while new dentures are made. If the mucosa does not respond naturally to the release of pressure (and most do) surgical removal of the excess mucosa may be necessary.

Q1. Chronic irritation by a denture can lead to an overgrowth of mucosa called denture hyperplasia.
True or false?

Q2. Denture hyperplasia is treated with which of the following?

    a. oral surgery
    b. reducing the denture flange
    c. removing the excess mucosa
    d. making new dentures

How well did you do?
    A1.True   A2.a,b,c,d

Gerodontology

While reading the text answer the following;

Q1. What is gerodontology?

Q2. What oral problems are associated with the aging process?

Gerodontology is the study of aging effects on the mouth and teeth. The oral health of the elderly is becoming increasingly important as people are not only living longer but are retaining their natural teeth.

ORAL HYGIENE OF THE ELDERLY

As patients get older they may find it harder to maintain a high level of oral hygiene. The deterioration of functional capacities such as gripping a toothbrush makes cleaning difficult. Electric toothbrushes make cleaning easier as the patient needs minimal manual dexterity and the chunky handle is easier to grip.
Decrease in saliva production can lead to widespread decay especially if the patients suck boiled sweets to moisten their mouths.
The oral status of the institutionalised elderly is often poorer that than those still living at home in the community.

ORAL HEALTH

Certain oral diseases increase with age. Periodontal disease increases with age. It progresses more rapidly if the patient becomes debilitated.
Recession increases the risk of root decay. Root decay is exasperated if the salivary flow decreases.
The risk of oral cancer increases with age. Even edentulous patients should be reviewed annually to check the oral mucosa.

GENERAL HEALTH

As people get older they are more likely to suffer from medical disorders. For example arthritis can result in greatly decreased manual dexterity. A decrease in mental faculties often leads to general neglect of the body and a greater reliance on others. The elderly may not be good at explaining their dental complaint especially if they are forgetful making consent and diagnosis more difficult.
Older people may be on several medications and may have complicated medical histories. It is often wise to confer with their doctor before finalising the treatment plan.
Also the decline in oral health may lead to periodontal disease which has been related to heart disease and strokes.

DRUGS

Elderly patients may need lower doses of medicine as they may have some kidney or liver impairment. They may also be on several medicines already which may react badly if a further drug is added. Some elderly patients may be forgetful or have difficulty reading the instructions or opening childproof bottles.

PATIENT MOBILITY

As the elderly are often less mobile there is a greater need for domiciliary (home) visits. This requires portable equipment. The range of treatment is limited by the limited facilities outside a dental surgery.
Within the surgery more time should be allowed to help the elderly into the dental chair. Elderly patients may use crutches, walking frames or wheelchairs. These patients should be able to easily access the dental chair whilst using these mobility aids.

FRAIL

The patient may need extra support in the chair. For example curvature of the upper spine may mean that the patient needs a cushion as well as a fully extended neck rest. Be aware of this when reclining the patient to avoid neck injury. Often the patient may not be comfortable when laid flat and the nurse and dentist may need to work with the patient upright.
The skeleton is much weaker in the elderly. This includes the jaw. The dental team must be aware of this particularly during extractions to avoid fractures or dislocation of the mandible.

FAMILY PRESSURE

The patient should always be treated in their best interest. There may be pressure placed on the dentist by relatives of the elderly patient to do treatment which is not in the patient's best interest. For example the patient may be perfectly content to have an edentulous mandible. They may manage on a softer diet and be unconcerned about the appearance. However their relatives may be embarrassed by the lack of teeth and push for a denture. Always remember who the patient is. Treat the patient not the relatives.

COST

As the elderly are often retired cost of dental treatment is important. High costs may limit the patient's choices.

The need for oral health care among the elderly is increasing and this demand needs to be addressed.

Q1. Gerodontology is the study of which discipline?

a. the health of the elderly
b. the health of children
c. the oral health of the elderly
d. the oral health of children

Q2. Which of the following oral conditions become more pronounced with age?

a. dry mouth
b. root caries
c. oral cancer
d. strong bones

How well did you do?
A1.c   A2.a,b,c

181

17. Mouth Cancer

While reading the text answer the following;

Q1. What is the most common form of mouth cancer?

Q2. Who has a high risk of getting oral cancer?

The most common cancer of the mouth is squamous cell carcinoma. This affects the soft tissues. However rarer cancers can occur such as cancers of the bone, salivary glands or even developing teeth.

WHO'S AT RISK?

CAUSES OF MOUTH CANCER

A substance (or agent) that causes cancer is called a carcinogen. The main carcinogens of mouth cancer are;

1. Tobacco
    Smoking cigarettes, cigars or pipes or chewing betel nut, paan or gutkha all put the patient at risk of oral cancer. The habit of holding tobacco in the buccal sulcus causes cancer of the adjacent mucosa.

2. Alcohol
    People with a high alcohol intake are more likely to suffer oral cancer. People who smoke and drink heavily are at greatest risk.

3. Sun radiation.
    Sun damage may cause cancer of the lips, especially the lower.

Patients over 40 years old are more likely to have oral cancer than younger people. Also more men get mouth cancer than women. However the number of women with mouth cancer is increasing.

Q1. What is the most common mouth cancer?

    a. squamous cell carcinogen
    b. squamous cell carcinoma
    c. squamous cell oesteoma
    d. squamous cell lymphoma

Q2. Who has a high risk of getting mouth cancer?

    a. cigarette smokers
    b. heavy drinkers
    c. older people
    d. sunbathers

How well did you do?
    A1.b   **A2.a,b,c,d**

WHAT SHOULD THE PATIENT LOOK FOR?

SYMPTOMS OF MOUTH CANCER

While reading the text answer the following;

Q1. How does mouth cancer usually present?

Q2. List six causes of mouth ulcers.

Mouth cancer usually presents as a painless ulcer that does not heal properly. People can get ulcers for a variety of reasons and the majority of these will be non-cancerous. The most distinguishing features of cancerous ulcers are that they do not heal (ordinary ulcers heal within 2 weeks) and they are not painful (most ulcers are painful or sore). Mouth cancer is usually only painful when it is far advanced. Oral ulcers caused by cancer often have a rolled border.
Sometimes the patient presents with a white patch (leucoplakia), red patch (erythroplakia) or red and white patch (erythroleukoplakia) on the oral mucosa which later develops into cancer.

CAUSES OF ORAL ULCERS

1. Trauma
    e.g. from hard food such as crusty bread or from a rubbing denture
2. Burns
    e.g. from melted cheese
3. Chemicals
    e.g. aspirin
4. Infection
    e.g. herpetic ulcers or bacterial abscesses
5. Autoimmune response
    e.g. recurrent aphthae
6. Cancer

Q1. How does mouth cancer usually present?

    a. painful ulcers
    b. non painful ulcers
    c. ulcers which do not heal
    d. ulcers which heal but then reoccur

Q2. Which of the following causes mouth ulcers?

    a. biting the inside of your cheek
    b. burning your mouth whilst eating pizza
    c. squamous cell carcinoma
    d. recurrent aphthae

How well did you do?
    A1.b,c   **A2.a,b,c,d**

EXAMINATION

While reading the text answer the following;

Q1. What does a raised lymph gland indicate?

Q2. How would you describe a lesion?

Q3. What does toluidine blue dye stain?

Q4. Why is it sometimes necessary to re-dye the patient's mouth two weeks later?

Q5. What is a mouth map?

EXTRA-ORAL EXAMINATION (outside the mouth)

As soon as the patient steps into the surgery the dentist will notice any unusual swelling in the neck. When the patient is seated the neck is palpated for lumps. This is done methodically and follows the chain of lymph glands found there. Lymph glands increase in size if fighting infections or if they have cancer cells within. A raised lymph gland in the neck may also indicate that there is cancer elsewhere e.g. breast cancer. The original site of the cancer is called the primary tumour. If the cancer spreads, tumour cells can be found in other regions of the body. These are called secondary tumours. Cancer cells can spread through the circulation and lymphatic systems.

INTRA-ORAL EXAMINATION (inside the mouth)

The dentist uses a mirror to look all around the mouth and uses gauze to hold the tongue while checking around it. This way any abnormal lumps can be felt. Any suspicious ulcer, white, red or red and white lesion can be referred for a biopsy. A lesion is an abnormality in the mucosa. Any lesions or lumps should be recorded in the patient's notes on a mouth map along with a written description and the date. The description should include the colour, size and shape, if it is flat or raised, whether it has a rolled, smooth or irregular border and if ulceration is present.

BIOPSY

If at any time the dentist suspects cancer the patient is immediately referred to the oral surgeon as an **urgent** case for a biopsy. The word "urgent" should be clearly written on the referral letter. A biopsy is an investigative procedure which involves the removal of a small amount of tissue which is then made into a slide and viewed under a microscope by a pathologist. During disease, cells and tissues change shape. A pathologist can diagnose the disease by recognising the pattern of tissue change, seeing if any unusual cells are present and noting any abnormal increase in the number of cells. If the lesion is small it is totally removed during biopsy with a border of healthy looking tissue. If the lesion is large the most abnormal section along with a margin of healthy tissue is removed. The margin between healthy and unhealthy tissue shows the pathologist if the border is invasive or not.

If the dentist takes a biopsy the dental nurse will need to prepare a suture tray and local anaesthetic. It is often best for the dentist to grab the tissue undergoing biopsy with a suture rather than tissue forceps as this causes less tissue damage. The dentist must have the appropriate tissue container to send the labelled sample to the pathology laboratory.

TOLUIDINE BLUE DYE TEST

The toluidine blue dye test e.g. OraTest™ can be used by the dentist to check high risk patients. This dye will stain the tongue and plaque as well as any lesions (damaged areas) that are present. It will not stain fillings or porcelain crowns. It shows up more lesions than can be seen with the naked eye alone. Before the test the patient should be told that this is normally a two stage procedure. The dentist examines the stained mouth. If no lesions have stained blue the patient can be reassured immediately and told that the second test will not be necessary. However if there are lesions present these are precisely recorded on a mouth map.

The patient should be asked to swill the dye around the mouth thoroughly and then GENTLY spit it out into a large plastic cup. The dental nurse can then pour this down the centre of the drain.

Q1. What may a raised lymph gland indicate?

    a. The patient has been eating too much sugar.
    b. There may be an infection present.
    c. There may be a primary tumour present.
    d. There may be a secondary tumour present.

Q2. Which of the following terms are used to describe a lesion?

    a. raised
    b. irregular border
    c. ulcerated
    d. white

Q3. What does toluidine blue dye stain?

    a. plaque
    b. traumatic ulcers
    c. cancerous ulcers
    d. tissue lesions

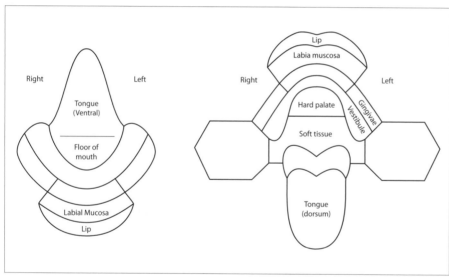

Figure 17.1 Diagram of mouth map. (Courtesy of Zila Ltd.)

Q4. If blue lesions can be seen after the initial dying the patient is asked to repeat the process two weeks later to either eliminate or confirm the suspicion of cancer. True or false?

Q5. A mouth map shows which of the following?

    a. caries
    b. periodontal disease
    c. soft tissue lesions
    d. plaque

The patient is told to return in two weeks for another routine blue dye test. (At this stage the patient must be reassured that it is routine to avoid unnecessary worry.) After two weeks the mouth is then stained again and any lesions present are compared with those recorded on the mouth map. If a lesion is seen to have persisted, the patient must be referred immediately for a biopsy. The reason for two tests is that the blue dye will stain any damaged tissue. But as you know non-cancerous lesions will heal within two weeks. Any lesion staining twice has a real chance of being cancerous and must be acted upon promptly.

Nursing tips! There are actually three rinses for the patient to take. The first and third cleanse the mouth and are acetic acid (vinegar!) so taste unpleasant but must be held in the mouth for 20 seconds. Pre-warn the patient of the taste. The middle rinse is the blue dye and again is rinsed around the mouth for 20 seconds. The dental nurse does the timing. This dye will stain clothes and work surfaces. The patient must be warned of this. The patient must wear a large disposable waterproof bib and protective glasses.

How well did you do?
    A1.b,c,d   **A2.**a,b,c,d   **A3.**a,b,c,d
    A4. True   **A5.**c

184

WHAT HAPPENS IF THE RESULTS ARE POSITIVE?

TREATMENT OF MOUTH CANCER

While reading the text answer the following;

Q1. What is the treatment for mouth cancer?

Q2. What is the aftercare?

Oral cancer can occur anywhere on the mucosa or tongue. Common areas are the lateral borders of the tongue, the floor of the mouth and the retro molar region. The cancer usually needs to be surgically removed. The patient often needs a course of radiation or chemotherapy before or after the surgery.
Likewise parotid gland tumours are excised and then irradiated. Almost all radiation therapy has oral side effects. The more radiation needed the greater the chance of side effects developing. It can affect the salivary glands resulting in a dry mouth which may be permanent. Now it is possible to be very precise and some tumours can be irradiated leaving the surrounding healthy tissue untouched. This allows normal saliva production to continue.
The larger the tumour the poorer the prognosis as it may have invaded underlying structures or spread to other parts of the body. During excision of any tumour the surgeon takes a surrounding layer of healthy tissue. This is then examined under the microscope to make sure all was removed.

However in the head and neck there are many important structures. (Remember your dental anatomy of the maxilla and mandible.) The oral surgeon must dissect the tumour away from important structures such as arteries and nerves. After the surgery the patient may have a course of radiation therapy or chemotherapy. The areas removed may be replaced with reconstructive surgery. The dentist may be required to make new dentures, bridges or place implants. Plastic surgery may be needed to restore or improve the patient's appearance. The patient may need help to rehabilitate. For example if part of the tongue is removed a speech therapist is required to help them readjust and learn to produce certain sounds again.
Psychologically the patient may feel that part of their identity has been taken away. They may feel anxiety, depression or a loss of self esteem due to their altered body image. Counsellors help patients overcome this. Treatment of cancer takes several months and involves many specialities. The patient is then recalled periodically by the oral surgeon to ensure that the area is still healthy and the cancer has not returned. The lesson is twofold; prevention is better than cure and the sooner the diagnosis the simpler the treatment and the greater the prognosis of complete cure.

A cancerous ulcer of the lower lip may be treated by the oral surgeon taking a wedged shaped section out and then stitching the lip together again. This may sound disfiguring but a patient can lose one third of their lower lip and still have a normal shaped mouth once healing is complete. Sometimes a section is not necessary and removing a "slither" of the top surface of the lip can solve the problem by removing the sun damaged tissue.

Q1. The treatment for mouth cancer is usually oral surgery followed by radiation or chemotherapy therapy. True or false?

Q2. What is the aftercare for mouth cancer?

a. reconstructive surgery
b. speech therapy
c. rehabilitation
d. regular reviews by the oral surgeon

How well did you do?
A1.True   A2.a,b,c,d

WHAT'S OUR ROLE?

While reading the text answer the following;

Q1. Why is it necessary to get the patient dentally fit before radiation or chemotherapy?

Q2. What are the side effects of cancer therapy?

Q3. What dental treatment may be required after cancer therapy?

1. GETTING THE PATIENT DENTALLY FIT BEFORE STARTING CANCER THERAPY.

Before radiation and chemotherapy the patient should have any dental work required. After radiotherapy or chemotherapy the mouth will be sore, more prone to decay and infections and will take longer to heal. There may be stiffness in the jaw making opening and closing the mouth difficult. Any decay or gum infections should be treated two weeks prior to radiotherapy to allow the mouth to heal after the dental work.

2. SYMPTOM RELIEF DURING THERAPY

Side effects from the cancer therapy can be problematic to the patient. Tooth brushing may be difficult or painful at first. A lack of saliva means that the patient is more prone to decay. Topical fluoride in toothpaste or mouthwash prevents caries. Antibacterial mouthwashes such as chlorhexidine are useful to prevent infections developing especially after surgery. A soft toothbrush or even a child's toothbrush may be necessary. Spicy foods are best avoided when the mouth is sore. Artificial saliva for example Glandosane™ helps alleviate the symptoms of dry mouth. Patients are also advised to sip water regularly through a straw if necessary. Sucking on ice chips can be soothing. Anti-inflammatory sprays may be needed to relieve a sore mouth or throat which may be ulcerated. Petroleum jelly keeps the lips moist. Exercising the jaws will relieve muscle stiffness. In the long term, lip salves with sun blocks should be used.

3. RECONSTRUCTION

After the cancer therapy is over and the patient has recovered, prosthetic work can begin. This may involve new dentures, bridges or implants. It not only restores the function of the teeth but begins to allow the patient to feel whole again. The patient's morale is boosted by being able to smile once more.

Q1. The patient should be made dentally fit two weeks before radiation or chemotherapy so that there is enough time for the mouth to heal after the dental work. True or False?

Q2. What are the side effects of cancer therapy?

a. dry mouth
b. mouth ulcers
c. stiff jaw muscles
d. delayed healing

Q3. What dental treatment may be required after cancer therapy?

a. deconstruction
b. reconstruction
c. implants
d. dentures

How well did you do?
Q1.True   Q2.a,b,c,d   Q3.b,c,d

HOW CAN I AVOID GETTING ORAL CANCER?

PREVENTION OF MOUTH CANCER

While reading the text answer the following;

Q1. How can mouth cancer be avoided?

Q2. What is the advantage of early diagnosis of cancer?

Q3. How can we help a patient who wants to stop smoking?

For the last 80 years the five year survival rate of mouth cancer has remained at less than 50%. However our ability to reconstruct the mouth and surrounding tissues has greatly improved. Still, prevention is far better than cure!

1. **Stop smoking or chewing tobacco**. This is easier said than done! However smoking is becoming more anti-social and recent changes in the laws are making people review their smoking habits. The patients themselves need to want to give up the habit. There are now products available to help them to quit such as nicotine patches, nicotine chewing gum or prescribed tablets that reduce the cravings of nicotine withdrawal. It is also useful for the patients to take up new interests, especially a sport, to take their mind off their cravings and to combat the initial tendency to put on weight. There are also help lines and help groups to assist, relaxation clinics and even hypnosis.

2. **Decrease alcohol consumption**. Excessive alcohol consumption by itself can lead to cancer. However drinking and smoking greatly increases the chances of getting a tumour. Unfortunately often the two go hand in hand. People are also often surprised by how much they actually drink.
Making a diary of your drinking habits can be quite revealing. Drinks at home and parties tend to involve more units of alcohol as glasses are often larger and are continually topped up. A guideline to reasonable quantities of alcohol per week is 14 units for women and 21 units for men.
When a patient is a smoker and drinks excessive alcohol the increased risk of mouth cancer is greater than the sum of both.

3. **Routine dental check-ups**. Patients are visually screened for cancer every time they have a routine dental examination regardless of their age or smoking and drinking habits. The dentist examines the soft tissues with a mirror before looking at the teeth and gums. In the patient's notes a comment is recorded about the soft tissue. It is usually normal. Patients should see a dentist at least once a year to screen for cancer. Even edentulous patients should be checked annually. Nervous patients can be reassured that the dentist will only use a mirror.

4. **If an ulcer does not heal within two weeks**.
If the patient is at all concerned they should contact their dentist whether or not they are due for a dental check-up. Sometimes the patient will only voice their concerns to the nurse (as they are frightened of getting bad news from the dentist). In these cases you must inform the dentist and reassure the patient that they made the right decision to get it checked. Early diagnosis leads to a better chance of successfully treating the disease. Also many patient's fears of having cancer are unfounded and they can be reassured by the dentist if this is so.

5. **Use lip sun screens**.
This is very important when outside in the summer. The lower lip is much more likely to develop cancer than the upper lip as the lower faces the sun's rays. Lip cancer can occur in young, non smoking, non drinking adults as the cause is specifically due to sun damage. It can be an occupational hazard to people who work outside in sunny climates or airline pilots who not only fly to sunnier climes but are exposed to the sun's radiation at altitude in the cockpit. These patient's tend to have a higher risk of skin cancer for the same reasons.

Q1. How can mouth cancer be avoided?

a. use sun block on the lips
b. stop smoking
c. decrease your alcohol intake
d. have regular dental check-ups

Q2. The advantage of early diagnosis of cancer is that it is easier and less traumatic to treat and a successful prognosis is greatly increased.
True or false?

Q3. What is available to help a patient who wants to stop smoking?

a. nicotine patches
b. prescriptive antismoking tablets
c. help lines
d. hypnotism

How well did you do?
A1.a,b,c,d   A2.True   A3.a,b,c,d

NURSES ROLE

Cancer is a very emotional subject and needs to be handled carefully and sensitively.
Dental nurses can talk generally to patients about the causes of oral cancer and how to prevent it but should ALWAYS refer the patient to the dentist when the patient asks specific questions about their own oral cancer. Cancer frightens most people. A lot of psychology goes into the best way to communicate with patients so that the information is given to them in a form which they can absorb without heightening their alarm or misinforming them. It should be specific to their situation.
ONLY THE DENTIST CAN ANSWER SPECIFIC QUESTIONS ABOUT THE PATIENT'S OWN CANCER.

18. Children's Dentistry

Eruption Dates and Charting

188

DECIDUOUS TEETH

While reading the text answer the following;

Q1. When do deciduous teeth erupt?

We have two sets of teeth. Our first set of teeth can be called our primary, deciduous, baby or milk teeth!

These teeth tend to be smaller, softer and whiter than the permanent teeth. They have very large pulp chambers and thinner enamel so decay can progress through the tooth rapidly.

There are 20 baby teeth in total (adults have 32). Adult teeth are referred to by number whereas primary teeth are usually referred to by letter.

A = central incisor
B = lateral incisor
C = canine
D = first molar
E = second molar
There are no deciduous premolars.

ERUPTION

AGE GUIDE OF DECIDUOUS TOOTH ERUPTION

The primary teeth start to form within the jaw in the foetus. The teeth start to erupt from the age of 6 months. There is some variation but a guide to eruption ages is;

A central incisors = 6 months
B lateral incisors = 8 months
C canines = 18 months
D first molar = 12 months
E second molar = 24 months

The baby teeth are smaller than their permanent successors. The upper deciduous molar teeth have three roots and the lower molars have two. However all deciduous molars have widely divergent roots because the crowns of the permanent premolars form between them. As the child grows older the deciduous roots become resorbed. As this happens the baby teeth become wobbly and fall out. The permanent teeth then erupt.

AGE GUIDE OF PERMANENT TOOTH ERUPTION

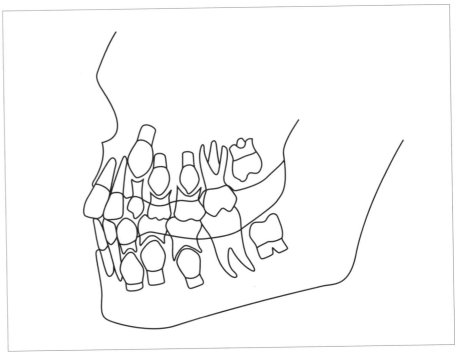

Figure 18.1 *Mixed dentition of a child aged 8 years.*

1 central incisor = 7 years
2 lateral incisor = 8 years
3 canine = 9 years (lower), 11 years (upper)
4 first premolar = 10 years (lower), 9 years (upper)
5 second premolar = 11 years (lower), 10 years (upper)
6 first molar = 6 years
7 second molar = 12 years
8 third molar = 18+ years

- The primary incisors and canines are replaced by the permanent incisors and canines.
- The primary molars are replaced by the permanent premolars.
- The permanent molars erupt as the jaws grow and lengthen.

CHARTING DECIDUOUS TEETH

Either the Palmer or FDI system is used.

PALMER TOOTH NOTATION

The mouth is divided into four quadrants:

Upper right (UR)	Upper left (UL)
Lower left (LL)	Lower right (LR)

The tooth is described by the quadrant it is in followed by it's letter.
> e.g. lower right deciduous first molar
> = LRD

FDI SYSTEM

The mouth is divided into four quadrants which are numbered;

quadrant 5	quadrant 6
quadrant 8	quadrant 7

The teeth are also designated numbers;

> 1 = central incisor
> 2 = lateral incisor
> 3 = canine
> 4 = first molar
> 5 = second molar

Every tooth can be described using a two-digit number: the number of the quadrant followed by the tooth number.

> e.g. lower right deciduous first molar
> = 84

Q1. When does the deciduous canine erupt?

   a. 6 months
   b. 12 months
   c. 18 months
   d. 24 months

How well did you do?
   A1.c

Management

While reading the text answer the following;

Q1. List three areas that the dental nurse oversees while treating young children.

Q2. How should young children be treated?

Q3. During the procedure why is it important for the nurse to predict what the dentist needs?

Q4. How can we prepare a parent / guardian for their child's first dental appointment?

Before describing the different dental procedures for deciduous and young permanent teeth it is imperative that the dental nurse understands their role.
A dental nurse must manage and oversee three areas when treating a child, especially a young or nervous child.

1.   The child patient.
2.   The dental procedure.
3.   The escort, whether this is the parent, guardian, grandparent, au pair or the whole family!

THE YOUNG CHILD PATIENT

De-clutter the surgery.
The nurse should put away unnecessary items. These are distracting for a child as the child may not realise that not everything on display will be used. Unnecessary items may cause anxiety. However, all the instruments and materials required should be ready on the nurse's worktop. Children do not tolerate long appointments so the dental nurse has to be focused and organised. As always the instruments on the dentist's bracket table should be covered with a tissue.

Children do not forget.
The dentist often feels under pressure to finish a procedure. Parents may also apply pressure on the dentist to "get it over with". Both parties may justify this by telling themselves that the child will soon forget. However, children do not forget. Childhood memories often last a lifetime. Many adults with dental phobias will relate their phobia to an upsetting childhood dental experience. Dental phobic adults often delay attending the surgery and often suffer painful abscesses and loose teeth prematurely as a result.

Some children are shy and take time to build up confidence. They need more time to get used to the dental setting before accepting treatment. They may need to see their siblings, friends or soft toy in the dental chair before they will sit down. Encourage these young children to bring their favourite toy or comfort blanket to the surgery so that they feel more secure.

It is important to allow the child to become part of the clinical team. Let them know what is happening before it happens. Build up trust. Let them stop the dental procedure by raising their hand.
The dental team must stop when the child raises their hand even when they know the child is just testing them. Give the child control.

Children want to know what they will feel, hear, taste, smell and see.

With young children, you must never assume that they know what to expect. They are too young to have any past experiences on which to draw on so, from their perspective, the sensation of dental procedures are more important than the process itself or the end product. For example, coating a glass ionomer with varnish may be upsetting because they were not warned about the strong odour. It is better to use petroleum jelly.

Young children also have little concept of time and tend to live in the present. They may not be able to differentiate between 10 minutes and half an hour. It may be better for the dentist to count aloud to three then stop or stop at the end of a story or rhyme.

Children can hear what you are saying about them.

Children are not stupid or deaf. However, they will probably have a limited understanding of conversations held between the dentist and parents. Overheard conversations may cause anxiety or confusion. It is often best for the dental nurse to take the child out of the room while the parent and dentist discuss the treatment options. Children may not understand that several treatment options will be discussed but only one may happen. They may not understand that you are discussing possible treatment several years in the future.

Talk in words which are appropriate for the age of the child.

Do not use technical terms and be very careful of the words you use.
Telling a child that they are "very brave" when the dentist is looking at their teeth is inappropriate. It is appropriate to tell them that they are "very good". How would you feel if someone told you that "you are very brave" just before you were about to embark on something completely new to you?

Dental nurses should not discuss "needles", "injections" or "drills" unless the child uses those terms. The child may have overheard an adult conversation at home or nursery. If the child talks in these terms the dentist will deal with the subject openly and honestly but in a non intimidating form.

Children do feel pain.

It is often best to painlessly numb up a child before starting an invasive procedure. Deciduous teeth do have a nerve supply. If the child complains that they feel pain during a procedure believe them. Adults know when something hurts, so do children. Even if you are sure the tooth is completely anaesthetised it is important to believe the child and not break trust. The child must be given dignity and respect.

Often parents do not understand the need to fill a baby tooth that is going to fall out. The dentist may need to explain that the baby tooth is not due to be shed for several years and if the decay is left the tooth will probably become abscessed causing pain and infection for the child.

THE DENTAL PROCEDURE

The dental nurse must know the dental procedure inside out and back to front! The nurse should be able to **predict** which instruments are required without being prompted by the dentist.
Sometimes a dentist can feel like a driving instructor having to give a constant stream of verbal instructions to their dental nurse though out a dental procedure even though they have both performed the same procedure together many times before.
This is unacceptable when handling small children and nervous patients. When performing **routine** dental procedures the dental nurse should be able to **predict** which instruments the dentist will require and when they will need them. There are three reasons for this;

- It enables the procedure to flow in a calm assertive manner. The gentle rhythmic chatter of the dentist to the child will not be interrupted by commands to the nurse which would break the rapport.
- It also saves precious time. Small children cannot tolerate staying still for long appointments so the dentist has to work quickly. The dental nurse must not hold up the procedure. This is particularly true towards the end of an appointment so the nurse should be efficient at mixing liners and filling materials and passing the curing light.
- By completely knowing your role in the dental procedure, you will hand instruments back and forth automatically which will enable you to focus on the child's wellbeing.

THE ESCORT

Remember that as soon as the child walks into your surgery you are being closely monitored by the child themselves and their guardian. Their guardian at that moment may be their parent, grandparent, legal guardian or au pair. A parent, whether natural or adoptive, will be highly protective of their child in this foreign environment. If the parent is nervous of dentistry they will perceive the dental environment (and that includes you) as a potential threat. This fear may well be inadvertently transmitted to the child even though the parent may try their best to cover their own anxiety.

The **non verbal communication** of the clinical team is paramount in conveying a kind, trustworthy, competent message to both the child patient and guardian. The nurse must ensure that the situation flows. As well as being attentive to the dentist and predicting what the dentist will need, the nurse must be aware of the parent and their emotions. Are they showing signs of anxiety? Are they gripping their child's hand or just holding it? Do they look anxious? The nurse may have to be put the parents at ease while the dentist is building a rapport with the child. The nurse should just calmly and quietly invite the parent to sit in the escort chair and give them a magazine to read before returning to the dentist and child. It is definitely not the time to leave the room to develop radiographs or autoclave instruments - too much is going on!

It is often wise for the practice to send a letter to all parents of new young patients. Sometimes the parent does not know what is expected of them. To show their support for their child they may crowd the dental chair preventing the clinical team from doing their job. Other times parents can inadvertently make comments which are far from helpful. The following is an example of the content of such a letter.

Dear Mrs X

Many parents wonder what they should say or do to prepare their child for their first visit to the dentist. We have found that the following advise is most helpful for developing a pleasant childhood experience of dentistry.

What should I say to prepare my child?

Tomorrow we are going to the dentist. The dentist helps us keep our teeth clean, strong and healthy. First the dentist will look at mummy's teeth and then the dentist will look at yours. The dentist will polish your teeth to make them clean and shiny. At the end you can choose a sticker for you and your doll / toy.

What not to say.

Tomorrow you must go to the dentist. I want you to be good and stay still and then it won't hurt.

My child always asks lots of questions. How should I answer them?

It's natural for children to ask lots of questions and we love to explain what we are doing as we are going along in a manner that your child understands and accepts. Most parents find these questions tricky to answer. Please make a note of your child's questions and ask us when you arrive. We'll happily answer them.

What will happen at the surgery.

At the surgery you and your child will meet the dentist. First we will look at your teeth and let your child watch and just get used to the new surroundings. After your examination you will get a sticker! We will then invite your child and their favourite toy to sit in the dental chair. If they don't want to sit there at first we will not push. Your child's experience of this visit is important to us. We may look at your child's teeth out of the chair where they feel more comfortable. If your child is willing, we will clean their teeth with our tickly toothbrush. Whatever is done, your child will be rewarded with a sticker, just like mummy / daddy.

How should I act?

Your child really appreciates your presence and support. We would like you to sit in the surgery and relax. We'll give you a magazine to read. It is important for the dentist to build a rapport with your child. We would like you to remain silent so that we can develop this rapport. Trying to help us may have the opposite effect so please stay in the background. Your physical presence will be enough to support and reassure your child.

We look forward to meeting you both.

Q1. Which areas does the dental nurse oversee while actually treating young children?

   a. the test run of the autoclave
   b. changing the tanks in the film processor
   c. the well being of the child
   d. the dental procedure

Q2. How should young children be treated?

   a. with authority, children should obey adults
   b. with consideration for their needs and perspective
   c. without anaesthetic, deciduous teeth do not need to be anaesthetised
   d. in silence

Q3. During the procedure why is it important for the nurse to predict what the dentist needs?

   a. to use time efficiently
   b. to enable the flow of the procedure to continue without interruption
   c. to allow the dentist to continue their rapport with the patient
   d. so the nurse can dictate to the dentist the filling material to use

Q4. How can we prepare a parent / guardian for their child's first dental appointment?

   a. with a letter explaining their role
   b. by criticising them in front of their child
   c. by shutting them out of the surgery
   d. by bossing them around

How well did you do?
   A1.c,d   A2.b   A3.a,b,c   A4.a

Dental Procedures

Children have two sets of teeth. The two sets are treated differently mainly because the deciduous teeth will normally be shed after a few years of use whereas the permanent teeth should last for the rest of the patient's life. There are also anatomical differences between the two sets of teeth. Deciduous teeth have large pulps and little dentine. The age of the child, their previous dental experiences and their ability to cope with dental treatment will all influence treatment options.

Procedures for Young Children with Deciduous Teeth

While reading the text answer the following;

Q1. What information does the dental nurse require from the receptionist?

Q2. How can the nurse help the dentist during the child's dental appointment?

Q3. What are the advantages of the dentist discussing the treatment options without the young child present?

THE FIRST VISIT TO THE DENTIST-THE DENTAL EXAMINATION

All patients should be managed correctly from the moment they first make contact with the practice. This is usually when they telephone to arrange an appointment. The receptionist should note the age of the child and if it is a routine check-up or if there is a problem. They should make a note if this is the child's first visit or if the child is anxious or had a previous bad experience. This information is usually volunteered by the parent. As always this information must be passed on to the clinical team. The receptionist may verbally tell the nurse but it must also be recorded in the patient's records and highlighted on the dentist's day sheet. Obviously, the best initial experience is a simple check up appointment rather than an emergency appointment!

The dentist will focus on the child, talking to them and building a rapport. The patient is treated kindly and courteously by the dentist. The nurse can take a medical history of the child from the parent. The dentist seats the child in the chair if they are happy to do so. The dentist gives a running commentary on every thing that they do before they do it so that the child knows what to expect. The dentist shows the child the mirror and explains that they use a little mirror to look at little teeth. The dentist often gives the child a hand mirror for the child to hold so they can see what the dentist is doing. The child is asked to open their mouth wide like a crocodile. The child may be happy to sit in the dental chair but may not want to lay back. In this situation the examination would be carried out with the chair upright. At the end of the appointment the dentist congratulates the child and suggests that at the next check-up they will be big enough to lie in the chair as they will be older.

Sometimes little children are too unsure to sit in the dental chair especially at the first appointment. The child may be upset and the parent, wanting the child to co-operate may try and force the child into the chair. In this case the dentist immediately takes control and informs both the parent and child that there is no need to sit in the dental chair this visit. This immediately takes the "pressure to perform" off both the parent and child.

The dentist asks the parent to sit in the escort's chair. The parent stands their young child in front of them between their legs. The dentist gives the parent a hand mirror for them to hold with the child. The child now feels secure as their parent's arms are around them while they both hold the mirror. The child is holding the mirror and looking at their own mouth so they are now actively involved in the examination. The dental nurse should have unobtrusively moved the dentist's chair to the dentist so that they can sit down and be at the same eye level as the standing child. The dental nurse should also quietly place a dental mirror in the dentist's hand. If the dental nurse can do these two things without being asked, the dentist and child can remain focused on the examination without interruption. This allows the procedure to flow and a successful outcome is more likely. Again the child is shown the dental mirror and the dentist explains that a small mirror is used to look at little teeth. Again they are asked to open wide like a roaring lion and the dentist examines their mouth with or without the dental mirror as they deem appropriate. The child still feels in control as they can see what the dentist is doing in the hand mirror.

When viewing the upper teeth it is better if the child moves their head up. The dentist may put up one of their hands to get the child to look up. As soon as the dental nurse sees the dentist doing this, they should put up their hand with a sticker on it next to the dentist's raised hand. This allows the dentist to drop their hand and continue the examination with two free hands. If the nurse does not do this, as soon as the dentist drops their hand the patient's head drops as it follows the dentist's hand, making the examination difficult for the dentist. The dentist needs to see the teeth and mouth clearly as young children are not good at giving a dental history. They often find it difficult to express what they are feeling. They can easily get confused by different questions and sometimes they are so eager to please they give the answer that they think the dentist wants to hear. This can be very misleading!

At the end of the examination the nurse should take the child (or children) out of the surgery to look for stickers as a reward for their (hopefully good) behaviour. This allows the dentist to have a private word with the parent. Many dentists discuss young children's treatment plans in front of the children. However this is unfair. Children are not deaf and they may suffer anxiety listening to a conversation which they do not fully understand. Also the parent may find it hard to speak openly in front of their child. When the dentist and parent speak privately the parent can focus completely on what the dentist is saying. They then have the opportunity to discuss frankly how they want their child to be treated, what options are available, what they feel their child will cope with and any remaining anxieties that the parent has from their own childhood experiences.

(These are often inadvertently passed onto the child by the parent.) This enables the dentist and parent to tailor-make a treatment plan for the patient with the child's best interests at the fore front of everyone's mind. The dentist can explain exactly how the treatment will be performed and how the parent can prepare the child. This empowers the parent and builds trust with the dentist. It also prevents confusion for the young child patient as they have not overheard several different treatment possibilities.

At the end of the examination, if all the family has been present in the surgery, it is often best for the dentist to explain to the parent and child patient that at the next (treatment) appointment one parent will be allowed in the surgery with the child but the rest of the family should remain in the waiting room. The dentist can then explain to the young child what will happen at the next appointment.

Q1. What information does the dental nurse require from the receptionist?

    a. the reason for the appointment
    b. the age of the child
    c. the past dental experience of the child
    d. the orthodontic stasis of the child

Q2. How can the nurse help the dentist during the child's dental appointment?

    a. by allowing the dentist to build up a rapport with the child
    b. by seating the parent
    c. by being attentive to the needs of the dentist
    d. by casting up the previous patient's alginate impressions

Q3. What are the advantages of the dentist discussing the treatment options without the young child present?

    a. both dentist and parent may speak openly about the child's concerns and needs
    b. various treatment options can be discussed
    c. the parent can concentrate on the conversation knowing that the nurse is supervising the child
    d. the parent can discuss their own dental phobias without upsetting their child

How well did you do?
    A1.a,b,c   A2.a,b,c   A3.a,b,c,d

193

HOW TO GIVE LOCAL ANAESTHETIC TO SMALL CHILDREN

While reading the text answer the following;

Q1. How can dental injections be administered painlessly in children?

Q2. Where should the dental nurse stand during the injection?

Children feel pain. It is often best to numb a child even for a deciduous tooth before placing a filling. All injections should be pain free. As always a running commentary should be given to the child by the dentist in terms they understand. Children are surprisingly co-operative when they know what is happening. The dentist will explain that they need to put the tooth to sleep so that they can mend it. They then explain that first they need to put the gum to sleep with a magic paste that tastes of bubblegum (or what ever flavour it is.) Always order a fast acting and flavoured topical anaesthetic. (The actual anaesthetic drug has a bitter taste.) While the dentist is explaining this the nurse should put the topical on a small cotton wool roll. The dentist holds this in the patients mouth for 30 seconds while they explain that the gum may start to tingle as it falls to sleep. The patient is sat up to rinse. The nurse should help the child to do this. Remember to only half fill their cup to prevent spills. The child should be told that the tooth will also feel tingly and big when it is asleep. As the child is laid back the dentist explains that they will now put the tooth to sleep with a special wand. The child can be shown the syringe with the needle covered if they ask. The nurse should load the syringe with a warmed cartridge. Cartridge warmers warm the local anaesthetic to body temperature.

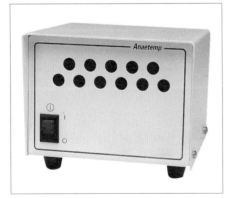

Figure 18.2 *Cartridge warmer. (Courtesy of Minerva.)*

The dentist asks the patient to close their eyes and think of something nice for the tooth to dream about. From chatting to the child beforehand, you will have discovered their favourite topic such as their pet cat, football team or favourite television program and the dentist and nurse can chat about this while injecting. The dentist injects slowly so that it is painless. The nurse should hold the patient's hand as this is reassuring. It also allows the nurse to position themselves between the patient and the parent so that they **shield the parent's view**. Most parents want to be in the surgery during treatment to support their child. Children appreciate their presence. However most adults do not like needles or injections so the nurse should shield their view.

If your practice has inhalation sedation, the child can be given a couple of minutes of sedation before the local anaesthetic injection.

Often with young children it is possible to anaesthetise lower deciduous teeth by infiltration rather than block so only a short needle is required. Discuss this with the dentist **before** the child enters the room. As a general rule it is possible to achieve anaesthesia of the lower deciduous molars by infiltration up to the age of 5 years.

As always, the nurse must have the topical anaesthetic and the loaded syringe ready to discreetly pass to the dentist on time and without prompting so that the rhythmic flow of conversation with the patient is not interrupted.
When a patient cannot feel pain they relax and the parents relax.
Remember after the dental treatment the child must be warned not to bite their lip. An adult should keep an eye on them over the next couple of hours to ensure this.

Q1. How can dental injections be administered painlessly in children?

    a. warming the cartridge
    b. injecting slowly
    c. using an infiltration injection rather than a block in children less than 5 years old
    d. using plenty of topical anaesthetic

Q2. Where should the dental nurse stand during the injection?

    a. behind the dentist
    b. between the patient and parent
    c. reassuringly close to the parent
    d. where they can holding the patient's hand

How well did you do?
    A1.a,b,c,d   A2.b,d

HOW TO FILL A DECIDUOUS TOOTH

While reading the text answer the following;

Q1. What instruments and disposables are required for filling a deciduous tooth?

Q2. How should the procedure be demonstrated to a child?

Q3. What is the nurse's role?

Q4. Describe two situations whereby a decayed deciduous tooth may not require a filling.

Hand instruments come in children's size for small mouths. Handpieces are available with small heads for easier access in children's mouths or tight spaces in adult's mouths for example the wisdom tooth region. Burs with shorter shanks should be used. When setting up children's trays also use narrow cotton wool rolls and small Dry Guards™.

While the child is numbing, the dentist explains that the soft tooth decay must be washed away with water jets and, so that the child's mouth does not fill up, the nurse will take the water away with a tiny hover. The child is warned that the hoover and water jets are very noisy but that is OK. The dentist picks up the child's hand and the nurse first of all puts the "hoover" on the dentist's hand then on the child's. Always demonstrate on the dentist first. The patient is laid back and the dentist explains that they will put the hoover in the mouth to show the child what it is like. The dentist next explains that they will use the hoover and the water jet to the count of three and then stop. The dentist then explains that they will be stopping and starting as they work but there is no need to count as the child is doing so well. If the dentist needs to use the slow handpiece the dentist explains that they are about to use the tooth tickler which is very good at cleaning teeth but tickles. The dentist picks up the child's hand and first runs the slow bur on their own fingernail before running it on the child's. Most children cope well when they know what is going on and they feel involved and in control. While all this is happening the dentist and nurse will also be chatting about the patient's favourite topics. The banter will be light and casual but the dentistry must be highly professional. This is not the time for the nurse to relax so much that they fail to predict the dentist's next moves in the procedure!

Children produce a lot of saliva and work must be done quickly if the area is to remain dry. Some children like having the straw (saliva ejector) in their mouth whereas others will not tolerate it. Towards the end of the procedure the child may become tired or fidget. The dentist may pop them up for a mouth rinse to give them a break while telling them, "Almost finished and the last part is easy so I know you'll do really well". The nurse must quickly mix the calcium hydroxide while the dentist lays back the child. The child is told that there will be a puff of air (as demonstrated on their hand) and the "cream" is then placed. As soon as the nurse has handed the dentist the calcium hydroxide they quickly mix the glass ionomer. This is quickly placed in the tooth and light cured with the magic blue wand. Light cured materials are better than chemically cured ones as they set more quickly.

Deciduous teeth have large pulps and little dentine. A pinpoint exposure of a vital tooth should be pulp capped with calcium hydroxide before filling.

If the child is older and there is no pain or infection there may be no need to fill a carious deciduous tooth. Both the child and the parent should be told that decay is present but that the baby tooth will be shed before the decay causes any problems so that there is no need to fill this time. Oral hygiene instructions and dietary advise should be reiterated and the child should be aware that if the decay was in a permanent tooth, the tooth would have to be filled.

If the child is young and particularly shy or nervous but the parent is willing to change the diet and improve the oral hygiene, regular fluoride applications may be enough to stabilise some dental decay. The decay will darken to become arrested decay. This requires a lifestyle change for the family in order to be successful. These teeth must be closely monitored by the dentist.

Extensive widespread decay in a young child may necessitate several extractions under one general anaesthetic in a hospital. This may have later consequences such as delayed eruption of the permanent teeth, orthodontic treatment or teasing at school. Parents and children must not rely on extractions under general anaesthetic as a way to solve all dental problems.

Q1. What instruments and disposables are required for filling a deciduous tooth?

    a. small headed drills
    b. child size Dry Guards™ and narrow cotton wool rolls
    c. routine hand instruments
    d. shorter burs

Q2. The procedure should be demonstrated on the child's hand first and then on the dentist's. True or false?

Q3. When treating children, the nurse's role is to chat continually to the mother leaving the dentist to cope with the child on their own. True or false?

How well did you do?
    A1.a,b,d   **A2.False**   **A3.False**

STAINLESS STEEL CROWNS

While reading the text answer the following;

Q1. What are the advantages of stainless steel crowns?

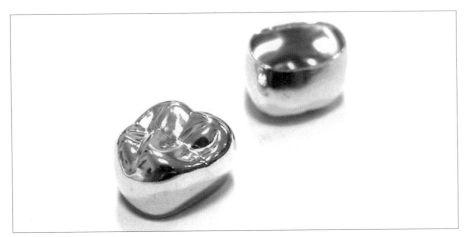

Figure 18.3 Stainless steel crowns. (Courtesy of Minerva and 3M ESPE.)

Fillings in small children are often compromised. If the deciduous molars have more than minimal decay then ideally a stainless steel crown should be placed. Studies show that stainless steel crowns have a higher success rate in deciduous teeth than all other restorative materials.

- The deciduous tooth is anaesthetised.
- The decay is removed and the crown is prepared with a tapered diamond burs in the high speed handpiece.
- The dentist chooses the correct size stainless steel crown. The crowns may be adjusted with contouring pliers and bee bee scissors.
- The tooth is lined with calcium hydroxide.
- The nurse mixes chemically setting glass ionomer to a thin paste.
- The cavity is filled with glass ionomer by the dentist while the nurse lines the crown with the remaining glass ionomer cement. The crown is quickly passed to the dentist who places it on the tooth. The child is asked to bite together to ensure that the crown is fully seated.

- Excess glass ionomer is removed with a flat plastic and probe. The nurse should have a wet tissue to wipe the hand instruments.

Q1. What are the advantages of stainless?

   a. more success than placing a restorative filling in deciduous molars
   b. more success than placing a restorative filling in permanent molars
   c. no special equipment is required
   d. great cosmetics

How well did you do?
   A1.a

VITAL PULPOTOMIES

While reading the text answer the following;

Q1. When is a vital pulpotomy performed on a deciduous tooth?

Q2. What materials are used for a vital pulpotomy?

Q3. When is a non-vital pulpotomy performed on a deciduous tooth?

Q4. What materials are used for a non-vital pulpotomy?

Vital pulpotomies are required when the deciduous tooth is alive but an area larger than a pinpoint has been exposed. The concept is to remove the coronal pulp but maintain the vitality of the radicular pulp (found in the roots). Vital pulpotomies are preformed when there is no infection present, the tooth is pain free and the pulp is bleeding when it is exposed.

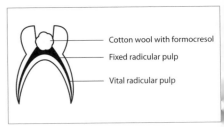

Figure 18.4 Vital pulpotomy.

- The deciduous tooth is anaesthetised.
- The decay is removed and the pulp chamber opened with a high speed handpiece.
- The coronal pulp is removed with a rose head bur in the slow handpiece or a large excavator.
- The pulp chamber is washed with sterile saline or sterile water in a disposable syringe and dried with cotton wool pledgets.

- The nurse mixes 1 drop of formocresol with 4 drops of glycerol in a glass dappens pot. The nurse dips a cotton wool pledget in the solution and passes it to the dentist. The dentist places it in the pulp chamber for 5 minutes. This solution is hazardous and should be handled with care. Five minutes is a long time for a small child so the dentist and nurse must be entertaining to make the time go quickly.
- The pledget is removed. If the bleeding continues the process is repeated. If the bleeding has stopped the tooth is filled with zinc oxide and eugenol and a stainless crown may be placed immediately or at a later appointment.

NON-VITAL PULPOTOMIES

Non-vital pulpotomies are preformed on deciduous teeth with a history of infection and pain. Indeed, the surrounding mucosa may be red and swollen and the tooth may be mobile and tender to bite on. The necrotic coronal pulp is removed and the radicular pulp is disinfected. This usually takes two appointments.

FIRST APPOINTMENT

- The decay is removed with friction grip burs in the high speed handpiece and the pulp chamber is opened.
- The coronal pulp is removed with a rose head bur in the slow handpiece or large excavator.
- The pulp chamber is washed with sterile saline or sterile water in a disposable syringe and dried with cotton wool pledgets.
- The nurse places beechwood creosote in a glass dappens pot. The nurse dips a cotton wool pledget in the beechwood creosote and passes it to the dentist.

- The dentist places the pledget in the pulp chamber and seals it in with a temporary of zinc oxide and eugenol.
- This is left in place for 7 to 10 days. A second appointment is made.

SECOND APPOINTMENT

- The temporary is removed and the tooth is checked for signs of persistent infection. If infection is still present the process is repeated.
- If the tooth is free from infection, it is filled with zinc oxide and eugenol and a stainless steel crown is placed.

Q1. When is a vital pulpotomy performed on a deciduous tooth?

    a. when infection is present
    b. when the tooth is pain free
    c. when the exposed pulp is bleeding
    d. when the tooth is mobile

Q2. What materials are used for a vital pulpotomy?

    a. calcium hydroxide
    b. glycerol
    c. formocresol
    d. beechwood creosote

Q3. When is a non-vital pulpotomy performed on a deciduous tooth?

    a. when infection is present
    b. when the tooth is pain free
    c. when the exposed pulp is bleeding
    d. when the tooth is mobile

Q4. What materials are used for a non-vital pulpotomy?

    a. calcium hydroxide
    b. glycerol
    c. formocresol
    d. beechwood creosote

How well did you do?
    A1.b,c   A2.b,c   A3.a,d   A4.d

PREVENTION OF DECAY AND GINGIVITIS IN YOUNG CHILDREN

While reading the text answer the following;

Q1. List six ways to prevent dental disease.

Q2. What specific preventative advise should be given for toddlers?

1. DIET
- If the young child needs a comfort bottle to get to sleep this should contain water only. Even milk can cause decay as the deciduous molars are bathed in lactose throughout the night. As saliva flow decreases when we sleep the milk is not washed away. This often results in bottle caries.
- Decrease the quantity of sugar in the diet.
- Decrease the frequency of sugary snacks. Sugar-free snacks such as cheese can be eaten between meals. (Note young children should not be fed nuts as they may inhale them.)
- The parents should be advised not to dip teething rings or dummies in syrup before placing them in the baby/toddlers mouth. This results in rampant caries of the anterior teeth which often decay as they erupt. The parents often believe that the teeth came through black and do not associate it with the syrup.
- Sticky sugary foods that stay around the teeth for a long time should be avoided.
- Sugar consumption should be confined to mealtimes.
- Be aware that sugar-free fizzy drinks are acidic and will erode the enamel. Many young children initially do not like fizzy drinks but are persuaded to drink them by adults and older children! Water, milk, diluted fruit juices or diluted sugar-free squash are alternatives.

2. ORAL HYGIENE

- Children's teeth need to be brushed as soon as they start to appear. Baby tooth brushes are available and these are very soft as the gums may be tender.
- The young child will not have the manual dexterity to brush their teeth effectively and will need the parent to do this for them after breakfast and just before going to bed. Very little toothpaste should be used as toddlers tend to suck on the toothbrush and cannot rinse out. Always use children's toothpaste. As the child gets older the parents may allow them to brush their own teeth while being supervised.
- Young children should not be allowed to run around or play with toothbrushes in their mouths.
- From the age of 12 years children may be shown how to floss.

3. FLUORIDE

- This toughens the enamel making it harder to demineralise. This is very effective in developing teeth.
- The dentist may apply fluoride to children's teeth to strengthen the teeth and to perform a confidence-building, non-invasive procedure.
- Fluoride encourages remineralisation of porous enamel and, along with improvements in diet and oral hygiene, may arrest caries.

4. FISSURE SEALANTS

- Fissure sealants form a physical barrier over pits and fissures of permanent teeth preventing decay. Fissures not only provide a stagnation area for plaque but the occlusal enamel is very thin in the depth of a fissure. It does not take long for the bacteria to reach the amelodentine junction under the fissures.
- Fissure sealants do not protect the remaining surfaces of the tooth and the patient and parents should be informed of this.

5. REGULAR DENTAL EXAMINATIONS

- Enables the detection of demineralisation and early decay allowing it to be arrested by non intrusive methods such as fluoride applications or minimal restorations to conserve the remaining enamel and dentine.
- Decay must be detected early as it spreads very rapidly through children's teeth. Treating children who have been up all night with an abscess is not easy and everything should be done to prevent carious infections.
- Regular examinations allow the dentist to monitor the oral hygiene and sugar consumption and re-educate the parents and children when necessary.

6. PATIENT EDUCATION

- As mentioned, the adult accompanying the child may be a grandparent or au pair and the dental team may not get to meet the parents. This makes education difficult as you are relying on an intermediary to get the message across. Grandparents may feel they know best and neglect to pass on the dentist's dietary advise especially if they like to buy their grandchildren sweets. An au pair may not feel that they have the authority to tell the parents how they should look after the children's teeth.

Q1. List six ways to prevent dental disease.

    a. regular dental appointments
    b. regular sleep
    c. regular consumption of sticky, sugary foods
    d. fissure sealants

Q2. What specific preventative advise should be given for toddlers?

    a. dip teething rings in soothing honey
    b. lactose in milk may decay teeth if the toddle goes to sleep with a bottle of milk
    c. floss daily
    d. fissure sealants are often placed to protect the deciduous molars

How well did you do?
    A1.a,d   A2.b

Procedures on Older Children with Immature Permanent Teeth

FISSURE SEALANTS

While reading the text answer the following;

Q1. Why are pits and fissures vulnerable to decay?

Q2. What is required to place a fissure sealant?

Q3. What are the patient instructions for mouth guards?

As you know pits and fissures collect plaque, cannot be cleaned thoroughly and have only a thin layer of enamel. Children usually get their first permanent molars at the age of 6 years, before they have shed any of their deciduous teeth. Often the parents do not realise that these are new adult teeth and so may not brush them efficiently. These molars are right at the back of a small mouth and so are more difficult to reach with a toothbrush. It is no surprise that the most common area to decay in the permanent dentition is the occlusal surfaces of the first molars. Decay in all pits and fissures can be prevented with fissure sealants.

Ideally the posterior teeth should be sealed as soon as they erupt. For example the first permanent molars are usually sealed at 6 years of age. Fissure sealing has the added advantage of performing a dental procedure without the need for injections or drills and so building the confidence of the child.

As with all young children the procedure is fully explained beforehand in appropriate terms. While the patient is sitting upright in the dental chair, the dentist will explain every detail, showing the etchant gel on their finger, then the child's, placing the sealant on their finger, then the child's, using the suction on their finger, then the child's and so on.

- The child is reclined and the dentist gives a commentary on the proceedings.
- The teeth are polished with pumice or prophy paste in a dappens pot. The child is warned that this will feel gritty but they will be allowed to rinse out in a minute.
- The patient is allowed to rinse and then reclined again.
- The dentist explains that a straw (saliva ejector) will be placed in their mouth. The dentist shows the child the Dry Guards™ before placing them.
- The child is forewarned that they will have to keep their mouth open for a few minutes. The etchant is placed on the child's tooth and after the required time washed and dried with the 3-in-1 syringe.
- The nurse must keep the suction close to the tooth to keep it dry.
- The sealant is placed with a syringe or applicator and the tooth is light cured. The nurse holds the protective orange shield.
- The process is repeated for the other teeth. The child is praised and allowed to rinse.

- Both the child and parents are reminded that sealants only protect the biting surfaces and that the teeth still need to be cleaned diligently to prevent decay in other areas.

MOUTH GUARDS

Mouth guards protect the teeth against trauma during contact sports and boisterous play.
Before taking an impression the procedure is fully explained and a bib placed. The patient is told that the tray will be in their mouth for a couple of minutes until the soft paste has set. First the unloaded tray is placed in the mouth and then the tray loaded with alginate. The impression is taken, cleaned, disinfected, rinsed and sent to the laboratory.
The patient normally returns a week later to have the mouth guard fitted. The patient is told to clean the mouth guard in cool water. Hot water and bleach will damage the mouth guard. Mouth guards can be soaked in mouthwash to disinfect and freshen them. The mouth guard should be stored in the box provided when not in used.

Q1. Why are pits and fissures vulnerable to decay?

 a. they retain plaque
 b. the enamel is thin in the depths of a fissure and pit
 c. six year olds may not have the dexterity to clean the first permanent molars well
 d. sticky, sugary food is easily trapped in pits and fissures

Q2. What is required to place a fissure sealant?

 a. pumice or prophy paste
 b. etchant
 c. dentine bonds
 d. curing light

Q3. What are the patient instructions for mouth guards?

 a. use the mouth guard in any situation where the teeth may be knocked
 b. disinfect the mouth guard with boiling water
 c. bleach is used to clean the mouth guards
 d. store in the box provided

How well did you do?
 A1.a,b,c,d   A2.a,b,d   A3.a,d

TRAUMATISED TEETH

While reading the text answer the following;

Q1. How may the patient present?

Q2. Why is the maturity of the tooth important when treating fractured teeth?

Q3. How is a wire and composite splint placed?

Q4. What instructions would you give over the phone to a patient with an avulsed tooth?

It is the nature of children to have a few falls and tumbles. The elastic bone of children can absorb most knocks however some playground and sporting accidents result in more extensive damage. Dentists often need to repair fractured incisors of immature permanent teeth. Children can traumatise their permanent incisors from the age of 7 years. With immature teeth the root is still forming and the root apex is open. An open apex allows a good blood supply to the tooth but poses problems if root treatment is required.

With any traumatic injury it is important to enquire if the child is immunised against tetanus especially if the wound is contaminated with soil.

When a child has been involved in an accident there are often lacerations to the lips, bruising, swelling and bleeding. Both the child and parents (or guardian) may be in emotional shock and anxious. By being calm and competent both the child and adults will begin to relax as they realise they are now in safe hands. Adults can feel very guilty that a child under their care has been injured, and perhaps even more so if the child is not their own.

ASSESSMENT OF THE EXTENT OF THE INJURY

These appointments are usually emergency appointments and both the dentist and the nurse will be expected to work efficiently. The dentist will prioritise treatment. The dentist will immediately assess the extent of the injury. Is the bone fractured? Do the soft tissues need suturing or will they heal naturally? Is the fractured tooth lodged in the lip? What is the extent of the tooth injury? Radiographs help the dentist in their assessment.

COMPOSITE BONDING

If the enamel and dentine have been fractured but the pulp is not exposed the tooth can be repaired in the routine manner with dentine bonds, acid etch technique and composite.

PULPAL INVOLVEMENT

If there is a clean pinpoint pulpal exposure the tooth can be pulp capped with calcium hydroxide before restoring with composite. A bigger exposure in a tooth with an open root may also survive as the open root means that the tooth has a good blood supply which promotes healing. Keeping the wound clean with sterile water or saline is important during this procedure. An extensive fracture that exposes the pulp in an immature tooth has a bad prognosis. Root treatment of an open apex root has been described in detail in Chapter 15 Endodontics. In the long term an implant

or adhesive bridge will provide more predictable solutions. If the root apex is closed root treatment is the treatment of choice followed by composite bonding. A permanent crown may be placed when the child is 16 to 18 years old.

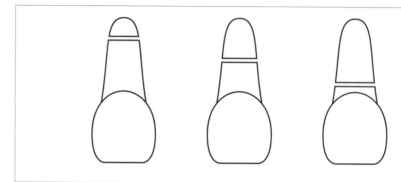

Figure 18.5 Fractured roots.

FRACTURED ROOT

If the tooth is fractured in the apical one third, the tooth will not be mobile and no treatment is required. If the tooth is fractured in the middle or coronal third the crown will be mobile and the teeth will need to be splinted until they become firm. If a fracture is close to the gingival crevice the prognosis is poor. In these cases a decision is made to either remove the coronal portion and root treat the remaining root and make a post and crown or to extract both portions.

COMPOSITE AND WIRE SPLINT

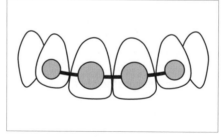

Figure 18.6 Composite and wire splint.

- Cotton wool rolls and a saliva ejector are used to keep the area as dry as possible.

- Etchant is applied to the mobile and neighbouring teeth. After 30 seconds the etch is removed by the 3-in-1 syringe and suction. The teeth are washed and dried.

- Enamel bond is applied with an applicator and cured with the curing light. The nurse shields the light with the orange screen.
- A piece of orthodontic wire is cut to span the number of teeth involved. The wire is curved to the required shape.
- The wire is held against the teeth and composite is placed over the wire and bonded to the labial surfaces of the teeth with the curing light.
- The patient is asked to eat a soft diet over the next few days and to avoid the traumatised teeth.
- The splinting period depends upon the injury sustained. If the periodontal ligament is damaged the splint may only be required for 1 week if at all. If the alveolar bone is fractured the split may be required for 1 month. If the root is fractured, the splinting period may be 2 or 3 months.

- In the case of fractured roots, sometimes little or no repair takes place. The fracture site becomes filled with inflamed granulation tissue and the tooth remains loose. In these cases the tooth is extracted and a temporary denture is made. Long term solutions include adhesive bridges or implants.

DISPLACED PERMANENT TEETH

Displaced teeth should be anaesthetised and repositioned before splinting. Teeth that have been displaced labially or palatelly or have been extruded can be gently pushed back into position and splinted. If there has been delay in seeking treatment or the tooth is intruded they will need to be repositioned by orthodontic means. For the first few days the patient should have a soft diet and avoid chewing on that region.

If the root has an open apex, the pulp may survive. These teeth should be radiographed periodically for root resorption. If the root has a closed apex, the pulp will invariably die and the tooth should be root treated quickly to avoid root resorption. Again these teeth must be radiographed periodically, initially every 2 to 3 months.

AVULSED PERMANENT TEETH

Sometimes the blow to the mouth is strong enough to avulse the tooth (knock the tooth out of it's socket). The first person to hear about this is usually the receptionist. The receptionist should tell the patient to put the tooth in milk and to come to the surgery immediately to have it put back in. The patient should not wash the tooth or handle it excessively. They should simply pick it up by the crown, put it in milk and get to the surgery as soon as possible. The receptionist should immediately inform the nurse that the patient is on their way. This patient has priority over patients with appointments.

As with all traumatised teeth, there is a risk of resorption. The prognosis is most favourable if the tooth is reinserted within half an hour of avulsion and if the periodontal tissues attached to the root were kept moist and undisturbed.

The dentist will immediately replant the tooth. This is often painful even with a local anaesthetic. The patient should be warned of this. The tooth should then be splinted to the neighbouring teeth. At the end of the procedure, the patient must be reassured that future appointments will be pain free. This appointment is often emotionally charged as the patient may be in emotional shock, they may be annoyed with a friend who they feel caused the accident, the tooth hurts and the procedure often hurts. Reassurance is vital at this stage. The patient is asked to return to the surgery in two weeks to have the splint removed and the tooth root treated pain free.

For the first few days the patient should have a soft diet and avoid chewing on that region. Again these teeth should be periodically radiographed for signs of resorption.

If the patient or parents are willing, and can differentiate between the palatal and labial surfaces, the receptionist can tell the patient to reinsert the tooth themselves and report to the surgery immediately to have it splinted.

All traumatised teeth must be monitored closely. There is always a risk of future pulpal death or root resorption. The traumatised teeth should be vitality tested if appropriate and radiographed periodically. The parents and patient should be warned that tooth ache, discolouration or the appearance of a sinus should be reported immediately.

Q1. How may a patient with traumatic tooth injury present?

    a. they may have lacerated lips
    b. there may be bruising and swelling
    c. the alveolar bone may be fractured
    d. the tooth may just be chipped

Q2. The pulp has a better chance of surviving trauma if the apex is open. True or false?

Q3. How is a wire and composite splint placed?

    a. using dentine bonds
    b. using the acid etch technique
    c. using orthodontic wire
    d. the mobile teeth are bonded either side to the healthy teeth

Q4. What instructions would you give over the phone to a patient with an avulsed tooth?

    a. wash the tooth then put it in milk
    b. put the tooth in milk and bring it to the surgery immediately
    c. put the tooth in water and bring it to the surgery immediately
    d. pick the tooth up by the root, put it in milk and bring it to the surgery immediately

How well did you do?
**A1.a,b,c,d   A2.True   A3.b,c,d
A4.b**

19. Orthodontics

This chapter was written in conjunction with Mr P J Turner MSc., MOrth RCS Eng., FDS RCS Ed. Consultant Orthodontist Birmingham Dental Hospital.

Orthodontics is the branch of dentistry that is concerned with the correction of irregularities of the teeth. Orthodontists are also concerned with the wider subjects: such as monitoring the developing dentition and assessing facial growth.

For many dentists orthodontics is out of the scope of their general dental practice. Dentists with post graduate qualifications may practice orthodontics. In this chapter these dentists will be referred to as orthodontists.

When all the teeth are of a normal shape and size, perfectly aligned and meet in the correct fashion then the patient is said to have an 'ideal' occlusion. In fact an ideal occlusion is very rarely seen. Most people have some minor irregularities and are said, therefore, to have a 'normal occlusion' with minor variations from the ideal which are acceptable. Where the variation becomes unacceptable then the patient has a 'malocclusion'

You will appreciate that a dental malocclusion can therefore vary from minor displacements of the teeth to severe irregularities of the teeth and jaws.

ORTHODONTIC TERMS

While reading the text answer the following;

Q1. What is the overjet and overbite?

Q2. Which teeth are important in determining Angle's classification?

Q3. List four different types of malocclusion.

OVERJET

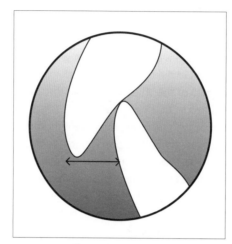

Figure 19.1 The overjet.

The overjet is the horizontal overlap of the upper and lower incisors in relation to the patient's occlusal plane. It is usually measured in millimetres using a steel rule.

OVERBITE

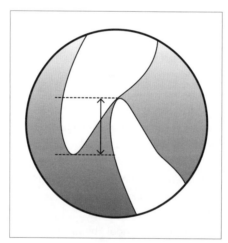

Figure 19.2 The overbite.

The overbite is the vertical overlap of the upper and lower incisors in relation to the patients occlusal plane. The overbite is described as being normal, increased or decreased. It may be complete where the lower incisors touch the upper incisors or incomplete where the lower incisors do not touch the uppers.

PROCLINED INCISORS

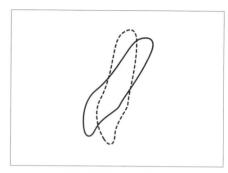

Figure 19.3 Proclined incisor.

Proclined incisors tilt further forward from the normal, expected inclination.

RETROCLINED INCISORS

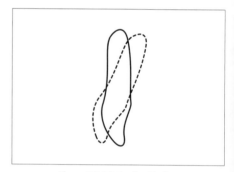

Figure 19.4 Retroclined incisor.

Retroclined incisors tilt backward.

ROTATIONS

Where teeth have significant rotations, these are noted. A rotation is where a tooth is rotated around it's own axis.

CLASSIFICATION OF OCCLUSION/MALOCCLUSION

It is helpful to classify a patient's occlusion or malocclusion by describing how their front teeth meet on closing: this is termed the "Incisor Classification" and has been used for many years.

Another way to classify occlusion and malocclusion is to describe how the upper and lower first molar teeth meet. This is termed 'Angle's Classification and is still used, as it is useful to know when planning treatment, but Angle's original premise was incorrect in assuming that the first molar teeth reflected how the jaws relate to each other.

1. INCISOR CLASSIFICATION

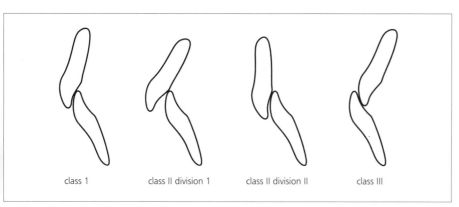

class 1   class II division 1   class II division II   class III

Figure 19.5 Incisor classification.

2. ANGLE'S CLASSIFICATION

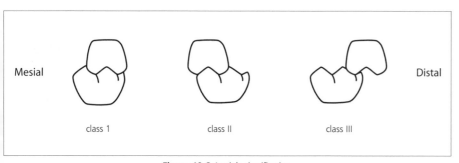

Mesial   class 1   class II   class III   Distal

Figure 19.6 Angle's classification.

CLASS 1 MALOCCLUSION

- A class 1 occlusion is regarded as a 'normal' incisor relationship where the overjet is 2mm. The overbite is normal and complete. This means that the lower incisor edges occlude with the middle third of the palatal aspect of the upper incisors.

- However even though there is a normal overbite and overjet, discrepancies can still occur in the dental arches, such as crowding or missing teeth.
- Angle's classification states that the mesiobuccal cusp of the upper first permanent molar occludes with the buccal groove of the lower first permanent molar.

CLASS II DIVISION 1 MALOCCLUSION

- The overjet is increased and the upper incisors are usually proclined.
- The lower incisors bite or would bite behind the middle third of the palatal surface of the upper incisors – either onto the palatal third of the incisor or onto the palatal mucosa.
- The lower lip often rests behind the upper incisors.
- There is often an Angle's class II molar relationship.

CLASS II DIVISION II MALOCCLUSION

- The upper central incisors are usually upright or slightly retroclined. The lateral incisors may be retroclined or proclined and are often rotated.
- The overbite is usually increased and complete and may be traumatic. A traumatic bite occurs where the lower incisors bite onto the palatal mucosa. This may be damaging to the palatal gingivae but only where the patient also has poor oral hygiene.
- Typically the molars are Angle's class II.

CLASS III MALOCCLUSION

- Strictly speaking, a Class III incisor relationship exists where the overjet is reduced. However, often there is a reversed overjet so that the lower anterior teeth lie in front of the upper anterior teeth.

- The molar relationship tends towards Angle's class III.

Q1. Overbite can be described in which of the following ways?

    a. as the horizontal overlap of the upper and lower incisors
    b. as the vertical overlap of the upper and lower incisors
    c. as normal, increased or decreased
    d. as complete or incomplete

Q2. Which teeth are important in determining Angle's classification?

a. incisors
b. canines
c. first molars
d. second molars

Q3. Which of the following are characteristics of a Class II division II malocclusion.

a. the lower incisors occlude with the middle third of the palatal aspect of the upper incisors
b. the overjet is increased
c. the overbite is increased
d. the overjet is reversed

How well did you do?
A1.b,c,d   A2.c   A3.c

CAUSES OF MALOCCLUSION

While reading the text answer the following;

Q1. List nine causes of malocclusion.

Malocclusion is thought to be caused by a combination of genetics and the environment but debate still rages on the relative importance of each. An example where genetics plays a role is where an individual inherits a large lower jaw in Class III malocclusion. An environmental example is a patient with a digit sucking habit that causes the upper incisors to procline.

1. CROWDING AND SPACING
   When there is insufficient room for the teeth within the jaws crowding occurs. In essence the size of the teeth do not match the size of the jaws. Some individuals have the opposite condition: the teeth, whilst all present are spaced in the dental arches and patients seek treatment to close these spaces.

2. JAW SIZE DISCREPANCIES
   Jaw discrepancies are an imbalance in the position or size of the jaws and are an important factor in causing many malocclusions.

For example a Class III jaw relationship (where the mandible is further forwards relative to the maxilla) can be caused by any combination of the following;

- The maxilla is small in relation to the mandible.
- The maxilla is set back in relation to the mandible.
- The mandible is large in relation to the maxilla.
- The mandible is set forwards in relation to the maxilla.

Where jaw discrepancies are small this can be compensated for by a change in the angulation of the teeth – a phenomenon that nature achieves. Minor jaw discrepancies may be 'camouflaged' by changing the angulation of the teeth using orthodontic appliances. However beyond a certain point such compensation is not possible and the only way to fully address a malocclusion is by a combination of orthodontics and jaw surgery.

3. IMPACTED TEETH
   Teeth may be prevented from erupting for various reasons. There may be a lack of space, the teeth may have developed in an abnormal (ectopic) position or there may an obstruction, such as retained deciduous teeth or a supernumerary tooth.

4. CONGENITALLY MISSING TEETH
   Some people never develop certain teeth. The most common teeth to be missing are the third molars. Other teeth that tend to be absent are the upper lateral incisors, the second premolars and the lower central incisors. The term used for missing teeth is hypodontia. If six or more teeth are missing (apart from the third molars) then the patient is said to have severe hypodontia,

5. SUPERNUMARY TEETH
   Some people develop extra teeth called supernumerary teeth. They are common in the upper midline and can prevent the permanent central incisor teeth erupting or create a diastema. Sometimes supernumerary teeth look exactly like a normal erupted tooth and are termed supplemental teeth.

6. THUMB/FINGER SUCKING
   A persistent thumb or finger sucking habit, if practised often enough by the patient, will cause a malocclusion. Typically the upper teeth are proclined, there is an anterior open bite and anterior asymmetry in the bite. The back teeth are often in crossbite as well. In some cases the thumb also prevents the upper incisor teeth from fully erupting.

7. RETAINED DECIDUOUS TEETH
   Some patients present for assessment partly because have held onto their deciduous teeth. This may purely be owing to delayed dental development but may also be a sign of missing adult teeth.

8. ANKYLOSIS

Occasionally the deciduous teeth become directly attached to the jaw bone as the periodontal ligament is lost over an area of root surface. In this situation the teeth become 'stuck' to the bone. These teeth will no longer erupt and can not be moved orthodontically. Classically the adjacent adult teeth continue to erupt which gives the appearance of the deciduous teeth 'submerging'.

9. EARLY LOSS OF TEETH

Early extraction of deciduous teeth may cause crowding of the permanent teeth. If deciduous canines are lost early on one side, the dental midline may move across. Early loss of deciduous molar teeth can result in the permanent molar teeth drifting forwards which would result in later crowding in the buccal segments.

Q1. Which of the following are causes of malocclusion?

a. crowding
b. thumb sucking
c. early loss of deciduous teeth
d. jaw size discrepancies

How well did you do?
A1.a,b,c,d

AIMS OF ORTHODONTIC TREATMENT

While reading the text answer the following;

Q1. Why do patients seek orthodontic treatment?

Q2. What are the potential risks of orthodontic treatment?

The benefits of orthodontic treatment can include the following:

1. Most patients seek orthodontic treatment to improve the appearance of their teeth.
    This tends to increase their confidence.
2. To correct the bite so that the front teeth meet on closing and the back teeth mesh together.
    This improves eating and biting.
3. To reduce the likelihood of damage to prominent teeth. If the front teeth protrude they are more likely to fracture if the patient sustained an blow to the face, for example fell over or sustained a sports injury.
4. To improve the patient's ability to maintain oral hygiene by removing stagnation areas due to crowding.
5. To align the teeth to allow a crown, bridge or implant to be placed.

THE POTENTIAL RISKS OF ORTHODONTIC TREATMENT

*   If the patient does not maintain a high standard of oral hygiene demineralization of the tooth enamel (white patches and marks), decay and periodontal disease may result.
*   It may be difficult or impossible to achieve the desired orthodontic result, especially if the patient does not fully comply with treatment.
*   There is a possibility of trauma to the mucosa from intra-oral appliances during treatment.
    This is usually transient.
*   Occasionally the roots of the teeth may be resorbed during treatment. This happens to a small degree in all patients but for about one patient in a hundred significant resorption takes place, resulting in shorter roots.
*   On completion of treatment, patients are invariably given retainer appliances to hold the result whilst the surrounding tissues adapt. For a significant number of patients the teeth relapse back to their original position to a varying degree.

Q1. Why do patients seek orthodontic treatment?

a. to straighten their teeth
b. to improve the way the teeth meet
c. to align the teeth prior to bridge or implant placement
d. to improve the appearance of the teeth

Q2. What are the potential risks of orthodontic treatment?

a. root resorption
b. relapse of the teeth back to their former position
c. not being able to eat
d. transient trauma to the mucosa

How well did you do?
A1.a,b,c,d   A2.a,b,d

ORTHODONTIC ASSESSMENT

While reading the text answer the following;

Q1. How important is patient compliance?

Q2. What is noted during the extra oral examination?

Q3. What is noted during the intra oral examination?

PATIENT COMPLIANCE

A vital aspect of orthodontic assessment is to ascertain the degree of concern that a patient has for their teeth and their potential level of compliance if they were offered orthodontic treatment. It is important to assess how keen the patient is as orthodontic treatment requires co-operation from the patient over several months often spanning a couple of years.

EXTRA ORAL EXAMINATION

It is important to examine the patient's face and jaws before examining the teeth. This allows the orthodontist to start building a picture of the reasons why a particular malocclusion has arisen-its cause.

Firstly the jaws (the hard tissues) are assessed in three planes of space: from the side (anteroposterior), in height (vertically) and from the front (transversely). In the latter case the orthodontist is looking for possible facial asymmetry.

Anteroposteriorly, the skeletal pattern is described as either Skeletal I (the jaws are in balance), Skeletal II (the lower jaw is behind the upper jaw) or skeletal III (the lower jaw is in front of the upper jaw).

Vertically the height of the face is assessed and may be short (low angle) or increased high angle).

Next the lips and facial musculature are assessed. How the lips meet at rest is of utmost importance in influencing how the teeth may meet and whether or not they will stay in a stable position when corrected. Clinicians talk in terms of a competent lip pattern-where the lips meet at rest-or an incompetent lip pattern-where the musculature is strained when the lips meet. Some individuals have a tongue to lower lip swallow, which influences the position of the front teeth and invariably results in an incomplete overbite.

INTRA ORAL EXAMINATION

The orthodontist records the following points, usually by dictation to the dental nurse. Many orthodontists use a proforma when undertaking an orthodontic assessment.

- Oral hygiene.
- Soft tissues. This involves recording the facial profile and the function of the facial muscles for example during swallowing.
- Evidence of active disease such as decay or periodontal disease. This has to be treated before orthodontic treatment can be considered.
- Any evidence of incisor trauma.
- The teeth are carefully charted. The orthodontist notes how many teeth are present, for example, if there are supernumeries or if some teeth have already been extracted. Heavily filled teeth are extracted in preference to healthy, unfilled teeth when space is required.
- The incisor teeth of each dental arch is assessed in turn for:
  Crowding/spacing.
  Inclination of the teeth (normal, proclined or retroclined).
  Rotations of the teeth.
- The buccal teeth are also commented on. For example crowding, spacing, rotations and retained deciduous teeth are noted.

EXAMINATION OF THE TEETH IN OCCLUSION

- The incisor relationship is described in terms of
- overjet (in millimetres)
- overbite (normal, increased or decreased, complete or incomplete) From this the incisor classification is given.
- Is there a traumatic overbite where the lower incisors occlude with the palatal mucosa?
- Anterior crossbites. Sometimes one or more teeth may be in cross bite.
- Any centerline shifts (and their possible cause).
- The molar relationship is described separately using Angle's classification.
- The presence of unilateral or bilateral crossbites. A unilateral crossbite is on one side only whereas a bilateral is on both sides.
- Any displacements (which are often associated with a crossbite). A displacement is when the patient bites into initial occlusion and then slides into centric occlusion. Centric occlusion is where there is maximum habitual intercuspation of the teeth.

X-RAYS REQUIRED FOR ORTHODONTIC ASSESSMENT

A panoramic radiograph is a useful screening x-ray for orthodontic purposes and is clinically justified where there is a suspicion of either dental disease, a dental anomaly or where orthodontic treatment is being contemplated. The dentist looks for the following;

- The presence or absence of unerupted teeth.
- Dental disease such as caries or other pathology.
- The stage in dental development, paying attention to the developmental stage of the unerupted teeth and the sequence in which the dentition is changing.

- The position of any unerupted teeth and whether they are impacted.
- Supernumery teeth.
- Pathological lesions such as cysts.

STUDY MODELS

This involves taking upper and lower alginate impressions and a bite to record the occlusion. Study models provide a reference when studying the progress of orthodontic treatment. It also allows the dentist to view the teeth from every angle and decide the best treatment plan for the patient.

ORTHODONTIC REFERRAL

Many dentists prefer to refer patients to an orthodontist for an opinion and possible treatment. The dentist will send a referral letter stating their observations during the initial examination and any relevant radiographs. The index of orthodontic treatment need (IOTN) may be required by the orthodontist. It is most helpful if the referring dentist can give an indication of the patient's possible future compliance.

Q1. Good patient compliance consists of which of the following?

a. missing a couple of appointments will not matter
b. good oral hygiene is not expected when there is so much wire in the mouth
c. it does not matter if the child patient is not keen as long as the parents are
d. the patient must be keen to have orthodontic treatment

Q2. What is noted during the extra oral examination?

a. vertical face height
b. lips and facial musculature
c. how the patient swallows
d. oral hygiene

Q3. What is noted during the intra oral examination?

a. oral hygiene
b. crossbites
c. crowding
d. displacements

How well did you do?
A1.d   A2.a,b,c   A3.a,b,c,d

TOOTH MOVEMENT

While reading the text answer the following;

Q1. How do teeth move?

There are several ways in which teeth can be moved. By this we mean the type of tooth movement carried out. It is important to appreciate the type of tooth movement as this has a direct bearing on which appliance system is subsequently selected to carry out the treatment.

TIPPING MOVEMENTS

This is where the teeth are tipped about a fulcrum point, thought to be one third the way along the root from the apex. Removable appliances are often used in situations where a malocclusion can be corrected by tipping teeth alone.

BODILY MOVEMENT

Fixed orthodontic appliances move the entire tooth bodily through the bone. This is where all parts of the root move the same amount. Such a movement can only be carried out using fixed appliances.

EXTRUSION

Sometimes teeth need to be extruded by the application of orthodontic force, for example where an ectopic tooth has been exposed and brought down into the line of the arch.

INTRUSION

Sometimes teeth require intrusion. Forces should be kept very light where this is contemplated.

ROOT TORQUE

Again this can only be carried out with fixed appliances and is used where the crown of the tooth is in the correct position and the orthodontist wishes to move the root apex.

HOW TEETH MOVE

When pressure is applied to a tooth the periodontal ligament is stretched one side and compressed the other. Osteoblasts will lay down bone on the side being stretched while osteoclasts will resorb bone on the side being compressed so that gradually the tooth moves. Slow constant pressure allows this process of remodelling to take place without damage to the periodontal ligament and bone or resorption of the roots. However if the tooth is moved to quickly damage occurs and the rate of tooth movement actually decreases.

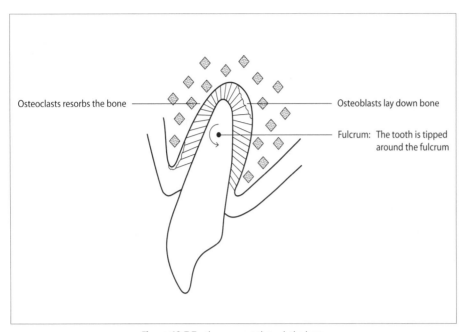

Osteoclasts resorbs the bone

Osteoblasts lay down bone

Fulcrum: The tooth is tipped around the fulcrum

Figure 19.7 *Tooth movement through the bone.*

After the teeth have been moved into a new position they are held there using simple retainer appliances for a period of time. This allows the surrounding bone to reorganize and the gingivae to adapt to the new position. This phase of treatment is is called retention and is required in the vast majority of treated cases.

Q1. How do teeth move?

    a. extrusion
    b. tipping
    c. repulsion
    d. bodily movement

How well did you do?
    A1.a,b,d

ORTHODONTIC TREATMENT

COMPLIANCE

All orthodontic treatment involves a great deal of co-operation from the patient over a long period of time. It is important for the patient to understand this from the onset and to know what is expected of them. Patients have a duty to show that they can maintain a high standard of oral hygiene before the brace is fitted as there is greater potential for food and plaque to collect with an appliance in place. Both the patient and their parents or guardians must understand that the patient will need to see the orthodontist every 4 to 6 weeks for many months and must arrange their lifestyle and transport around this. The orthodontist should explain to patients if extractions are required, including which teeth are to be extracted and how.

TYPES OF APPLIANCE

While reading the text answer the following;

Q1. Name three types of appliance.

Q2. What are the patient instructions for a removable appliance?

Q3. What is extra-oral traction?

REMOVABLE APPLIANCES

As the name implies, removable appliances can be taken out of the mouth by the patient. These appliances cannot bodily move the teeth through bone. They can only tilt the teeth into position. This restricts their use to simple malocclusions where tipping movements only are required to correct the malocclusion.

Removable appliances are composed of an acrylic baseplate which is closely adapted to the palate. The baseplate helps retain the appliance, supports all the components of the appliance and contributes to the orthodontic anchorage. Retention is obtained with stainless steal clasps such as Adams cribs. Also attached to the baseplate are the active components. These include springs, labial bows and screws.

IMPRESSION APPOINTMENT

Alginate impressions are taken of the upper and lower jaws together with a wax bite. The impressions are washed, disinfected, rinsed and sealed in a labelled plastic bag by the dental nurse. The orthodontist draws a diagram and provides a written description of the appliance. The nurse enters the return date on the instructions and checks that the patient's name and dental practice are clearly marked on the label before sending these to the technician.

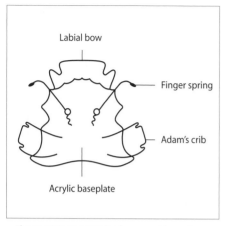

Labial bow

Finger spring

Adam's crib

Acrylic baseplate

Figure 19.8 An example of a removable appliance.

FIT APPOINTMENT

Figure 19.9 Adams universal pliers and spring forming pliers.

The dentist tries in the removable appliance. An acrylic trimming bur in a straight handpiece is used to adjust the acrylic baseplate if necessary. The Adams cribs are adjusted if necessary with Adams universal pliers: some adjustment is often required to ensure adequate retention. Spring forming pliers are used to adjust and activate the springs. The patient is given the instructions to care for their appliance.

PATIENT INSTRUCTIONS FOR REMOVABLE APPLIANCES

- The patient and parents are shown how to insert and remove the appliance. The patient then demonstrates that they can do this.
- The patient is shown how the appliance works and given clear instructions that it must be worn all day and night even at meal times otherwise the teeth will not straighten. It may be taken out for contact sports and swimming and stored in a rigid container to avoid breakage.
- Where necessary instructions are given on the fitting of elastics or extra oral traction. If there is a screw on the baseplate the patient is shown how to use the key to turn it and how often this should be done.
- The patient must take the appliance out after every meal to clean both the appliance and their teeth. They should be shown how to clean it carefully. The appliance must be reinserted immediately after cleaning.
- The patient is reassured that they will adjust to the appliance within a few days and the initial speaking and eating difficulties will disappear.
- Both patient and parents should understand the importance of keeping to the monthly / six weekly review appointments and the next appointment should be arranged. They should be reassured that if there are any problems between these reviews they can contact the surgery. The surgery should be contacted as soon as possible if the appliance is broken or lost.
- Patients should also continue to have their routine dental check-ups.

MONITORING AND ADJUSTMENT OF REMOVABLE APPLIANCES

The nurse sets out the notes, radiographs, study models and instruments. The dentist usually requires Adams pliers and Spring forming pliers for adjusting springs and clasps. A straight handpiece and an acrylic bur may be needed to trim the acrylic. The oral hygiene is checked and the patient encouraged to keep good plaque control. Mid-treatment models and x-rays may be taken.

FINAL APPOINTMENT

Once the teeth are in the correct position the original removable appliance can sometimes be adapted and used as a retainer. More commonly impressions are taken to construct a retainer appliance. The severity of the original malocclusion and the type of tooth movements carried out determine how much and for how long a retainer should be worn. Typically with upper removable appliance treatment a retainer would be worn at night for six months, followed by alternate nights and eventually one or two nights a week up to eighteen months. Final study models, x-rays and photographs may be taken.

FUNCTIONAL APPLIANCES

Functional appliances are used in the growing patient for correction of their incisor relationship. They are either fixed or removable and predominantly work by forcing the patient to close their mouth and bring the mandible forwards into a protruded position. Muscle forces act to try and bring the jaw back to its normal resting position: these forces create a force, transmitted by the appliance to the teeth, which has the net affect of tending to retract the upper teeth and procline the lower teeth (in Class II malocclusion).

It is commonly observed that in growing patients, there is often some improvement in the jaw relationship at the same time. However there is no evidence to show that functional appliances themselves can produce any extra jaw growth.

Functional appliances come in several different designs. All have their advantages and disadvantages. More recently the Twin Block functional appliance has become popular: this is composed of upper and lower removable appliances, each carrying an inclined bite plane to effect the necessary protrusion.

To construct a functional appliance, the dentist again requires good quality impressions, extended into the sulcus, a normal wax bite and a special 'functional bite' where the patient's teeth are recorded meeting in a protruded position.

HEADGEAR AND EXTRA-ORAL TRACTION

Headgear provides a force to the teeth from outside the mouth. Headgear has two main uses.

1. It may be used as anchorage reinforcement to hold certain teeth in position while other teeth are being moved.
2. It can be used to create space by moving the posterior teeth backwards one by one on either side of the upper jaw. This is called extra-oral traction.

Headgear may attached to either removable, functional or fixed appliances. Extra-oral traction may consist of a head strap, neck strap, face bow and extra oral elastics or modules.

Figure 19.10 *Headgear.*

The facebow usually inserts into tubes on the molar teeth – either soldered to an Adams clasp on a removable appliance or as part of the attachment on a fixed appliance molar band.

A variant is J hook headgear where the facebow is replaced by two J shaped whiskers which attach to hooks on the front of the appliance.

For extraoral anchorage, where the posterior teeth are being held back, patients' typically wear the headgear for 8-10 hours a day using forces of 150-250 grams on each side. For extra-oral traction wear is required for 12-14 hours a day with forces of 350-500 grams.

Typically headgear forces are applied by means of elastic bands which are manufactured in a range of sizes. The orthodontist can measure the force being applied using a small gauge.

Q1. Which of the following are types of orthodontic appliance?

    a. removable appliance
    b. stationary appliance
    c. functional appliance
    d. dysfunctional appliance

Q2. What are the patient instructions for a removable appliance?

    a. if the appliance is lost or broken wait for your next appointment to discuss this with the orthodontist
    b. the appliance should not be worn at night
    c. the appliance should not be removed even when brushing the teeth
    d. the appliance should be worn during meals

Q3. What is extra-oral traction?

    a. force from outside the mouth
    b. may consist of headgear, neck strap, facebow and elastics
    c. moves the buccal teeth forward
    d. moves the buccal teeth backwards

How well did you do?
    A1.a,c   A2.d   A3.a,b,d

FIXED APPLIANCES

Fixed appliances are attached to the teeth using dental composites or cements. Their main components are brackets, bands and wires which are directly attached to the patient's teeth. Fixed appliances are used to treat severe malocclusions and are able to move teeth in any direction through the bone.

COMPONENTS OF FIXED APPLIANCES

While reading the text answer the following;

Q1. Name four components of a fixed appliance.

Q2. What are the patient instructions for separating elastics?

Q3. List thirteen instruments/materials needed to place a fixed appliance.

.   BRACKETS
Traditionally brackets are made of
stainless steel. Over recent years other
materials have been used in attempt
to create a more aesthetic bracket.
The most popular of these materials is
ceramic brackets. Adult patients often
prefer the more discrete tooth
coloured bracket. The brackets are
bonded to the teeth with acid etched
composites or glass ionomer. They
have a slot for the arch wire to run
through and tie wings on which to
place modules and other auxiliary
components. Hooks may be attached
to the brackets to allow the
attachment of intra oral elastics.

Another recent trend is so-called self
ligating brackets. These have a locking
mechanism integral to the bracket for
holding the archwire in place.

2. ORTHODONTIC BANDS
Orthodontic bands are metal rings
that fit around the posterior teeth.
They are cemented in place using a
glass ionomer cement and have
buccal tubes for the arch wire to sit.
Bands come in several sizes (which
are different for each manufacturer)
and are presented in
compartmentalized boxes to facilitate
selection when the orthodontist is
choosing the correct size. Typically
two or three bands are tried in for
each tooth before the correct size is
found for a particular tooth. A well
fitting band should be closely adapted
to the tooth, without any obvious
gaps, and be fairly self retentive even
before it is cemented into place.
Attention to detail at this point
almost eliminates band failure.

3. ARCH WIRE
The arch wire sits in the grooves of
the brackets and bands. It is the
archwires that actually move the
teeth. Contemporary fixed appliance
techniques use a succession of alloy
aligning wires of increasing dimension
to align the teeth, leading on to a
steel 'working archwire' which is
strong enough to support elastics and
other auxiliary forces for moving
blocks of teeth.
There are various sizes of archwire
dimension and materials used and
these should be kept neatly and in
order to facilitate their retrieval.

4. ELASTIC MODULES AND WIRE
    LIGATURES

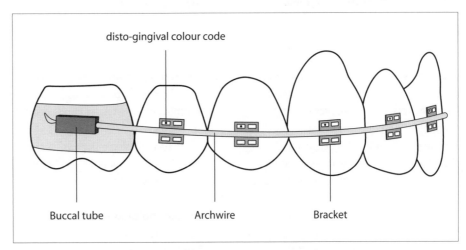

disto-gingival colour code

Buccal tube   Archwire   Bracket

Figure 19.11 *Fixed orthodontic appliance.*

The function of elastic modules and wire
ligatures is to attach the wire to the
brackets. Elastic modules are the
commonest way that archwires are held in
the bracket slot. The module is placed over
the four wings of the bracket.

PLACEMENT OF SEPARATING ELASTICS

This appointment is usually arranged a
week before fitting the bands. The
separating elastics push the teeth gently
apart so as to open up the contact point
and facilitate the placement of orthodontic
bands. The dental nurse places the elastics
on the separating pliers and hands them
to the dentist. The dentist places the
separating elastic between the contact
points.

INSTRUCTIONS FOR SEPARATING ELASTICS

1. The patient should expect some
    discomfort for 24-48 hours. This
    quickly passes but may be controlled
    with mild analgesics such as
    paracetamol.
2. The patient can eat as normal and
    brush as normal.
3. After a few days one or more elastics
    may fall out. This is expected because
    as the contact opens there is nothing
    to hold the elastics in place. The
    patient does not need to return
    before their next visit.

SEPARATING ELASTIC REMOVAL

Figure 19.12 Briault probe.

At the next appointment, the separating
elastics are removed and the orthodontic
bands are placed. The elastics should be
accounted for: patients can usually recall
how many elastics have been lost and
those still in place are easily removed with
a briault probe. The dentist should however
check carefully that no elastic has sunk
beneath the gingival margin: if an elastic is
missed in this position it can damage the
gingival attachment and even cause a
localized periodontal abscess.

INSTRUMENTS REQUIRED TO PLACE A
FIXED APPLIANCE

1. **Arch-form card**
    The dentist should form the archwires
    to the patient's own archform and
    dimension: this is done using the
    original pre-treatment study models,
    which should be available at each
    appointment. However arch-form
    cards are also useful to check for
    shape and symmetry in the archwires.

2. **Chinagraph pencil / wax sticks**
    The chinagraph pencil is used to mark
    on the arch wire where bends need
    to be made.
    More recently single-use wax sticks
    have become popular. These reduce
    the chances of cross-infection.

3. **Bracket holding pliers**
    Bracket holding pliers or tweezers are
    used to pick up and pass the brackets
    to the orthodontist. A slightly
    modified tip is used for picking up
    bondable molar tubes.

4. Howe pliers

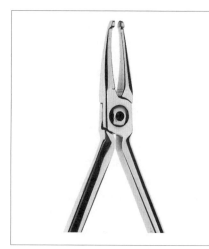

Figure 19.13 Howe pliers.

Howe pliers is an example of a type of
pliers used to hold the archwire.

5. **Band seater and band pusher**
    These two instruments are used when
    selecting and fitting orthodontic
    bands.

6. **Distal end cutter**
    These cut the arch wire. They are
    designed to hold the free end of the
    cut wire and so prevent inhalation or
    trauma when used in the mouth.

7. **Light wire pliers**
    Used to bend the arch wire. These
    pliers are the standard instruments
    used for adjusting and placing
    archwires. A heavier version for
    bending rectangular archwires is
    called Bird-beak pliers.

8. Bracket removing pliers / debonding pliers

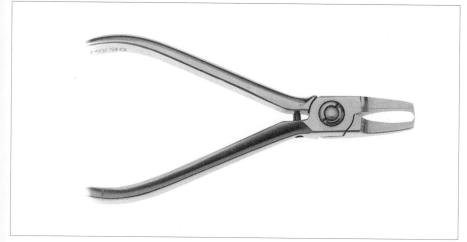

Figure 19.14 *Bracket removing pliers.*

There are two or three different design of bracket removing pliers. The classic design is where two angled tips are placed as close to the base of the bracket as possible. The operator squeezes the pliers and this transmits a shear force across the composite and breaks the bond.
An alternative design of debonding plier lassoes one of the bracket tie wings and literally pulls the bracket away from the tooth surface.

9. Mosquito artery forceps

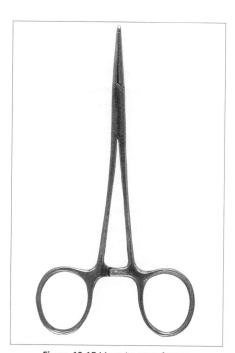

Figure 19.15 *Mosquito artery forceps.*

Mosquito artery forceps are often used for placing elastic tie modules.

10. Coombe's Ligature lockers / Mathieu needle holders

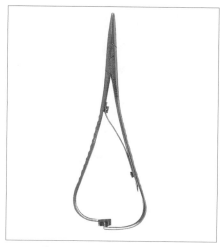

Figure 19.16 *Mathieu needle holder.*

Ligatures are another means of securing the archwire in the bracket slot. They are placed either with ligature lockers or using Mathieu needle holders.

11. Ligature tuckers
The tuckers tuck the sharp ends of the wire ligatures under the bracket where they cannot traumatise the oral mucosa.

12. Ligature cutters
These cut the wire ligatures. An important point is that this is the only wire that should be cut by these cutters. If they are used for cutting archwires, the tip is blunted very quickly which makes them useless for their primary role.

13. Soft Wax
Soft transparent wax is given to patients following fixed appliance placement and instructions are given to push a small piece of wax over the appliance wherever it is rubbing.

Q1. Which of the following are components of a fixed appliance?

a. ligature cutters
b. brackets
c. Howe pliers
d. wire ligatures

Q2. What are the patient instructions for separating elastics?

    a. the patient should expect severe pain for the first couple of days
    b. the patient should not brush their teeth for a week
    c. if an elastic falls out pop it back in
    d. one or more of the elastics may fall out before their next visit

Q3. Which of the following instruments are needed to place a fixed appliance.

    a. distal end cutters
    b. band seater
    c. ligature tucker
    d. dental mirror

214

How well did you do?
    A1.b,d   A2.d   A3.a,b,c,d

PLACEMENT OF THE FIXED APPLIANCE

While reading the text answer the following;

Q1. How are fixed appliances placed?

Q2. What are the patient instructions for fixed appliances?

Q3. What may happen during an adjustment appointment?

Different orthodontists may place a full upper and lower fixed appliance following a slightly different sequence. Where extractions or minor surgery is required prior to fixed appliance fit, the operator should ensure the patient is seen two weeks or so after these procedures for appliance fit. This is to ensure that the extraction spaces are not lost and space closure can be controlled by the appliances.

As mentioned, prior to fitting bands, the teeth concerned should have separators placed to open up the contact points at least 3 days previously. Many orthodontists therefore arrange three successive appointments one week apart for fixed appliance fit.

1.   Separation
2.   Band placement
3.   Bracket bonding and wire placement.

However there are variations to this sequence. Some orthodontists may place the brackets and separators in one appointment and bands and wires on a second appointment. Alternatively it is possible to separate on one appointment and then place the full upper and lower fixed on the second appointment.

The bands may be cemented to the teeth using glass ionomer cement and the brackets using composite and the acid etch technique. Diligent moisture control is required at this stage to ensure adequate bond strength. Moisture control is invariably achieved using cheek retractors and a device to hold the tongue back, which usually also supports a low volume suction tube.

Contemporary fixed appliances invariably have individual brackets designed for individual teeth. This is because orthodontists believe that each tooth in the mouth has a precise position in terms of how it is angled and inclined, in order for all the teeth to meet in an ideal relation and to achieve the best aesthetic and functional result.

Every bracket therefore must be identifiable and this is usually achieved by the brackets carrying a colour-coded dot or dash on the disto-gingival corner. The coding for a particular bracket product is never difficult to learn and it allows the dental nurse to identify and orientate the brackets before passing them to the orthodontist.

When an orthodontist places a fixed appliance the orthodontist should firstly inform the nurse which teeth they are bonding and in what sequence. The nurse then places the relevant brackets onto a sticky pad ready for loading and passing to the orthodontist.

PATIENT INSTRUCTIONS FOR FIXED APPLIANCES

- The brace is fixed to the teeth and the patient should be warned that they will not be able to remove it.
- The patient will need to be seen every 4 to 6 weeks to have the appliance adjusted. They should also continue their routine check-ups with their regular dentist.
- Most orthodontic treatments take 12 to 24 months. Missed appointments and repeated breakages of the fixed appliance may extent the treatment time.
- The patient should be warned that every time the fixed appliance is adjusted the teeth are likely to feel sore. If necessary, the patient should take a painkiller such as one they would take for a headache. If the brace rubs the cheeks or lips the patient is instructed to use the wax given to stop this.
- The patient should be shown how to place and wear elastics and headgear if this is applicable. Headgear is normally worn after school and at night. Elastics are worn all the time.
- The patient should be reassured that they will be able to eat normally. However patients should avoid sticky, sugary and hard food.
- Sticky food such as toffees and chewing gum may damage the brace.
- Sugary food and fizzy drinks may cause extensive decay and demineralisation.
- Hard foods can damage the brace. These include crunchy apples and crusty bread.

- The teeth must be brushed three times a day (after every meal). Tooth brushing will take longer. Interdental brushes are useful. A fluoride mouthwash should be used every evening after brushing, before the patient goes to bed. Failure to maintain a good level of oral hygiene may result in intrinsic staining of the teeth.
- A gumshield should be worn during sports.
- Children who play wind instruments may find this difficult with a fixed appliance.
- The patient must take reasonable care of their brace. If the brace breaks the patient should contact the surgery so that it can be repaired as soon as possible. Patients should not wait until their next appointment to report the damage.
- Once the active phase of the treatment has been completed the patient will need to wear a retainer. This may be a removable appliance or a wire fixed behind the front teeth. The time retainers need to be worn varies from case to case.

MONITORING AND ADJUSTMENT OF FIXED APPLIANCES

At each successive appointment the patient should be asked how they are getting along with the fixed appliances. Any breakages or areas where the appliance is rubbing should be identified and repaired.

It is also a matter of routine that the patient's oral hygiene should be checked and, if deficient, measures should be instigated immediately to improve this. If a patient demonstrates a consistently poor level of oral hygiene then the appliances should be removed.

At each appointment the operator assesses the progress of treatment. Typically a progression of aligning wires are placed. With contemporary fixed appliances these are usually flexible alloy wires and later on steel wires. Typically, after four of five visits the 'working archwires' are placed which allows the operator to place elastics to move blocks of teeth.

An essential aid to monitoring progress is by referring to the patient's original study models which the nurse should have ready at the chairside for every appointment. The orthodontist will observe whether the mechanics applied at previous visits is having the desired affect.

The wires are changed to become progressively thicker and stronger. They also change from being round in cross-section to rectangular. The routine use of safety glasses by the patient and dental team is particularly important when cutting wire. The remnant wire clippings should be discarded in the sharps bin.

Once the fixed appliance has been built up into working archwires and where an incisor relationship is being corrected it is common for the patient to be directed to wear intra-oral elastics. These come in various sizes (which alters the force applied) and invariably patients are asked the wear the elastics for 24 hours a day and change them every two days, unless one breaks in which case it should be changed straight away.

Using a hand mirror patients are carefully shown how to place the elastics. The elastics are supplied in packets and typically two packets are given, to last the patient between appointments.

For some patients, mid-treatment records (so-called stage records) are taken. These may involve an x-ray and/or study models. These records allow the orthodontist to assess the progress of treatment and plan the next stage.

COMPLETION OF FIXED APPLIANCE THERAPY

The orthodontist will have determined the aims of treatment before the fixed appliances were placed. In many cases these goals are to a correct a malocclusion to a Class I incisor relationship with normal overjet and overbite, and a Class I molar relationship. However there are many instances when the treatment aims will be limited for legitimate reasons. For example there may be limited tooth correction in an adult patient. The orthodontist's treatment plan may be restricted as the patient has stopped growing.

Brackets are removed using orthodontic debonding pliers: these are designed to place a shear force across the composite bond. Band removing pliers are designed to remove the bands. Most operators will remove the fixed appliance from each dental arch in one piece, without dismantling it first.

Any remaining composite or cement on the tooth surface should be removed separately. This is most commonly done using a straight cut tungsten carbide bur in a slow handpiece. When used carefully, these burs will remove composite without damaging the enamel surface.

Study models and photographs are taken after the appliance has been removed. The same alginate impressions can be used by the technician to construct the patients' retainer appliances. X-Rays, if required, are usually taken towards the end of active treatment (not at debond) so that the appliances are still in place to rectify any discrepancies in tooth position detected on the x-ray.

Q1. How are fixed appliances placed?

    a. bands are bonded to the teeth with composite

    b. bands are cemented to the teeth with glass ionomer

    c. the colour coded dot on the disto-gingival corner allows the nurse to identify and orientate the bracket

    d. the colour coded dot on the mesio-gingival corner allows the nurse to identify and orientate the bracket

Q2. Which of the following are instructions for fixed appliances?

    a. the patient may eat toffees if they suck them slowly

    b. there is no need to brush the teeth as long as the patient uses a fluoride mouthwash

    c. the brace may be removed after meals to clean

    d. a gumshield should be used when playing sport

Q3. What may happen during an adjustment appointment?

    a. oral hygiene is checked

    b. treatment progress is checked against the patient's original study models

    c. the wires are changed to progressively become thinner

    d. the wires are changed from being round in cross section to rectangular

How well did you do?
    A1.b,c   A2.d   A3.a,b,d

216

RETENTION

While reading the text answer the following;

Q1. Why is retention of newly moved teeth necessary?

Q2. What oral hygiene instructions are given to orthodontic patients?

Following active appliance therapy a retainer appliance is required. This is because initially the teeth tend to move back to their pre-treatment positions: the bone through which the teeth have just moved is immature and the gingival fibres are stretched and take a long time to remodel. Retainers hold the teeth whilst these tissues reorganize and settle down. Another reason why the corrected malocclusion may change is the later effects of facial growth. Also, if the teeth have been moved into a potentially unstable position again they may move.

The retainer may be removable or fixed. For a removable retainer an alginate impression is taken at the previous appointment. This is sent to the technician who makes the removable retainer. If a bonded retainer is used a selection of thin or twist-flex wires are required. Howe's pliers and wire cutters are used to cut the wire to the correct length. The teeth are dried and the acid etch technique is used to bond the wire to the teeth with bond and composite. Fixed retainers are usually placed on the lingual surface of the lower anterior teeth and the palatal surface of the upper anterior teeth.

ORAL HYGIENE INSTRUCTIONS FOR ORTHODONTIC PATIENTS

Any appliance in the mouth tends to collect plaque. This is especially true to appliances with many intricate parts that can harbour bacteria. The patient needs to maintain a high standard of oral hygiene and preferably reduce their sugar intake so that plaque cannot form so quickly. The patient must also be aware that working parts of an appliance such as the springs and bows must be cleaned with care to avoid distortion.

ASSESSING ORAL HYGIENE

Plaque scores and disclosing the teeth can help with the initial assessment of oral hygiene. BPE scores should always be taken for adult patients or those patients recognized as having current or previous periodontal disease. Orthodontic treatment should not be contemplated unless the orthodontist is satisfied that the required standard of oral hygiene can be achieved. If a patient does not have a standard of oral health that can support appliance wear then active treatment should not be offered: either a compromise treatment should be considered or the malocclusion accepted.

ORAL HYGIENE ADVISE

The Bass tooth brushing method should be used gently with a small headed, medium textured toothbrush. Interdentally brushes of the appropriate sizes may be used to clean in between the teeth especially when fixed appliances are worn as the patients will not be able to floss. The patient should be shown how to clean around the brackets and underneath the wires with their various brushes. Dental floss can be used with removable appliances as normal.

ASSESSING THE PATIENT'S DIET AND DIETARY ADVISE

A convenient way to analyse the diet is to ask the patient to write down everything they eat and the time it was eaten over a 24 hour period. It is useful to review this diet sheet with the patient and parents / guardian. Areas that contribute to demineralisation, decay and erosion are highlighted and the patient's eating habits are readjusted where necessary. Sugary foods should be kept to a minimum and only eaten at mealtimes. Fizzy drinks should be cut out if possible or only allowed on special occasions. Sticky foods such as toffees and chewing gum should not be eaten as they may damage appliances prolonging treatment. During orthodontic treatment hard food should be cut up into small pieces to avoid damage to the appliance when chewing.

FLUORIDE MOUTHWASH

A fluoride mouthwash is routinely recommended for all patients who are undergoing orthodontic treatment. A good time to suggest its use is just after cleaning the teeth at night. Fluoride has been shown to harden the enamel, reduce the amount of bacterial plaque and encourage remineralization.

After orthodontic treatment patients tend to continue with the high standard of oral hygiene. For the following reasons;

• Their routine has become ingrained.
• Hygiene maintenance is easier now the teeth have been straightened and the appliances removed.
• They are motivated by their new smile.

Q1. Why is retention of newly moved teeth necessary?

a. the gingival fibres have been stretched and need time to remodel
b. the bone through which the teeth have moved is immature and needs to remodel
c. to prevent the teeth returning to their former positions
d. to extend patient treatment times

Q2. What oral hygiene instructions/dietary instructions are given to orthodontic patients?

a. normal dental floss can be used with fixed appliances
b. interdentally brushes should be used
c. fluoride mouth rinse should be used after brushing the teeth at night
d. chewing gum is useful to keep the appliance and teeth clean

How well did you do?
A1.a,b,c   A2.b,c

20. Implants

This chapter was written in conjunction with Jo Lakeman Course Tutor from Nobel Biocare.

While reading the text answer the following;

Q1. What is an implant made of?

Q2. What is osseointegration?

Q3. How may implants be used?

AN IMPLANT

A dental implant is a titanium screw which is surgically placed in the jaw and integrates with the surrounding bone. This integration is called osseointegration. A fixed or removable prosthesis can be placed onto the implant to replace the missing tooth or teeth. Titanium has excellent biocompatible properties.

OSSEOINTEGRATION

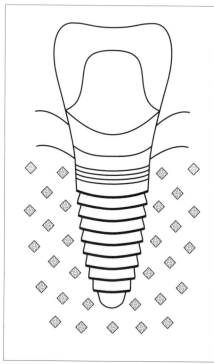

Figure 20.1 *Osseointegration.*

Osseointegration is a direct structured and functional connection between ordered living bone and the surface of a load carrying implant.

REASONS FOR PLACING AN IMPLANT

When a permanent tooth or teeth are lost they leave a gap. Unless the patient had the extraction for orthodontic reasons they generally have the following options;

1. LEAVE THE GAP
    When one tooth is lost often the function of two teeth is lost as the opposing tooth can no longer be used for chewing. With time the opposing tooth may over erupt and the adjacent teeth may tilt into the gap making future restoration difficult if the patient changes their mind and would like the missing tooth repaced. Tilted and overerupted teeth also increase the stagnation areas for plaque.
    Many patients will not tolerate a gap at the front of the mouth for cosmetic reasons.

2. PLACE A DENTURE
    Dentures require patient skill to use. Many patients do not feel confident wearing a denture in case it moves when they laugh or eat. Some people are embarrassed to remove it at night. Dentures tend to cover a large area of mucosa and trap food, increasing the risk of decay and periodontal disease. However they can be removed for cleaning and are inexpensive compared to the alternatives. More teeth may usually be added to an existing denture. Also dentures can be replaced with bridges or implants at a later date.

3. PLACE A CONVENTIONAL BRIDGE
    This involves preparing the abutments. This may be an advantage if those teeth have large restorations but a disadvantage if they are healthy and unfilled.

4. PLACE AN ADHESIVE BRIDGE
    This involves minimal preparation to the abutments. Adhesive bridges are useful if the abutments are healthy unfilled teeth. (Approximately 20% of crowned abutments need future root treatment. An adhesive bridge reduces this number.) They also allow for the patient to have a denture, conventional bridge or implant at a later date. However they have limited applications and can debond which may be embarrassing and inconvenient for the patient.

5. PLACE AN IMPLANT
    This is like having a new tooth. An advantage is the adjacent teeth are not necessarily involved in the implant restoration. However implants do have disadvantages as they involve long treatment plans spanning several months and are expensive. Implant placement requires surgery and may require sedation or general anaesthetic. Implants have many uses;

SINGLE TOOTH IMPLANT

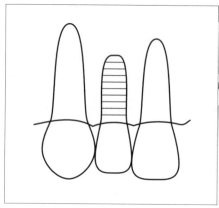

Figure 20.2 *Single tooth implant.*

218

IMPLANTS UNDER BRIDGES

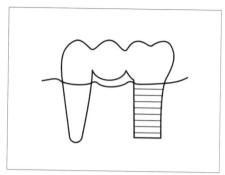

Figure 20.3 Implant under a bridge.

IMPLANT RETAINED DENTURES

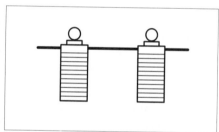

Figure 20.4 Implant under a denture.

In conclusion the two most important reasons for having implants from the patient's view point are;

1. The psychological advantage of effectively having "a new tooth" that looks good and gives the patient confidence.
2. Having the tooth function restored. For example the patient's denture is no longer loose or their crown and bridge is now built on a solid foundation.

Q1. What is an implant made of?

a. gold
b. titanium
c. stainless steal
d. porcelain

Q2. Osseointegration is a direct structured and functional connection between ordered living bone and the surface of a load carrying implant. True or false?

Q3. How may implants be used?

a. to retain fillings
b. to support crowns
c. to support inlays
d. to retain dentures

How well did you do?
A1.b   A2.True   A3.b,d

TREATMENT PLANNING FOR IMPLANTS

While reading the text answer the following

Q1. How are patients assessed prior to implant placement?

Q2. What type of consent is required?

Q3. What is a stent?

1. MEDICAL HISTORY
- General health. Patients with a variety of systemic conditions may be successfully treated with implants. However it may be wise for the dentist to seek advise from the patient's doctor first. Also both the dentist and nurses should be aware that in general, patients undergoing implant surgery are at the greatest risk of having a medical emergency in the dental chair.
- Smoking. Implants may be placed in patients who smoke. However some studies show a higher failure rate in smokers compared to non smokers. The probability of failure has been shown to increase with the extent of smoking. Smoking reduces the blood flow which has a detrimental affect on healing. Smokers should be encouraged to stop smoking altogether or at least to stop for several weeks before and after the surgical placement of the implants.

- Diabetes. If the diabetes is controlled implants may be placed. Again diabetes can affect the vascular system.
- Facial pain. The cause of facial pain needs to be diagnosed as an implant may become the focus for this pain.
- Psychological disorders. These patients need to be carefully assessed before agreeing to place implants.
- Radiotherapy. Patients who have had radiotherapy to the jaws have a lower success rate due to impaired bone healing. These patients should be referred to specialist centres for implants.

2. DENTAL HISTORY
It is important to know why the tooth or teeth were lost. The patient should be dentally fit before implant placement. Active caries and periodontal disease increases the number of bacteria in the mouth and suggests future loss of further teeth. Severe periodontal disease results in a loss of alveolar bone which may hinder implant placement. The patient's oral hygiene should be adequate to provide a "clean" surgical field and maintain the final prosthesis. Implants are expensive, require surgery and often require treatment spanning several months so the patients must be keen and co-operative.

3. CLINICAL EXAMINATION
The extra-oral examination should include the temporomandibular joints, muscles of mastication, the facial profile, the lip support and the smile line. The intraoral examination includes assessing the general condition of the mouth such as the occlusion, any parafunction and the prognosis of the remaining teeth. The implant site must be examined to assess the thickness and shape of the ridge, the thickness of the mucosa and to check that there is enough height for the implant abutment and crown/bridge/denture.

21

4. RADIOGRAPHS

Intra-oral radiographs will show fine details of the proposed implant site. A panoramic radiograph is always required. Some surgeons also take CAT scans to get a clearer indication of the bone depth, width and the relative position of nearby structures such as the inferior dental nerve and maxillary sinus.

Ideally good quality bone is required at the implant site. This is often hard to assess pre operatively even with CAT scans. The quality of the bone is assessed during surgery by the feel of it's resistance to the drilling and placement of the implant.

5. CONSENT

As always the consent must be informed consent. Various treatment options should be discussed each with their clinical advantages, disadvantages, risks and cost. The consent must be written consent. The patient should be given the form to take home with them to study. It is best if the patient signs the consent form in advance and not on the day of surgery as, on reflection, the patient may be deemed to have been too nervous to have understood it completely.

It is worth adapting a standard consent form to the individual patient so that both parties clearly understand the procedure being used, from where extra bone will be harvest if this is found necessary, if local anaesthetic alone, sedation or general anaesthetic are to be used, how many implants are to be placed, the name and telephone number of the patient's escort and that the patient agrees to follow pre and post operative instructions.

6. PREOPERATIVE IMPRESSIONS

Upper and lower alginate impressions and an occlusal record (bite) are taken in the routine manner. The nurse washes, disinfects, rinses, wraps in damp tissue and seals the work in a labelled plastic bag. This is sent to the technician to cast up and to make a surgical stent for the implant. The nurse should put a return date on the laboratory form that allows the dentist plenty of time to study the models before the patient's surgical appointment.

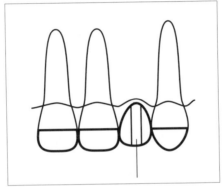

Figure 20.5 The stent.

The technician makes a wax up of the false tooth on the model. This shows where the implant may be placed to achieve a good aesthetic and functional restoration. A stent is made of the area. The stent is usually made of acrylic and fits precisely over the neighbouring teeth. The stent has a channel drilled into it exactly over the proposed implant site. During surgery the dentist will place the stent over the patient's teeth and use this channel as a guide to the correct position and direction to drill the hole for the implant.

Q1. How are patients assessed prior to implant placement?

a. with a panoramic x-ray
b. by taking a comprehensive medical history
c. by examining the thickness and shape of the bone
d. by biopsy

Q2. What type of consent is required?

a. implied
b. verbal
c. written
d. informed

Q3. What is a stent?

a. a type of impression
b. a model of the site
c. an acrylic guide for the correct position of the implant
d. an acrylic guide for the correct direction of the implant

How well did you do?
A1.a,b,c   A2.c,d   A3.c,d

SURGERY APPOINTMENT

While reading the text answer the following;

Q1. What equipment is required for implant surgery?

Q2. Name the roles of the two dental nurses.

When the patient arrives the nurse should check that there is a signed consent form and that there has been no change in the patient's medical history. At this stage the nurse will confirm the escort's name and contact number if they have not accompanied the patient and the patient is being sedated. The nurse may find it prudent to give the escort a courtesy phone call to give them the expected time of completion of the operation. This allows the nurse to confirm that there is an escort organised!

It is good practice to give the patients antibiotic cover one hour before implant surgery. This may be amoxicillin 3 grams or clindamycin 600 mg if the patient is allergic to penicillin. The patient may have a light meal up to 2 hours before the procedure (unless they are due to have a hospital general anaesthetic whereby they should have fasted). The patient should go to the toilet before the procedure. Any lipstick or nail varnish should be removed. If the patient is having intravenous sedation the pulse oximeter will not be able to get a reading through nail varnish (or nail extensions-in this case the pulse oximeter may be placed on the patient's toe). The patient should wear loose comfortable clothing as they may get hot underneath the surgical drape. They should remove their glasses or dentures if these are worn. To avoid alarming the patient, the nurse should explain that the dental surgery will look different this visit as it has been set up for implant surgery. The patient should also be informed that they will be covered with surgical drapes to maintain a sterile surgical field.

The patient should not be in the surgery as you are setting up. It takes time to set up the surgery. The extra time should be written into the appointment book so that the set up is not compromised. The patient is often numbed up in a separate room. Prior to their local anaesthetic they should swill a Corsodyl™ mouthwash for three minutes.

PREPARATION OF THE SURGERY

First the nurse clears away everything off every surface. This includes books, notes, plants and unnecessary equipment which should all be stored away. Every surface is then disinfected. This includes all work surfaces, chairs and overhead light. The nurse checks that all the equipment is present and working. A mayo table or bracket table should be available for surgical instruments. There should be a viewer for radiographs and one sink is designated as the sluice for scrubbing up. The taps should be operated using the elbows not hands.

EQUIPMENT REQUIRED FOR IMPLANT SURGERY

- Surgical instruments autoclaved.
- Drilling unit and motor assembled. In some models the motor can be sterilised. If this is true of yours always remember to fit the protective cap onto the motor first to prevent steam from entering and coil the tubing loosely to prevent long term damage to the internal wiring.
- Disposable hose set for irrigation.
- Saline infusion bag. Sterile water can be used as an alternative as both will keep the bone cool. Saline is closer in consistency to saliva but may clog the internal tubing of the handpiece.
- Slow speed handpiece autoclaved.
- Disposable drills if using the Branmark System™.
- Implant surgical kit autoclaved.
- Metal pot for harvest bone.
- Dense bone drills autoclaved.
- Drape kit. Some drape kits come with caps but some do not and so these may have to be ordered separately. It is possible to order the sterile gowns, suction tips, suction tubing, sterile swabs and a connector for the suction individually.
- Face masks and theatre caps.
- Sterile surgical gloves. Know the hand size of the dentist and yourself.

- Patient protective glasses. The nurse should soak these in disinfectant such as Corsodyl for at least one hour prior to surgery.
- Implants.
- Healing abutments or similar if a single stage procedure.
- Disinfectant for scrubbing such as Hibiscrub™ or iodine.
- Sterile scrub brushes such as the single use EZscrub™.
- No.15 scalpel blades/scalpels.
- Needle and suture.

Many dentists have two nurses present when placing implants; the scrub nurse and the circulating nurse. The scrub nurse will don surgical gowns and assist the dentist. The circulating nurse wears the standard dental nurse uniform and assists the scrub nurse. The circulating nurse must not touch any sterile surface.

The scrub nurse removes any jewellery and puts on an operating cap, glasses and mask. Some masks come with visors attached. The scrub nurse then proceeds to scrub their hands.

Q1. Which of the following equipment is required for implant surgery?

    a. drape kit
    b. drilling unit and motor
    c. sterile surgical gloves
    d. metal pot

Q2. Name the two types of dental nurse.

    a. circulating nurse
    b. scrub nurse
    c. assisting nurse
    d. disinfecting nurse

How well did you do?
    A1.a,b,c,d   A2.a,b

THE SURGICAL HAND WASH

While reading the text answer the following;

Q1. Describe the surgical hand wash.

The scrub nurse should open the drape kit on the work surface taking care to only touch the outer surface of the package. The circulating nurse assists, again only touching the outer surface. The wrapper is spread out to form a sterile drape with the contents on top. Sterile tape from within the pack can be used to tape the edge of this drape to the wall so that nothing within the kit can become contaminated from touching a non-sterile surface.

The circulating nurse opens the sterile single use scrubbing brush pack. The circulating nurse takes care to only touch the outside of the packaging. The scrub nurse takes the sterile scrubbing brush and starts hand washing with a liquid disinfectant such as Hibiscrub™. The fingernails are scrubbed and then the rest of the hands for 1 minute. The hands should be held up at a higher level to the elbows throughout the process so that the water drains away from the hands. The hands and forearms are then rinsed in running water. The hands and forearms are then washed starting with the fingers and moving down the forearms towards the elbows again using a liquid disinfectant for a further 2 minutes. The scrub nurse should operate the soap dispenser and taps with the elbows.

The scrub nurse can now pick up the sterile paper towels from the drape kit and may dry both hands.

Q1. During a surgical hand wash which of the following should occur?

a. the scrub nurse should open the scrubbing pack
b. the hands are initially washed for 1 minute with a bar of soap
c. the hands should be held higher than the elbows
d. the hands and arms are washed for a further 2 minutes with liquid disinfectant

How well did you do?
A1.c,d

PUTTING ON THE SURGICAL GOWN

While reading the text answer the following;

Q1. How does the scrub nurse put on the sterile gown?

Q2. Describe the closed glove technique.

The scrub nurse then puts on the gown. Allow plenty of room to do this. The gown is packed inside out so that it is possible to put on without contaminating the outside. The scrub nurse puts each hand in the sleeves. The surgical gown will unfold as the scrub nurse works both hands down to the end of the sleeves. The hands should NOT go through the end of the sleeves at this stage. The circulating nurse closes the gown at the back by knotting the ties and closing the velcro at the neck.

THE CLOSED GLOVE TECHNIQUE

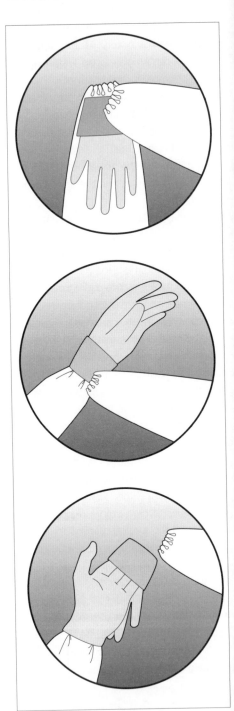

Figure 20.6 The closed glove technique.

The scrub nurse is now ready to put on the surgical gloves. The circulating nurse opens the pack of sterile gloves and drops them onto the sterile drape. The scrub nurse opens the sterile inner paper without taking their fingers out of the sleeves of the surgical gown. Inside will be two gloves marked left and right. Turn the pack of gloves around so that the fingers point towards you. You will notice that the cuffs of both gloves are turned down to reveal the inner surface of the glove. Pick up the inside of the left hand glove up with your right hand and place it on the left hand which should have the palm facing upwards. With your covered right hand put your cover left hand into the glove and still using your covered right hand pull the glove on. Allow the fingers of your left hand to go through the sleeve of your surgical gown to seat fully to the end of the glove. With your covered right hand fold the cuff of the left glove high over the sleeve of your surgical gown.
Next with your gloved left hand pick up the right glove by putting your fingers under the folded cuff of the glove. Place the right glove on the right palm and repeat the process.

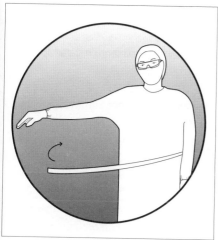

Figure 20.7 *Securing the long tie.*

After the gloves are on the scrub nurse takes hold of the card on the front of the surgical gown and hands this to the circulating nurse. This card is attached to the long tie. The circulating nurse leads this tie around the scrub nurse's waist. The scrub nurse takes the end of the tie leaving the card in the circulating nurse's hand. This card can now be discarded in the waste bin while the scrub nurse knots the tie at the side.

The scrub nurse is now fully surgically dressed. The scrub nurse MUST NOT TOUCH ANY NON STERILE SURFACE from this point. It often helps to clasp your hands in front of you to prevent yourself from inadvertently touching a contaminated surface for example when waiting for the patient to be brought in by the circulating nurse.

Q1. How does the scrub nurse put on the sterile gown?

    a. allow plenty of space
    b. only touch the outside of the gown
    c. put your hands through the end of the sleeves before you put on the gloves
    d. the circulating nurse closes the velcro at the neck

Q2. Which of the following steps occur in the closed glove technique.

    a. the circulating nurse opens the pack of sterile gloves
    b. the scrub nurse opens the inner paper containing the sterile gloves
    c. pick up the inside of the left hand glove with the right hand
    d. fold the cuff of the gloves high over the sleeves of your surgical gown

How well did you do?
    A1.a,d   A2.a,b,c,d

PREPARING THE SURGERY

While reading the text answer the following;

Q1. How does the nurse ensure that every surface used in the surgery is sterile?

The scrub nurse proceeds to drape the Mayo stand or bracket table with the sterile Mayo stand cover from the kit. This cover can also be used as a bag for the disposable items after surgery. The scrubbed nurse's gloved hands must not touch the Mayo stand/bracket table, only the sterile cover.

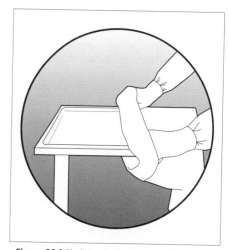

Figure 20.8 *Placing a sterile drape on a Mayo table.*

The overhead light handles should be covered for sterile handling. Again the scrub nurse must not touch the light handles when putting on the sterile covers. The scrub nurse joins the sterile irrigation tubing to the handpiece while the circulating nurse joins the other end to the saline bag. The scrub nurse covers the drilling unit with the transparent drape. The circulating nurse assists by holding the motor and cord to one side.

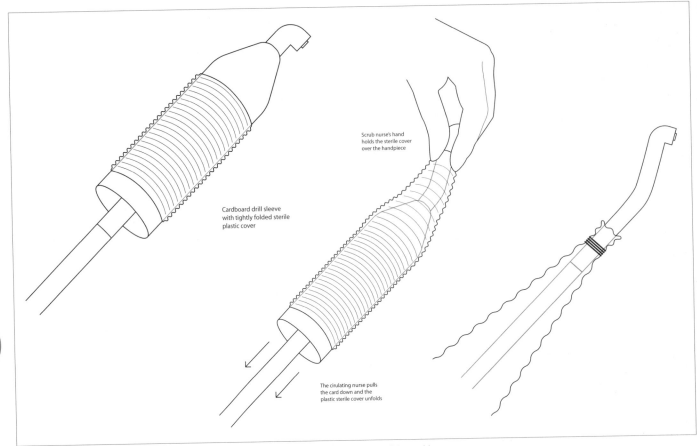

Figure 20.9 *Covering the handpiece tubing.*

Use the drill sleeves to cover the irrigation tubing, motor and handpiece. The circulating nurse opens the sterilising pouch and drops the handpiece onto the sterile drape. The scrub nurse picks it up. Together both nurses place the handpiece on to the motor; the scrub nurse holding the sterile handpiece and the circulating nurse holding the motor so that there is no contamination.

The scrub nurse then places the drill sleeve over the handpiece. The scrub nurse holds onto the handpiece and the end of the plastic. The circulating nurse pulls the card backwards along the tubing and the plastic cover unfolds. The scrub nurse uses an elastic band to secure the plastic cover to the end of the handpiece ensuring that the motor is totally covered.

The scrub nurse finally arranges the sterile instruments in the order that they will be used on the draped bracket table.

Both the stent and patient's glasses are taken out of the chlorhexidene where they have been soaking for one hour. They are held by the scrub nurse while the circulating nurse pours sterile saline over to rinse them. They are then dried with sterile gauze by the scrub nurse. The stent is placed on the bracket table.

Q1. How does the nurse ensure that every surface used in the surgery is sterile?

  a. by covering every surface with sterile drapes
  b. by covering the handpiece hosing with a sterile drill sleeve
  c. by covering the drilling unit with a sterile plastic drape
  d. by soaking the stent for half an hour in chlorhexidine

How well did you do?
  A1.a,b,c

PREPARING THE PATIENT

While reading the text answer the following;

Q1. How is the patient prepared for implant surgery?

The patient is brought into the surgery by the circulating nurse. The circulating nurse places a surgical cap on the patient.

The patient sits in the dental chair and the scrub nurse places the glasses over the patient's eyes. The patient has either had their Corsodyl™ mouth rinse previously or may have one now.
The patient is laid back. The scrub nurse uses swabs dipped in Corsodyl™ to wipe the lower half of the patient's face. A sterile drape is then folded and placed under their head. The corners of the top layer are then crossed over the patient's forehead and secured with sterile tape.

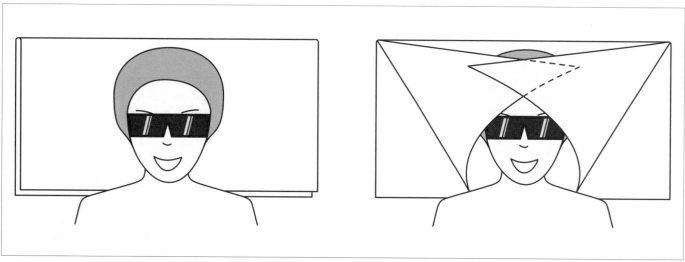

Figure 20.10 *Patient with head drape.*

The big sterile sheet/drape is placed over the patients body. The scrub nurse places the top of the drape under the patient's chin and unfolds it down the patient's body. The circulating nurse takes the end of the drape by holding the underside to cover the patient's feet.

Sterile suction tips are placed on the sterile suction tubes by the scrub nurse while the circulating nurse attaches the other end to the main suction supply. The suction tube is clipped onto the patient's drape by the scrub nurse to prevent it falling on the floor. (It is wise to keep spare tubing in case this happens.)

The nurses, surgery and patient are now ready for implant surgery.

Q1. How is the patient prepared for implant surgery?

    a. giving antibiotic cover 1 hour beforehand
    b. swabbing around the patient's mouth with chlorhexidine
    c. placing a surgical cap on the patient
    d. covering the patient with a sterile drape

How well did you do?
    A1.a,b,c,d

IMPLANT DESIGN

While reading the text answer the following;

Q1. How is an implant shaped?

Q2. Above what temperature will bone die?

Q3. Why is the surface of an implant treated?

Q4. What are the features of an implant?

IMPLANT SHAPE

The basic design of an implant may be tapered or straight.

1.   TAPERED

Figure 20.11 *Tapered implant.*

The advantage of the tapered implant is that it can be placed next to curved roots. The disadvantage is that it requires copious amount of irrigation to prevent the bone from overheating. The area is kept cool by internal irrigation.

2.   STRAIGHT

Figure 20.12 *Straight implant.*

The straight implant has a cutting edge and may not generate as much heat as the tapered implant. The straight implant may be cooled by external irrigation.

The bone temperature should never be allowed to exceed 47°C, regardless of the implant used, as bone death will occur.

THE SURFACE OF THE IMPLANT

The surface of the implant is important as this is where osseointegration occurs. Different implant manufacturers have researched different methods of promoting osseointegration. Most methods involve increasing the surface area of the implant to achieve a greater area for osseointegration to take place. Different methods have involved machining, coating, sand blasting and acid etching the implants. For example Nobel Biocare™ uses a tiunite surface. The titanium implant is dipped in a chemical and electrolysed. This expands the outer surface into a honeycomb mesh. The honeycomb layer allows the bone to grow into it. This allows the implant to be immediately loaded when placed in good bone.

IMPLANT CONNECTORS

1. INTERNAL CONNECTION
The abutment connects internally to the implant. The internal connection may be a lug design or an internal hex.

Figure 20.13 Diagram of an internal connection showing the three "lugs".

One of the lugs should face the buccal surface so that the abutment seats in the correct position.

2. EXTERNAL CONNECTION
The abutment connects externally to the implant. An example is the external hex.

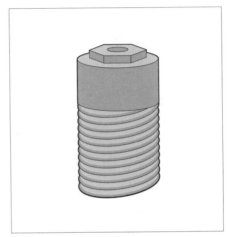

Figure 20.14 External hex.

3. MORSE TAPER CONNECTION

Figure 20.15 Morse taper.

THE LENGTH OF THE IMPLANT

Shorter implants fail more often than longer ones. The dentist will always use the longest implant possible without compromising nearby structures such as the inferior dental nerve.

THE PLATFORM/DIAMETER OF THE IMPLANT

The load bearing surface of an implant is called the platform. The size of the platform depends on the widest diameter of the implant.

Figure 20.16 The shaded area is called the platform.

Narrow diameter implants can be used in small spaces. Wider diameters are generally used in the posterior part of the jaw.

There are several different brands of implants available. Each brand has their own specific surgery kits. For the teaching purpose of this textbook the NobelReplace™ tapered system will be demonstrated as an example of implant placement.

Q1. How is an implant shaped?

    a. tapered
    b. straight
    c. hex
    d. lug

Q2. Above what temperature will bone die?

    a. 27°C
    b. 37°C
    c. 47°C
    d. 57°C

Q3. The surface of an implant is treated to promote Osseointegration.
True or false?

Q4. Which of the following are the connectors of an implant?

    a. internal connection
    b. external connection
    c. Morse taper
    d. platform

How well did you do?
    A1.a,b A2.c A3.True
    Q4.a,b,c

THE IMPLANT SURGICAL KIT
(NobelReplace™ tapered system)

While reading the text answer the following;

Q1. What is the function of the twist drill?

Q2. What is the function of the direction indicator?

Q3. Describe the procedure of selecting the correct implant.

THE IMPLANTS

The diameter of the implants and drills are based on the diameter of the platform. There are different sized implants to replace the various sized teeth and fit into the amount of bone available. The dentist will normally aim to fit the longest and widest implant possible.

THE SURGICAL PROCEDURE

THE 2MM TWIST DRILL

Figure 20.17 *Disposable twist drill with depth gauge.*

A full thickness mucoperiosteal flap is raised and the bone is exposed. The dentist uses the stent as a guide to place the implant. A narrow disposable twist drill is used to drill a narrow hole in the bone to the required depth. The twist drill is usually 2mm in diameter and has depth markings on the side to help the dentist. The scrub nurse assists with the suction.

THE DIRECTION INDICATOR

The dentist then uses a direction indicator to confirm the future direction of the implant. The direction may be modified in the early stages. The direction indicators are different diameters to suit the diameter of the drilled hole. Direction indicators are small and could inadvertently be dropped and swallowed or inhaled by the patient. To prevent this the scrub nurse should thread a piece of suture thread or sterile non waxed floss through the hole in the indicator.

IMPLANT DRILLS

The bone preparation uses drills of increasing diameter to gradually widen the hole/site. The aim is to produce a site into which a slightly wider sized implant is threaded.

For example the dentist chooses the narrow platform drill (ø3.5mm) of the required length (for example 13mm) and drills through the initial hole modifying the direction if necessary. Again the scrub nurse always assists with the suction while the dentist is drilling as the bone needs to be cooled with profuse irrigation. The drill is rotating slowly at 800rpm to prevent excess heat. The scrub nurse should collect any harvested bone in a sterile stainless steel pot. This pot may contain a drop of saline to prevent the harvest bone from drying out or a damp sterile gauze may be placed over the top. The circulating nurse should record which drills are being used. The drills should be replaced after they have been used twenty times as they will become blunt. (Blunt burs generate extra heat.)

The dentist rechecks the direction with the appropriate direction indicator.

The dentist then uses the regular platform drill (ø4.3mm) of the required length (in this example 13mm). The dentist may stop here if this is the sized implant that is going to be placed. If not, the direction would be rechecked and the wide platform drill (Δ 5.0mm, length 13mm) would then be used and so on.

If the bone is particularly dense a dense bone drill can now be used to widen the bone a little. This prevents excess heat being generated when the implant is placed.

THE DRILLING UNIT AND IMPLANT DRIVER

The bone is now ready for the implant. The speed of the drilling unit is greatly reduced to about 25-50rpm. A stable implant should be placed at 35 Newton per cm (Ncm). This is a measure of resistance. The drilling unit is programmed to 35 Ncm and will cut out/stall once 35Ncm has been reached to prevent the bone being under too much pressure and dying.

Implants are very expensive. They must be used or disposed of once their packaging has been opened. The dentist will ask for the precise implant required. For example the regular platform ø4.3mm, length 13mm tapered implant. The circulating nurse should **show the dentist** the implant container **before opening** it so that there is no misunderstanding. The circulating nurse opens the package and drops the contents onto the sterile drape. The implant used is then recorded in the patients notes. The implant packaging label is stuck in the patient's records. This records the batch number and article number of the implant.

The implant is surrounded by a titanium casing. The scrub nurse places the implant onto the implant driver. At this stage the titanium casing is still protecting the implant. The scrub nurse hands the implant driver to the dentist. The dentist takes off the titanium casing and places the implant into the bone. At no stage is the actual implant touched as this may affect osseointegration. The hand wrench is used by the dentist to make fine adjustments to the placement of the implant.

Q1. What is the function of the twist drill?

    a. to drill a narrow hole in the bone to the correct depth
    b. to widen the hole/site
    c. to place the implant in the bone
    d. to make fine adjustments to the placement of the implant

Q2. What is the function of the direction indicator?

    a. to check the direction of the drilled hole
    b. to place the implant in the bone
    c. to make fine adjustments to the placement of the implant
    d. to harvest bone

Q3. Which of the following are part of the procedure of selecting the correct implant.

    a. the implant chosen is shorter than the hole drilled
    b. the implant chosen is the same width as the hole drilled
    c. the dentist chooses which implant to use
    d. the circulating nurse should show the dentist the implant before opening the packet

How well did you do?
    A1.a   A2.a   A3.b,c,d

TREATMENT OPTIONS AFTER THE IMPLANT HAS BEEN PLACED

While reading the text answer the following;

Q1. After the implant has been placed what are the three treatment options?

Q2. What are the post operative instructions?

Q3. How is the equipment cleaned and sterilised?

There are three treatment options at this point;

1.   TITANIUM COVER SCREW
    A titanium cover screw is placed. The flap is sutured over the implant and the mouth is left to heal for the next three to six months. This option is used if there is any doubt about the stability of the implant at the time of placement, if the bone is of poor quality, if the patient has a history of failed implants or if the dentist is being cautious.

This necessitates a second surgical procedure to reveal the implant. The implant is revealed by raising a mucoperiosteal flap or by using a tissue punch. A healing abutment is then attached. The healing abutment is left for several weeks while the soft tissues heal before the final prosthesis is fitted.

2.   HEALING ABUTMENT
    A healing abutment is placed. This retains the soft tissue contour and is useful for single anterior implants. This avoids a second surgical procedure as the healing abutment protrudes through the mucosa. Six months later the permanent prosthesis is fitted.

3.   IMMEDIATE PLACEMENT
    A temporary abutment and crown are placed. For immediate placement the dentist must be satisfied of the following;

- The bone is of good quality.
- 35Ncm was achieved.
- The temporary crown is out of occlusion.
- The implant surface had been appropriately treated e.g. has a tiunite surface.

POST OPERATIVE INSTRUCTIONS FOLLOWING IMPLANT PLACEMENT

- No mouth washing for 24 hours.
- If bleeding occurs, roll up a clean handkerchief and bite on this continuously for 10 minutes.
- If bleeding persists contact your dentist.
- Take your usual analgesics for any pain but do not exceed the stated dose.
- After 24 hours use hot salt water mouthwashes 3 to 4 times a day particularly after meals for the next week.

- The patient should make an appointment to return to the surgery for the removal of sutures one week later. If any sutures come out before the next appointment the patient should contact the surgery.

CLEANING AND STERILISING THE INSTRUMENTS AND EQUIPMENT

HANDPIECE MAINTENANCE

- Scrub the handpieces under running water.
- Take the handpiece apart and oil with a good quality handpiece oil.
- Autoclave. Vacuum autoclave is best. If the autoclave has a drying cycle the handpiece may be bagged before autoclaving. If there is no drying cycle then it is recommended that the handpiece is autoclaved immediately prior to surgery and taken directly from the autoclave to the sterile operating field.
- Autoclave temperature should reach 134°C for 3 minutes and then dry for a minimum of 20 minutes.

MPLANT SURGICAL KIT

- The implant surgical kit should be cleaned with a scrub brush and a soap solution under running water. The individual bur slots may be cleaned with an interdental tooth brush. Keep the plug in the sink to avoid loosing drills.
- The irrigation needle is used to clean any debris from the internal irrigation channels which run through the various drills. The irrigation needle is pushed through these channels to remove large debris. A 10ml syringe is attached to the irrigation needle and used to flush out smaller particles.
- Drills and other loose components should then be placed in a pyrex beaker with detergent and placed in an ultrasonic bath for 10 minutes.
- Any items placed in the ultrasonic bath must be rinsed in cold water before drying.

- All items should be fully dried before reassembling in the organiser.
- The whole organiser is then bagged and autoclaved.
- The implant wrench should be dismantled into it's separate components before sterilising.
- Again, if there is no drying cycle then it is recommended that the organiser is autoclaved immediately prior to surgery and taken directly from the autoclave to the sterile operating field.
- Titanium instruments and stainless steel instruments must be kept separate throughout cleaning and sterilising.

ROLE OF THE DENTAL NURSE

PRE OPERATIVE

- Ordering.
- Ensuring that the x-rays, patient's records and stent are ready.
- Preparation of the equipment and instruments.
- Sterilisation of the equipment.
- Patient preparation and care.

DAY OF THE OPERATION

- Clean and prepare the surgery.
- Patient care on arrival.
- Preparation of the instruments and sterile field.
- Assist during the procedure.
- Suction and irrigation control.

POST OPERATIVE

- Cleaning, sterilising and maintenance of the equipment.
- Post operative patient care and instructions.
- Re-ordering stock.

Q1. After the implant has been placed what are the three treatment options?

    a. place a gold cover screw
    b. place a healing implant
    c. place an temporary abutment
    d. place a healing abutment

Q2. What are the post operative instructions?

    a. if bleeding occurs bite on a rolled up handkerchief for 10 minutes
    b. if bleeding persists contact your dentist
    c. take over-the-counter painkillers for discomfort at the recommended dose
    d. after the first week rinse with hot salt water mouthwashes 3 to 4 times a day

Q3. How is the equipment cleaned and sterilised?

    a. implant surgical kit should be scrubbed with a scrub brush and a soap solution
    b. floss is used to clean the individual bur slots
    c. the irrigation needle is pushed through the internal irrigation channels of the drills
    d. a 10ml syringe is attached to the irrigation needle to flush out small particles

How well did you do?
    A1.c,d   A2.a,b,c   A3.a,c,d

PROSTHETIC PROCEDURES

While reading the text answer the following;

Q1. Name two types of impression taken with implants.

Q2. What complications can occur?

The ease of the restoration depends on the position of the implant. When the implant placement has been compromised, a compromise in the prosthetic function or appearance usually follows.
Handling the soft tissue correctly during surgery is important to maintain the interdental papillae and avoid "black triangles" occurring. This blunting of the interdental papillae is more likely to occur when multiple implants are being placed.

ABUTMENTS

There are various designs of abutment available depending on the final prosthesis required. The final prosthesis may be a single unit, a multi-unit for example a screw retained bridge or an over denture. The abutments available for over dentures are ball or bar abutments.
The abutment is placed using the appropriate screwdriver. A manual torque wrench is then used to achieve the required preload on the abutment screw to prevent it loosening during function.
A periapical radiograph is then taken to ensure that the abutment is fully seated.

ABUTMENT LEVEL IMPRESSION

This may be taken in an open or closed tray. An open tray is a standard stock tray that has been adapted by the dentist to accommodate the height of the impression by making a window in it. The abutment is placed on the implant and a torque wrench used to achieve the required load. An abutment level coping is placed on the abutment and the rubber impression is taken. When the impression material has set the impression is removed from the mouth. It will have the impression coping incorporated within it. This is washed, disinfected, dried and labelled before being sent to the aboratory.

IMPLANT LEVEL IMPRESSION

These impressions are used for customised abutments. The impression is taken with an open tray. An impression coping is screwed onto the implant head and the impression is taken. After the impression material has set the impression coping is unscrewed to allow the impression to be removed from the mouth. The impression is washed, disinfected, dried and labelled before being sent to the laboratory where a customised abutment is produced.

SURGICAL COMPLICATIONS OF IMPLANTS

The most common complications are the relatively minor complications associated with surgery and include swelling, bruising and discomfort. The patient should be warned of these before surgery. Mild post operative pain should be controlled by non-prescriptive analgesics.

FAILURE TO INTEGRATE

This may be due to infection. The implant can be mobile. A radiograph may show a gap between the bone and the implant. Sometimes the implant feels solid as there is no bone on one side only but elsewhere integration has taken place. The implant can be drilled out with equipment which resembles an apple core cutter. The area is left to heal while the treatment is re-planned.
The implant should be sterilised and returned to the manufacturer with a description of the signs and symptoms. The implant is examined to try and find a cause.

FRACTURED IMPLANT

The implant may fracture if it was incorrectly placed or the patient has a particularly heavy bite for example nocturnal clenching. Again the sterilised implant should be returned to the manufacturer with a completed fracture form to try to find an explanation.
If bone loss continues after the implant has been placed this may result in implant fracture. After surgery a set of radiographs should be taken to provide a baseline by which subsequent review radiographs may be judged.

DAMAGE TO THE INFERIOR DENTAL NERVE

Damage to the inferior dental nerve can result in paraesthesia. Damage to the nerve due to direct trauma or as a result of excess heat may result in a permanent feeling of numbness of the lower lip. The implant may not necessarily be touching the nerve. Transient paraesthesia may result from bruising and swelling.

AN IMPLANT IS LOST IN THE MAXILLARY SINUS

This is most likely to occur when placing an upper implant immediately after a molar tooth has been extracted. It can also be caused by forgetting to reduce the speed of the drilling unit when placing the implant. The implant should be retrieved from the sinus during the implant surgery.

CONTAMINATED IMPLANT SURFACE

The oxidised outer layer of the implant will begin to breakdown if it is touched. For example if it is inadvertently dropped on the sterile drape.
This will hinder osseointegration.

THE ABUTMENT WILL NOT SEAT

There are three main reasons why the abutment will not seat;

1. The abutment is upside down. Turn it the right way and it will seat.
2. Soft tissue or bone is in the way. Clear the platform and the abutment will seat. A bone mill is used to carefully remove the bone.
3. The wrong sized abutment is being used for that platform.

PROSTHODONTIC COMPLICATIONS OF IMPLANTS

Complications are either surgical or prosthodontic. Prosthodontic complications include fracture of the prosthesis due to stress places on poorly placed prostheses, excessive loading or the poor design of the metal framework. Loosening or fracturing of screws may occur if there was excess or insufficient tightening of screws. Fractured screws may also occur if there was an overload or poor fit of any component.

In summary the success of implants relies on excellent cross infection control procedures and following the correct protocols. The dental nurses each have a critical role to play.

Q1. Name two types of impression taken with implants.

   a. abutment level impression
   b. prosthesis level impression
   c. implant level impression
   d. bone level impression

Q2. What complications can occur?

   a. failure to integrate
   b. damage to the facial nerve
   c. fractured implant
   d. contaminated implant

How well did you do?
   A1.a,c   A2.a,c,d

21. Cosmetic Dentistry

While reading the text answer the following;

Q1. What is cosmetic dentistry?

Q2. What constitutes a great smile?

Q3. What is the buccal corridor?

Q4. When do black triangles form?

Cosmetic dentistry is improving the appearance of the smile and teeth. This may include rectifying underlying problems such as decay but the final restoration is not only functional but pleasing to the eye.

WHAT CONSTITUTES A GREAT SMILE?

THE "IDEAL" SMILE

1. TOOTH COLOUR AND BRIGHTNESS
   Lighter teeth give a more youthful appearance as teeth naturally darken with age as the labial enamel wears thin revealing the darker colour of the underlying dentine.

2. THE LENGTH OF THE TEETH
   Short teeth appear more ageing as teeth naturally wear as we get older. When the patient says "f" or "v", the incisal edges of the upper centrals should lightly touch the wet/dry border of the lower lip. If the central incisors are lengthened beyond this, speech will be affected.

3. SYMMETRY

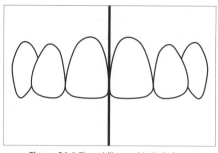

Figure 21.1 The midline and incisal plane.

Symmetry is particularly important at the midline. The upper central incisors should be mirror images of each other. The hardest porcelain crown to match to its enamel neighbour is a single upper central incisor. A line drawn between the upper central incisors should coincide with the facial midline and be perpendicular to the horizon.

4. THE UPPER LIP LENGTH

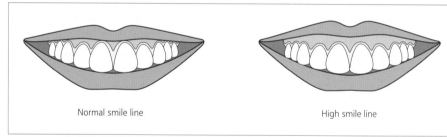

Normal smile line   High smile line

Figure 21.2

The upper lip line should follow the gingival line from upper canine to canine at full smile. This occurs in about 70% of the population. 10% have a high smile line and 20% have a low one. A short upper lip causes a high smile line with the patient showing more gum when they smile.

5. INCISAL PLANE
   The incisal plane is the line drawn from the tip of the upper right canine to the tip of the upper left canine. When a straight line is drawn from the tip of the upper right canine to the tip of the upper left canine, this line should be parallel to the horizon.

7. BLACK TRIANGLE

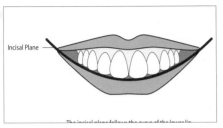

Figure 21.3 The smile line follows the curve of the lower lip.

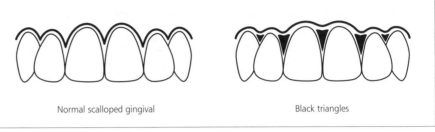

Normal scalloped gingival

Black triangles

Figure 21.5

However the incisal plane is not flat but has a curve that parallels the curve of the lower lip at full smile. All of the incisal edges of the upper anterior teeth should be see in full smile.

6. BUCCAL CORRIDOR

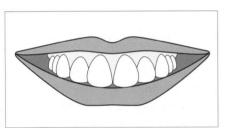

Figure 21.4 The width of the smile has been shortened as only the canines and incisors were veneered.

The buccal corridor is the space between the buccal surfaces of the upper posterior teeth and the cheek. In a full smile the buccal corridor is almost filled with teeth. The width of the smile should be taken into consideration when deciding how many teeth are going to be veneered. Sometimes when only the upper anterior teeth are veneered, the upper posterior teeth become lost due to the brightness of the new restorations and the width of the smile is inadvertently shortened. This is avoided by veneering one or more posterior teeth either side of the canines.

The gingival margin forms a scalloped edge around the teeth. If the interdental papillae are lost or the contact points between the teeth are too close to the incisal edge, an unnatural appearance of black triangles result. It is actually just an enlarged space which looks black as you are looking into the dark interior of the mouth.

8. SHAPE OF THE TEETH

Curved incisal edges look feminine. Square incisors look more masculine.

Q1. Cosmetic dentistry includes which of the following?

    a. root fillings
    b. composite fillings
    c. amalgam fillings
    d. bleaching

Q2. What constitutes a great smile?

    a. high upper lip
    b. an incisal plane that follows the curve of the upper lip
    c. an incisal plane that follows the curve of the lower lip
    d. asymmetry

Q3. The buccal corridor is the space between the upper back teeth and the cheek. True or false?

Q4. When do black triangles form?

    a. when spinach gets caught between the teeth.
    b. when the scalloped gingival margin is lost
    c. when the contact point is too close to the incisal edge
    d. when the contact point is too close to the neck of the tooth

How well did you do?
    A1.b,d   A2.c   A3.True   A4.b,c

SHADE SELECTION

While reading the text answer the following;

Q1. How does lighting effect our colour perception?

Q2. During an appointment when should the shade be taken?

Q3. What is the difference between hue and value?

Q4. What part of the tooth tends to be translucent?

Q5. How can the shade be recorded for the technician?

233

It is important to be as precise as possible when selecting the correct shade for a tooth. The hardest tooth to match is the upper central incisor when one is to be rebuilt with porcelain and the other is to remain in it's natural enamel form. The nurse's opinion of the shade may be sought from the dentist or indeed the patient themselves so it is important to know how to use a shade guide.

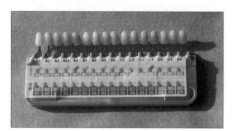

Figure 21.6 A typical shade guide.

The first requirement to choosing the correct shade is the correct lighting. Normal fluorescent tubes emit a green light which distorts our colour perception. Colour corrected fluorescent tubes that mimic natural daylight are recommended for dental surgeries. It is best to view the teeth in several different lights for example with and without the overhead light, with the overhead light dimmed to different intensities and by the window in natural day light.

HUE/COLOUR

The hue is the basic colour of the tooth. The shade should always be taken at the **beginning** of an appointment because by the end the patient's enamel will have dried out and will appear whiter than normal.

To get the basic colour of any tooth you must look at the centre of the tooth and compare it to the colour at the **centre** of the shade guide tooth.

The main colour of a tooth comes from the colour of the dentine. As you know, even though enamel is whiter than dentine, it is translucent and allows the hue of the dentine to show through.

The basic under lying colours are yellow, orange, grey and brown which are shades A, B, C and D on the shade guide. Often the tooth is made up of several shades. Is the neck of the tooth the same colour as the body? Are there white speckles within the teeth?

When veneering or crowning all of the upper anterior teeth the final colour and shape of the teeth look best when they match the tone of the skin and shape of the face. Be aware that striking lipstick and tanned skin can alter your perception of the tooth shade.

VALUE

The value is how light or dark a tooth appears. As you remember, the enamel is thickest at the incisal tip and thins out to a knife-edge at the neck of the tooth allowing the dentine colour to show through. This is why teeth are darker at the neck and become lighter towards the edge. The value is represented by a number. For example A1 is lighter than A2 which is lighter than A3 etc.

The darkest teeth in the mouth are the canines. (These teeth can also be quite yellow/orange in colour.) However if the patient is having all the upper anterior teeth crowned they usually want all the teeth to be the same colour and value. The patient's wishes overrides that which would normally be found in nature!

All patients requiring isolated anterior porcelain work should be informed that these restorations cannot be bleached. If they would like their teeth lightened they should get them bleached before they have a new crown, veneer or bridge.

OPACITY AND TRANSLUCENCY

Basically, enamel is translucent and dentine is opaque. Any part of the tooth that is composed of enamel only, tends to be more translucent e.g. the incisal edge. If the teeth are worn the enamel on the incisal edges will have been ground down and the incisal edges will then be opaque as the remaining enamel will be resting on dentine.

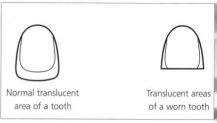

Normal translucent area of a tooth   Translucent areas of a worn tooth

Figure 21.7

The more colour the enamel has the more opaque the tooth will appear. Sometimes the enamel has very little colour and the tooth has a very translucent appearance. This can be hard to match. Very thin labial enamel will also make the tooth look opaque as the dentine shows through more.

LABORATORY SHEET

The required shade of a tooth is written on the laboratory sheet for the technician. Always include the name of the shade guide used as these can vary slightly between different brands.

The more descriptive the dentist, the easier it is for the technician to produce a lifelike tooth. This is best explained in diagrammatic form.

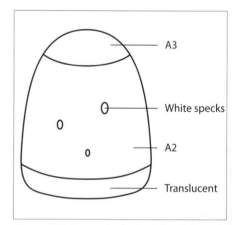

Figure 21.8 An example of a description of the tooth shade for a technician.

Photographs can be useful but unfortunately the camera flash tends to bleach out the colour of teeth so the technician always requires a colour description. However a photograph of the patient's teeth with the selected shade guide in the frame can be useful.

There are now dental chromometers available that record the various colours and values within an individual tooth taking the human factor out of shade selection.

Q1. Colour corrected fluorescent tubes that mimic natural daylight are recommended for dental surgeries. True or false?

Q2. The shade should always be taken at the end of the appointment. True or false?

Q3. What is the difference between hue and value?

a. value is the colour and hue is the darkness
b. value is the darkness and hue is the colour
c. value is the opacity and hue is the darkness
d. value is the translucency and hue is the colour

Q4. What part of the tooth tends to be translucent?

a. the parts comprising of enamel only
b. the body of the tooth
c. the incisal edge
d. the neck

Q5. How can the shade be recorded for the technician?

a. by written instructions
b. by a diagram
c. by a photograph of the teeth only
d. by a photograph of the teeth and the corresponding shade guide

How well did you do?
A1.True   A2.False   A3.b
A4.a,c   A5.a,b,d

TREATMENT PLANNING AND MOCK UPS

While reading the text answer the following;

Q1. What are the advantages of using study models?

Q2. How can photographs be used in dentistry?

Mock ups show the patient how their teeth will look after a cosmetic procedure. Many cosmetic procedures involve crowning, bridging or veneering several teeth. This is expensive and the patient will want to know if the change is worth the investment. They also allow the dentist to experiment and decide upon the best cosmetic approach.

1. COMPUTER IMAGING
    A digital photograph is taken of the patient's smile and downloaded to the surgery computer. Aesthetic changes are then made on screen for the patient to view.

2. WAX-UP ON A STUDY MODEL
    Study models are useful diagnostic aids. They show the teeth from every angle and how the upper and lower jaws relate to each other. By using tooth coloured wax to alter the teeth on the models the dentist can visualise how different adjustments would look. This can be shown to the patient for their approval. Also when making the chairside temporary, if the dentist takes an impression of the mock up rather than the patients actual teeth, this can be used to make the temporary in the patient's mouth. The patient is then able to see how the final restoration will look in situ. If the patient approves the appearance, the mock up can be sent to the technician to copy. Also by wearing the mock-up-temporary the patient is testing the function of the new teeth before the final restoration is fitted. This is useful when the teeth are being lengthened.

3. COMPOSITE MOCK-UP IN THE MOUTH
    This concept is similar to using a wax mock up on a study model. Here, composite is used to create a mock up in the mouth. No etchant is used so that the composite mock-up can be flicked off afterwards. This technique is useful for simple procedures such as diastema closure.

4. PHOTOGRAPHS
    Preoperative photographs of the patient's smile can help the technician. However, as stated, the camera's flash often "bleaches" the colour of the teeth so it is wise to give a written description of the shade and to include the chosen guide shade within the picture.
    Cheek retractors are used to expose as many teeth as possible.

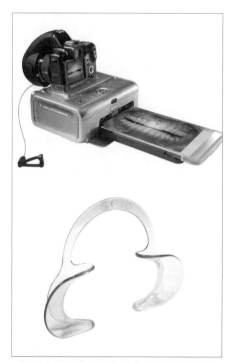

Figure 21.9 *A photograph of the patient's teeth and cheek retractors.*

Some patients may want to view photographs of the dentist's previous work to check their ability. Care must be taken not to breach confidentiality.

Pre- and post-operative photographs are a good way of documenting the treatment and should be kept in the patient's records.

Q1. What are the advantages of using study models?

  a. the teeth can be viewed from every angle
  b. they show how the upper and lower jaws relate to each other
  c. a wax mock can be used to predict the final result
  d. a temporary can be made from the wax mock up

Q2. How can photographs be used in dentistry?

  a. as part of the patient's dental records
  b. as a portfolio showing the dentist's work
  c. to record the progress of the patient's dental work
  d. digital photographs can be viewed and enhanced on a computer screen during treatment planning

How well did you do?
  A1.a,b,c,d   A2.a,b,c,d

Bleaching

Please note different countries have different legislation as to the concentration of bleaching agents allowed for tooth whitening. The concentrations discussed in the text are the ideal clinical concentrations. However these concentrations may have legal restrictions in some countries.

While reading the text answer the following;

Q1. What is intrinsic and extrinsic staining?

Q2. How does the bleaching agents whiten teeth?

Q3. What preoperative instructions should be given to the patient?

Bleaching or tooth whitening is a popular, non invasive method of enhancing a smile. The teeth are whitened with different strengths of hydrogen peroxide or carbamide peroxide. Carbamide peroxide is hydrogen peroxide with urea. It is important to distinguish the two as 10% carbamide peroxide contains approximately 3% hydrogen peroxide and 7% urea and so it is weaker than 10% pure hydrogen peroxide.

There are basically two types of stain; intrinsic and extrinsic. Extrinsic stains form on the surface of the tooth and may be removed by scaling and polishing the teeth. Red wine, tea, coffee and tobacco cause extrinsic staining. However intrinsic stains are within the enamel and dentine and need to be bleached to remove for example fluorosis and tetracycline stains. Bleaching lightens teeth by oxidising the organic matrix within enamel and dentine to remove chromatic (colour producing) materials.

PREOPERATIVE INSTRUCTIONS AND EXPECTATIONS

- Patients should be warned that their teeth may become sensitive temporarily during tooth bleaching.
- Bleaching will not damage existing restorations such as fillings or crowns.
- White fillings and porcelain do not bleach. These restorations will have to be replaced to match the new shade after bleaching has finished.
- If the patient is considering having any anterior porcelain work they should always be forewarned that it cannot be whitened by bleaching at a later date.
- The patient should be given a hand mirror so that they can see the shade being taken at the original appointment and subsequent reviews. Remember the patient is not an expert at taking shades. It is helpful to have the shade guide organised light to dark as below, as this will make more sense to the patient.

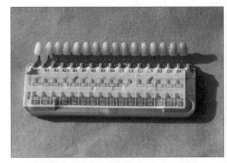

Figure 21.10 *Reorganised shade guide.*

Whitening normal teeth only requires a couple of weeks. However whitening teeth discoloured by tetracycline takes longer. It is very effective but the patient must be forewarned of the time needed. The alternative is porcelain veneers which is destructive to enamel and several times more expensive. Also there is greater success if the tetracycline stain is towards the incisal edge. Heavily stained teeth in the gingival one third have the poorest prognosis for complete lightening. When bleaching white speckled teeth the white speckles may become more pronounced for the first couple of nights before the whole tooth lightens and the speckles disappear. Brown spots may bleach up to become white spots at first. Patients usually find these an immediate improvement.

Q1. Which of the following are examples of intrinsic staining?

   a. fluorosis
   b. coffee stains
   c. tetracycline stains
   d. tobacco

Q2. Bleaching lightens teeth by oxidising the organic matrix within enamel and dentine to remove chromatic materials. True or false?

Q3. What preoperative instructions should be given to the patient?

   a. the teeth may become permanently sensitive
   b. bleaching lightens porcelain and composites
   c. bleaching can dissolve fillings
   d. it is best to bleach first before placing an anterior crown

How well did you do?
  A1.a,c A2.True A3.d

HOW DO WE LIGHTEN TEETH?

METHODS OF BLEACHING

While reading the text answer the following;

Q1. List three methods of vital bleaching.

Q2. What are the advantages and disadvantages of in office bleaching?

Q3. What are the advantages and disadvantages of at home bleaching?

Q4. What instructions should be given for home bleaching?

Q5. When should over the counter bleaching trays be worn?

Q6. Why do non vital teeth darken?

Q7. How are non vital teeth bleached?

BLEACHING VITAL TEETH

The surface of the teeth must be totally clean to ensure that the bleaching agent is actually in contact with the tooth surface. However the teeth may be left for two weeks after a hygienist appointment before bleaching to allow any gingival or tooth sensitivity to abate.

1.   IN OFFICE BLEACHING
The teeth are isolated using a rubber dam or gauze and a resin dam. First the nurse coats the patient's lips with a sun block. The dentist places a plastic disposable lip retractor and then several layers of gauze to cover the exposed mucosa. Finally the gingival margins are covered precisely with a resin dam which hardens by sweeping the blue curing light over it. A high concentration (e.g. 35% carbamide peroxide) of bleach is accurately placed on the teeth with a syringe and brush. The lamp is then placed over the teeth and the teeth are lightened over a 15 minute period. The light is used to activate the bleach. Alternative systems can use heat to activate the bleach. Sometimes the nurse is left to monitor the patient during this period. After the 15 minutes are up the nurse hands the dentist cotton wool buds which are pre-soaked in gel remover. The bleach is removed and refreshed with new bleach and the lamp replaced over the patient for another 15 minutes. This is repeated until the teeth have lightened. If the teeth become sensitive the process can be stopped and continued another day. The teeth should never be anaesthetised prior to bleaching for this reason. Individual teeth can be lightened by leaving the others free of bleach. Afterwards the final bleaching gel is removed and a desensitizer is placed on the teeth and then varnish. The resin dam is pealed off and the gauze and plastic lip retractor removed. The gingivae should appear normal. However if some of the bleaching gel managed to touch the gum the gingival margin will appear white at that point. The patient should be reassured that no treatment is required and it will return to normal soon.

This method gives the patient noticeably lighter teeth within a couple of hours with minimum patient compliance. The disadvantages of this method are that the fee is usually higher as more chairtime is required, there is a possibility of soft tissue damage from the stronger bleach used and the results may not be as good as the slower at-home method. To overcome this last factor, patients are also given trays (specifically made for them from alginate impressions) to use as top-up bleaching trays along with instructions for their use.

2.   AT HOME BLEACHING
At home bleaching uses lower concentrations of bleach (e.g. 10% carbamide peroxide) in well fitting custom trays.

IMPRESSION APPOINTMENT

Alginate impressions of the upper and lower arches are taken. These are washed, disinfected, rinsed, wrapped in wet tissues and a labelled plastic bag and sent to the technician who casts the impressions and makes the trays.

FITTING THE BLEACHING TRAYS AND GIVING WHITENING INSTRUCTIONS

The soft neat trays are fitted. Because these trays are soft and not bulky most patients have no difficulty sleeping with them. The patient is given the appropriate number of syringes of bleach at the required concentration. They are told to gently but thoroughly clean the teeth before wearing the trays. They are shown how to place the bleach in the trays and the small amount that is required. After seating the trays in their mouth any excess bleach should immediately be removed from the gums with the sweep of a finger. The patient should then wash their hands and go to bed. The next morning they remove the tray, rinse their mouth with water and brush their teeth with a desensitizing toothpaste. The bleaching trays should be cleaned with cold running water. The process is repeated each night until the desired shade has been achieved. Individual teeth can be bleached by applying bleach to that part of the tray only before seating. The patient should not smoke or eat and drink foods that stain while they are bleaching their teeth as this defeats the object.
Patients should be forewarned that their teeth may temporarily become more sensitive while bleaching. If the teeth become too sensitive they can have a night off from bleaching. The patient does not have to bleach their teeth every night but obviously they will whiten quicker if they do. If they are still sensitive, the teeth can be smeared with a thin layer of desensitising toothpaste and the empty tray seated in their mouth before going to sleep. An alternative to toothpaste is desensitising gel.

The patients should be advised to keep the trays for future "top up" bleaching. Tooth whitening is quite stable. However many patients like to "top up" by bleaching their teeth for a couple of nights every 6 to 12 months or before a special occasion such as a wedding. The trays can be kept fresh by soaking in an antibacterial mouth rinse for a few minutes before rinsing with cold water.

3.   OVER THE COUNTER BLEACHING KITS
Much cheaper bleaching kits are available over the counter. These trays are not custom made. A low concentration of bleach is used. These trays should not be worn whilst sleeping but worn for half an hour after cleaning the teeth.
Over the counter bleaching kits are effective and do whiten teeth. The disadvantage is that as the patients are unsupervised they may attempt to bleach decayed teeth. If a patient uses a home bleaching kit after a porcelain crown has been fitted, the unaware dentist may be incorrectly blamed for the consequent mismatch in shade.

BLEACHING NON VITAL TEETH

Dead teeth can darken due to trapped blood products. This ranges from a slightly more yellow/orange colour to a deep blue/black shade. This is frustrating to the patient when it occurs in anterior teeth which have been root filled but have sufficient dentine left not to require a crown. This is easily remedied by internal bleaching.

The nurse prepares a routine filling tray. Obviously no local anaesthetic is required. The dentist drills a palatal access cavity down to the gutta percha root filling. The root filling is protected with a layer of glass ionomer. The dentist then places the bleach into the cavity and seals this in place so that it cannot leak into the patients mouth. The patient is given an appointment a week later to review the shade. The process is either repeated or if satisfactory the temporary is replaced with a permanent composite filling.

In a small number of cases root resorption can occur and patients need to be warned of this risk.

Q1. List three methods of vital bleaching.

   a. at home
   b. in office
   c. over the counter
   d. non vital

Q2. What are the disadvantages of in office bleaching?

   a. more expensive
   b. greater possibility of soft tissue damage
   c. the result may not be as good as at home bleaching
   d. bleaching trays may still be required

Q3. What are the advantages of at home bleaching?

   a. cheaper as less chair time
   b. the patient has control over the final shade
   c. the patient has control over sensitivity
   d. it is quicker than in office bleaching

Q4. What instructions should be given for home bleaching?

   a. there is no need to wash the teeth first
   b. excess bleach should be removed from the gums
   c. bleaching trays can be cleaned with hot water
   d. it is best to stop smoking

Q5. When should over the counter bleaching trays be worn?

   a. every night
   b. all night
   c. for 30 minutes after tooth brushing
   d. for several hours during the day

Q6. Non vital teeth darken due to trapped blood products. True or false?

Q7. Both vital and non vital teeth can be bleached internally. True or false?

How well did you do?
**A1.a,b,c A2.a,b,c,d A3.a,b,c
A4.b,d A5.c A6.True
A7.False**

Composite Bonding

While reading the text answer the following;

Q1. What technique is used during composite bonding?

Q2. What equipment is required?

Q3. Give five uses for composite bonding.

Q4. When opening the bite how many teeth are built up at any one time?

Q5. How would you use an occlusal matrix?

Bonding is the build up of tooth surfaces using bonds with little or no tooth preparation but with the help of etches, primers and bonds.

Impressive cosmetic changes can be made in a single appointment at a fraction of the cost of porcelain. If the patient does not like the change or would like it modified this is easily achieved. Indeed the teeth can even be returned to their former state. Although many different problems can be solved with composite bonding the same **acid etch technique** is used. The nurse needs to set up a routine filling tray with clear celluloid matrix strips. The dentist will need to polish the teeth first to provide a clean enamel surface so have a prophy brush and polish available. The nurse must also have the shade guide, acid etchant, enamel bonds and applicators and both dentine and enamel shades of composite ready. Discs and composite finishing and polishing burs will be needed. Composite polishing paste will give a smooth finish. Good moisture control is imperative. Local anaesthetic is not required.

CLOSING DIASTEMAS

Some patients have gaps between their teeth called diastemas. These are often advantageous as debris and plaque cannot collect interdentally. However psychologically some patients are self conscious of these spaces. The most common is the upper midline diastema which is due to the labial fraenum inserting between the upper centrals. Diastemas can be closed in three ways;

1. Surgery and Orthodontics
    The labial fraenum is surgically removed under local anaesthetic and then a fixed upper appliance is used to bring the upper centrals together over a few weeks. They are then permanently retained with a neat fixed retainer hidden on the palatal surface.

2. Porcelain veneers
    Alternatively porcelain veneers can be placed within a couple of appointments. This is quicker than moving the teeth but it is still expensive. The cosmetic result is normally excellent.

3. Composite bonding
    This the quickest, cheapest and least invasive method of closing a diastema. No local anaesthetic is required. The tooth shade is taken and the teeth are polished to remove any plaque. Then the teeth are isolated by rubber dam or cotton wool rolls and the saliva ejector. Phosphoric acid etchant is applied to the two teeth adjacent to the diastema. They are washed for 1 minute and dried with the 3-in-1 syringe during which the nurse aspirates with the high powered suction. An enamel bond is applied and light cured. Clear celluloid strips are used to keep the teeth separate. The teeth are built up with composite using the dentine shades first and finally an enamel outer coat.

They are finished and polished with composite finishing burs and Soflex™ discs.

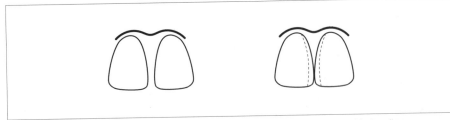

Figure 21.11 Before; patient with a midline diastema. After; diastema closed by bonding.

COMPOSITE VENEERS

The shape of a tooth can be altered with porcelain or composite veneers. Again the advantage of composite is that it is a quick, cheap and non invasive technique.

1. **Peg laterals.**

Figure 21.12 Before; peg lateral.   After; peg lateral built up by bonding.

Some people develop peg laterals. These lateral incisors are short, thin, and peg shaped-hence the name. These teeth can be built up with composite using the above technique. Some times the dentist uses half of a clear acetate crown form filled with composite and placed over the labial aspect of the tooth to get the correct shape. The composite is light cured and then the clear crown form is removed. The restoration is neatened at the margins with finishing burs.

2. Instanding teeth.

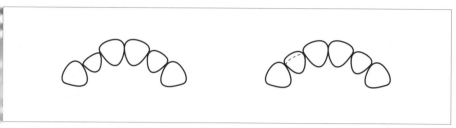

Figure 21.13 *Before; The instanding lateral incisor.* *After; With the composite veneer.*

It is not uncommon to have an instanding upper lateral incisor ruining an otherwise well aligned arch. This can also be remedied by orthodontics or porcelain or composite veneers.
Once again the composite is bonded to the enamel using the acid etch technique.

CHANGING THE SHAPE OF TEETH

 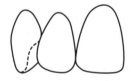

Figure 21.14 *Before and After.*

Some people have rotated upper canines. When they smile they show the mesial aspect of the canine giving a pointed, fang-like appearance. By bonding composite to this aspect the tooth can be reshaped to give a normal appearance.

BUILDING UP WORN TEETH

Many people grind their teeth. They may grind from side to side wearing down their canines and posterior teeth or backwards and forwards wearing the anteriors. Some patients can present with very worn dentitions with over one third of the anterior teeth worn away. They are usually suddenly made aware of this when they see a photograph of themselves at full smile with no teeth showing! On other occasions patients present with temporomandibular joint (TMJ) problems such as clicking, TMJ pain or headaches. These patients may be unaware that they grind their teeth at night and that their TMJ problems are due to their worn dentition.
It is possible to restore these teeth with crowns but the worn bite must be opened up by the correct amount first. This can be achieved by placing composite on the occlusal surfaces of the posterior teeth. Alternatively, the patient can have their teeth restored by composite bonding. Before starting the treatment the patient should always be warned that they will take a couple of weeks to adjust to the new bite.
Restoring a worn dentition requires a long appointment as 6 to 8 teeth need to be built up in one sitting. (Either all the upper anteriors, all the lower anteriors, all the upper posteriors or all the lower posteriors.) This ensures that any occlusal stress is distributed evenly through out several teeth and that the bite is always balanced maintaining the health of the TMJs.
Again the acid etch technique is used to build up the incisal or occlusal surfaces of the teeth in the usual manner.
When producing the correct occlusal contour in posterior teeth **occlusal matrices** can be used. An occlusal matrix is simply a thin transparent plastic film (e.g. cling film). The posterior teeth are built up to the required height in composite which is then cured.

241

The dentist then places another layer of composite over the occlusal surface and then a layer of bond. This time the dentist places the occlusal matrix over the top. The patient is asked to close and grind from side to side and then open. The occlusal matrix is carefully pealed away. The uncured composite now has the imprint of the opposing dentition. The edges of the composite are neatened and the composite is cured. This gives the occlusal surface the correct intercuspal relationship with the cusps of the opposing teeth. This is repeated with the other posterior teeth until a balanced occlusion has been achieved. This is verified with fine articulation paper in Miller's forceps. As stated, either the anterior or posterior teeth are built up-whichever are worn. (If all the teeth are worn then all the teeth can be built up to replace the lost enamel.) The patient is then warned that they will take approximately two weeks to adjust to the new bite. The patient can manage this with no harm to the TMJs as long as both the right and left sides of the new occlusion are balanced.

If the anterior segment has been built up then over the next few weeks the posterior teeth over erupt into occlusion and likewise if the posterior teeth were built up the anterior teeth will over erupt into occlusion.

The advantage of using composite rather than crowns is that the composite can easily be reduced or further built up until the patient is happy. Obviously composite is also much cheaper than crowns or onlays.

In cases such as bulimia where very little enamel remains dentine primers and bonds are used. By building up the anterior teeth and restoring the smile a bulimic patient gets a psychological boost which restores their confidence. This along with counselling can help them along the road to recovery.

Q1. What technique is used during composite bonding?

a. acid etching
b. bleaching
c. porcelain veneering
d. crowning

Q2. What equipment and materials are required?

a. matrix strips
b. etchant
c. shade guide
d. amalgam carrier

Q3. Which of the following are uses for composite bonding.

a. veneers
b. building up worn teeth
c. changing the shape of teeth
d. closing diastemas

Q4. When opening the bite how many teeth can be built up at any one time?

a. all the teeth on the right hand side
b. all the teeth on the left hand side
c. all the back teeth
d. all the front teeth

Q5. An occlusal matrix is used to help contour the occlusal surface of posterior teeth. True or false?

How well did you do?
**A1.a   A2.a,b,c   A3.a,b,c,d
A4.c,d   A5.True**

Porcelain Veneers

While reading the text answer the following;

Q1. Give seven uses for porcelain veneers.

Q2. What is the function of a depth cut bur?

Q3. How is a temporary veneer made?

Q4. What equipment is needed to fit a porcelain veneer?

Q5. What post operative instructions are given to a patient after fitting a veneer?

A porcelain veneer is a thin layer of porcelain that is bonded to the enamel of a tooth to improve it's appearance. They can also be used to repair anterior teeth without the need to remove as much tooth material as a crown.

USES

1.   To lighten intrinsically stained teeth e.g. tetracycline staining.
2.   Peg laterals-to give them a normal appearance.
3.   Instanding teeth-to bring them into alignment.
4.   Rotated teeth-to make them appear aligned.
5.   Diastemas-to close the gap.
6.   Fractured incisors-to repair the tooth.
7.   To repair decayed incisors where the decay extends to the incisal angle.

Porcelain veneers are indirect restorations and require two appointments: the preparation and fit appointments. In between the appointments the technician constructs the veneer.

PREPARING A PORCELAIN VENEER

EQUIPMENT

The nurse prepares a normal restorative instrument tray. The dentist uses tapered crown burs and also depth cut burs. It is important for the veneer preparation to stay within enamel for maximum strength during bonding. Depth cut burs can only penetrate a certain depth. They create grooves in the enamel. The dentist uses these first and then uses the regular crown burs to remove the enamel between the grooves.

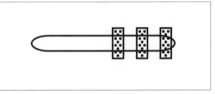

Figure 21.15 Diamond depth cut bur.

The nurse also prepares the rubber impression material, impression trays, retraction cord and haemostatic agent and the temporary resin gun syringe.

PREPARATION

The patient is anaesthetised and the shade is taken before the tooth dehydrates. The patient is numbed as dentine may be exposed for example in a fractured incisor. However the preparation must be kept to enamel as much as possible for the veneer to be successful. Ideally all the margins should be in enamel. The margin must not rest on composite or the restoration will fail.

A slither of enamel is removed from the labial surface using depth cut and tapered crown burs. The amount of enamel removed depends on the angulation of the tooth and how dark the tooth is stained. The darker the tooth the more porcelain is needed to mask it. An instanding tooth needs very little preparation.

The preparation may also include the incisal edge especially if the teeth are going to be lengthened.

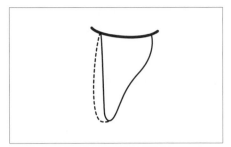

Figure 21.16 Porcelain veneer preparation involving the labial surface only.

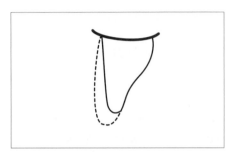

Figure 21.17 Porcelain veneer preparation involving the incisal edge.

The retraction cord soaked in haemostatic agent is place around the prepared teeth to gently widen the gingival crevice. After 4 minutes it is removed and a silicone or polyether impression taken. This can be taken in an anterior triple tray. If it is taken in a perforated stock tray the bite and an alginate impression of the opposing dentition must also be taken. Which ever trays are used the nurse must apply the appropriate fixative first. The "rubber" impression is disinfected, washed and dried. The alginate is disinfected, washed, wrapped in damp tissue and sealed in a labelled plastic bag.

TEMPORARY VENEER

1. A temporary veneer can be made by placing just a dot of etchant on the labial surface (or no etchant at all). This is then washed after 15 seconds and dried. Thin enamel bond is applied and light cured. A ball of composite is then lightly patted into place and light cured. By using so little etch the temporary can be flicked off at the next appointment.

2. If several veneers have been prepared a resin temporary is made using an alginate impression of the unprepared teeth in the same way that temporary crowns are made. This is trimmed. It is then cemented with a polycarboxylate cement.

FITTING A PORCELAIN VENEER

Porcelain veneers are fragile and fiddly to fit. They take just as long to fit as to prepare. You will need to prepare an instrument tray with a mirror, tweezers, probe, carver, flat plastic, excavator, brushes, matrix strips and articulation paper. On your work top the porcelain veneer bonding kit. (Please note that there are slight variations between the different kits available and the following method of placement gives the general principles of bonding. Always follow the manufacture's instructions precisely.) The kit usually contains water soluble try-in pastes, different shades of bond, etchant and porcelain primers. If the porcelain veneer is thin the dentist will want to use a light cured bond. If the veneer is quite thick a duel cured bond is used. Ask the dentist which system will be required. Make sure that the laboratory work arrived that morning.

The patient is anaesthetised and the teeth are isolated with the saliva ejector, cotton wool rolls and retraction cord or rubber dam and retraction cord.

TRY-IN

The temporaries are removed along with all traces of cement or composite. They are flicked off with an excavator or flat plastic. The teeth are washed and dried and the veneers are tried in to check the fit and appearance. About 80% of the shade comes from the actual porcelain veneer and 20% comes from the bond. This enables the dentist to lighten or darken the veneer at the fitting stage. The final shade can be determined using water soluble try-in pastes. These come in a variety of shades which correspond to the bond shades. Once you have the patient's approval the porcelain veneers are removed. The try-in resin is removed with brushes dipped in acetone until the veneers are completely clean.

VENEER PREPARATION

The porcelain veneers are then dried. Silane is placed on the fitting surface and left to dry.
(The fitting surface of the veneer is the inner surface and appears rough or frosted.)

TOOTH PREPARATION

The teeth are cleaned with pumice and washed and dried.
Acid etchant (30% phosphoric acid) is placed on the tooth and after 20 seconds the tooth is washed and dried with the triple syringe. Clear plastic matrix strips are placed interdentally. Thin layers of primers and bonds are applied according to the manufacture's instructions. If tints or opaque are necessary they are placed on the tooth in the appropriate areas and light cured for 90 seconds.

Before fitting the veneer the nurse should check that the overhead light is on a dim setting. On the dentist's command the dental nurse places an even layer of the correct shade of bond on the fitting surface of the veneer and hands this to the dentist on the flat of an outstretched palm. Timing is important. If you place the bond on the veneer before the dentist is ready it will start to set outside the patient's mouth and will be unusable. The dentist slides the porcelain veneer onto the tooth eliminating air bubbles. The excess is quickly removed with a flat plastic or small brush. The veneer is "tagged" into position by shining the curing light on it for a few seconds. The dentist carefully flicks away any partially cured flashes of composite with a carver while still supporting the veneer. The veneer is then fully cured. During this stage you should be close by with the curing light and a clean dry tissue ready to wipe and hold hand instruments.

FINISHING

Any remaining flashes of bond or composite can be removed with a No.12 scalpel. Interproximal polishing and finishing strips can be used. The nurse should have floss ready for the dentist to check the contact points.

POST OPERATIVE INSTRUCTIONS

- Foods and drinks which can stain teeth can also stain the veneer margins. For example tea, coffee, tobacco.
- Habits such as ice chewing or fingernail biting must be avoided as they can fracture porcelain veneers.
- Patients who are nocturnal grinders must wear a bite guard.

A **non cosmetic** use of veneers is when they are placed on the palatal surfaces of upper anterior teeth to replace eroded enamel. These are made of metal (gold) or composite. Gold, unlike porcelain, avoids wear on the lower teeth. Composite is used if there is a chance that the gold would show through at the incisal edge.

Q1. Which of the following are uses for porcelain veneers.

  a. to make rotated teeth appear aligned
  b. to make peg laterals appear larger
  c. to close diastemas
  d. to replace missing teeth

Q2. A depth cut bur helps to keep the veneer preparation within the enamel? True or false?

Q3. How is a temporary veneer made?

  a. by etching all the preparation and bonding composite
  b. by making a resin temporary and permanently bonding it to the tooth
  c. by spot etching and then bonding composite to the prepared surface
  d. by spot etching and the cementing the temporary resin with polycarboxylate cement

Q4. What equipment is needed to fit a porcelain veneer?

  a. clear matrix strips
  b. porcelain veneer kit
  c. retraction cord
  d. 30% phosphoric acid etchant

Q5. What post operative instructions are give to a patient after fitting a veneer?

  a. no need to wear a sport's guard during contact sports
  b. nail biting can fracture the veneers
  c. red wine may stain the margins
  d. night guards should be worn by nocturnal grinders

How well did you do?
A1.a,b,c   A2.True   A3.c
A4.a,b,c,d   A5.b,c,d

All Ceramic Crowns and Bridges

When excellent aesthetics are required, dentists prefer to use all ceramic crowns. Excellent aesthetics are needed for anterior crowns in patients with a high smile line / short upper lip.

However traditional porcelain jacket crowns cemented with traditional luting cements such as zinc phosphate and polycarboxylate were too weak for some bites. These crowns would easily fracture.

Porcelain is brittle and has been traditionally strengthened by fusing it to metal to produce porcelain bonded crowns. Porcelain bonded crowns often show a thin metal line at the margin. Dentists always try to hide the labial margins of upper anterior teeth within the gingival crevice. However the slightest recession may reveal the metal margin. Also the gingival margin on anterior teeth is often thin and translucent. In these cases the metal border would appear as a "bruised" gingival margin. This frustrated both dentists and patients.

Today new ceramics have been produced that are intrinsically stronger than traditional porcelain. These ceramics can be used to make metal free crowns.

In fact the tooth coloured material Zirconium is strong enough to make certain fixed-fixed bridges without the need for any metal substructure.

However traditional porcelain still provides the best aesthetics. It is now possible to use traditional porcelain by bonding it firmly to the dentine and hence increasing the overall strength of the restoration.

These are called dentine bonded crowns. The fitting surface of the porcelain is etched. A coating of silane is placed on the etched porcelain and left to dry. The crown is then bonded to the tooth with a dentine bond such as Panavia F. The crown, bond and tooth become one solid unit.

"Today the technician also has less problems masking dark cores as the dentist can use composite rather than amalgam to build up the tooth and white fibre posts instead of cast metal post and cores. Dark non-vital teeth may be bleached prior to crowning.

22. Conscious Sedation and the Anxious Patient

THE "RELAXED" PATIENT

While reading the text answer the following;

Q1. List ten ways to provide a relaxed but professional environment in the surgery.

A dental surgery is a very strange room for most people, filled with all sorts of unfamiliar equipment, noises and smells. The very nature of dentistry means that the patient is lying down in a vulnerable position with two people working over their face while intruding on their body space and taking away their ability to speak. Just reading this may be making you feel a little anxious and that's before I mention needles and drills!
It should be taken for granted that all patients will feel at least mildly uncomfortable in this predicament. This is why for every patient, whether anxious or not, we do the following;

1. WHAT WOULD THE PATIENT LIKE US TO DO?
The first question the dentist asks the patient is " What can I do for you?" It is important to gauge the patient's requirements and priorities as these may differ from ours. The patient needs to see that we are interested in them as a human being not just as a set of teeth. This is where trust is built. The patient can then actively participate in their treatment plan as there is usually more than one way to solve any problem. This gives the patient control in their treatment and confidence in the dental team.

2. SITTING THE PATIENT UPRIGHT DURING DISCUSSIONS
You will notice that the dentist always sits the patient upright when discussing treatment plans or their medical history. This puts the patient at an equal eye level to the dentist so that the treatment can be discussed adult to adult rather than the patient lying down in a submissive position.

3. FULL DISCUSSION OF THE TREATMENT OPTIONS
Again this allows the patient to voice any concerns that they may have. When the patient is talking the dentist will look at them to show that they are listening. Often the nurse will record the main points of the conversation on the computer while it is happening so that the dentist can concentrate on listening. By this stage the patient is often confident enough to voice any anxieties.

4. KEEP INSTRUMENTS OUT OF VIEW
All instruments look alien and hostile when you are on the receiving end. Keep the instruments on the bracket table covered with a tissue before the patient sits down and pass all instruments low down under the chin out of the patient's line of vision.

5. SPEAK IN A CLEAR CALM VOICE
This signals to the patient that you know what you are doing and everything is going well.

6. USE SMOOTH FLUID MOVEMENTS
Again this signals that you know what you are doing and you are not rushed.

7. GIVE THE PATIENT CONTROL TO STOP THE PROCEDURE
Before starting any dental procedure the patient should know that they can stop you at any stage by raising their hand.

8. CONSTANTLY MONITOR AND REASSURE THE PATIENT
This lets the patient know that however technical and involved the procedure may be, you haven't forgotten that you are working on a human being. This is largely the nurse's role as the dentist is concentrating on the procedure.

9. LIGHT BANTER BETWEEN THE DENTIST AND NURSE
Light banter and a radio in the background helps to "normalise" the setting.

10. EXPLAIN WHAT YOU ARE DOING AND THE SENSATIONS THEY MAY EXPECT
For example before placing topical anaesthetic tell the patient that it tastes of bubble gum and will start to numb the gum. Before using the slow handpiece explain that it's very gentle but it vibrates. Giving a running commentary is reassuring to the patient as there are no surprises.

Q1. Which of the following provide a relaxed but professional environment in the surgery?

    a. revving up the drill as the patient is speaking
    b. lay the patient flat while talking to save time
    c. use fluid movements
    d. give a simple running commentary so that the patient knows what to expect

How well did you do?
A1.c,d

THE ANXIOUS PATIENT

While reading the text answer the following;

Q1. List four additional ways to minimise the anxiety of the dental phobic patient.

These patients feel a strong sense of anxiety or frank panic in the dental surgery. It usually takes them a lot of will power to go to the dentist. This should be respected. Anxious patients usually declare their anxiety immediately. However, as a dental nurse, you should monitor all patients for signs of anxiety such as sweating, feeling and looking hot/flushed, talking too much and too rapidly, looking anxiously around the room or keeping one foot permanently on the floor while lying back in the chair (psychologically for a quick get-away). When managing an anxious patient it is important to do the following;

1. DISARM!
    Keep dental instruments to a minimum to make the dental surgery less intimidating.
    The patient should be reassured that this is just a check-up appointment unless they specifically ask for immediate treatment, for example to make them pain free. If possible the dentist will hold the consultation in a separate room to the surgery or while the patient is sitting in the chaperone's chair rather than the dental chair. Nervous patients focus better on conversations when away from the perceived "danger zone" of the dental chair.
    During the examination the nurse should only place a mirror and periodontal probe on the bracket table. No other instruments should be near the patient. In this first appointment reassure the patient that the dentist is only assessing the mouth. The dentist shows them the instruments before using them. Diagnostic x-rays and a blood pressure reading may be taken during this examination.

The patients will start to relax as soon as they know that, in this appointment, the only aim is to gather information so that the dentist can then discuss the best treatment options. By discussing their fears and suggesting ways in which they can be treated in a comfortable manner anxious patients begin to develop trust and confidence.

2. ESTABLISH THE CAUSE OF THEIR ANXIETY
    This should be done before the examination. Sometimes the patient is quite specific about the cause of their anxiety and this can be addressed. For example;
    Needles - Give the patient some topical anaesthetic to put on the tip of their tongue. This demonstrates how effective it is.
    Drills/noise - Encourage the patient to bring their iPod to the next appointment. Reassure the patient that the noise cannot hurt them.
    Childhood experiences - reassure them that dentistry has progressed. Give the patient control to stop the procedure.
    However it is more difficult if the total dental experience frightens the patient or their specific fears are terrifying. Then they may need some form of sedation.
    It is important for the whole dental team to be reassuring and sensitive to the patient's needs. This should be routine for all patients and start at the reception when they first book an appointment. Any information about the phobia must be relayed to the dentist. The patient may only confide in the waiting room to the nurse as this may be less intimidating. The more open the patient becomes the more we can help by selecting the correct treatment.

3. ESTABLISH THE MAGNITUDE OF THEIR FEAR
    What help will the patient need to get them through a dental procedure-reassurance, oral sedation, relative anaesthesia or intravenous sedation? For example some people are needle phobic but can cope if they are given plenty of topical anaesthetic and reassurance as they know that this part of the treatment takes only a few seconds. However other patients could not cope with a needle anywhere near them. Some again can easily cope with an injection in their arm but definitely not in their mouth.

4. DISCUSS THE TREATMENT PLAN AND OBTAIN WRITTEN CONSENT
    Nervous patients usually want as few appointments as possible. If the patient is to be sedated the treatment should aim to be completed in one or two appointments. However the patient must have a full understanding of the sedation procedure and must be given written instructions to take home. The patient should be allowed to go away and think before giving written consent. However it is better to get written consent prior to the day of treatment as the patient will be anxious and, on reflection, it may be deemed that they were incapable of making an informed decision.

Q1. Name the additional ways to minimise the anxiety of the dental phobic patient.

   a. tell them not to be so silly
   b. establish the cause and extent of their fear
   c. discuss the appropriate treatment options including sedation
   d. only give verbal sedation instructions – if they're that scared they will remember

How well did you do?
A1.b,c

247

SO WHAT IS CONSCIOUS SEDATION?

While reading the text answer the following;

Q1. What is conscious sedation?

Q2. What are the main uses of conscious sedation?

Q3. Name three types of conscious sedation.

DEFINITION OF CONSCIOUS SEDATION

Conscious sedation is the use of drugs to relax the patient by depressing their central nervous system enough to allow dental treatment without the patient loosing consciousness. In this modified state of mind the patient can still speak, respond to commands and retain their natural protective reflexes.

BASIC PRINCIPLES OF CONSCIOUS SEDATION

- The patient is relaxed enough to accept local anaesthetic and dental procedures.
- The patient remains conscious at all times.
- The patient can understand, respond and reply to verbal instructions throughout the procedure.
- The patient retains their natural protective reflexes.

USES OF CONSCIOUS SEDATION

1. For anxious patients who could not cope with dental treatment without sedation.
2. For long or unpleasant procedures which would be stressful to a patient.
3. To avoid a general anaesthetic. General anaesthetic has a very small but real risk factor. For this reason it is avoided whenever possible for routine dental treatment.

TYPES OF CONSCIOUS SEDATION

There are three types of sedation;

1. Oral sedation
2. Inhalation sedation
3. Intravenous sedation

MEDICAL HISTORY

A full medical history is recorded. It is especially important to note cardiovascular disease, respiratory disease, liver or kidney disease and psychiatric conditions. Pregnant women can be sedated with inhalation sedation in their second and third trimesters only. Pregnant women should not be given oral and intravenous sedation.
Care must be taken with older patients. Elderly patients should be physically fit. Intravenous sedation is not predictable for children and early teenagers and is not used in patients under the age of 16 years. All medication that the patient is currently taking should be recorded. This includes alternative remedies and recreational drugs as well as prescribed drugs. Drugs which depress the central nervous system should be given special notice. Allergies to the sedative drug would contraindicate its use. The patients blood pressure must be taken regardless of their medical history.

AMERICAN SOCIETY OF ANAESTHESIOLOGY CLASSIFICATION OF PHYSICAL STATUS (ASA)

The ASA classification helps to identify the severity of the patients medical condition. Only by knowing the patients medical status can the dentist decide which sedative method to use and whether it is best provided in the surgery or in hospital. The Dental Sedation Teachers Group (DSTG) and the Society for the Advancement of Anaesthetic in Dentistry (SAAD) recommend the following;

ASA 1 = Normal healthy patient.

ASA 2 = A patient with mild systemic disease, for example mild asthma, well controlled epilepsy or well controlled diabetes.

ASA 3 = A patient with severe systemic disease limiting activity but not incapacitating, for example epilepsy with frequent fitting, uncontrolled high blood pressure or a recent heart attack.

ASA 4 = A patient with incapacitating disease that is a constant threat to life.

ASA 5 = Moribund patient not expected to live more than 24 hours with or without treatment.

Patients in categories ASA 1 and 2 may be treated in general practice. ASA 3 patients should be treated in hospital. ASA 4 and 5 patients are usually hospitalized or bed ridden and generally only seek emergency dental treatment.

Q1. Which of the following apply to conscious sedation?

a. the patient may become unconscious briefly
b. the patient can understand but is unable to respond to verbal instructions
c. the patient retains their protective reflexes
d. the patient is in a relaxed state

Q2. What are the main uses of conscious sedation?

a. dental phobia patients
b. all children
c. for long unpleasant dental procedures
d. to avoid general anaesthetic

Q3. What types of conscious sedation are available.

a. topical
b. intravenous
c. local
d. oral

How well did you do?
A1.c,d   A2.a,c,d   A3.b,d

ORAL SEDATION

While reading the text answer the following;

Q1. What are the advantages of oral sedation?

Q2. What are the disadvantages of oral sedation?

USES OF ORAL SEDATION

This is useful on adult patients who are nervous of dentistry and need sedative drugs to be in a relaxed state of mind but who do not need the amnesic effects of intravenous sedation to cope with dental treatment.

ADVANTAGES

1. No special equipment is necessary.
2. Oral sedation does not involve needles or nose masks which may in themselves be frightening.

DISADVANTAGES

1. Like all conscious sedation the patient needs to be escorted home afterwards.
2. Oral sedation is effective in conjunction with the continual reassurance from the dental team.
3. As with all conscious sedation local anaesthetic is required.

PROCEDURE FOR ORAL SEDATION

1. The patient arrives at the surgery 1 hour before treatment.
2. The patient's medical history is checked. The patient does not need to fast but should not have had alcohol.
3. The patient takes 20mg temazepam table with water. The patient remains in the waiting room for the sedative to take effect. It is helpful if the patient is pre-warned to take a book or i-pod with them to keep themselves occupied. The patient is reminded that they will not fall asleep but simply be in a more relaxed state.
4. After 1 hour the dental nurse escorts them to the surgery for their dental treatment.
5. Throughout the procedure the dentist and nurse are continually reassuring and comforting.
6. After the dental treatment the patient and their escort are given the following verbal and written instructions to obey for the remainder of the day;
- They must not drive, cycle, operate machinery or go back to work.
- They must not sign legal documents.
- They must not drink alcohol.

INHALATION SEDATION (RELATIVE ANALGESIA)

While reading the text answer the following;

Q1. What gases are used for inhalation sedation?

Q2. What are the advantages of inhalation sedation?

Q3. What are the disadvantages of inhalation sedation?

Q4. What is the role of the dental nurse in relative anaesthesia?

249

Inhalation sedation uses a mixture of two gases, nitrous oxide and oxygen, which is administered to the patient through a nasal mask. The nitrous oxide is analgesic. It comes in a light blue cylinder. The oxygen is supplied in a black cylinder with a white top. Both cylinders are housed in a special anaesthetic machine which ensures that the concentration of nitrous oxide never exceeds 50% and the oxygen never falls below 30%.

USES OF RELATIVE ANALGESIA

Inhalation sedation can also be known as relative analgesia. It is particularly useful for nervous children.

ADVANTAGES OF INHALATION SEDATION

1. Relative analgesia is very safe.
2. It is useful for patients with needle phobia as the sedative is inhaled through a mask.
3. The level of sedation is easily increased or decreased.
4. The patient recovers within minutes at the end of treatment.
5. Inhalation sedation is suitable for children.
6. Good for patients with asthma and high blood pressure as inhalation sedation eases the symptoms of both. Can be used on pregnant women in their second and third trimesters.

DISADVANTAGES OF INHALATION SEDATION

1. The specialised equipment required can be bulky and intrusive to the clinical team.
2. The nitrous oxide needs to be continually administered throughout the treatment.
3. The nasal mask may lead to restricted access for the dentist.
4. Scavengers are required to prevent exhaled nitrous oxide effecting the dental team.

5. Inhalation sedation is only effective in conjunction with continual reassurance from the clinical team. It is often ineffective with adults as they are more resistant to suggestion than children.
6. For sedation to be effective the child must inhale through their nose. Mouth breathing makes inhalation sedation ineffective. This also applies to any nasal obstruction e.g. the common cold.
7. There is some analgesia but local analgesia is almost always required.

PROCEDURE FOR INHALATION SEDATION

1. Before the patient arrives the nurse should check that both gas cylinders are full, there are spare tanks if necessary and that the equipment is working. Both nitrous oxide and oxygen should flow at the various levels required. The scavenging system should be checked to ensure it is working and the resuscitation kit should be nearby.
2. Read the medical history. Make sure that the child has not developed a respiratory infection such as a cold.
3. All pre-operative instructions must have been obeyed.
   • The patient may have a light snack up to two hours before treatment.
   • The patient must have an adult escort.
4. The patient is seated and the procedure is explained. The patient is allowed to handle the nasal mask before it is placed on their nose and they are laid back.
5. Both dentist and nurse should give continual praise and encouragement throughout.
6. At first 100% oxygen is given by the dentist.
7. 10% nitrous oxide is added and the patient is told that they will begin to feel pleasantly relaxed.

8. Increments of 5% nitrous oxide are added and plenty of soothing encouragement until the patient is relaxed enough to numb up and treat.
9. The nurse continually monitors the patient while carrying out the routine duties of dental nursing such as providing suction and passing instruments.
10. When the dental treatment is complete the nitrous oxide is switched off and the patient is given 100% oxygen for 2 minutes.
11. The patient is congratulated for their co-operation.
12. After 2 minutes the nasal mask is removed and the patient is sat up.
13. After 15 minutes the patient may leave the surgery but must stay with the escort for a further 15 minutes.

POST OPERATIVE INSTRUCTIONS

For the remainder of the day the patient should obey the following instructions;

• They must not cycle/drive, operate machinery or go back to school/work.
• They must not sign legal documents.
• They must not drink alcohol.

Q1. What gases are used for inhalation sedation?

   a. carbon dioxide
   b. oxygen
   c. nitrous oxide
   d. carbon monoxide

Q2. What are the advantages of inhalation sedation?

   a. suitable for most adults
   b. patients recover quickly
   c. good for needle phobia
   d. good for mask phobia

Q3. What are the disadvantages of inhalation sedation?

    a. scavengers are required
    b. equipment is bulky
    c. site of sedation is away from the mouth
    d. cannot use on asthmatics

Q4. What is the role of the dental nurse in relative anaesthesia?

    a. to administer the inhalation sedation
    b. to monitor the patient
    c. to soothingly reassure the patient
    d. to stock the gas cylinders

How well did you do?
    A1.b,c   A2.b,c   A3.a,b
    A4.b,c,d

INTRAVENOUS SEDATION

While reading the text answer the following;

Q1. What is intravenous sedation?

Q2. What are the advantages of intravenous sedation?

Q3. What are the disadvantages of intravenous sedation?

Q4. What is the nurse's role during intravenous sedation?

Q5. Name an intravenous sedative and it's antidote?

Q6. What are the post operative instructions for conscious sedation?

During intravenous sedation a tranquilliser is injected into a vein to relax the patient. The tranquilliser used is benzodiazepine. The dentist may legally administer a sedative if a second appropriate person is present. The second appropriate person may be an anaesthetist, another dentist or **a dental nurse who has attained a recognised level of proficiency in conscious sedation**. There are advanced dental nursing courses which enable a nurse to attain a Certificate in Dental Nursing Sedation. However an unqualified nurse may be present to assist the dentist if an anaesthetist or second dentist is present to monitor the patient.

USES OF INTRAVENOUS SEDATION

Intravenous sedation is particularly useful for highly nervous patients who want to be "put out" for dental treatment. The patient actually never looses consciousness but as they often cannot remember the procedure they feel as though they have. It is also a good alternative to general anaesthetic for unpleasant or prolonged procedures such as the placement of implants.

ADVANTAGES OF INTRAVENOUS SEDATION

1. The site of injection is away from the mouth allowing the dentist access to do the dental work.
2. Onset of sedation is rapid.
3. Often only a single does is required however further doses can be administered easily through the same site by keeping the vein patent.
4. Less co-operation is required from the patient. This technique does not rely on suggestion.
5. Intravenous sedation has an amnesic effect on the patient which is useful as the patient cannot remember the procedure.
6. The sedative used, benzodiazepine / midazolam (Hypnoval™), can be reversed by another drug called flumazenil. This is useful in a medical emergency.

DISADVANTAGES OF INTRAVENOUS SEDATION

1. Intravenous sedation involves an injection which is off putting for those with needle phobias.
2. Intravenous sedation can only be used on people over the age of 16 years. The effect of benzodiazepine is unpredictable on children.
3. The patient needs to be closely monitored which involves special equipment and two operators who are trained for intravenous sedation.
4. Once injected the sedative cannot be stopped.
5. Overdose of the sedative may result in respiratory depression.
6. The sedative may accidentally be injected into the artery instead of the vein.
7. In a small number of people intravenous sedation has the opposite effect and may increase anxiety.

PROCEDURE FOR INTRAVENOUS SEDATION

1. Prepare the monitoring equipment and check that it is functioning. The nurse ensures that the resuscitation equipment is ready including the antidote, flumazenil.
2. Read the medical history and make sure that the patient is still fit for intravenous sedation.
3. The nurse checks that the following pre-operative instructions have been obeyed;
- The patient has not eaten in the last 2 hours.
- They have an escort to take them home and someone to look after them while they fully recover there.
4. The sedation procedure is explained to the patient. The oximeter is explained and attached to the patient's finger and the patient is laid back in the chair. The oximeter may bleep and the patient is reassured that this is normal.

5. The dentist administers the sedation via a vein in the back of the hand or the inside of the elbow (antecubital fossa). A special needle is used which allows further medication to be delivered if necessary. It is taped to the patient's arm.

6. The sedative is given in timed increments. The patient is carefully monitored as these increments are given. Different patients need different amounts of sedative. The patient must still be able to carry out instructions but will show a slower response than normal. Their speech may become slurred and they will noticeably relax.
The nurse records the name of the drug administered and the dose and time of the increments given.

7. Local anaesthetic can now be given and the dental treatment can proceed. The nurse continually monitors the patient. This includes taking the pulse at regular intervals and recording the blood oxygen levels periodically and monitoring the respiration rate and colour of the patient. The dentist is **immediately** informed of any changes.

8. When the dental treatment is complete the patient should be given sufficient time to recover. They can be lead to a recovery room where they can lie down. Recovery takes about 1 hour from the last increment of sedative. The patient must not be left unsupervised during this time. The nurse supervises the recovering patient until the dentist gives permission for them to be taken home. Any indwelling needle can be removed by the dentist and a dressing applied. Even after 1 hour the patient will still feel the effects of sedation and must be escorted home and have someone who can stay with them for the rest of the day.

9. The patient and escort are given both verbal and written instructions for the next 24 hours.
- They must not drive, cycle, operate machinery or go back to work.
- They must not sign legal documents.
- They must not drink alcohol.

Q1. What is intravenous sedation?

a. a sedative is injected into an artery
b. a sedative is injected into a vein
c. a sedative is injected into the mouth
d. it is relative anaesthesia

Q2. What are the advantages of intravenous sedation?

a. rapid onset
b. rapid recovery
c. there is an amnesic effect
d. useful for children

Q3. What are the disadvantages of intravenous sedation?

a. the patient needs continual monitoring
b. onset is slow
c. needs three trained operators
d. it requires an injection

Q4. What is the nurse's role during intravenous sedation?

a. to administer the sedative drugs
b. to administer the local anaesthetic
c. to monitor the patient
d. to judge when the patient can go home

Q5. The intravenous sedative is called flumazenil and it's antidote is benzodiazepine. True or false?

Q6. What are the post operative instructions for conscious sedation?

a. do not drive
b. go back to work
c. do not sign legal papers
d. drink less alcohol

How well did you do?
**A1.b   A2.a,c   A3.a,d   A4.c
A5.False   A6.a,c**

MONITORING CONSCIOUS SEDATION PATIENTS

While reading the text answer the following;

Q1. List five ways in which a patient under sedation can be monitored.

Q2. What is cyanosis?

Q3. What does an oximeter measure?

Q4. What is the normal oxygenation of blood?

Q5. Name two methods of taking blood pressure.

1. BREATHING

- Regular chest movements indicate normal breathing.
- The patient can be reminded to take deep steady breaths if required.

2. SKIN COLOUR

- Observe the colour of the face, fingers and lips.
- The patient should not be wearing make-up, especially lipstick or nail varnish.
- Pink skin colour is normal
- A blue tinge signals oxygen deficiency. This is called cyanosis.
- Pallor and sweating signals a severe deficiency.
- **Any change in colour must be noted and acted upon immediately.**

3. OXYGEN SATURATION OF THE BLOOD

- This is measured by a pulse oximeter.
- This is clipped onto the patients finger and continually measures the pulse rate and oxygenation of the blood.
- It relies on the transmission of light through the skin so nail varnish must be removed.
- It is good practice for the nurse to record the pulse oximeter readings at regular 10 minute intervals.
- Normal oxygenation is 100%
- If it drops below 90% the cause should be found and rectified immediately.
- The machines usually bleep a warning if the oxygenation is too low.

4. PULSE

- The nurse needs to monitor and record the pulse at regular intervals. The carotid pulse in the neck can be used but it is often more practical to use the wrist as this does not crowd the dentist's space.
- The rate, regularity and strength of the pulse is recorded at 10 minute intervals.
- The normal pulse of a resting adult is between 60 to 90 pulses per minute.

5. BLOOD PRESSURE

- A sphygmomanometer and stethoscope or an automatic blood pressure monitor are required to measure the blood pressure.
- The average reading for a healthy young adult at rest is 120/80.

METHODS OF TAKING BLOOD PRESSURE

1. TRADITIONAL

A cuff is firmly fitted around the upper arm. The anticupital fossa is a depression found between the upper arm and forearm. This should be at the same height as the heart. The cuff is inflated. This stops the flow of blood to the lower arm. A stethoscope is placed in the fossa where the artery runs. The cuff is slowly deflated. The pressure reading is recorded when the first sound is heard. This is the systolic pressure and represents the ventricular contraction. The cuff continues to be slowly deflated. The sound increases and then suddenly stops. The pressure at this point is recorded. This is the diastolic pressure. This shows the ventricular relaxation between heart beats. The cuff can now be removed.

2. AUTOMATIC

Automatic blood pressure monitors have a cuff which must be correctly placed around the patient's upper arm. Again the fossa must be at the same height as the heart. The cuff is inflated by pressing the start button on the monitor. The machine inflates the cuff and releases it automatically, reading the systolic and diastolic pressures as it does so. This is shown on the monitor screen.

Q1. Which five ways can a patient under sedation can be monitored.

a. observing their breathing
b. taking their pulse
c. taking their blood pressure
d. taking a blood sample

Q2. What is cyanosis?

a. the skin goes blue
b. the skin goes bright red
c. there is too much oxygen in the blood
d. there is too little oxygen in the blood

Q3. An oximeter measures the blood pressure. True or false?

Q4. What is the normal oxygenation of blood?

a. 90%
b. 100%
c. 80/120
d. 120/80

Q5. The stethoscope is placed in the anticupital fossa when taking blood pressure. True or false?

How well did you do?
**A1.a,b,c   A2.a,d   A3.False
A4.b   A5.True**

GENERAL ANAESTHETIC

While reading the text answer the following;

Q1. What is general anaesthetic?

A brief mention of general anaesthetic (GA) will be mentioned here as general anaesthetic can only be preformed in hospital as it is illegal to do so in general dental practice.

During general anaesthetic the patient is unconscious, has complete loss of feeling and no protective reflexes. Some patients are very anxious about dental procedures and would not be able to cope with local anaesthetic alone. However for simple dental procedures a general anaesthetic cannot be clinically justified. Conscious sedation is a useful alternative.

Fewer routine dental patients are being referred for GA as most procedures can be preformed under sedation. However complicated wisdom teeth extractions and major oral surgery are preformed in hospital under GA usually by an oral surgeon.

ADVANTAGES OF CONSCIOUS SEDATION COMPARED TO GA

- There is no need to wait for a hospital referral for GA.
- GA is safe but conscious sedation is safer.
- A separate anaesthetist is not necessarily required for conscious sedation. The dentist may legally administer the sedative if a second appropriate person is present.
- There is no need for a long period of fasting before sedation. There is with GA.
- The patient is at all times conscious, co-operative and retains their protective reflexes during conscious sedation.

Q1. Which of the following are true of general anaesthetic?

a. the patient is unconscious
b. the patient maintains their protective reflexes
c. the patient may be slow but can obey simple instructions at all times
d. the patient still requires a local anaesthetic

How well did you do?
A1.a

23. Health and Safety in the Dental Practice

While reading the text answer the following;

Q1. What is the difference between a clinical audit and peer review?

Q2. List the areas of practice management that are covered by the Health and Safety at Work Act.

Many specific aspects of health and safety have been covered in other parts of the book under the relevant topic. For example the rules and regulations governing ionising radiation have been stated in the chapter on radiology. This chapter covers the remaining aspects of health and safety.

The practice principle should have a quality assurance system for radiation protection, infection control and health and safety. This practice quality assurance system should be written down and a member of staff should be appointed to operate this system. All clinical staff are required to continue their professional development through training.

Clinical audits and peer reviews allow dentists to assess different aspects of their practice and make improvements where necessary. Clinical audit is made by individual dentists whereas peer review is made by a group of dentists.

HEALTH AND SAFETY AT WORK ACT

All dentists have a legal requirement to provide a safe environment for their patients and staff. All staff are legally bound to cooperate with their employer with regards to health and safety requirements and to take reasonable care for their own and others' health and safety.

Health and safety involves the following areas;

- Ionising radiation legislation.
- First aid and medical emergencies.
- Cross infection control.
- Disposal of clinical and special waste.
- Fire regulations.
- COSHH.
- RIDDOR.
- Security in the workplace.

Q1. A clinical audit is made by a group of dentists whereas peer review is assessed by an individual dentist. True or false?

Q2. Which of the following areas are covered by the Health and Safety at Work Act?

    a. disposal of sharps
    b. security
    c. fire regulations
    d. needlestick injuries

How well did you do?
    A1.False   A2.a,b,c,d

FIRE REGULATIONS

While reading the text answer the following;

Q1. List the types of fire extinguishers that may be found in the practice.

Q2. What would you do in the event of a fire at the practice?

- Emergency exits must be kept unlocked during work time and free of obstruction.
- Emergency exits should be clearly marked by green "Fire exit" signs and must lead directly to a place of safety.
- Emergency doors should open manually in the direction of the escape.
- Emergency lightening may be necessary.

- Smoke detectors are advised.
- Staff should be trained in the use of fire extinguishers and what to do in an emergency.
- At least two of the following extinguishers should be present in the practice;
- Water/red extinguisher-for all fires except electrical.
- Carbon dioxide/black extinguisher-safe on electrical fires.
- Dry powder/blue extinguisher-safe on electrical fires.
- The fire extinguishers must be inspected annually.

Dental practices should have a written fire safety policy which should be read and signed by all members of staff.

EXAMPLE OF A FIRE POLICY

On discovering a fire;

1. Raise the alarm.
2. Either contain the fire immediately with the equipment available (extinguishers, safety blankets etc.) or call 999 and ask for the fire brigade.
3. Evacuate everyone from the premises and take a register to confirm that everyone is out of the building. (Day sheets or appointment books are useful.)
4. Do not use the lifts.
5. If possible windows and doors should be shut when vacating individual rooms and ideally the main gas and electricity switches should be turned off. However, no unnecessary risks should be taken.
6. Inform the fireman of the location of any gas cylinders within the building. This includes oxygen cylinders.

Q1. Which of the following are types of fire extinguishers that may be found in practice?

    a. green extinguisher
    b. carbon dioxide
    c. blue extinguisher
    d. dry powder

Q2. What would you do in the event of a fire at the practice?

    a. panic
    b. finish the dental procedure
    c. leave the surgery by the closest exit
    d. leave through the automatic doors

How well did you do?
    A1.b,c,d   A2.c

COSHH (CONTROL OF SUBSTANCES HAZARDOUS TO HEALTH)

While reading the text answer the following;

Q1. What does COSHH stand for?

Q2. Who should have access to the COSHH file?

COSHH is a legal requirement. All potentially hazardous substances such as chemicals, drugs and poisons that are used in the workplace are assessed for risk of injury to the staff. These reports are kept in a file labelled COSHH and kept in a place which is accessible to every member of staff. This file should be kept updated. With the help of the manufacturer's instructions, each substance is written up in the following manner;

- Name of the substance.
- How it is hazardous.
- Who may be harmed. This is usually the staff who use the chemical.
- The nature of the risk. For example, is it inflammable, poisonous, biological or chemical.
- How it may cause harm. For example, on skin contact, inhalation, swallowing etc.
- Evaluate the risk of the substance. For example the exposure limits.
- How these risks can be controlled or reduced. The precautions needed for safe handling and use such as ventilation, eye protection, gloves, storage, disposal, special training or health monitoring (e.g. mercury exposure or needlestick injury).

- The first aid measures taken if the substance is ingested, inhaled or makes skin or eye contact.
- All members of staff should read these sheets and sign them to show that they have understood them.

Q1. COSHH stands for "containment of substances harmful to health". True or false?

Q2. Who should have access to the COSHH file?

    a. only the dentist
    b. only the dentist and manager
    c. only the clinical staff
    d. all staff

How well did you do?
    A1.False   A2.d

RIDDOR (REPORTING OF INJURIES, DISEASES AND DANGEROUS OCCURRENCES)

While reading the text answer the following;

Q1. What does RIDDOR stand for?

Q2. What circumstances are covered by RIDDOR?

All workplaces including dental surgeries must report any accident that causes a major injury or dangerous occurrence to the Health and Safety Executive.

These include;

- Bone fractures.
- A lack of oxygen severe enough to cause unconsciousness.
- Any injury requiring 24 hours hospital admission for treatment.
- Acute ill health due to infectious material.
- A major mercury spillage.
- The explosion of an autoclave or compressor.

- An explosion or fire due to inflammable substances causing 24 hours of stoppage.
- An electrical overload causing 24 hours of stoppage.

Assaults or attacks at the surgery should be reported to the police.

Q1. RIDDOR stands for "reporting of injuries, diseases and dangerous occurrences". True or false?

Q2. Which of the following circumstances are covered by RIDDOR?

    a. the compressor exploding
    b. fractured scull
    c. a minor mercury spillage
    d. accidentally setting off the fire alarm

How well did you do?
    A1.True   A2.a,b

FIRST AID

While reading the text answer the following;

Q1. What is found in the first aid kit?

Q2. How would you treat a severely bleeding arm?

Q3. How would you treat an eye injury?

All practices should have a basic first aid kit and every member of staff should be trained in basic first aid. It is recommended that practices nominate a person to be in charge of first aid. All practices should also have an accident book to record all incidents whether they involve a patient or member of staff.

FIRST AID KIT

The first aid box is traditionally a green box with a white cross.

It contains the following;

- Plasters, adhesive tape and safety pins.
- Sterile dressings of various sizes.
- Bandages and gauze.
- Scissors and tweezers.
- Disinfectant to cleanse wounds.
- Sterile eye pads and sterile eye wash.
- Disposable gloves.

FIRST AID PROCEDURES

Always remember to put on clean gloves before treating any open/bleeding wounds.

CUTS AND GRAZES

- Clean the cut under running water and wash the surrounding skin with a liquid soap.
- If possible raise the affected area above heart level while patting the graze dry with a sterile dressing.
- Cover the cut completely with a plaster or sterile dressing.

SEVERE BLEEDING

- The first aid principle with bleeding is to reduce the amount of blood lost.
- Apply immediate pressure to the wound with a sterile dressing.
- Raise and support the cut limb above heart level if possible. If you suspect a broken limb be gentle.
- Lay the patient down as they may be in shock.
- Bandage the dressing firmly to control bleeding but not to stop the circulation to the fingers or toes. If blood comes through the bandage, do not remove it but bandage another over the first. If blood seeps through both bandages remove both and replace with a fresh set applying pressure as you do. Phone 999.

OBJECTS IN THE CUT

- If there are small objects in the wound wash or swab them away.
- If there is a large object embedded in the wound, leave it in place.
- Apply firm pressure either side of the object.
- Raise and support the limb above heart level.
- Lay the patient down to treat for shock.
- Gentle cover the wound with a sterile dressing and build up padding around the object. When the padding is higher than the object, bandage carefully.
- Call 999 or take the patient to casualty.

EYE INJURIES

- The patient should sit down facing the light.
- Gently separate the eyelids with your finger and thumb of your left hand if you are right handed.
- If the foreign object can be seen on the white of the eye, flush it away by pouring clean water from a beaker with your right hand.
- If this is unsuccessful lift the object with the damp corner of a clean tissue.
- If the object still remains, seek medical advise.
- If a chemical substance splashes into the eye, refer to the COSHH sheet for that substance and the required treatment.

Q1. What is found in the first aid kit?

a. bandages
b. adrenaline
c. sterile dressings
d. sterile eye wash

Q2. How would you treat a bleeding arm with glass embedded?

a. apply pressure to the wound
b. apply pressure either side of the wound
c. raise the arm
d. lay the patient down

Q3. How would you treat a foreign object in the eye?

a. flush the object out with clean water
b. flush the object out with sterile eye wash
c. remove the object with the corner of a damp clean hanky
d. seek medical help for an embedded object

How well did you do?
A1.a,c,d   A2.b,c,d   A3.a,b,c,d

257

FRACTURES

While reading the text answer the following;

Q1. How would you treat a fracture

Q2. How would you treat a scald?

Q3. How would you react if someone's tunic caught fire?

- The first aid principle is to prevent further damage by restricting movement.
- Reassure the patient. Ask them to keep still. It is best not to move the patient.
- Call an ambulance.
- If there is bleeding control the flow with pressure.
- If the leg has a suspected fracture, put padding between the ankles and knees and then gently and firmly bandage the injured leg to the good leg at the ankles and knees. Then bandage above and below the injury.
- If the arm has a suspected fracture, use a sling to support the arm close to the body.
- Do not give the patient anything to eat or drink in case an operation is necessary.

MINOR BURNS AND SCALDS

- The first aid principle with scalds and burns is to prevent infection of the exposed tissues and to prevent shock due to blood serum loss.
- Burns may be caused by heat, chemicals or radiation. Scalds are caused by steam or hot fluid.
- Hold the burn under cold running water for at least 10 minutes or until the pain subsides.

- Remove jewellery before swelling occurs.
- Do not puncture any blisters that may develop.
- Cover the burn with a clean, non-fluffy material such as a plastic bag or plastic film.
- If the burn is greater than the size of a postage stamp, it will require medical treatment.

SEVERE BURNS

- Hold the burn under cold running water for at least 10 minutes to start cooling the wound.
- Call 999.
- Lie the patient down to treat for shock.
- Pour copious amounts of water over the wound for at least a further 10 minutes.
- Remove jewellery and clothing from the area that could cause constriction if the region swells. However, do not remove clothing if it is sticking to the burn.
- Cover the burn with a clean, non-fluffy material such as cling film. Do not use adhesive dressings.

CLOTHING ON FIRE

- Stop the patient from panicking or running as these actions will fan the flames.
- Drop the patient to the ground, cover with a coat or blanket and roll them along the ground to smother the flames.
- Call 999.

Q1. How would you treat a fractured leg?

    a. move the leg to see if it is fractured or sprained
    b. call 999
    c. bandage the fractured leg to the healthy leg to keep it immobilised
    d. give the patient a sweet drink to stop them going into shock

Q2. How would you treat a scalded hand?

    a. hold the hand under warm water
    b. hold the hand under cold running water
    c. cover the scald with an adhesive dressing to protect it from infection
    d. remove all jewellery except a wedding ring

Q3. How would you react if someone's tunic caught fire?

    a. drop the patient to the ground, cover them with a heavy coat and roll them
    b. smother the flames
    c. tell them to wave their arms around
    d. call 999

How well did you do?
    A1.b,c   A2.b   A3.a,b,d

ELECTROCUTION

While reading the text answer the following;

Q1. How would you react if you witnessed someone being electrocuted?

Q2. How would you treat someone who had ingested a poison?

Q3. How can you maintain practice security?

- An electric current through the body may interfere with the heart beat causing fibrillation or the heart to stop beating altogether. Electrocution also causes burns.
- Cut off the electricity supple. Every member of staff should know where the mains switch is.
- Call 999.
- Treat the patient for burns and shock.
- Basic life support may be necessary.

POISONS

- The effects of poisoning depend on the substance swallowed. Poisons include bleach, detergent and drugs.
- There may be vomiting, pain or burning sensation, impaired consciousness or restricted breathing due to swelling.
- Call 999.
- If conscious, ask the patient what they have swallowed and give as much information as possible to the ambulance men.
- Refer to the COSHH folder for the information on that chemical substance.
- Be reassuring.
- Do not try to induce vomiting.
- If unconscious, maintain the airway. Give basic life support if necessary with a pocket mask so that you do not come into contact with the poison.

SECURITY

Dental practices are busy places with many people walking in and out of the building on a daily basis. The security of the practice and safety of the staff may be enhanced by considering the following;

- Keep the number of key holders to a minimum.
- Ensure that money is banked daily to decrease the incentive for burglary or at least minimise the amount taken.
- Have an adequate alarm system and ensure that it is set correctly at the end of each day.
- Make sure that the practice door is locked if you are alone in the building. Lock away drugs, needles and prescription pads at the end of the day. Make sure all windows and entrances are closed and secure before leaving the practice at the end of the day.

Q1. How would you react if you witnessed someone being electrocuted?

    a. immediately drag the person away from the cause
    b. immediately cut off the electricity supply
    c. call 999
    d. treat the patient for burns and shock

Q2. How would you treat someone who had ingested a poison?

    a. encourage them to vomit
    b. call 999
    c. gather as much information about the substance swallowed
    d. give basic life support if necessary with a pocket mask

Q3. How can you maintain practice security?

    a. bank money daily
    b. duplicate spare keys in case a staff member looses their key
    c. ensure the door is locked if you are alone in the building
    d. keep a spare key under a flower pot

How well did you do?
    A1.b,c,d   A2.b,c,d   A3.a,c

24. Consent, Complaints and Records

CONSENT

While reading the text answer the following;

Q1. List three principles which ensure that consent is valid.

Q2. What are the three types of consent?

Dentists have a legal and ethical obligation to get valid consent before examining or treating the patient. The patient has the choice whether or not to accept the dental advice or treatment as it is the right of the patient to choose what happens to their own body.

There are three principles to getting consent to ensure that it is valid.

1. Informed consent.
   - The patient should understand the proposed treatment, alternative procedures and what may happen if no treatment is carried out.
   - The patient should be told the risks and benefits of all the options.
   - The patient should know whether the treatment can be provided by the NHS or not and the cost.

2. The patient has to make the decision voluntarily.
   - The patient has the right to refuse dental advise and treatment. They should not be pressurised to accept treatment and they are allowed to consent to only part of the proposed treatment.
   - Once given, the patient has the right to withdraw consent at any time.
   - Giving consent is an ongoing process between the dentist and patient.

3. The patient must have the ability to make an informed decision.

The person carrying out the treatment is responsible for getting the patient's consent. This may be the dentist or hygienist.

There are three types of consent.

1. Implied consent.
   - e.g. The patient is sitting in the dental chair.

2. Verbal consent.

3. Written consent.

Q1. Which of the following are principles which ensure that consent is valid?

   a. consent must be voluntary
   b. consent must be informed
   c. the patient must be insured
   d. the patient must have the ability to make an informed decision

Q2. Which of the following are types of consent?

   a. supplied
   b. relied
   c. implied
   d. verbal

How well did you do?
   A1.a,b,d   A2.c,d

COMPLAINTS

While reading the text answer the following;

Q1. How should complaints be dealt with?

Complaints arise when patients do not get the service they expect. Complaints may be about clinical issues or service issues such as a lack of politeness.

Complaints should be dealt with quickly, efficiently and as smoothly as possible before they have time to grow. It is best to respond to a complaint in writing or by telephone as soon as it is received and certainly no longer than 10 days. The dentist may need time to investigate the complaint fully and fairly. This should be explained to the patient and the anticipated timescale it will take. All information received should be held in confidence.

It is important to listen to the patient in a polite manner. The patient should be involved in the process of sorting their complaint out. Every point raised in the complaint should be sorted. Problems are resolved quicker and more smoothly when the practice attitude is open and helpful rather than defensive.

It is important to apologise to the patient when something has gone wrong. An apology does not mean you are admitting responsibility but rather that you are concerned and understanding. Often an apology will resolve the issue.

Every practice should have a simple effective complaints procedure which every member of staff should know about. The complaints procedure should be kept where patients can see it. Patients should know who to contact if they have a complaint. This is often the dentist or practice manager.

A written log of complaints should be kept to monitor the performance of handling such matters and to identify areas for improvement.

If the patient is unsatisfied with the practice's efforts to sort the matter out, they have the right to complain to the Local Primary Care Trust for NHS treatment or to the Dental Complaints Service for private treatment. Serious complaints such as allegations of professional misconduct may be investigated by the General Dental Council. The resolution of a complaint by a third party relies strongly on complete and accurate dental records. The importance of good record keeping should never be underestimated.

Q1. How should complaints be dealt with?

   a. in a polite, defensive manner
   b. never apologise as you will be admitting responsibility
   c. respond to the complaint as quickly as possible
   d. have a simple, effective complaints procedure

How well did you do?
   A1.c,d

RECORDS

While reading the text answer the following;

Q1. What do the patient's records comprise of?

Q2. Why is it important to maintain complete and comprehensive records?

PATIENT RECORDS

Patient records provide a comprehensive, up-to-date case history of every patient's medical history, examination results and treatments. These records include paper records, computer records, radiographs, photographs, study models, referral letters, consent forms, estimates, accounts and all other correspondence between the patient and practice.

Patient records are legal documents. Incorrect treatment or failure to provide treatment may occur if these records are inaccurate or incomplete. This may result in serious legal difficulties. Patient records should be retained for at least 11 years or until the patients reach the age of 25 years, whichever is the longer. After this time they may be incinerated or shredded.

The nurse may be required to record information given by the patient or dictated by the dentist. This is often true when computers are used. When a practice relies on written notes the dentist can face the patient while taking written notes. However, when using computers, dentists often find it more reassuring to the patient if they face the patient when the patient is talking to them, while the dental nurse (often with their back to the patient) records the gist of the conversation on the computer. The nurse should focus on **recording the patient's actual words** to describe their symptoms and record all **decisions made by the patient**. The nurse should **never** put this information into the history records. At the end of the appointment the dentist should add relevant information and edit the notes. **The records are the dentist's legal responsibility and only the dentist should put them into history.** Whether written or computer records are used, the nurse is invariably expected record dental and periodontal chartings and should be proficient at doing this.

THE LAW

The Data Protection Act protects the patients by ensuring that the records are accurate, relevant, kept securely and not disclosed to unauthorised people. The dentist is obliged to register under the Act. They must also keep back-up copies of computer records and store them and all manual records in a secure, fireproof container. It may be the nurses duty to back-up the computer at the end of the working day.

The Freedom of Information Act allows the patient access to their records. Patients have the right to correct any inaccuracies and alter other entries or, if refused, have their requests noted in the records.

CLERICAL RECORDS

Clerical records include purchase and service records for dental equipment, bills and accounts from various suppliers, materials and drugs used, dental laboratory receipts, waste disposal documents and staff personnel records.

Q1. What do the patient's records comprise of?

   a. radiographs
   b. computer records
   c. referral letters
   d. study models

Q2. Why is it important to maintain complete and comprehensive records?

   a. it is a legal requirement
   b. they provide a comprehensive, up-to-date case history of every patient
   c. the records must be kept for 18 years
   d. the Data Protection Act demands this

How well did you do?
   A1.a,b,c,d   A2.a,b,d

List of Illustrations

Glossary

A

Abscess An infection resulting in a collection of pus in the tissue.

Abrasion Wearing of the teeth from an abrasive substance.

Abutment The tooth or part of the implant used to support a fixed or removable prosthesis.

Aesthetic Of pleasing appearance.

Allergen A substance which causes an allergic reaction.

Allergy Unusual sensitivity to a normally harmless substance.

Alveolar bone The part of the jaws that support the teeth.

Amelodentinal junction Where the enamel meets the dentine in a tooth.

Amnesia Memory loss.

Anaesthetic A drug that removes all feeling.

Analgesic A drug that remove pain.

Anaphylaxis A severe, life threatening allergic reaction.

Anaphylactic shock Anaphylaxis which is so severe it results in a large drop in blood pressure and unconsciousness.

Antibody This is a protein produced by certain white blood cells in the presence of an antigen. Antibodies attach themselves to the antigen to weaken or destroy it. This is an immune response to infectious micro-organisms.

Antigen A substance on the surface of a micro-organism that stimulates the production of an antibody.

Anti-inflammatory Medicine that reduces the effects of inflammation.

Aseptic Sterile Free from infection and disease causing micro-organisms.

Aspirate To suck up fluid via a syringe or the suction apparatus.

Asymptomatic Without symptoms, usually no pain. This means that the patient is unaware of a dental problem.

Attrition Tooth wear caused by tooth to tooth contact such as grinding.

Autoimmune disease The patients own antibodies/immune system start to attack the body.

Avulsed When the complete tooth is knocked out of its socket due to trauma.

B

Bacteraemia Bacteria in the blood stream. This happens during scaling, extractions, oral surgery and endodontics.

Bite 1 The occlusion, how the teeth meet.

Bite 2 Registration of the occlusion.

Buccal Near the cheek.

Bur The rotator cutting bit used in a handpiece/drill.

C

Calcific barrier A barrier that forms after calcium applications.

Cancellous bone The interior of bone that looks like sponge. Also called spongy bone.

Carcinogen Cancer producing, e.g. radiation.

Caries Dental decay.

Cariogenic Caries/decay producing, e.g. sugar.

Cast A model made from an impression.

Ceramic Item made from porcelain.

Clinical audit The evaluation of a clinical system to optimise the care of patients.

Composite A strong tooth coloured filling material.

Coronal Relating to the crown.

Cross-bite When the upper teeth occlude inside the lower teeth rather than outside.

Cyanosis A bluish colour of the skin due to lack of oxygen.

D

Deciduous Primary tooth.

Debilitated Weakened health.

Defibrillation Restoration of a normal heart beat with controlled electric shocks.

Demineralised Loss of minerals from a hard tissue.

Dentate With natural teeth.

Dentition The teeth.

Diastema A gap between teeth.

Distal The back of an object.

Distilled Purified water.

E

Edentulous Without natural teeth.

Electrosurgery Cauterisation.

Erosion Chemical wearing of teeth.

Eruption Teeth moving through the bone and gum into the oral cavity.

Etchant Acidic fluid or gel.

Exfoliate Natural loss of a deciduous tooth.

Exposure To reveal the pulp.

F

Fissure The natural groves found in the enamel.

Flange The part of the denture that occupies the sulcus.

Fluorapatite This is the crystal structure of the enamel which has absorbed fluoride making it tougher.

Fluorosis Discolouration and mottling of the tooth due to excessive fluoride.

Foramen An opening in the bone through which nerves and blood vessels can pass.

Furcation The area of a multi-rooted tooth where the roots separate.

G

Gag To retch without vomiting.

General Dental Council The governing body of the dental profession.

Gingivae The gums.

Gingival crevice The natural groove between the gum and tooth.

H

Handpiece The drill.

Haemostasis To stop bleeding.

Hydroxyapatite Crystal structure of enamel.

Hypertension High blood pressure.

Hyperventilation High rate of breathing resulting in an imbalance of carbon dioxide.

Hypoxia Deduced oxygen in the blood.

I

Impaction An unerupted or partially erupted tooth is stuck against bone or another tooth and cannot fully erupt.

Implant A titanium screw surgically placed into the jaw onto which a prosthesis is fixed.

Inflammation A tissue reaction to injury producing redness, swelling, heat, pain and loss of function.

Inlay An indirect filling made outside the mouth and cemented into the tooth.
Inoculation Vaccination.
Intravenous An injection into the vein in order to introduce a drug
Interproximal In between the teeth. Usually the mesial or distal surface of a tooth.
Irreversible pulpitis Inflammation of the pulp which will not recover but leads to the death of the pulp.

L

Lance To pierce an abscess to allow the pus to drain.
Lateral canal A minor canal branching off the main root canal.
Lesion Diseased tissue.
Light curing The hardening of a dental material with a curing light.
Lingual Near the tongue.
Lymph gland Glands producing the clear body fluid lymph. These glands tend to swell when infection is present.

M

Malocclusion When the variation from normal occlusion becomes unacceptable.
Mandible Lower jaw.
Mandrel Rotary metal shank to which polishing discs are attached.
Maxilla Upper jaw.
Microleakage/Marginal leakage Microscopic gaps between the tooth and restoration allowing saliva to penetrate. This leads to secondary/recurrent decay or the dissolving of luting cements.
Micro-organism Bacteria, viruses, fungi and spores.
Mastication Chewing.
Mesial Towards the midline.
Mixed dentition When primary and secondary teeth are present in the mouth, usually from 6 to 12 years.
Mucosa The epithelial lining of the mouth.
Mucoperiosteum The layer of mucosa and underlying periosteum lining the jaw bones.

N

Necrosis Area of dead tissue.
Non-vital Dead pulp/tooth.

O

Occlusal The biting surface of posterior teeth.
Occlusion The bite. The contact surface of the teeth of one jaw with the opposing jaw.
Odontoblast Cells that produce dentine.
Operator The person carrying out the dental procedure e.g. dentist, orthodontist, hygienist or dental therapist.
Overhang Excess filling material protruding into the gum.the teeth of one jaw with the opposing jaw.

P

Palatal Near the palate/roof of the mouth.
Paraesthesia "Pins and needles" sensation.
Peg lateral Abnormally small upper lateral incisor.
Periapical Around the apex of the root.
Pericoronitis Inflammation of the gum around the crown of a partially erupted tooth.
pH How acidic or alkaline a substance is.
Phobia Overwhelming anxiety or fear.
Pit A depression in the enamel.
Plaque A biofilm of bacteria and sticky matrix which adheres to the teeth causing decay and gum disease.
Plastic A dental material which is soft when it is first inserted into a tooth allowing it to be manipulated.
Pontic The unit/s in a bridge which replaces the missing teeth.
Post A metal or fibre rod placed in the prepared root canal to support a crown.
Posterior At the back.
Prognosis Expected outcome.
Prophylaxis Treatment to prevent a disease.
Prosthesis Artificial body part.
Psychological Relating to the mind.
Pulpectomy Total removal of the pulp.
Pulpotomy Partial removal of the pulp.

Q

Quality assurance A system to make sure a consistently high standard of treatment is achieved.

R

Radicular pulp The part of the pulp that lies in the root.
Recession The gum shrinking away from the tooth revealing the root surface.
Remineralisation When minerals are absorbed into softened/porous enamel to make it hard again.
Retraction Holding back the soft tissue to allow physical and visual access.
Retroclined The incisors slope backward.
Reversible pulpitis Inflammation of the pulp which can be resolved without the death of the pulp.

S

Saline Salty water with a similar concentration to body fluid.
Scavenger A machine that removes waste gases to purify the air.
Sedative A drug to reduce anxiety and make the patient feel calm.
Shock A sudden drop in blood pressure. If left untreated there may be a lack of blood/oxygen reaching the tissues which may be fatal.
Silane agent This is a substance that allows composite to bond to porcelain.
Sinus Antrum in the maxilla.
Sinus tract A connection from an infected area, such as the apex of a tooth, to the oral cavity.
Stagnation area Any area of the mouth which is not self cleaning and allows plaque to build up.
Sterile Having no micro-organisms.
Subgingival Beneath the gingival margin of the tooth.
Supernumary Extra tooth-like structures.
Supragingival Above the gingival margin of the tooth.
Suture Surgical stitch.
Symptom A change that the patient notices that indicates a disease/disorder.

T

Toxin Poisonous substance.

Transillumination Shining a light through teeth to detect interproximal decay.

Trismus Inability to open the mouth fully. This is often due to inflammation or infection.

Tubules Small dentinal tubes.

U

Undercut cavity The base of the cavity is wider than the opening. This is one method of retaining a filling.

V

Vaccine A dead virus or weakened virus is injected into a healthy person so that they can develop specific antibodies to the virus without suffering from the illness. The patient is then protected from that disease if they come into contact with the living virus at a later date.

Vasoconstrictor A drug which constricts/narrows the blood vessels.

Veneer A facing that covers part of the natural crown of a tooth.

Vital Alive.

X

Xerostomia Long term dryness of the mouth due to a decrease or lack of saliva.

Notes

Notes

Notes